The
SHAKESPEARE
Dictionary

The
SHAKESPEARE
Dictionary

Edited by Sandra Clark

NTC *Publishing Group*
Lincolnwood, Illinois USA

USA

1996 Printing
This edition first published in 1994 by National Textbook Company, a
division of NTC Publishing Group, 4255 West Touhy Avenue,
Lincolnwood (Chicago), Illinois 60646-1975 U.S.A.
Published in the United Kingdom by Helicon Publishing.
Manufactured in the United States of America.
Library of Congress Catalog No. 94-65121

4 5 6 7 8 9 BC 9 8 7 6 5 4 3 2 1

CONTENTS

PREFACE

No playwright has at any time been the subject of so much interpretation as Shakespeare. His plays are vitally alive both in the theatre and on the printed page, and his language is, though we may not always know it, often on our lips. Critics and scholars, especially in our own century but also for more than two hundred years earlier, have debated his style, his language, his sources, his characters; they have argued about his use of dramatic structure and his lack of it, his Christianity and his skepticism, his morality and his bawdiness, his reliance on stereotyped characters and traditional situations, and his deep understanding of human nature. In the midst of this abundance and diversity, this book is designed to serve a specific purpose: to make available to the student and the general reader the basic information necessary to a better understanding and enjoyment of Shakespeare's writings.

In order to make the information easily accessible, the major portion of the book is arranged in the form of an alphabetical list covering all of Shakespeare's plays and all of the characters in those plays, as well as persons and places mentioned in the plays; the principal actors, acting companies, and theatres of the time; other playwrights, writers, and historical figures of Elizabethan times important to Shakespeare's works; contemporary writings that mentioned Shakespeare; and much more. Each play entry contains a discussion of possible sources for the play and some stage history of the play, a list of characters in the play, and a plot summary. Each of the characters in the plays is given a separate entry, which may be read in conjunction with the play entry or may serve in itself as an immediate means of identification.

Preceding the alphabetical listing is a separate section containing essays on the life of Shakespeare, on play production in Elizabethan times, and on Shakespeare's major poetry. The articles provide a general background and a context within which to place Shakespeare's works. They afford an insight into Shakespeare's theatrical world, and also into the complexities of his creative genius. This section is followed by an annotated bibliography in five parts, compiled especially with the needs of students in mind.

A SHORT BIOGRAPHY OF SHAKESPEARE

The early years, 1564–c. 1587

The exact date of Shakespeare's birth is not known; tradition has it that it took place on St. George's day, April 23, 1564, and from all evidence, it is unlikely that he was born more than two or three days before April 26, when his baptism was recorded in the parish register of Stratford-on-Avon. He was the eldest son of John Shakespeare, then a prosperous Stratford businessman, and Mary Arden, his wife. John Shakespeare, the son of a farmer, had left the land in about 1550 and had come to live in Stratford, at that time a town of some 2,000 inhabitants. In some documents he is called a yeoman (a freeholder of land to the annual value of fifty shillings), but at different times he was also a glover and a leather-worker, a seller of barley and timber, and perhaps a wool-dealer. After moving to Stratford, he became a man of importance in the community and held numerous civic offices, including those of constable, chamberlain, and alderman. When Shakespeare was four his father was bailiff of Stratford and as such was empowered to grant licenses to companies of traveling players. He owned four houses in Stratford, two purchased in 1556 and two in 1575. The house now designated as Shakespeare's birthplace was not purchased until 1575, and it is possible that Shakespeare was actually born in the adjoining house, to which John Shakespeare had held title since 1556. This prosperity for the Shakespeare family did not last, and from 1577 onward local records suggest that John Shakespeare had begun to run into debt. In 1578 he mortgaged and sold some property that his wife had inherited, and eight years later (1586), he was deposed from his office as alderman because of failure to attend council meetings regularly. By 1596, however, his eldest son's success as a playwright brought the restoration of the family fortunes.

Shakespeare's mother, Mary, was a gentlewoman and the youngest daughter of Robert Arden, who had leased the land that John Shakespeare's father farmed. The Ardens were one of the oldest families in the West Country, and Robert Arden was sufficiently wealthy at the time of his death in 1556 to make provision

1

for his eight daughters as well as for his second wife. Mary's inheritance included a valuable piece of land at Wilmcote, outside Stratford, called Asbies, which she brought with her to her marriage. Altogether they had eight children: Joan and Margaret, who died in infancy before William was born, William himself, Gilbert (b. 1566), Joan (b. 1569), Anne (b. 1571), Richard (b. 1574), and Edmund (b. 1580), the youngest; Joan, who died in 1646, was the only one of the eight to outlive William.

The details of William Shakespeare's early life are still a matter of conjecture, since the only documentary evidence from this time consists of the records of his baptism and his marriage. Although Shakespeare became a famous man in his own day, no biography of him was written until Nicholas Rowe's account in 1709. Rowe's work does not pretend to be scholarly and it is not always accurate; he was a playwright, not an historian. As Shakespeare gained recognition as a playwright, his public life became increasingly well documented in terms of published work, Court appearances of his dramatic company, legal cases, and property dealings, but there is no fully reliable account of his personal affairs. Some of his contemporaries did record their reactions to him as a man, including Ben Jonson, often his rival, who said he was "honest, and of an open, and free nature." John Aubrey, the antiquarian, who was not born until after Shakespeare's death but was well acquainted with the Shakespeare mythos, in his *Brief Lives* provides details that may have some historical basis: "He was a handsome well shap't man: very good company, and of a very readie and pleasant smooth Witt." It is from such incidental remarks and what can be inferred from his public life that we must piece together the outline of Shakespeare's character.

There are no factual records of Shakespeare's childhood, but Rowe says that he went to a free school, that is, a local grammar school with little or no tuition charges, where the children were instructed in Latin, rhetoric, religion, and possibly some Greek. According to Rowe, Shakespeare left before his education was completed because of straitened family circumstances and "the want of his assistance at Home." But since John Shakespeare's financial troubles seem to have started only about 1577 and schooling was free for the sons of burgesses, it is assumed that Shakespeare was able to complete much of his education there. Other accounts of his life at this time are equally undocumented. Aubrey recounts that "his father was a Butcher, & . . . when he was a boy he exercised his father's Trade, but when he kill'd a Calfe, he

would doe it in a *high style*, & make a Speech."[1] Some of Shakespeare's biographers think it very likely, though there is no substantial evidence, that his youth was not one of "sobriety and
self-restraint."[2] One story has it that as a youth he got drunk one
night with the "sippers" of Bidford and slept under a crabtree. His
plays suggest a familiarity with field sports such as falconry, hawk-
ing, and hunting and an interest in horsemanship that he is unlikely
to have acquired during his years in London. And many of his
writings have descriptive passages that recall the countryside
around Stratford. But accounts of the way he spent his youth can
be no more than conjecture.

The only other documentary evidence of his life during this
period are the marriage license and bond he obtained in November,
1582 to marry Anne Hathaway. Even these documents are not
without their mysterious side. The register of licenses gives the
bride's name as Anne Whateley of Temple Grafton, whereas in
the marriage bond she is named as Anne Hathaway of Stratford.
The discrepancy is generally laid to the confusion of the clerk who
made out the licenses, since Rowe and others who knew nothing
of the bond recorded Anne's name as Hathaway. The identity of
her family is not certain, but she may well have been the daughter
of Richard Hathaway of Shottery, who in 1581 left a bequest to
his daughter Agnes (which name was then regarded as a form of
Anne). The church where the ceremony took place has never been
identified, but it was not, as might have been expected, the parish
church of Stratford. The marriage seems to have been performed
somewhat hastily, for a bond was filed on November 28, 1582,
with the Bishop of Worcester, in whose diocese the town of Stratford lay, freeing him from liability since the marriage was to be
solemnized without the usual threefold asking of the banns in
church. Had Shakespeare and Anne been obliged to undergo this
formality they could not have married before mid-January, since
by church law the marriage ceremony could not be performed
during Advent. At the time of the ceremony Anne was about three
months pregnant, and the young Shakespeares's first child, Susanna, was baptized in the parish church on May 20, 1583. William
was then nineteen, Anne eight years his senior. Nearly two years
later Anne gave birth again, to the twins Judith and Hamnet, who

1. Quoted in E.K. Chambers, *William Shakespeare: A Study of Facts
and Problems*, Oxford, 1930, ii, 252–3.
2. T.M. Parrott, *William Shakespeare, a Handbook*, New York, 1934,
15.

were baptized on February 2, 1585. The unusual names suggest that they may have been christened after Shakespeare's neighbor Hamnet (or Hamlet) Sadler, a Stratford baker, and his wife Judith. Hamnet Shakespeare died when he was eleven, but Judith outlived her own children to die at the age of seventy-seven.

Sometime after mid-1584, Shakespeare left Stratford and eventually made his way to London. Aubrey thought he came to London in 1584, and perhaps he was already there by the time the twins were baptized; however, there is nothing to indicate even the year-date of his departure, so he may have remained in Stratford for several years after their birth. There has been much speculation as to his reasons for leaving Stratford. Some writers have postulated domestic difficulties, but there is no evidence of this and, since there seems to have been a general economic decline in Stratford about this time, it may have been the necessity to support his family that brought him to London. Rowe connects Shakespeare's departure from home, in a story that is attested to by other sources, with his poaching of deer in the park at Charlecote, which belonged to Sir Thomas Lucy, a local landowner of some importance. So great was Sir Thomas's anger, says Rowe, especially since Shakespeare saw fit to add insult to injury by lampooning the knight in a ballad, "probably the first Essay of his Poetry,"[3] that the young man had to flee to London for safety. Inevitably, doubt has been cast upon this account, especially since it was later discovered that Sir Thomas had no park at Charlecote at that time, only a free-warren. And while some biographers have suggested that Shakespeare was remembering this escapade when he gave Judge Shallow the same heraldic device as the Lucy family, and made him complain, in *The Merry Wives of Windsor* (I.i.), that Falstaff had beaten his men and killed his deer, it is equally possible that the tradition that Rowe and others report derives at least partially from the play. Another account, from William Beeston, whose father Christopher was an actor and member of Shakespeare's company, has it that Shakespeare was for a time a country schoolmaster. A Mr. Dowdall, writing in 1693, said that Shakespeare ran away from Stratford to escape his apprenticeship to a butcher.[4] In fact, we know nothing more of Shakespeare until 1592, when he had already become known as an actor and playwright in London.

3. Quoted in E.K. Chambers, *William Shakespeare*, ii, 265.
4. See E.K. Chambers, ii, 259.

Some have thought that during these lost years Shakespeare visited Italy, but there is no evidence, not even hearsay, to support the idea. More likely, once he reached London, he earned his living doing theatrical hackwork, revising the plays of others, adding speeches, reworking old material, collaborating—in general, learning the techniques of his trade. Aubrey says that he "was an Actor at one of the Play-houses and did act exceedingly well."[5] This too is very plausible. It is essential to presuppose some groundwork laid for Shakespeare's very rapid rise to fame and success after 1592, and not very surprising to find no record of it. There was no reason for anyone to pay much attention to the early efforts of an obscure young man up from the provinces.

Life in London to 1595

London in the 1590's was a vast, magnificent city by the standards of the rest of England at that time. About a quarter of a million people lived there, mostly in the area known now as the City of London, bounded by Finsbury Fields to the north, the Inns of Court to the west, Aldgate to the east, and the river Thames to the south. Literary men tended to know each other and maintain close friendships and well-defined enmities. The first printed reference to Shakespeare comes in a pamphlet by Robert Greene, one of the most notorious members of London's literary coterie. Greene —poet, playwright, and pamphleteer—an exceptionally prolific writer, testified in one of his last pamphlets to the fact that Shakespeare had already begun to make his name in the literary world of London. At that time Greene, only a few years older than Shakespeare, was dying in poverty; in *Greene's Groatsworth of Witte* (1592) he recalled his own life and described, not without a slight reveling in the melodrama, the circumstances of his miserable end, warning his friends Marlowe, Peele, and Nashe to avoid the vices of the world and in particular to distrust actors, for they were treacherous fellows who would desert a playwright, however well he had provided them with parts, as soon as they saw a newer one:

There is an vpstart Crow, beautified with our feathers, that with his *Tygers hart wrapt in a Players hyde*, supposes he is

5. Quoted in E.K. Chambers, ii, 253.

as well able to bombast out a blanke verse as the best of
you: and beeing an absolute *Iohannes fac totum*, is in his
owne conceit the onely Shake-scene in a countrey.[6]

The reference to Shakespeare was unmistakable and unflatter-
ing. He seems to have taken offense at the pamphlet, as did Marlowe, whom Greene had openly accused of atheism. Greene died
before the pamphlet was published, but Henry Chettle, who saw it
into print, made an apology to Shakespeare in the preface to his
own pamphlet, *Kinde-Harts Dreame*, which came out at the end of
the same year:

> My selfe haue seene his demeanor no lesse
> ciuill than he exelent in the qualitie he
> professes: Besides, diuers of worship haue
> reported his uprightnes of dealing, which
> argues his honesty, and his facetious grace
> in writting, that aprooues his Art.[7]

By 1592, then, Shakespeare was known as an actor and as a
playwright. There has been much speculation as to what he had
written by this time. *Greene's Groatsworth* parodies a line from *3
Henry VI*: "O tiger's heart wrapped in a woman's hide" (I.iv.137),
so this play was known by 1592, although it was not printed until
1595. The first and second parts of *Henry VI* had also been written
by this time; *1 Henry VI* was produced by Philip Henslowe for
Edward Alleyn's company on March 3, 1592. At this time, Shakespeare may have been acting with Alleyn, or with the Earl of Pembroke's Men, who went bankrupt in 1593. Exactly how his stage
career began is not known; anecdotes of his beginning by looking
after the patrons' horses outside the playhouse door cannot be
substantiated. It was not, however, a prosperous time for the
theatre in London, since plague and civic disorder were so wide-
spread that the playhouses hardly opened between June 1592 and
the summer of 1594. The chief companies toured the provinces
during this time, but Shakespeare may have stayed in London to
write, since in 1593 he appeared for the first time in print with his
erotic narrative poem *Venus and Adonis*, following it the next
year with *The Rape of Lucrece*. Both were dedicated to Henry

6. Quoted in E.K. Chambers, ii, 188.
7. Quoted in E.K. Chambers, ii, 189.

Wriothesley, Earl of Southampton, a young, handsome, and wealthy nobleman who was a member of the Court and a favorite with the Queen. If Shakespeare did not know Southampton when he wrote the first poem it is possible that the two men became acquainted in the year that passed before the second, as the dedication to that mentions the patron's favor. Both poems were popular; *Venus and Adonis* went through nine editions in Shakespeare's lifetime, *The Rape of Lucrece* six. From this time on, Shakespeare's name began to appear in print more and more frequently.

It is possible that he also began to write his sonnets at this time (although they were not published until 1609), since this was the great decade of the English sonnet, with sequences by Sir Philip Sidney (*Astrophel and Stella*, published in 1591, though probably written in 1582), Samuel Daniel (*Delia*, 1592), Henry Constable (*Diana*, 1592) and Edmund Spenser (*Amoretti*, 1595), among others. If, as many have thought, Southampton was "Mr. W.H." to whom the sonnets were dedicated, then this period is all the more likely for their composition. But again there is no proof of when they were written, although we do know that some of the sonnets had circulated privately among Shakespeare's friends by 1598.

When the theatres reopened in 1594, there was a general regrouping of the members of the chief companies, from which emerged two companies that were to exist as rivals for some time to come: the Lord Admiral's Men, headed by Edward Alleyn, and the Lord Chamberlain's Men, whom Shakespeare joined as a shareholder (possibly one of the original ones) in 1594. He remained with them as actor and playwright for the rest of his London career, and after joining them he wrote for no other company. The Lord Chamberlain's Men was a closely knit group that continued to prosper during the time that Shakespeare was part of it. In 1594 the company included Richard Burbage, the great tragedian, Will Kempe, the clown, John Heming, later to become one of the editors of Shakespeare's first folio, Thomas Pope, Augustine Phillips, and George Bryan. Kempe was replaced by Robert Armin in 1599, but Burbage, Heming, and Henry Condell, who joined in about 1598, were still with the company when Shakespeare retired from it in 1610 or 1611, and he commemorated the long friendship with bequests to them in his will. In the ten years from 1599 to 1609 only five new actor-shareholders joined the company, two coming as replacements for actors who died. During Elizabeth's reign they were to give thirty-two performances at Court, as against twenty by the Lord Admiral's Company. When James I came to the throne, royal favor continued, and the company then (1603) became the King's Men.

In the winter of 1594 the Lord Chamberlain's Men performed twice for the Queen at Court, and a warrant for payment for these performances, issued on May 15, 1595, names Shakespeare, Richard Burbage, and Will Kempe as the payees for the company. From this it can be assumed that by 1595 he had an assured status in the theatre and in his company, and a certain financial security. He had written historical plays and comedies—*The Comedy of Errors, The Taming of the Shrew*, and perhaps *Love's Labour's Lost* date from this period—as well as narrative poems and his first tragedy, *Titus Andronicus*. He was thirty, and on the verge of greatness.

Shakespeare and his company, 1595–1603

The years from 1595 to 1600 were eventful ones for Shakespeare. In August of 1596, Shakespeare's son Hamnet died. His sorrow at the death of his only son may be reflected in the moving lines spoken by Constance in the play *King John*, written at this time:

> Grief fills the room up of my absent child,
> Lies in his bed, walks up and down with me,
> Puts on his pretty looks, repeats his words,
> Remembers me of all his gracious parts,
> Sniffs out his vacant garments with his form;
> Then have I reason to be fond of grief.
>
> (III.iv.93–8)

In the same year (1596) John Shakespeare, recovered from his earlier financial straits, successfully applied to the College of Heralds for a grant of arms to the family and was assigned a golden shield with the design of "a Bend Sables, a Speare of the first steeled argent. And for his creast or cognizaunce a falcon his winges displayed Argent standing on a wrethe of his coullers."[8] With this, the Shakespeare family officially became members of the gentry.

8. E.K. Chambers, ii, 19.

In 1597 Shakespeare bought a residence to suit this advance in rank, New Place, a decayed but elegant house in Stratford, restored by him and his family to such magnificence that Queen Henrietta Maria stayed there when she came to Stratford during the Civil War (1642–1646). In London he was fast becoming the foremost playwright. Francis Meres, an otherwise obscure man of letters, wrote in his *Palladis Tamia, Wit's Treasury* (1598) that not only was Ovid reborn in "mellifluous and hony-tongued" Shakespeare but also that "among the English" Shakespeare was the most excellent in both comedy and tragedy. Meres cites specifically the comedies *Two Gentlemen of Verona, The Comedy of Errors, Love's Labour's Lost, A Midsummer Night's Dream, The Merchant of Venice,* and the ever mysterious *Love's Labour's Won* (possibly an early version of *All's Well that Ends Well* or *Much Ado About Nothing*), and the tragedies *Richard II, Richard III, Henry IV, King John, Titus Andronicus,* and *Romeo and Juliet.* This comprises a complete list of all that Shakespeare is thought to have written up to that time, with the exception of *Henry VI, The Taming of the Shrew,* and perhaps *The Merry Wives of Windsor.*

During this time the Lord Chamberlain's Men were engaged in finding themselves a new playhouse. They had been performing for some years at the Theatre, a building erected in Finsbury Fields in 1576 by James Burbage, the father of the tragedian. The site was held on a 21-year lease due to expire in April 1597. The Burbages had hoped to move the company to a more fashionable neighborhood inside the city limits, to Blackfriars, an indoor theatre that James Burbage had refurbished before his death in February 1597. Men of the theatre might be prosperous gentlemen, but at that time theirs was still not a respectable profession, and the residents of the Blackfriars area successfully petitioned the Privy Council to prevent the Lord Chamberlain's Men from moving in. Meanwhile, Giles Alleyn, who owned the lease of the ground on which the Theatre stood, was procrastinating about a renewal, and the company was performing in the nearby Curtain, an old and shabby building. At the end of 1598 Richard Burbage and his brother Cuthbert, realizing that Alleyn hoped to acquire for himself the Theatre building, pulled it down themselves, carried the timbers across the frozen Thames, and began to build their new playhouse, the Globe, on a site they had bought in Southwark. To provide the necessary capital, Cuthbert Burbage devised a scheme that was new in his day; he formed a stock company for the theatre consisting of ten shares, five for himself and his brother Richard, and one each for five members of the company—Heming, Phillips, Pope, Kempe, and Shakespeare. This meant that Shakespeare owned a tenth part of the new playhouse as well as his own share in the company and had now three sources of revenue—the plays that he wrote for the company, his pay as an actor plus a share of all the profits made by the company, and also a tenth of the rent that the company as a whole paid to the owners of the playhouse.

The Globe opened in the summer of 1599. Shakespeare had turned from history to comedy, and his "happy" comedies *Much Ado About Nothing, As You Like It,* and *Twelfth Night* were among the first plays to be put on there. He was also writing tragedy again, and *Julius Caesar,* performed in September 1599, was perhaps the first of his Globe plays. *Hamlet* was to follow at the turn of the century, about the time when Shakespeare's own father died.

The company became, probably unwittingly, involved in affairs of state when the Earl of Essex commissioned them to perform Shakespeare's *Richard II* on February 7, 1601. In the judicial examination of the players that followed the event, Augustine Phillips, the company's spokesman, said that they had not wanted to play *Richard II* because it was "so old & so long out of vse as that they shold have small or no Company at yt."[9] However, the Earl's representative, Sir Gelly Meyrick, offered them £2 as an inducement, and so the show went on. It was intended as a prelude to a rebellion against the throne, but the real event was much less well-planned and successful than the one in the play. On February 8, Essex and his friend and follower, the young Earl of Southampton, having returned from a disastrous expedition to quell the unrest in Ireland and out of favor with Elizabeth, rode into London at the head of a body of 200 men, determined to raise the city against the old queen. At this stage of her reign she was much less popular than she had been a decade or so earlier, but even so the earls found no support. They never reached her palace at Whitehall where she sat waiting for them. Instead, they were arrested the same day at Essex House and brought to trial a week later. Both were condemned to death, but at the last moment Southampton was reprieved. Essex went to the block on February 25. The Lord Chamberlain's Men were summoned by the Privy Council to account for their part in the uprising but were acquitted of any responsibility. As a result of this, however, a ban was placed,

9. E.K. Chambers, ii. 325.

for a time, on the production of plays dealing with England's history.

At this same time, the Lord Chamberlain's Men was not without its professional problems. They were facing strong competition from the increasingly popular companies of boy actors, especially the newly formed Children of the Chapel, the "little eyases" that the players in *Hamlet* feared as rivals; the children were then performing at the Blackfriars theatre, from which the Lord Chamberlain's Men had been prohibited. Another source of competition, the Rose theatre, the home of the Admiral's Men, was in close proximity to the Globe on the Bankside location. Shakespeare's friend and rival, Ben Jonson, was writing for both the Admiral's and the Chamberlain's, but with his unruly temper, could keep peace with neither. He moved on to the children at the Blackfriars and in his comedy *The Poetaster* (1601) he satirized his fellow playwrights Marston and Dekker and poured scorn on the players and their "wormwood comedies." The Lord Chamberlain's Men retaliated by commissioning a satire from Dekker and in the same year presented *Satiromastix* in which Jonson is represented as an empty boaster. Shakespeare seems to have kept out of this literary infighting, and perhaps because of this emerged with credit. An anonymous play put on at Cambridge in the Christmas season of 1601–1602 compliments him on putting down all his rivals, especially the irascible Jonson: "Our fellow Shakespeare hath given him a purge that made him bewray his credit." Nonetheless, Shakespeare and Jonson did not bear grudges. Shakespeare acted, probably for the last time, in Jonson's tragedy *Sejanus* at Christmas 1603; it was hissed off the stage by a bored audience, unimpressed by Jonson's observance of classical decorum. When the play was published, two years later, Jonson took care to note that the text was not that of the stage version, "wherein a second pen had good share," but was entirely his own. The second pen has sometimes been thought to have been Shakespeare's, but there is no evidence of this.

At Elizabeth's court the Lord Chamberlain's Men were a favorite company. Their production of *Twelfth Night* was chosen for the Christmas festivities of 1600–1601 in preference to Jonson's *Cynthia's Revels*, and they played (there is no record of which play) for Elizabeth on the night in 1601 before Essex was executed. They were three times at Court in the Christmas of 1601–1602, and they performed the last play Elizabeth was ever to see, in February 1603 at Richmond Palace.

London, 1603–1610

Immediately after his accession, James I took Shakespeare's company under his patronage and they became known as the King's Men. Nine of them, including Shakespeare, were promoted to the rank of Grooms of the Bedchamber and as such were employed at Court from time to time. In 1604 they acted as part of the Spanish ambassador's entourage when he came to negotiate for peace, and Shakespeare and his fellows, as the Master of the Great Wardrobe records, were each given four yards of red cloth, presumably to wear as the livery of the monarch's servants when James proceeded in state through London on March 15, 1604.

James was an even keener patron of the theatre than Elizabeth had been; Shakespeare's company performed at Court 177 times in the period from 1603 to 1613. In the Christmas season of 1604–1605 alone, James saw *The Merry Wives of Windsor, The Comedy of Errors, Love's Labour's Lost, Henry V,* and *The Merchant of Venice,* Shakespeare's new plays, *Othello* and *Measure for Measure,* and two plays by Jonson. James also favored the boy players and in 1604 gave a Royal Patent to the Children of the Chapel, known as the Children of the Queen's Revels until 1605, when they lost the Queen's patronage by performing *Eastward Ho,* a comedy by Chapman, Jonson, and Marston in which the Scots were indiscreetly satirized. James particularly favored extravagant and expensive masques, which Jonson readily supplied for him, though Shakespeare never did.

Shakespeare was now forty. He had given up acting, and all of his professional attention was directed toward writing plays. E.K. Chambers ascribes no plays at all to the theatrical season from autumn 1603 to summer 1604, but just before this Shakespeare had probably written two of his melancholy comedies or "problem plays," *Troilus and Cressida* and *All's Well that Ends Well;* the third, *Measure for Measure* came in the autumn of 1604, followed by the great tragedies, *Othello, King Lear,* and *Macbeth.* In the year of James' accession, the plague was so severe that the theatres were closed from May 7, 1603, to April 9, 1604, and the city was deserted. About a sixth of the population died. Perhaps Shakespeare recalled these times in *Macbeth*:

> The dead man's knell
> Is there scarce asked for who, and good men's lives

Expire before the flowers in their caps,
Dying or ere they sicken.

(IV.iii.170–4)

The King's Men toured the provinces, visiting Bath, Shrewsbury, Coventry, Ipswich, and Oxford, and their royal patron provided them with subsidies to supplement the diminished profits.
We do not know if Shakespeare traveled with the company, but
in December 1603 he was present when they performed at Wilton
House, the home of Sir Philip Sidney's sister, the Countess of
Pembroke, who wrote to her son urging him to solicit the King's
presence at a performance of *As You Like It*, for "we have the
man Shakespeare with us."

Records of Shakespeare's private affairs show that he was
growing increasingly prosperous. He had inherited the Henley
Street houses in Stratford after his father's death in 1601, and in
1602 he bought two more pieces of Stratford property, amounting
to 107 acres of arable land, for £320. In 1605 he made his most
sizable transaction, the purchase of the lease of certain Stratford
tithes for £440. He was amassing considerable personal wealth,
and he preferred to spend it in putting down roots in the country
rather than in bringing his family to London. During his twenty
or more years in the city he had always lived in rented lodgings.

In about 1604 he was living in Cripplegate, in the heart of
the City, in the house of Christopher Mountjoy, a Huguenot tire-
maker (headdress maker). Legal records show that Shakespeare
was involved in arranging a marriage between Mountjoy's daughter Mary and his apprentice, Stephen Bellott, and also in the lawsuit that took place in 1612 when Stephen Bellott sued his father-
in-law for a part of the marriage portion that had not been paid.

Between 1604 and 1608, when Shakespeare was writing some
of his great tragedies, we have little knowledge of his movements.
The King's Men toured the provinces and performed at Court as
well as in the Globe theatre, but Shakespeare may not have accompanied them on their travels, since he was no longer acting.
Augustine Phillips, one of the original Globe shareholders, died in
1605, leaving a 30-shilling piece to Shakespeare in his will, and
John Heming took over as business manager. Aubrey tells of
Shakespeare making annual visits to Stratford and lodging during
the trip at Oxford, in the inn of John Davenant and his wife. The
Davenants' son, William, who was born in 1606 and became well-
known in the Restoration as a playwright and theatre manager,

liked to encourage the rumor that Shakespeare was his natural father. Several eighteenth-century writers record the anecdote, based on an old jest, that the young William Davenant, referring to Shakespeare as his godfather, was jokingly reproved by an old man with the words, "Fie, child . . . why are you so superfluous? Have you not learned yet that you should not use the name of God in vain?"[10] This rumor is now generally held to be untrue.

By 1607 Shakespeare had removed from the Mountjoys' house and was living south of the river. Meanwhile, his family group was altered. In 1607, his illegitimate infant son Edward died. Several months later, in the winter of 1607, his youngest brother Edmund, also an actor, died at the age of twenty seven. Perhaps it was William who paid the twenty shilling fee for a "forenoon knell of the great bell" at Edmund's funeral in the actors' church, St. Saviour's, Southwark. Earlier that year Shakespeare's elder daughter Susanna was married to John Hall, a Stratford doctor, and in February 1608, during one of the hardest winters for many years, Susanna gave birth to a daughter, Elizabeth, Shakespeare's first and only granddaughter. In September of 1608 Shakespeare's mother died.

Meanwhile, Shakespeare's professional life was also changing. In August 1608 the King's Men at last acquired the lease of the Blackfriars Theatre, from Henry Evans, the manager of the Children of the Chapel, who had fallen from the royal favor by allowing not only the presentation of *Eastward Ho* but also *The Conspiracy of Byron*, by Chapman, in which the royal family were unflatteringly portrayed. The Blackfriars was an indoor theatre, and it became the winter home of the King's Men. They continued to play at the Globe in the summer, but the new playhouse brought them far more profit. Shakespeare's own income was probably considerably increased by this transaction. He still owned his share in the Globe, now about one-twelfth,[11] and he held over one-seventh of the shares in the Blackfriars, along with Condell, Heming, William Sly, Henry Evans, and the Burbage brothers. The venture was financially most successful; in a lawsuit of 1612 it was claimed that the King's Men "gott & as yet dothe, more in one Winter in the said great Hall by a thousand powndes than they were used to gett in the Banckside."[12] The price of admission at the Blackfriars

10. From Joseph Spence, anecdote of 1742–1743, quoted in E.K. Chambers, ii, 272.
11. E.K. Chambers, ii, 67.
12. E.K. Chambers, ii, 69–70.

was higher than at the Globe and the audience was less mixed. With the Children of the Chapel, Blackfriars' audiences had been used to sophisticated plays, satire, and tragi-comedy; accordingly, Shakespeare wrote for them the plays that are known as his romances, or last plays: *Pericles* (probably only in part), *Cymbeline*, *The Winter's Tale*, and finally *The Tempest*. Before this, however, his powers had reached their realization in the writing of the great tragedies: *King Lear* was followed by *Macbeth* and *Antony and Cleopatra*; then came *Timon of Athens*, a play full of unsublimated bitterness and pessimism.

The years 1607 and 1608 were a time of personal upheaval for Shakespeare, and once the company was established in the Blackfriars, Shakespeare's output decreased and he began to spend more time in Stratford. His cousin, Thomas Greene, the town clerk of Stratford, with his wife and family, had been lodging in Shakespeare's house, New Place, with Anne and the still unmarried Judith; in 1610 the Greenes moved out and it seems likely that Shakespeare, then aged forty six, returned after more than twenty years to live in his home town.

The last years, 1610–1616

For a time Shakespeare kept up his London contacts. He was still writing, although no longer at the rate of two plays a year, and he continued to visit London. In May, 1612 he was in the city to make a deposition in the Bellott-Mountjoy case. The next year he was there in March, when he bought for £140 the Blackfriars gatehouse and at once mortgaged it. In the same month he designed an *impresa*, a symbolic device with a motto, for Francis, Earl of Rutland, to display at a Royal Tournament and was paid 44 shillings for it. Tradition has it that he coached the actor John Lowin of the King's Men for the leading part in his own *Henry VIII*, and if so, he may have stayed till June for the première. His last visit was in November 1614 when he came with his son-in-law, Susanna's husband John Hall, to discuss Stratford property matters with Thomas Greene.

During 1611, *Cymbeline*, *The Winter's Tale*, and *The Tempest* were all performed in London, the third at Court in November. If *The Tempest* was intended as Shakespeare's farewell to the stage, then somehow he was persuaded to go back on this final gesture, perhaps by John Fletcher, who with, and sometimes without, his partner Francis Beaumont, had begun to write the tragi-comedies and romances that became so popular with middle-class London playgoers. *The Two Noble Kinsmen* (1612–1613) is probably mostly Fletcher's but contains some parts thought to be by Shakespeare. Fletcher had a hand, too, in Shakespeare's last play, *Henry VIII*, a Globe but not a Blackfriars production. The first performance of this play began with great ceremony and splendor in the afternoon of June 29, 1613, but it proceeded no further than the first act. At an entrance of the king in the play, a "sound-effect" cannon behind the stage fired, a small piece of burning material caught in the thatched roof over the galleries, and in no time the whole place was ablaze. The audience and actors escaped, but the entire building and probably a good part of the company's wardrobe were totally destroyed. The Globe was rebuilt and in operation a year later, but by that time Shakepeare had retired permanently from writing.

It was as a wealthy citizen and a respected gentleman that Shakespeare retired to Stratford. He had friends among the leading townspeople and the local gentry. The poet and playwright Michael Drayton, with whom he was acquainted, was a regular visitor at the home of Sir Henry and Lady Rainsford, who lived very near Stratford, and may well have found the time to call on him. Shakespeare became involved in the life of Stratford. He entertained a preacher in his home and was sent a quart of sack and a quart of claret by the town. In his garden that became famous, flourishing for over a century, he planted a mulberry tree. It must have been a quiet, orderly life after the busy years in London. Family affairs, inevitably, were to the fore. His two remaining brothers, Gilbert and Richard, died in Stratford in 1612 and 1613 respectively, both unmarried. His elder daughter, Susanna, was involved in court action in the Ecclesiastical Court at Worcester in 1613 to clear her name from a slander put about by John Lane of Alveston Manor. Accused of mismanaging her household and committing adultery, Susanna was legally vindicated and her accuser punished by excommunication.

Two months before Shakespeare's death his second daughter, Judith, then aged thirty, was married to Thomas Quiney, a tavern-keeper. The marriage did not have an auspicious beginning. It took place in February, a prohibited season, without a special license of the kind Shakespeare himself had obtained, and in consequence the couple were excommunicated. The next month a local girl called Margaret Wheeler died giving birth to a baby that also died, and Thomas Quiney confessed in court that he was the father. Shakespeare evidently altered the will that he had drafted in January on account of Judith's marriage. He signed the final settlement on each page (three of the six undisputed signatures of Shakespeare) on March 25, in the month when, according to tradition, the "merry meeting" took place between Shakespeare, Drayton, and Jonson that resulted in his death. It is possible that the three men did meet, since Drayton may well have been paying a visit to the Rainsfords and Jonson, a good friend, staying with him. Scholars accept or reject, according to temperament, the story reported by John Ward, vicar (1662–1681) of Stratford, in his notebook (c.1662) that Shakespeare drank too much at this "meeting" and as a result caught a fever. He died on April 23 and was buried in the chancel of the parish church.

His will was left in the form of a much-corrected draft and not a fair copy, perhaps because this was the practice of his lawyer, Francis Collins, or perhaps because of the need for haste if Shakespeare's death appeared imminent. The provisions do nothing to solve the many unanswered questions of his life. His property in Stratford and London went to his daughters, his granddaughter, and their heirs. His sister Joan and her sons were provided for. He made small bequests to the poor and to various local people, and he left twenty-eight shillings and six pence apiece to his old fellows Burbage, Heming, and Condell, to buy memorial rings. To Anne, his wife, he left only his second-best bed, knowing that she was well provided for by common law, which entitled her to a life interest in one-third of all her husband's heritable estates. This provision, made in an interlineation, seems curious and significant to us, but it need imply neither a lack of affection nor a deliberate slight; the best bed, which is not mentioned in the will, belonged in the master bedroom of New Place, and it went with the house to Susanna and her family, who lived there after Shakespeare's death. The hope that is implied in the terms of the will for the establishment and continuance of Shakespeare's family was not to be realized. When his granddaughter Elizabeth died in 1670, childless after two marriages, his direct line became extinct.

THEATRE AND PLAY PRODUCTION IN
SHAKESPEARE'S TIME

The Elizabethan theatre as we think of it began to develop in the 1570's. This is not to say that before that time there had been no tradition of organized drama in England. The highly complex and conventionalized medium of Marlowe, Jonson, and Shakespeare did not spring to life from a void. The beginnings of European drama have been traced back to musical elaborations of the Mass that took place during Easter ceremonies in the tenth century, in particular to the *Quem Quaeritis* trope, a musical sequence sung by a soloist representing the angel at Christ's tomb and singers representing the three Maries. This trope became a little play in its own right, and over the years other episodes were added, including those with no biblical warrant, becoming the basis for the Mystery plays; similar dramas evolved for other religious festivals. These were in Latin, but gradually, during the thirteenth century, drama detached itself from church worship and became secular in its organization and vernacular in its medium. From this time onward religious and moral plays were performed in public in the open air, in market places or on village greens or in processional manner on wagons. At Whitsuntide or Corpus Christi in England, cycles of Mystery plays based on biblical stories were performed in processional manner through the streets of such towns as Chester or York by members of the various local trade or craft guilds, who organized the whole venture, maintained the wagons ("pageants"), and paid the actors.

Many other kinds of performances took place during these centuries. The guilds performed Miracle plays, based on the lives of the saints and martyrs, and Moralities, didactic plays of various lengths in which the central subject is man's life and destiny, often represented in terms of conflict between personified virtues and vices. One of the last of these plays, *The Summoning of Everyman*, was written at the end of the fifteenth century, but like the Miracle and Mystery plays, Moralities continued to be performed in the sixteenth century. Folk plays or festivities connected with seasonal rites such as seed-sowing and harvest time were sometimes absorbed into the church plays and sometimes continued separately.

On May Day there was dancing round the maypole and the election of a May king and May queen; at Christmas time mummers would go from house to house, sometimes disguised with blackened faces and animal skins. The king and his court had their own ceremonies. Tournaments and jousts, which encouraged great displays of heraldry and special costumes for knights and their ladies, might go on for several days at a time. John Stow, the chronicler, records that in 1374, Dame Alice Perrers, dressed as the Lady of the Sun, "rode from the Tower of London, through Cheape, accompanied of many Lords and Ladies, every Lady leading a Lord by his horse bridle, til they came unto West Smithfield, and then began a great Just, which endured seven days after."[1] Under Henry VIII, court revels flourished, with all kinds of elaborately costumed spectacles, masques, dances, and interludes. Henry himself retained a troupe of eight players, the Lusores Regis, or Players of the King's Interludes, and paid them from the Exchequer.[2]

Professional entertainers such as minstrels, jugglers, conjurers, and ballad-singers traveled throughout the country to perform at fairs and in market places and, by invitation, at the homes of the rich. There were street pageants and processions, especially on festival occasions or for the entertainment of royalty or nobility; decorated wagons might be pulled through the streets or platforms set up on which would be posed a *tableau vivant*, a group of people costumed and arranged to represent an idea or theme. When Margaret of York came to Bruges to marry Charles the Bold in 1468 there were a number of *tableaux vivants* showing scenes on the theme of marriage: Adam and Eve, the wedding at Cana, Cleopatra marrying King Alexander.[3]

All these forms of theatre contributed in some way to the Elizabethan drama, but there were other more direct influences. During the sixteenth century, and probably earlier, boys in grammar schools and young men at Oxford and Cambridge and the Inns of Court acted in classical plays and also in plays, in both Latin and English, written by teachers and lawyers. Authors of such plays included Nicholas Udall, sometime headmaster of Eton, who wrote *Ralph Roister Doister*, and Sackville and Norton, the co-authors of *Gorboduc*. The companies of child actors, those "little eyases" that troubled the players in *Hamlet*, were already in

1. S. Joseph, *The Story of the Playhouse in England*, London, 1963, 8.
2. E.K. Chambers, *The Elizabethan Stage*, 4 Vols., Oxford, 1923, ii, 79.
3. G.R. Kernodle, *From Art to Theater*, 1944, 68.

existence in embryo early in the sixteenth century. The Children of the Chapel, originally choristers in the royal household, were first trained to act by their master, William Cornish (d.1523), who produced pageants, interludes, and entertainments of all kinds for the court of Henry VIII. Groups of boys from this institution played before Elizabeth I and in the seventeenth century acted in plays written for them by Ben Jonson. They were rivaled by the Children of Paul's, who also played both at Court and before a paying public under Elizabeth and her successor.

The Court was a friend and benefactor to the drama in this period, and royal patronage was particularly important during the 1570's, the early years of the permanent playhouses. At that time, the Church and the City Fathers, as the civic authorities of London were called, took every opportunity to attack the "sumptuous Theatre houses, a continuall monument of London's prodigalitie and folly,"[4] as well as the actors. Semi-professional companies of adult male actors began to appear in considerable numbers in the mid-sixteenth century. These companies were usually attached to the household of some nobleman or man of wealth, and they played at court and in the households of their patron and his friends, and from the 1550's, if not earlier, they traveled the countryside and also performed in London innyards. There were, as well, companies of strolling players who were not under the regular patronage of a nobleman but traveled in small groups, singing, clowning, acting, and providing entertainment as profited them most.

Legislation in the middle part of the century suggests that by then, amateur and semi-professional actors constituted a recognized element in the life of the country, especially in London. Censorship of interludes concerned with politics or religion began in 1533, and in 1543 there was a regulation that all interludes, books, and ballads that dealt with the interpretation of scripture were to be officially scrutinized. In 1553 the City Fathers issued an edict forbidding artificers and handicraftsmen to abandon their occupations and wander about singing in taverns and at weddings and feasts. But the most important legislation regulating the activities of actors came in the significant decade of the 1570's. In 1572 there was an act of parliament *"for the punishment of Vacabondes"* (14 Eliz. c.5) by which only those who held the rank of baron or above

4. Thomas White, quoted in F.P. Wilson, *The English Drama 1485–1585.* Oxford History of English Literature Vol. IV. Pt. 1, Oxford, 1969, 164–5.

were allowed to license players who "wandered abroad."[5] All those "Fencers Bearewardes Comon Players in Enterludes & Minstrels, not belonging to any Baron of this Realme or towardes any other Honorable Personage of greater Degree" who wandered the country were liable to be "adjudged and deemed Roges Vacaboundes and Sturdy Beggers" and punished accordingly. The act is notable in that it shows very clearly the stigma attached to the acting profession that lingered in the minds of many in this period despite the wealth and prestige that some men of the theater obtained. Even more significant is the fact that the act defined the actor's status and, by distinguishing between amateur and professional, encouraged the growth of a professional theatre.

One of the first companies formed in accordance with the statute was the Earl of Leicester's Men; it included Robert Wilson, famous for his wit, and James Burbage. Leicester was a great favorite of the Queen and a very wealthy man. He had maintained players in his household for several years before the statute, and his influence was available to win them many a hearing at Court. In 1574 his company received a license by royal patent.

The Elizabethan playhouse

At this time, the players had been performing in London for some years, but without any permanent headquarters for their performances. E.K. Chambers has presented the idea that, from 1557 onward, when the first performances of plays in London innyards were recorded at the Saracen's Head in Islington and the Boar's Head in Aldgate, some innkeepers so encouraged visits from the players, even modifying their premises for their convenience, that these inns gradually became "little less than permanent theatres."[6] References to inns such as the Bell and Cross Keys in Gracechurch Street, the Bull in Bishopsgate Street, and the Bel Savage on Ludgate Hill confirm their status as known playhouses for the rest of the century, sometimes perhaps as winter quarters for the major companies.[7] The importance of these inns is recognized in legislation of 1574, when the City Fathers issued a regulation specifically aimed at the control of "greate Innes, havinge chambers and secrete

5. E.K. Chambers, *The Elizabethan Stage*, iv, 269–71.
6. E.K. Chambers, *The Elizabethan Stage*, ii, 357.
7. G. Wickham, *Early English Stages 1300–1600*, Vol. ii, Pt. i, London, 1963, 188.

places adioyninge to their open stagies and gallyries" where "playes, enterludes, and shewes" lured the youth of the city and gave occasion for "ffrayes and quarrelles."[8]

While there is no denying that professional theatre was very much alive in London before the first playhouse was built, James Burbage's venture in building London's first permanent playhouse was nonetheless of great significance for the theater of his day. Burbage, a member of the Earl of Leicester's Men, was a bold and original man, and perhaps the confidence provided by so powerful a patron as Leicester was all that was needed to encourage him in his undertaking. No aristocrat or bourgeois, but an artisan, originally a joiner (carpenter), he designed a theatre and raised the money for it himself, without any monetary help from his wealthy patron—he gambled on the theatre's being self-supporting. His playhouse, the Theatre, was erected on a site in Shoreditch, outside the city limits, on land leased from Giles Alleyn for an annual rent of £14. It cost Burbage and his partner John Brayne £700 to build. Construction began in 1576, and the Theatre opened in 1577, before the work was actually complete; the last stages of the building were paid for out of the first takings. No illustrations of it have survived, but we know that it was round in shape, like the two rings for animal-baiting that existed on the south bank of the Thames, that it was built mainly of timber, and that contemporaries thought it very fine. A second theatre, the Curtain, was built the same year in the same locality. "It is an event token of a wicked time when plaiers wexe so riche that they can build such houses," remarked a disapproving contemporary.[9]

In Shakespeare's London there were eventually nine playhouses:

1. The Theatre, built in Shoreditch in 1576 by James Burbage. It was pulled down in 1597 when the ground lease expired.
2. The Curtain, built nearby in 1576. It was still in use in 1626.
3. A theatre at Newington Butts, built shortly after the Theatre and the Curtain. It was in use in the 1580's and early 1590's.
4. The Rose, built on the Bankside c.1587 by the financier Philip Henslowe. It was in use until about 1603.
5. The Swan, built on the Bankside in 1594 or 1595 by Francis Langley, a goldsmith. It was in use as a playhouse until about

8. G. Wickham, 195.
9. E.K. Chambers, *The Elizabethan Stage*, ii, 396, footnote.

1620. It is the only Elizabethan theatre of which a contemporary interior view exists. See cut following page 148.

6. The Globe, built on the Bankside in 1599 by the Burbages, out of the fabric of the old Theatre. It burnt down in 1613 and was immediately rebuilt.

7. The Fortune, built just outside Cripplegate in 1599–1600 by Philip Henslowe and Edward Alleyn as a rival to the Globe. Its building contract survived. It burnt down in 1621 and was rebuilt in brick in 1623.

8. The Red Bull, built about 1606 in Clerkenwell. It was later enlarged and probably roofed over, and continued in use after the Restoration, until 1663.

9. The Hope, built by Philip Henslowe and Jacob Meade in 1614 on the site of the old Bear Garden on the Bankside. The builder's contract, which survives, shows that it was designed to be used as both playhouse and bearbaiting arena, and had a removable stage. The shape was based on the Swan.

There existed also private theatres consisting of the halls of existing buildings, where performances took place by candlelight and a higher price was charged. The first of these was in Blackfriars, a large old building situated between St. Pauls and the river; it had once been used as a convent and later as a residence for important officials at court. In 1576, a few months after James Burbage signed the lease for the land where the Theatre was to be built, the upper story of Blackfriars was rented by Richard Farrant for the Children of Windsor and the Children of the Chapel to perform before the public. But the lessor of the rooms objected to the way they were used, and in 1584 the arrangement came to an end. The Burbages purchased a part of the building in 1596 and converted it for the use of the Lord Chamberlain's Men, but were prevented from using it as a theatre for adult actors by a petition of residents who objected to a common playhouse being set up within their select locality. For a time, the Burbages leased it to the Children of the Chapel, but in 1609 the Lord Chamberlain's Men, now the King's Men, managed to acquire the lease, and the company and its successors played there until the Civil War (1642–1646). Other private theatres existed at Whitefriars in an old monastic hall and in the Choir Singing School near St. Pauls.

The appearance and construction of these playhouses, especially of the public ones, is a matter of immense controversy. There have been a number of attempts at reconstruction, in particular of the Globe, which often differ very startlingly. Fashions in reconstruction come and go, to some extent according to the prevailing view of the theatre's architectural origins. Formerly, much stress was laid on the influence of the innyard on theatre design, and it was held that both auditorium and stage façade owed their characteristic features to those galleries, doors, windows, and yard that were an essential part of the sixteenth century inn. Other scholars have felt that since the Elizabethan playhouse was usually round or polygonal in shape while the traditional innyard square or rectangular, the innyard theory cannot be satisfactory. It has been suggested that the theatres owe much to those medieval and Tudor great halls in gentlemen's houses that were used by earlier players, and to the screens, often carved and ornate, that acted both as a shield between the guests in the main body of the hall and the doors to the kitchen, and as a background to the play.[10] Another possible influence is the tradition of street pageantry with its use of *tableaux vivants* and monumental sculpture, from which the structure and symbolism of the Elizabethan stage facade may be derived.[11]

At one time it was thought that there could be no classical influence on the Elizabethan theatre, despite the great Renaissance interest in classical architecture; but the fact that both foreign visitors and critical puritans were struck by the resemblance between the London public theatres and the auditoria of Greek and Roman amphitheaters seems significant. It is not impossible that James Burbage could have read of Vitruvius, the author of a book on architecture written in the first century A.D., whose theories were being studied in Renaissance Europe.[12] In this case, we should be justified in regarding Burbage's venture in 1576 as totally of the Renaissance, in its attempt to revive the classical theatre, rather than as a medieval survival.

Although contemporary evidence for the structure and organization of the Elizabethan theatre continues to be discovered, what we have is still fragmentary and not entirely consistent in its implications. This information consists of incidental references in letters, diaries, pamphlets, and so on, of the implications of the action and stage directions of plays themselves, and of documents such as the decrees of the Privy Council, the records of the Master

10. R. Southern, *The Seven Ages of the Theatre*, London, 1962, 128.
11. G.R. Kernodle, 150.
12. F. Yates, *The Theatre of the World*, London, 1969, Chs. VI and VII.

of Revels, accounts of litigation in various courts, and the contract for the building of the Fortune and Hope theatres. The diary of Philip Henslowe, the theatre owner and manager, who kept an account of the daily takings at the Rose theatre from February 1592 to November 1597, is a unique and invaluable source, not only of information about the theatres themselves, but also for the lives of the playwrights and actors who furnished their business. Foreigners who visited London in the period, such as Prince Lewis of Anhalt-Cöthen, Johannes de Witt, Paul Hentzner, and Thomas Platter of Basle often gave accounts of London's playhouses, sometimes contradicting one another. Pamphleteers and ministers of the church variously praised and condemned the phenomenon. Maps give interesting if unreliable testimony to the position, duration, and external appearance of the theaters. There is otherwise very little in the way of contemporary illustration to help us. There are a few title-pages and other engravings. Such factual details are extant as Inigo Jones's designs for scenery and costumes for his masques, and the drawing copied from one made by Johannes de Witt of the interior of the Swan, probably sometime after his visit to London in or about 1596.

Because of the lucky survival of its building contract, the Fortune is the only theatre whose dimensions and construction are known for certain. The building was square, 80 feet each way outside and 55 feet within. It was constructed of timber plastered over, on a foundation of brick and piles. The stage measured 43 feet by 27½ feet, large by modern standards, and is usually presumed to have been rectangular. There were three tiers of galleries in the auditorium, the lowest being 12 feet high, the next 11 feet, and the topmost 9 feet. Each was 12½ feet broad, and the upper two each extended ten inches over the one beneath. Each story contained four sections for "gentlemens roomes" and an unspecified number of "Twoe pennie roomes." In most respects the Fortune was designed, according to the contract, to resemble "the late erected Plaiehowse . . . called the Globe," except that "all the princypall and maine postes of the saide fframe and Stadge forwarde [presumably the stage front] shalbe square and wroughte palasterwise [made like pilasters]."[13] The carpenter, Peter Street, had assisted the Burbages when the Theatre was demolished and the Globe built out of its fabric, and it seems reasonable to suppose from this and from the wording of the contract itself, which con-

13. E.K. Chambers, *The Elizabethan Stage*, ii, 437.

stantly refers to the Globe as a model, that the two theatres were very similar in design. Alfred Harbage[14] conjectured that the Globe could hold nearly 2,500 spectators; Leslie Hotson[15] thinks more. De Witt, in the description of the Swan theatre that accompanies his drawing, said that it would take 3,000 people seated but did not mention how many could be accommodated standing in the yard. E. K. Chambers[16] thought this to be "merely the exaggerated round estimate of a casual visitor."

The other theatres doubtless differed from the Fortune in some ways, as modern theatres differ one from another. Most of the public theatres seem to have been approximately round or octagonal, and the halls at the Blackfriars and Whitefriars were rectangular. The Fortune was exceptional in being square. The roof of the Fortune was tiled, whereas that of the first Globe, to its misfortune, was thatched. The contract for the Hope theatre, which was to resemble the Swan, is less specific than the Fortune contract, but apart from features such as a removable stage and the absence of pillars supporting the stage covering, designed to provide for the dual function of playhouse and bear-baiting ring, it does not differ significantly. The Hope was constructed of timber on a brick foundation, with three galleries of the same height as the Fortune's, and a tiled roof.

Elizabethan stage and stagecraft

On the important matter of the construction of the stage both the Fortune (except for giving dimensions) and the Hope contracts are unfortunately silent, and the inconclusive evidence that survives has led scholars to differ, often quite widely, on certain matters. That the stage projected far out into the yard is certain, and it was probably rectangular rather than square. Part of the audience, the "groundlings," stood round three sides of it in the yard. The evidence that exists for the stage structure of the Swan, the Globe, the Fortune, and the Hope suggests that the construction in each case differed. It is thought that in the earlier houses, the Theatre and the Curtain, stages were built to be simple and easily removable, whereas they may have become more complex in the

14. A. Harbage, *Shakespeare's Audience*, New York, 1941, Appendix A.
15. J.L. Hotson, *Shakespeare's Wooden O*, London, 1959, 292–306.
16. E.K. Chambers, *The Elizabethan Stage*, ii, 526.

later theatres, when the financiers realized that permanent play-houses were no longer a risky enterprise.[17] The stage was about level with the tops of the heads of the spectators in the yard, and was supported on posts. There seems to have been a low rail around the edge, perhaps to discourage the groundlings from climbing onto it.

The area directly beneath the stage, which had many uses, was probably hidden from the audience in some way, perhaps by oak boards, as at the Fortune, or by hangings. The Swan drawing, however, appears to show the front of the stage supported on two very solid posts at either corner and the area beneath it uncon-cealed.[18] There was at least one trapdoor set in the stage, through which villains might descend to death or ghosts arise from the "cellerage."

The roof of the stage, or "heavens," was high above, probably supported on wooden pillars, except at the Hope, where the con-tract specified that it was "to be borne or carryed without any postes or supporters to be fixed or sett upon the said stage."[19] It may have covered all or only part of the stage. Over the heavens was built a hut, thatched at the Globe, tiled at the Fortune and the Hope, which maps and engravings usually show with windows. This is thought to have housed the machinery for raising and low-ering thrones, chariots, and other such properties onto the stage, though it is a matter of dispute as to whether such machinery actu-ally existed at the Globe.[20] The whole structure was topped by a flagpole, and a flag was flown at times of performance.

The construction of the building, usually called the tiring-house, at what we regard as the back of the stage is still more con-jectural. In general, it is agreed that this part of the building was divided into two or possibly three levels, perhaps equivalent in height to and level with the spectators' galleries, although again the Swan drawing shows no such thing. At the lowest of these levels were two doors through which the actors made their exits and entrances, as are clearly indicated in the Swan drawing. Con-troversy exists as to whether, between these doors, there was a curtained recess used as the "inner" or "rear" stage, a wider door or porch, or simply, as in the Swan drawing, a blank wall. A recess

17. G. Wickham, 300.
18. J.L. Hotson, 91, thinks these two "posts" may be windows.
19. C.W. Hodges, *The Globe Restored: A Study of the Elizabethan Theatre*, 2nd ed., Oxford, 1968, 19.
20. C.W. Hodges, 21.

would seem a most convenient location for those many scenes in Elizabethan plays that take place in some sort of alcove or removed place, as when Prospero reveals Miranda and Ferdinand playing chess in *The Tempest* or when Portia's caskets are discovered behind a curtain in *The Merchant of Venice*. However, such a recess would have been invisible to spectators in many areas of the theatre, and the term "inner stage," which seems the obvious way of describing it, was never used by the Elizabethans.

The use of the middle level of this tiring-house is also debatable. In the Swan drawing it seems to be shown as a spectators' gallery, divided into six compartments; but there are enough references to the "upper stage" in Elizabethan plays for us to be fairly sure that at least some part of this level was sometimes used by the actors. Indeed, as C.W. Hodges points out, "the business of vertical display, of building, mounting, and climbing upwards seems to have had a characteristic and symbolic importance in the Renaissance theatre as a whole."[21] How many scenes were played "aloft" in this gallery is a matter for conjecture. Again, it is hard to imagine that the space inside it was clearly visible to many in the audience, or that in general it would have been dramatically effective to leave the great area of the main stage unused while a sustained scene was played out in this enclosure. Both E.K. Chambers and C.W. Hodges propose that this gallery may have been used by musicians and by those spectators who could afford to pay for the privilege of being so near to the play and so visible to the rest of the audience, as well as by the actors Perhaps, as F. Yates suggests,[22] the central part of the gallery projected out over the stage, thus providing a readily visible balcony. If there was a higher gallery it may have been used for spectators or for musicians.

We do not know what sort of appearance this stage façade presented, but it was probably very ornate and decorative. The Fortune, the Hope, and probably the Swan featured columns as part of it, and it may well have been painted, perhaps to resemble the half-timbering of an Elizabethan house, or maybe in a more elaborate and symbolic way. G.R. Kernodle says that it was "more than an arrangement of side doors and inner and upper stages . . . [it was] a symbol of castle, throne, triumphal arch, altar,

---

21. C.W. Hodges, 51.
22. F. Yates, Ch. VII.

tomb, and several other shows long familiar in art and pageantry."[23] There was space backstage, between the stage façade and the outer wall of the playhouse, that was used in several ways: for dressing rooms, for the storage of costumes and properties, for actors to await their entrances, for the prompter and other attendants to carry out their offices, for the playwright to watch the enactment of his drama, for gallants and noblemen to chat with the actors. Most scholars are agreed that it is this whole backstage area behind the galleried façade that is meant by the term "tiring-house," although Leslie Hotson believes that the tiring-house was beneath the stage.[24]

Shakespeare disparaged his theatre and called it a "cockpit" and "an unworthy scaffold," but others, both defenders and detractors of the stage, wondered at its splendor. John Stockwood, a preacher, called the Theatre a "gorgeous Playing place," and Philip Stubbes, a Puritan, talked of "Venus' pallaces," while Thomas Nashe, a pamphleteer, compared the English stage favorably with the Roman one: "Our Sceane is more statelye furnisht than ever it was in the time of *Roscius*."[25] The modern taste in design for simple lines and muted furnishings was not the Elizabethan taste. Their theatres, with their painted pillars and pilasters, their carving and gilding, their arras and fine hangings, were colorful, decorative, even gaudy places, embellished in every possible way to appeal to an age that reveled in richness and display.

In what ways did this kind of theatre influence the plays that were written for it? Like many questions to do with the topic of the Elizabethan stage, this is not easily answered. To many of us, this large wooden platform with its formal tiered façade and painted pillars may seem so remote, even restrictive, that we are ready to ascribe all the most foreign and archaic features of Elizabethan drama to its effects. Yet the actors had frequently to perform in places other than their London playhouses—at Court, in country barns, in the halls of great houses, in innyards—so that plays and styles of acting had to be adaptable; moreover, as has been amply proven since, many Elizabethan plays translate readily to the picture-frame stage. Some modern critics have felt that the stage construction itself actually counted for much less than

23. G.R. Kernodle, 130.
24. J.L. Hotson, Ch. IV.
25. E.K. Chambers, *The Elizabethan Stage*, iv, 239.

we are accustomed to think.[26] Indeed, it may be that, as G.F. Reynolds asserts, "The principles of staging were, phrasing them not too exactly, those of the medieval stage."[27]

Of course there are some features of Elizabethan drama that must be related to the contemporary stage conditions. The neutrality of the stage is obviously a major point. The stage was free from any suggestion of a restricted location; at one moment it could represent Rome, at the next Egypt, without any pause in the action or change in its appearance. Neither space nor time had to be treated realistically. An actor might stand next to another and yet deliver an aside that was inaudible to him. A commentator could stand a few feet from the action that he was interpreting and yet not be observed by the other characters. The aside and the soliloquy are characteristic features of this drama. So too are various kinds of staging not possible in a realistically designed setting. For instance, in *Othello*, while Cassio and Bianca quarrel about Desdemona's handkerchief, Iago and Othello stand unobserved a little way off, misinterpreting the scene. In Shakespeare's *Troilus and Cressida* Cressida pleads with Diomede, watched separately by two different groups, the jeering Thersites to one side and the unhappy Troilus to the other. In *Richard III* the tents of the opposing leaders, Richmond and Richard, are simultaneously presented on the stage. In *King Lear*, Kent is placed in the stocks at the end of II.ii and left on stage, mute and sleeping during the next scene while Edgar soliloquizes, until he is discovered by Lear and his followers in II.iv.

Space and time expand according to the demands of the imagination. An hour can pass in the course of a thirty-line soliloquy, as it does at the end of Marlowe's *Faustus*, or a whole night in the course of a scene, as in *Othello* II.iii. On such a stage, where representation is unhindered by the need to create the illusion of actuality, the dramatist has no need to restrict himself to a few long scenes with plausible backgrounds. He can use as many scenes and locations as he likes and move back and forth from interior to exterior, from one country to another, without any slowing of the pace of the action, since there were no breaks between scenes. Where in a modern play a pause, a blackout, a curtain, a change of lighting, even a change of set, is used to denote the passage

26. For instance, B. Beckerman, *Shakespeare at the Globe 1599–1604*, New York, 1962, and G.F. Reynolds, *The Staging of Elizabethan Plays at the Red Bull Theater 1605–1625*, New York and London, 1940.
27. G.F. Reynolds, 189.

between one scene and the next, in an Elizabethan play one set of
actors had merely to go out and another set to come in. Location
boards may have been used to help the audience follow the changes
of scene where this was important. Sometimes the text makes the
scene change clear, with lines such as "This is Illyria, lady," in
Twelfth Night, or "Barkloughly Castle call they this at hand?" in
Richard II, but not always.

On this kind of stage, and in a theatre where sightlines were
by no means perfect, much emphasis fell on the spoken word. "We
are dealing with an aural theatre, not a visual one," writes Bernard
Beckerman.[28] While this is true, with implications for the style of
acting that are supported from other evidence, nonetheless note
should be taken of the Elizabethans' great love of stage spectacle
and the prominence of dumbshows, tableaux, processions, sword-
fights, and ceremonial dances.

Colorful and expensive costumes added to the brilliance and
visual appeal of the stage. Puritan critics were censorious of players who earned a mere "vi s. by the weeke" being able to "jet
under gentlemens noses in sutes of silk";[29] (it was said to be customary for the rich clothing of lords and noblemen to be handed
on after their deaths to the actors[30]). Philip Henslowe's invaluable
diary contains an inventory of costumes owned by the Lord Admiral's Men that included cloaks in scarlet and black velvet,
gowns, caps, suits and jerkins and doublets in silk, satin, and
damask, with trimmings of gold and silver tinsel and lace. Henslowe
records paying £6 for "a dublet of whitt satten layd thicke with
gowld lace, and a payer of rowne pande hosses [hose] of cloth of
sylver, the panes layd with gowld lace,"[31] and the then-extravagant
sum of £20.10.6. for a "black velvet cloak with sleeves embroi-
dered all with silver and gold."[32] Colors were often used symbolically on the stage, as for instance the white, red, and black tents
in Marlowe's *Tamburlaine*, the sable suit worn by Hamlet, and the
yellow stockings that signified Malvolio's role as a lover in *Twelfth
Night*.

Properties, too, were often elaborate. Henslowe provides a

28. B. Beckerman, 129.
29. G. Wickham, 118.
30. A. Gurr, *The Shakespearean Stage, 1574–1642*, Cambridge, 1970,
128–129.
31. R.A. Foakes and R.T. Rickert, eds., *Henslowe's Diary*, Cambridge,
1961, 325.
32. A. Gurr, 128.

useful list,[33] including such intriguing items as "the sittie of Rome" and "the clothe of the Sone & Mone," which were perhaps painted hangings, and "i Hell mought [mouth]" and "i dragon in fostes [Faustus]," which come directly from the trappings of medieval drama, as well as the tombs, crowns, and mossy banks that we know to have been standard properties. Despite the fact that the Elizabethans did not use movable scenery, there is much evidence that the stage was frequently decked out to represent certain conventional settings; an arbor or garden, a cave, a castle, or a tomb.[34]

But, obviously, the dramatist did have to rely very much on the words to create atmosphere and setting. In *A Midsummer Night's Dream* the evocation of moonlight and enchanted woods in the language of the fairies and the lovers makes a very deliberate contrast with the efforts of Bottom and his company to provide a moonlit setting for their play with such mechanical and symbolical aids as the man in the moon and his dog. The soldiers in the opening scene of *Hamlet* must evoke the eerie midnight atmosphere with their edgy dialogue, since they can have no assistance from lighting. It is, in fact, not so much the lack of scenery that the dramatist must compensate for, as the lack of lighting. In the public theatres plays were performed in the afternoon, and while the use of candles or tapers may have suggested nighttime scenes, there was no way of providing darkness or moonlight.

This lack of blackout and also of curtaining created another difficulty, that of the management of violence and climaxes; dead bodies had to be disposed of and the ending of the play had to be so contrived that the players all walked or were carried off. There was no chance to end with a final tableau. Shakespeare's tragedies *Hamlet* and *King Lear* present contrasting ways of dealing with this problem. In the last scene of *Hamlet*, five characters die onstage, with Hamlet himself last; Shakespeare cannot end with Hamlet's "the rest is silence," or yet with Horatio's epitaph, for the stage is piled with corpses—so Fortinbras enters and ends the play with the arrangements for the disposal of the bodies which Shakespeare, making a virtue of necessity, contrives appropriately:

> Bear Hamlet like a soldier to the stage,
> For he was likely, had he been put on,
> To have proved most royal.

33. *Henslowe's Diary*, 319–20.
34. G. Wickham, Ch. VI.

In *King Lear* most of the deaths take place before the final scene or else offstage; this makes the disposal easier but also leaves the stage free for Lear and his lamentations over Cordelia's body, so that attention is centred on the sight of father and daughter reunited in death, before Albany gives the order, "Bear them from hence."

One feature of Elizabethan stagecraft that does seem to result directly from the construction of the stage is the use of vertical movement. Hodges calls the use "of what seems to have been a permanent upper level . . . the most characteristic single feature of Elizabethan stage practice."[35] The upper stage could serve as a balcony or platform to which characters might climb (Romeo) or be conveyed (Antony); it might be an upper room, a city wall, a battlement, where characters could watch and comment on the action taking place below on the main stage. Richard II descends symbolically from the walls of his castle to the courtyard below where Bolingbroke awaits him. Richard III appears "aloft" in the company of two bishops. In *The Taming of the Shrew* Christopher Sly watches the whole play from the upper room, here representing the lord's bedroom in an inn. The trap door on the main stage provided for downward movement. Hamlet and Laertes could jump into it in their scuffle at Ophelia's funeral; the Jew of Malta might plunge down it into his burning cauldron. Devils, ghosts, and furies could arise from and descend into it. Just as the stage canopy was painted to represent heaven so the area below stage could represent hell, as indeed it was commonly called.

A play such as Marlowe's *Doctor Faustus* seems designed to make the fullest use of the stage's symbolic construction. Some plays, such as Thomas Heywood's *The Four Ages* exploited extensively the possibilities of movement between trapdoor and "heavens," with fireworks in the air, falling showers of rain, Jupiter and Ganymede descending on an eagle, devils rising out of hell, and Hercules sinking into it. In general, Shakespeare did not rely on such stage devices as these, but his stagecraft undoubtedly makes use of some of the possibilities of action on different levels.

The Elizabethan audience

The proximity of the audience may perhaps have been a factor in discouraging certain kinds of realism, but the idea that an open

35. C.W. Hodges, 51.

stage with the audience on three sides or all round totally destroys theatrical illusion is true only if the kind of theatrical illusion desired is that of slice-of-life realism. In this sense, of course, the Elzabethan drama had no pretensions to realism. A more significant feature than the proximity of the audience, which is after all not especially different in modern theaters, may have been its mixed character. It is still common to conceive of Shakespeare's audience as "composed largely of illiterate Londoners"[36] who were "primitive and undeveloped imaginatively."[37] But modern critics are more and more aware that if many in Shakespeare's audience were illiterate, they were not necessarily unintelligent or indifferent to the power of images and words. It is true that they crowded to watch bear-baiting and the executions of criminals, but as Alfred Harbage says: "Each age has its own brutalities. The Elizabethans were forced to live more intimately with theirs, and they acceded to the conditions of their existence."[38]

There is no doubt that the nobility and the uneducated alike attended the theatre, along with artisans, apprentices, students, foreign visitors, and the pickpockets and prostitutes of legend; the audience could not have been so dissimilar to that at a bear-baiting, and among those who were mentioned as present when Paris Garden, the bear-baiting arena, collapsed in 1583 were a baker, a clerk, several servants, a fellmonger, and several women. Plays had to appeal to a very heterogeneous crowd and undoubtedly this influenced their character, not necessarily for the worse. To this factor we can partly ascribe the wonderful variety of Elizabethan drama—the mixture of sophisticated wit and rhetoric, dazzling poetry, high comedy, clowning, farce, and all manner of spectacle. There were duels and fencing matches, dumbshows, conjuring, supernatural characters, music and songs, dancing, and much bloodshed. Shakespeare rejected some of these elements; we see very little conjuring, few magic tricks, few dumb-shows, and after the excesses of *Titus Andronicus*, not much bloodshed. But he never ceased to mix high and low comedy and to introduce fools and clowns at moments of the greatest dramatic tension, and his

36. A. Hart, "The Time Allotted for Representation of Elizabethan and Jacobean Plays," *Review of English Studies*, VIII, 1932, 412, quoted in A. Harbage, 150.
37. M.C. Byrne, "Shakespeare's Audience," in Shakespeare Association, *A Series of Papers on Shakespeare and the Theatre*, 215, quoted in A. Harbage, 157.
38. A. Harbage, 153.

use of music and dancing does not diminish but grows increasingly subtle and refined. Under the control of the Stuart kings the drama narrowed its scope and ceased to attract so wide and varied an audience; the theatre gradually lost its popular appeal, and so dwindled into decadence.

But in Shakespeare's time, despite or to some extent because of attempts from many sides to restrict and repress it, theatre flourished. Plays were advertised by bills posted in the city or distributed by hand. Since seats were not reserved, the audience would need to assemble early for a new or popular production, perhaps gathering fairly soon after the midday meal, as the performances started at 2 p.m. Performances lasted at least two hours, according to references such as that in the Prologue to *Romeo and Juliet* to the "two hours traffic of our stage," and longer, if it was followed, as was customary, by a jig. On dull days in winter the last act must have been played in the falling dusk.

During Shakespeare's time the cheapest price of admission to the public theater was a penny, which bought standing room out in the open in the yard. In days when a quart of ale cost 4d., a small pipe of tobacco or a very cheap meal 3d., such a price was not expensive. For the payment of a second penny the spectator might sit in the topmost gallery or one of the twopenny rooms. Pamphleteers and satirists made little distinction in their scorn between the "Twopenny Clients and Peny Stinkards."[39] Thomas Platter, a visitor to London from Basle in 1599, said that for 3d. one of the best seats, with a cushion, might be bought, but prices rose in the seventeenth century, and from 1604 onward there is evidence that the best seats could cost 6d., 12d., or even more. In Shakespeare's day these were genuinely popular prices, and the London artisan, who at the turn of the century earned between 10d. and 16d. a day, could afford them.

For the richest and most fashionable playgoer the place to sit was in one of the boxes over the stage, or better still, on a stool on the very stage itself. E.K. Chambers thought that the stools were placed at the sides of the projecting stage, thus obstructing the view of those in the yard and inviting their missiles and abuse. Leslie Hotson suggested that the stools were arranged beneath the Lord's gallery or upper stage, where according to other views the inner recess or central stage door would have been. Apparently it

39. T. Dekker, *Work for Armourers* (1609), quoted in E.K. Chambers, *The Elizabethan Stage,* ii, 533.

became most fashionable to sit on the stage, and by 1609 the Lords' room over the stage was being referred to as the haunt of the less reputable patrons. It is clear that those who sat on the stage made their presence felt to actors and audience alike. They blew smoke from their pipes onto the stage.They obstructed the actors. If they disliked the play or its author they might leave very conspicuously at some important point. Ben Jonson particularly objected to those capricious gallants who "have taken such a habit of dislike in all things, that they will approue nothing, be it neuer so conceited or elaborate, but sit disperst, making faces, and spitting, wagging their vpright eares, and cry filthy, filthy."[40] The rest of the audience was equally forthright in expressing opinions of the play. They clapped at what they liked, but they also booed, hissed, and "mewed." The vigor of their response was perhaps more akin to that of modern spectators at a sporting event than to the politeness of a twentieth century theatre audience. They wept without inhibition, and they roared with laughter and delight: "Player is much out of countenance, if fooles do not laugh at them, boyes clappe their hands, pesants ope their throates, and the rude raskal rabble cry excellent, excellent."[41]

Elizabethan actors and theatrical companies

An enthusiastic theatregoer might go several afternoons a week to the playhouse of his choice and see a different production each time, for the repertory system was a characteristic feature of the Elizabethan theatre. It was also a necessary feature, for the potential audience of the London playhouses was not large. In 1600 London itself had between 200,000 and 250,000 inhabitants; it has been calculated that perhaps 13 percent of these Londoners went once a week to the theatre. At times, three or even four public theatres might be in operation, and the rebirth of the children's companies at the turn of the century provided a serious source of competition for the adult companies. The repertory system was so arranged that over a period of two weeks the patron of a particular theatre might see a different play almost every day. Bernard Beck-

40. B. Jonson, *The Case is Altered* (before 1609), II.vii.
41. T.G(ainsford?), *The Rich Cabinet Furnished with Varietie of Descriptions* (1616), in W.G. Hazlitt, ed., English Drama and Stage, 230.

erman[42] has calculated that during the period from August 25, 1595, to February 28, 1596, 150 performances of thirty different plays were given at the Rose, where the Lord Admiral's Men performed. Of these plays, fourteen were new that season, and there were eighty-seven performances of these; eight plays were less than a year old and there were forty-six performances of these; the remaining eight that were more than a year old accounted for only seventeen performances, five of these being of Marlowe's *The Jew of Malta*, newly revived that season. This account illustrates the extent to which the theatre depended on new plays. It also shows what enormous demands were made of the Elizabethan actor. The system was such that every member of a theatrical company appeared in each production, sometimes in more than one part. Thus a leading actor in the Lord Admiral's company for that period would have had at least thirty roles at his command, nearly half of them newly learned. He would be also expected to retain a part over a long period, since he might have to wait several weeks or months between performances of the play.

E.K. Chambers lists twenty-four companies of adult actors performing in London and the provinces at different times between 1500 and 1620.[43] Ten or eleven of these were in operation in London during Shakespeare's time, and whenever the theaters were not closed on account of plague, civic disturbance, or Lent, there must have been at least two or three companies active simultaneously in the capital. The adult companies usually consisted of eight to twelve shareholders and from six to thirty hired men, plus boy apprentices, stagehands, and musicians. The Earl of Leicester's Men consisted of six actors in 1572, when they wrote to their patron to ask for appointment as his household servants in order to meet the terms of the act of Parliament that regulated the licensing of players. Queen Elizabeth's Men, formed in 1583, had twelve men and was the largest troupe. Some of these companies stayed together with very little change of personnel over long periods, continuing as a group under a succession of patrons; others played together for a short period, broke up, and re-formed under another name.

Conditions in the theatre were not stable for very long during the 1580's, especially since opposition to the development of the

---

42. B. Beckerman, 7–8.
43. E.K. Chambers, *The Elizabethan Stage*, ii, 77–260.

drama came from several fronts and the City Fathers did all they could to inhibit its growth. In 1583 a company was formed under the Queen herself. This became the leading group of the day until the death of Richard Tarlton, the great clown, in 1588, and the rise of the Lord Admiral's Men. Allied with the Lord Strange's Men, the Admiral's Men became the leading group in 1590. During 1594 there was a major reshuffle in which some minor or declining companies disappeared; the allied Strange's and Admiral's groups broke up, and two new companies were formed: the Lord Admiral's Men and the Lord Chamberlain's Men. Together, these two companies dominated the London stage for the next forty years. On his accession, James I became patron of the company to which Shakespeare belonged, the Lord Chamberlain's Men, which then became known as the King's Men. Royal patronage does not seem to have conferred any special benefits; Elizabeth did not save her men from financial loss or professional eclipse, and James's men had to defend themselves before the Privy Council for playing in the prohibited season of Lent. James himself exerted strong control over the theatre, and while on the one hand this was a protective measure and effectively silenced opposition from the City Fathers and from the Church during his reign, on the other it could be said that his influence was ultimately repressive and served to divorce the theatre from the popular audience and the topical subject matter that had given it life.

The Lord Chamberlain's Men were financially the most successful and also the most stable group of their time. They formed in 1594 and moved into their own new playhouse, the Globe, in 1599; there were then nine sharers: Thomas Pope, John Heming, Augustine Phillips, Richard Cowley, Richard Burbage, William Sly, Henry Condell, Robert Armin, and William Shakespeare. A company had three types of member: the sharers, who bought, for a down payment of perhaps £50, the right to a portion of the company's profits and usually, though not always, took the leading parts; the hired men, who were not permanent members of the company but worked with them for a time in whatsoever capacity was required and received a regular, if not very substantial, wage; and the apprentices, boys or young men who played the women's parts and meanwhile received dramatic training, apprenticed to one of the sharers. By no means all actors began as apprentices; many—perhaps Shakespeare himself—went directly into the theatre from some trade or profession. James Burbage who "by occupacion a joyner and reaping but a small lyving by the same, gave it over and became a common player in playes"[44] was untypical not in his change of career, but in the success he made of it. Robert Armin, the clown, was said to have once been a goldsmith's apprentice. John Heming called himself in his will a citizen and grocer.

There is some disagreement as to how far the actors specialized in roles, but it does seem fairly clear that the same actors constantly took the main parts. At the Globe, Burbage was always the straight lead, Robert Armin the comic lead, and Richard Cowley took secondary parts. Cast-lists for plays done by the King's Men survive from 1623–32, and the implications of these are that characters could be roughly categorized into types—the hero, the foil for the hero, the smooth villain, the dignitary or old king, the young man or lover, and the comic figure—and that the actors usually specialized in a particular type of role. A kind of star system was in operation, but actors cannot have been rigidly type-cast. Some doubling of parts was called for, and of course an actor had to be prepared to take over another's role in emergencies. Playwrights at times wrote on the assumption that certain players would take certain parts. Shakespeare may well have written *Richard III*, *Hamlet*, *Othello*, and *King Lear* in the knowledge that Richard Burbage would play the lead, but this, of course, only proves how far Burbage was from being type-cast.

The Elizabethan actor had to be versatile: he was above all an entertainer. Actors could sing, dance, fence, and perform acrobatic tricks; comic actors were expected to be able to improvise (which according to Hamlet they sometimes did too readily). Tarlton, whose quips were immortalized in print, was apparently so noted for his extempore wit that it was customary at the end of a play in which he appeared for the audience to shout out "themes" in rhyme for him to answer on the spot.

As the account of the repertory system shows, the actors had to work very hard for their money, retaining a large number of parts in their minds while constantly learning new ones. Some actors became very prosperous and sought to win respectability. Some of them, like Tarlton, who had Sir Philip Sidney as a godfather to his son, and Burbage, whose death in 1619 left his friend the Earl of Pembroke disconsolate, were on familiar terms with the great men of the realm. Shakespeare became a prosperous man and a property owner, but Edward Alleyn (of the rival Lord Admiral's Men), who took for his third wife a daughter of the poet Donne, by

---

44. E.K. Chambers, *The Elizabethan Stage*, ii, 305.

that time Dean of St. Pauls, was probably six times more wealthy. He was able to buy the manor of Dulwich for about £10,000 and found a college there, as well as becoming in old age a patron of writers and actors. But these were exceptional cases, and for the most part acting was a precarious profession. The sense of shame at being an actor that Shakespeare expressed in the sonnets—the "public means that public manners breed"—is part of a great body of evidence that testifies to the disrepute in which actors were held. Plays were commonly said to be "a speaciall cause of corrupting the youth, conteninge nothinge but unchast matters, lascivious devices, shiftes of Coozenage, & other lewd & vngodly practizes."[45] Players were called "the worste and daungerousest people in the world"[46] and "Schoole-masters in bawderie, and in idlenes."[47] Pamphleteers and playwrights themselves attacked the actors, perhaps jealous of their fame and success. The writer Robert Greene said they were "base minded . . . in their corse of life, for they care not how they get crowns, . . . how basely so they haue them."[48]

A study of the legislation concerning the theatre during this period shows the desire of citizens and civil authorities to repress the theatre growing all the stronger for its resilience. Some new law, some petition from powerful citizens against the actors was a constant threat in Elizabeth's reign; James's efficient appropriation into his own hands of control over the theatres regulated their activities no less than before.

During Shakespeare's time the plague was rarely long absent from London, so that whenever plague deaths amounted to more than thirty (later forty) a week the authorities were only too glad to close down the playhouses and send the actors off to exile in the country. This happened in 1583, 1592–3, 1594, and a great many times between 1603 and 1610, perhaps for almost thirty months.[49] Players and playwrights disliked these excursions; the country

45. The Lord Mayor of London and the Aldermen to the Privy Council, 1597, cited in A.M. Nagler, *A Source Book in Theatrical History*, New York, 1952.
46. S. Gosson, *The Ephemerides of Phialo* (1579), quoted in E.K. Chambers, *The Elizabethan Stage*, iv, 207.
47. A. Munday(?), *A Second and third blast of retrait from plaies and Theaters* (1580) quoted in E.K. Chambers, *The Elizabethan Stage*, iv, 212.
48. R. Greene, *A Quip for an Upstart Courtier* (1592), quoted in E.K. Chambers, *The Elizabethan Stage*, iv, 240.
49. F.P. Wilson, *The Plague in Shakespeare's London*, London, 1927, 124–5.

people were less sophisticated in their theatrical tastes than Londoners and companies did not risk new plays, so profits were lower. The companies had to reduce their establishments and dismiss hired men. Sometimes groups broke up as a result. Moreover the loss of dignity was great. In the city the more prominent actors were men of wealth and substance, but in the country all were reduced to the level of the wandering minstrel. "Players, by reason they shal have a hard winter, and must travell on the hoofe, will lye sucking there for pence and twopences, like young pigges at a sowe newly farrowed"[50] prophesied Thomas Dekker in 1609.

If the system was sometimes hard on the players, at least there were profits to be had by some; those who owned shares in a company, or better still, were "housekeepers" (that is, had a right to a percentage of all the company's takings, not merely those from certain sections of the house) had a good steady income, and there were sometimes bonuses of £10, £20, or more for a performance at court. Playwrights in general fared less well; perhaps they had a right to be jealous. At any rate Robert Greene, according to the famous passage in his pamphlet *Greene's Groatsworth of Wit* seems to have thought that playwrights had the worst of it, denouncing the players as "those puppets . . . that spake from our mouths, those Anticks garnisht in our colours." Plays were sold outright to theatrical companies or their managers. Some playwrights were contracted to individual companies and paid a fixed wage in return for writing a specified number of plays a year, while others sold their plays to whoever would buy them.

Philip Henslowe, who financed one of the two main companies between 1594 and 1602 and had dealings with many playwrights of his time, paid them about £6 for a play in the 1590's. Often he paid by installments of £1 or so as a batch of sheets came in, an arrangement that was much more advantageous to himself than to the wretched authors, who were constantly having to be bailed out of debtors' prisons. "Lent [paid] . . . to discharge Mr. Dicker [Thomas Dekker] out of the cownter in the Powltrey the some of fortie shillinges"; "Lent into harey chettel [Henry Chettle] to pay his charges in the marshallsey the some of xxxs"; "Lent vnto . . Wᵐ Harton [William Haughton] to releace hime owt of the clyncke [Clink prison] the some of xs."[51] These entries from Henslowe's

50. T. Dekker, *The Raven's Almanack* (1609), quoted in E.K. Chambers, *The Elizabethan Stage*, i, 332.
51. *Henslowe's Diary*, 86, 103, 131.

diary are typical of those dealing with playwrights.

Playwrights received no royalties for their work, and a play once sold became the property of the company to do with as it liked. The company was usually reluctant to allow its plays to be published, since there was no system of limiting acting rights and the plays could be appropriated for performance by another company. The Earl of Pembroke's Men only sold their playbooks to the printers in time of financial difficulties, in 1593. Plays were not generally regarded as of the same order of literature as poetry, and Ben Jonson was much ridiculed when he saw his collected plays through the press in 1616, calling them his "works." Playwrights supplemented their income from their own individual plays by hackwork or collaboration. During periods of theatrical prosperity, the demand for new plays was very great, and the Admiral's Men, between 1594 and 1600, needed one almost every two weeks. Often four or five authors would contribute to a single work. Thomas Heywood, who wrote for the Queen Anne's Men at the Red Bull Theater from 1605/6 to 1619, claimed to have worked on some 220 plays. Other occasional sources of income were court performances, for which a playwright might be paid between £15 and £30, or benefit performances, for which there is a little evidence.[52] Conditions for playwrights did improve in the seventeenth century, especially as a result of Ben Jonson's efforts to raise the standing of the dramatist, but it may be noted that greater stability and larger payments did not in general produce better plays.

A large number of forces combined to shape and develop the theatre of Shakespeare's day. The climate of criticism and repression by religious and civic authorities, and antagonisms between playwright and actor and between one company and another, the plague and legal restrictions, all served no less than the royal favor and the national love of rhetoric and spectacle to make the drama what it was. The drama had a fine flowering, but a short one; after the accession of James I the nature of control over the theatre changed, different kinds of plays were written, new dramatists appeared, and the nature of the audience changed. Shakespeare had the kind of relationship with his audience that no dramatist before or since has been lucky enough to find. Perhaps this was the major source of strength of the Elizabethan drama.

52. E.K. Chambers, *The Elizabethan Stage*, i, 373.

SHAKESPEARE'S MAJOR POETRY

Shakespeare wrote his first published poem, *Venus and Adonis*, in 1592, when he was twenty-eight. It can be seen from the pamphlet *Greene's Groatsworth of Wit* (1592) that he had, by this time, begun to make a name in London both as an actor and as a playwright. There are perhaps several reasons why he turned to poetry at a time when it must have seemed already apparent that his genius lay elsewhere. In that year, 1592, London was beset by bubonic plague, and this, along with civic disorders such as agitation against alien artisans in London, resulted in the closure of the theatres from the summer of 1592 intermittently for nearly two years. The players traveled in the provinces when they could not perform in London, but this brought in less money and required fewer new plays. Shakespeare did not travel with Edward Alleyn's group or with the Earl of Pembroke's Men or the Earl of Sussex's Men, the three troupes with which he is thought to have been associated by that time. It is most probable that he remained in London and occupied himself with whatever writing came to hand.

This intermission in his career, then, provided him with an opportunity to develop his talents outside the theatre, and to win a reputation in a literary field more respectable than that of play-writing. An erotic poem in a fashionable style dedicated to a well-heeled patron might at that time provide both money and literary credentials. So Shakespeare dedicated *Venus and Adonis* to Henry Wriothesley, Third Earl of Southampton, a wealthy, witty, and handsome young man, who had already been addressed in verse by the poet George Chapman. A year later, Shakespeare dedicated a second poem, *The Rape of Lucrece*, to Southampton, in terms that have suggested to some biographers that the two men had by then formed an intimate friendship; this may indeed be the case, but by the standards of Elizabethan compliment the second dedication was not especially effusive. It is subscribed, like the first, "in all duty." Nonetheless it is beguiling to consider the apparent results of Shakespeare's efforts. Rowe records that Shakespeare received "many great and uncommon Marks of Favour and Friendship" from Southampton, and Davenant says that Southampton gave him £1000, an improbably large sum. E.K. Chambers[1] thinks it

---

1. E.K. Chambers, *William Shakespeare*, i, 62.

more likely that Shakespeare received only £100, a generous sum in those times, and perhaps used it to buy a share in the Lord Chamberlain's Men.

Although these two poems are generally less highly regarded than Shakespeare's other work, the circumstances of their publication suggest that he himself thought well of them. They are the only works he published in which he laid claim to the status of a professional writer. He did not hasten to publish his plays and took no care with the texts of them, since plays were regarded as a different and much inferior kind of writing; many of them never appeared in print in his lifetime. Both poems, on the other hand, were carefully and accurately printed, probably from Shakespeare's own fair copies, by Richard Field, a man from Stratford.

Venus and Adonis is a poem of a type that enjoyed a short but immense popularity, mainly in the 1590's, the brief epic, or as it has sometimes been called, the epyllion. Based on stories from Ovid's *Metamorphoses*, the brief epic made considerable use of extravagant rhetorical devices and was witty, rich in its language, and erotic. The first such poem was called *Scilla's Metamorphosis*, by Thomas Lodge, published in 1589, but the most famous was Marlowe's *Hero and Leander*. Marlowe did not live to finish more than two sestiads, or sections, of his marvelous poem, and it was not published until 1598, five years after his death, when it appeared with a more moral and philosophical conclusion by George Chapman. But evidently Shakespeare saw Marlowe's part in manuscript, for it has clearly left its mark on *Venus and Adonis*.

Shakespeare combines several Ovidian tales in his poem, principally the story of the love of Venus for the great hunter Adonis (*Metamorphoses* x), in which the young man, warned by the goddess to beware of lions and boars, is fatally wounded in a boar-hunt, and the story of Salmacis and Hermaphroditus (*Metamorphoses* iv), in which a shy youth is wooed by an amorous water-nymph. The story of Narcissus (*Metamorphoses* iii), also a reluctant hunter pursued by a nymph, and punished for the sin of self-love, supplied another element in Shakespeare's poem. The story of Venus and Adonis was one of the most familiar of Ovid's tales and much used in the Renaissance. Book III of Spenser's *The Faerie Queene* (1590) describes a tapestry in Castle Joyeous that depicts, in four scenes, the love of the goddess for the youth. It shows Venus lasciviously gazing on Adonis while he bathes, hanging over him as he sleeps, and translating him into a "dainty flowre" after his goring by the boar. In the Garden of Adonis

(*The Faerie Queene*, Book III, canto VI) Venus and Adonis lie together in a flowery arbor:

> But she her selfe, when ever that she will
> Possesseth him, and of his sweetnesse takes her fill.

Shakespeare's account is much less idyllic. It begins with Venus hastening to Adonis at daybreak, as he is about to go hunting. She begins without delay to woo him, undeterred by his obvious reluctance. She ties up his horse, "seizeth on his sweating palm" (l. 25), and pushes him down into the grass. He "burns with bashful shame" (l. 49) and will say nothing, while Venus tries at length to persuade him of the pleasures and the wisdom of enjoying love when it is offered. Like Shakespeare himself in the sonnets, she urges procreation as nature's law:

> Torches are made to light, jewels to wear,
> Dainties to taste, fresh beauty for the use,
> Herbs for their smell, and sappy plants to bear:
> Things growing to themselves are growth's abuse.
>   Seeds spring from seeds, and beauty breedeth beauty;
>   Thou wast begot, to get it is thy duty.[2]
>
>   (ll. 163–8)

Adonis is disdainful; he speaks only to complain:

>   Fie, no more of love!
>   The sun doth burn my face, I must remove.
>   (ll. 185–6)

Venus grows more pressing, and offers herself without reserve in the kind of salacious metaphor that the Elizabethans had learned, from their love of Ovid, to cultivate:

> I'll be a park, and thou shalt be my deer:
> Feed where thou wilt, on mountain or in dale;
>   Graze on my lips, and if those hills be dry,
>   Stray lower, where the pleasant fountains lie.
>   (ll. 231–4)

2. All quotations from *Venus and Adonis* and *The Rape of Lucrece* are taken from the Arden edition, ed. F.T. Prince, London, 1960.

Adonis prepares to make his escape, but his stallion has been distracted by the sight of a "breeding jennet" (l. 260), a small female horse, and breaks his bonds to follow her into the wood. Venus, less successful than the horses in the appeasement of her desires, continues until nightfall with her blandishments. She begs and weeps, she faints, she takes advantage of a reluctantly offered goodnight kiss to pull Adonis into her arms, but all in vain. He plans to go hunting next day and is anxious to get his rest. Venus fears that he may meet his death without leaving the world his heir:

> What is thy body but a swallowing grave,
> Seeming to bury that posterity,
> Which by the rights of time thou needs must have,
> If thou destroy them not in dark obscurity?
> (ll. 757–60)

The theme of fruitless chastity and wasted life, so fully dealt with in the early sonnets, was already in Shakespeare's mind.

But Adonis coyly refuses to listen to Venus's arguments:

> Mine ears that to your wanton talk attended
> Do burn themselves, for having so offended.
> (ll. 809–10)

He finally breaks away, and Venus spends the night dolefully singing to herself. At this point Shakespeare is careful to prevent the mood of the poem from becoming either pathetic or foreboding by his description of Venus's lament:

> Her song was tedious, and outwore the night.
> (l. 841)

The next morning she hears the sounds of the chase; she runs, distracted, about the woods; she glimpses the boar, mad with rage and sees wounded hounds skulking in the thickets. Finally she comes upon the body of Adonis, gored in the thigh. She prophesies that, as a result of his death, love will henceforth be marred by sorrow, jealousy, and fear; no more will true lovers find contentment or love bring joy:

> It shall be cause of war and dire events,

And set dissension 'twixt the son and sire;
Subject and servile to all discontents,
As dry combustious matter is to fire.
  Sith in his prime death doth my love destroy,
  They that love best, their loves shall not enjoy.
                              (ll. 1159–64)

But again the possibility of pathos is rejected. The grieving goddess
is not presented as a figure for us to sympathize with. Indeed, her
grief is very short-lived. Adonis's body turns into a purple flower,
and Venus remarks on the appropriateness of this metamorphosis
since, like the self-centered youth, the flower's destiny is to "grow
unto himself" (l. 1180). She picks the flower and returns in her
dove-drawn chariot to the island of Paphos.

The poem has sometimes been disliked, partly because its
treatment of the subject is often unexpected. To a certain extent it
conforms to convention in the opulence of its language and the
delicacy of some of the fancy; it is amazingly eloquent. Some of
the lines astound us with their beauty:

Leading him prisoner in a red rose chain.
                              (l. 110)

Full gently now she takes him by the hand,
A lily prison'd in a gaol of snow.
                              (ll. 361–2)

Lo here the gentle lark, weary of rest,
From his moist cabinet mounts up on high,
And wakes the morning, from whose silver breast
The sun ariseth in his majesty.
                              (ll. 853–6)

Intricate and witty conceits lend the poem a complexity of
surface and relate it to the stream of Petrarchan love poetry popular in England at this time. Venus promises not to cloy Adonis with
her kisses, but alternately sting his lips red and drain them pale
with "ten kisses short as one, one long as twenty" (l. 22). Adonis's
mouth when about to utter bad news is like a "red morn that ever
yet betoken'd / Wrack to the seaman, tempest to the field" (ll. 453–
4) The boar meant not to wound Adonis, but to kiss him:

'Tis true, 'tis true, thus was Adonis slain:
He ran upon the boar with his sharp spear,
Who did not whet his teeth at him again,
But by a kiss thought to persuade him there;
   And nuzzling in his flank, the loving swine
   Sheath'd unaware the tusk in his soft groin.
                  (ll. 1111–16)

The combination of this sort of artifice with realistic imagery of country life is fresh, if not totally unusual. Shakespeare's range of feeling and mastery of language is revealed in the way he transmutes the sensuality of his story with brief and vivid glimpses of natural life. The shamefaced Adonis raises his eyes to confront Venus

Like a dive-dapper [dabchick] peering through a wave,
Who being look'd on, ducks as quickly in.
                  (ll. 86–7)

He is trapped in her arms like a bird in a net; his impotent anger overflows like a river overflowing its banks after rainfall. Venus describes the misery of hunted animals, especially, in a famous passage, the desperation of poor Wat, the hunted hare. And she starts back from the sudden sight of the dead boy, in an equally well-known description:

as the snail, whose tender horns being hit,
Shrinks backward in his shelly cave with pain.
                (ll. 1033–34)

Such comparisons are very frequent, and, despite the fact that Venus talks of lions and tigers in the forests being tamed by Adonis's beauty, the impression is strongly created of a countryside setting as truly English in its atmosphere as the enchanted wood in *A Midsummer Night's Dream*.

It is when such realism is applied directly to the behavior of the protagonists that difficulties of tone may arise. A statuesque and sensual Venus, such as the seductresses painted by Titian or Rubens, is acceptable, for Shakespeare's vision has clearly nothing to do with the elegant lassitude of Botticelli's Venus in "Venus and Mars." But a large and frankly lustful Venus who drags her lover from his horse and tucks him under her arm is another matter.

She pants and sweats and pulls Adonis down on top of her in her eagerness; she feeds on his breath "as on a prey" and she battens on him

> Even as an empty eagle, sharp by fast,
> Tires with her beak on feathers, flesh and bone,
> Shaking her wings, devouring all in haste,
> Till either gorge be stuff'd or prey be gone.
>   (ll. 55–60)

The animal imagery, as here, is frequently used to suggest the crudity and strength of sexual appetite. The episode of the stallion and the jennet portrays this objectively, but such words as "feed," "glutton," "devour," and "prey" used of Venus implicitly criticize the quality of her feelings. Adonis's comparison of love and lust (ll. 799–804) may recall for us Shakespeare's sonnet (129) on the same subject. And there may be something of the same disgust in Shakespeare's lines on Venus:

> And having felt the sweetness of the spoil,
> With blindfold fury she begins to forage;
> Her face doth reek and smoke, her blood doth boil,
> And careless lust stirs up a desperate courage,
>   Planting oblivion, beating reason back,
>   Forgetting shame's pure blush and honour's wrack.
>   (ll. 553–58)

The portrayal of Adonis makes things no easier. Shakespeare may have been striving after the effect Marlowe obtained with his erotic description of the innocent sensuality of Hero and Leander, but in general he only succeeds in making the young Adonis rude and loutish. He is sluggish and sullen; he "blush'd and pouted in a dull disdain" (l. 33), and he glowers and frowns "like the froward infant still'd with dandling" (l. 562). Venus pursues him "Like a milch doe, whose swelling dugs do ache / Hasting to feed her fawn" (ll. 875–6). On occasion Shakespeare seems to encourage the comic undertone that is often present in the physicality of the characters, with his emphasis on Venus's size and her eagerness. She is an effective antidote to the remote and icy mistress of Petrarchan poetry. But the broadness of the comic tone works against the sensuality of the poem; and the animal imagery, though it has been said to "temper" the eroticism, seems to introduce ideas and feelings that are hardly appropriate to an Ovidian poem.

"If the poem was not meant to arouse disgust, it was very foolishly written,"[3] writes C.S. Lewis, who charitably assumes that the poem may have failed because Shakespeare could not suspend his dramatist's habit of seeing events from a spectator's viewpoint. Nonetheless, Shakespeare's Elizabethan readers liked it, and it won for him a large following, especially among "the younger sort,"[4] who called him "sweet" and "hony-tongued." Apparently it became a kind of boudoir *vade mecum*, and for a decade after its publication Ovidian poets turned to it for a model. Nine editions of it were published in Shakespeare's lifetime.

The preoccupation with lust and its effects is an equally important feature of *The Rape of Lucrece*, published in 1594. The second poem is a kind of companion piece to the first, perhaps the "graver labour" referred to in the dedication of *Venus and Adonis*, promised for Southampton as a more fitting tribute. *Venus and Adonis* presents a woman's desire thwarted by a man's reluctance; in *The Rape of Lucrece* Shakespeare shows a man's lust enforced against a woman's integrity. Like *Venus and Adonis*, *The Rape of Lucrece* belongs to a recognized genre in Elizabethan writing, the Ovidian complaint, a combination of the medieval tales of the tragic downfall of one in high estate, such as *The Mirrour for Magistrates* (c.1555), with the decorative and opulent manner and sensuous subject matter of Ovid.

The first such hybrid poem was Samuel Daniel's *The Complaint of Rosamund*, published in 1592. It stood in the same relation to the complaint as Marlowe's *Hero and Leander* did to the Ovidian brief epic, and inspired a host of imitations. Daniel's use of a woman as the speaker and heroine of his tragic complaint provoked some adverse comment; Giles Fletcher, in a complaint attached to his sonnet cycle *Licia* and probably written the year before *The Rape of Lucrece*, specifically says that women are too light and trivial to be subjects of tragedy, or, as he put it, to be fortune's tennis balls. Nonetheless, Shakespeare followed Daniel's lead, although he divides the interest of his poem between Lucrece and her ravisher Tarquin, to whose mental struggle nearly half

3. C.S. Lewis, *English Literature in the Sixteenth Century (Excluding Drama)*, The Oxford History of English Literature, Vol. III, Oxford, 1954, 499.
4. Gabriel Harvey, quoted in E.K. Chambers, *William Shakespeare*, ii, 197.

the poem is devoted. Lucrece was a figure of more substance than Daniel's Rosamund and had always been regarded as an outstanding example of married chastity, a virtue in prominent literary vogue, with its celebration in Spenser's *The Faerie Queene*, Book III. In Chaucer's *The Legend of Good Women*, which Shakespeare certainly knew, Lucrece is regarded as a saint and martyr. In *The Rape of Lucrece*, Shakespeare does not explore the meaning of chastity as Spenser does in *The Faerie Queene*, but presents the story of a guilty act and its violent consequences with all the rhetorical heightening that he can muster.

The poem is an expansion of the legend recounted by Ovid, in 130 lines in Book II of the *Fasti*. Ovid's account supplies more preliminaries to the story than does Shakespeare's, but after the first sixty lines Shakespeare follows Ovid's narrative very closely, dilating, filling in, and moralizing on the terse outline at every point. Ovid takes eleven lines to get Tarquin from the military camp into Lucrece's bedroom, Shakespeare nearly four hundred. Ovid's Tarquin simply rises from his bed, draws out his sword, and strides into Lucrece's bedroom.

> Surgit: & auratum vagina liberat ensem:
> Et venit in thalamos.[5]

Shakespeare's character, in some of the most dramatic and tense lines of the poem, lies in his bed debating "The sundry dangers of his will's obtaining" (l. 128) Finally, he leaps up, "madly toss'd between desire and dread" (l. 171) flings on his mantle and lights a torch, but still he is held back, finding the "naked armour of still slaughter'd lust" (l. 188) an insufficient motive. Memory of Lucrece's beauty spurs him on; like Adonis, she alternates between blushing and pallor:

> O how her fear did make her colour rise!
>   First red as roses that on lawn we lay,
>   Then white as lawn, the roses took away.
>   (ll. 257–9)

But fear, shame, and the recognition that the satisfaction of his desires can be but the most temporary of pleasures—"A dream, a

---

5. *Fasti* II, 793–4, quoted from Appendix I of the Arden edition of *The Poems*, 197.

breath, a froth of fleeting joy" (l. 212)—hold him back. The weasels shriek, the broken locks creak, the wind blows smoke from his torch into his face, and he pricks his finger on a needle when he hastily picks up a piece of Lucrece's sewing; all the elements combine against him. At the very door of the room—Shakespeare gives the impression of Tarquin having penetrated to some inner sanctum—he pauses; he can hardly believe in the reality of the deed:

Thoughts are but dreams till their effects be tried.
(l. 353)

And then the moment:

This said, his guilty hand pluck'd up the latch,
And with his knee the door he opens wide.
The dove sleeps fast that this night-owl will catch.
(ll. 358–60)

The effect of this expansion of Ovid's brief lines is immensely dramatic; the detailed description of Tarquin's inner struggle involves us in his situation and introduces a strong element of tension. The evocation of the nocturnal sights and sounds—the sparks struck off a flint as Tarquin lights his waxen torch, the creaking as he forces lock after lock, the way he pushes open the door with his knee—is impressionistic and vivid. But not all Shakespeare's expansion of Ovid is done this way. Ovid's Lucretia is struck dumb with fear and can neither struggle nor cry out. She is totally impotent; Shakespeare's Lucrece is made of stouter stuff and reasons eloquently with her ravisher for ninety-two lines, calling upon his better nature to control his "rebel will" (l. 625). One of Shakespeare's central interests in this poem is the opposed aspects of human nature—flesh and spirit, will and reason, conscience and desire. "I sue for exil'd majesty's repeal" (l. 640), cries Lucrece, appealing to the reason and sense of honor that Tarquin has deliberately banished.

The rape itself is depicted with great economy. Tarquin "sets his foot upon the light" (l. 673) and gags his struggling victim; the deed done, he is satiated like "the full-fed hound or gorged hawk" (l. 694), but he achieves no contentment. His mind is still distraught and at odds with itself, and Shakespeare presents his condition in two ways; in the medieval manner he objectifies Tarquin's guilt by describing "troops of cares" (l. 720) mustering to

the ruins of his soul's temple to ask after the welfare of the soul,
"the spotted princess" (l. 721):

> She says her subjects with foul insurrection
> Have batter'd down her consecrated wall,
> And by their mortal fault brought in subjection
> Her immortality, and made her thrall
> To living death and pain perpetual.
>
> (ll. 722–26)

More characteristically, Shakespeare conveys the complexity of
Tarquin's situation through paradox; he is

> A captive victor that hath lost in gain,
> Bearing away the wound that nothing healeth,
> The scar that will despite of cure remain;
> Leaving his spoil perplex'd in greater pain.
>
> (ll. 730–33)

   At this point in the poem the focus of attention shifts to
Lucrece, and Shakespeare expands Ovid less dramatically and more
rhetorically. Lucrece passes the night in a lengthy lament (ll. 764–
1036), apostrophizing in turn night, shame, opportunity, and time.
Shakespeare gives her some fine lines, especially on time, a subject that evoked very similar passionate poetry from him in the
sonnets and in *Troilus and Cressida*:

> Time's glory is to calm contending kings,
> To unmask falsehood and bring truth to light,
> To stamp the seal of time in aged things,
> To wake the morn and sentinel the night,
>
> (ll. 939–42)

> To fill with worm-holes stately monuments,
> To feed oblivion with decay of things.
>
> (ll. 946–7)

She curses Tarquin in an eloquent execration that makes good use
of the rhetorical device of anaphora:

> Let him have time to tear his curled hair,
> Let him have time against himself to rave,

Let him have time of time's help to despair,
Let him have time to live a loathed slave.
                        (ll. 981–84)

It is splendid rhetoric and we are involved, not in pity for Lucrece's suffering, but in the energy of her passion. But in time this
palls; Lucrece is too eloquent. The self-conscious artistry of the
language robs the situation of any pathos or tension. Lucrece
greets the morning with continued lamentation. She summons her
maid, and the two weep together, the brief portrait of the sympathetic girl who cries without knowing why restoring some reality
to the situation. Lucrece then writes to her husband, even here debating about the style of the letter:

Conceit and grief an eager combat fight,
What wit sets down is blotted straight with will:
This is too curious-good, this blunt and ill.
                        (ll. 1298–1300)

Collatine's arrival, and the story's conclusion, is further delayed by a long digression, for which Ovid provides no source.
Lucrece, seeking some correlative for her woe, goes to look at a
painting of scenes from the fall of Troy, described in great detail.
She searches for some figure who epitomizes the extremity of sorrow, and finds it in Hecuba, whom Shakespeare was again to use in
Hamlet for the type of grief:

In her the painter had anatomiz'd
Time's ruin, beauty's wrack, and grim care's reign.
                        (ll. 1450–51)

Sinon, who betrayed Troy to the Greeks, appears to Lucrece like a
kind of Tarquin, with his handsome appearance concealing a
treacherous heart. Shakespeare may have taken the idea for this
painting from *Aeneid* I, 456–95, for Dido, herself betrayed by a
man, has a picture of the siege of Troy in her temple. The purpose
of this digression is to dilate the main theme with other examples
of grief and despair. At last Collatine arrives. He is amazed by the
change in his wife's appearance, and in a moment of realism husband and wife stand silent:

> Both stood like old acquaintance in a trance,
> Met far from home, wond'ring each other's chance.
>
> (ll. 1595–96)

Shakespeare continues to follow Ovid's hints to the very end. Lucrece tries three times to speak, and at last succeeds.

> Ter conata loqui: ter destitit: ausaque quarto.[6]

Then she stabs herself. The two lines in which Ovid describes the grief of her father and husband are expanded by Shakespeare into eight stanzas in which the two men compete awkwardly in grief. The poem ends with Brutus's vow of revenge and Tarquin's banishment.

It is a more ambitious poem than *Venus and Adonis*, and gives much more indication of the powers Shakespeare was to develop in his plays. C.S. Lewis's criticism of *Venus and Adonis*, that it suffers from inappropriate use of dramatic techniques, may also be relevant here. Shakespeare's desire to make Lucrece speak for herself in the manner of a tragic heroine weakens the poem, for her character is not sufficiently interesting or complex to sustain the vast amount of lamentation she is given. There is no intricacy of motive as in Tarquin's case; her feelings of grief and shame are basically very simple. The elaborateness of her rhetoric seems imcompatible with an intense sorrow; the emotion is trivialized by the manner of its expression. Ovid and Chaucer both avoid this problem by narrating Lucrece's story, allowing her the barest minimum of speech.

But if Shakespeare failed with Lucrece he certainly did not with Tarquin. In many ways, this character seems an early study for Macbeth, and the reference in the play to murder moving toward its design with "Tarquin's ravishing strides" (II.i.55) suggests that the earlier work was still at the back of Shakespeare's mind ten years later. Like Macbeth, Tarquin is an introspective man, fully conscious of what he stands to lose; the innocence of the victim and the horror of the deed weigh heavily with him. He tries to console himself with the thought of acting by night:

> The eye of heaven is out, and misty night
> Covers the shame that follows sweet delight.
>
> (ll. 356–7)

6. *Fasti*, II, 823.

He weighs in his mind the alternatives of going forward to accomplish his desire and allowing things to remain as they are, and it is his worse nature that impels him forward, "for himself himself he must forsake" (l. 157). Lady Macbeth comes to recognize the folly of sacrificing the realities of the present to the uncertainties of the future:

> Nought's had, all's spent
> Where our desire is got without content.
> 'Tis safer to be that which we destroy,
> Than by destruction dwell in doubtful joy.
> (III.ii.4–7)

Shakespeare moralizes on Tarquin's condition in a very similar way, even introducing the notion of ambition:

> So that in vent'ring ill we leave to be
> The things we are, for that which we expect;
> And this ambitious foul infirmity,
> In having much, torments us with defect
> Of that we have: so then we do neglect
>   The thing we have, and all for want of wit,
>   Make something nothing by augmenting it.
> (ll. 148–54)

The situation of guest and host is reversed in the two works, although both Tarquin and Macbeth betray their obligations when they act against their victims. The atmosphere of the night in *The Rape of Lucrece*, although it is much less intensely evoked, recalls the night of Duncan's murder.

The circumstances of the rape itself invite comparison with the similar situation in Shakespeare's later play, *Cymbeline*. Here the Roman soldier Iachimo, fired like Tarquin with an account of his friend's wife's purity, presents himself as a guest in the wife's home during the husband's absence. The wife Imogen, like Lucrece, welcomes the visitor and offers him hospitality. Iachimo enters her room by night, recalling Tarquin who "did softly press the rushes ere he waken'd / The chastity he wounded" (*Cymbeline*, II,ii,13–14), but does not in fact rape her. However, he misrepresents her chastity to her husband, as Tarquin had threatened to do, and causes a breach between husband and wife that is only healed after much misery.

The Rape of Lucrece has also some affinities with Shake-speare's tragedy, *Titus Andronicus,* which was probably written about a year earlier. The similarities between these two works, however, show some of the less attractive aspects of Shakespeare's writing. They share the preoccupation with lust and bloodshed and violated chastity, and something of the same morbidity and sen-sationalism. The description of Lucrece's death with her blood "bubbling from her breast" (l. 1737) and the separation of the flow into clotted black blood and flowing red blood, which is said to signify the tainted and the pure aspects of Lucrece's soul, seems designed for an age that reveled in Senecan horror. The imagery of this passage is not untypical in its inappropriate wit: the blood and the watery serum that separates out from the congealed blood is to be a token of pity for Lucrece's woe that will thereafter appear in all instances of bloodshed. Elsewhere in this poem the young Shake-speare fails embarrassingly to restrain his abundant invention; the description of Lucrece asleep in bed before the rape is a notable instance of his use of Elizabethan conceit:

Her lily hand her rosy cheek lies under,
Coz'ning the pillow of a lawful kiss;
Who therefore angry, seems to part in sunder,
Swelling on either side to want his bliss.
                              (ll. 386–89)

This kind of fertility is all part of the poem's rhetorical style, with its deliberate use of every kind of device for amplification; simple ideas are spun out at length and themes commonly stated in a few lines are played on for several stanzas. Moralizing digressions frequently slow the pace and vary the tone; when Lucrece and her maid weep together, Shakespeare takes three stanzas to discuss the helplessness of women. Lucrece's speeches are full of word-play and figures of speech, especially apostrophe and antithesis. Proverbial expressions elaborate the speech of both characters at moments of highest tension. Tarquin urges his passion on Lucrece in a series of gnomic lines:

I see what crosses my attempt will bring,
I know what thorns the growing rose defends;
I think the honey guarded with a sting:
All this beforehand counsel comprehends.
                              (ll. 491–94)

She replies in a similar manner:

> Mud not the fountain that gave drink to thee,
> Mar not the thing that cannot be amended.
> End thy ill aim before thy shoot be ended;
>   He is no woodman that doth bend his bow
>   To strike a poor unseasonable doe.
>   (ll. 577–81)

This sort of thing seems to have been very much to the Elizabethan taste, but we may feel that such rhetoric smothers the poem's dramatic potential. Yet Shakespeare's contemporary, Gabriel Harvey, coupled *The Rape of Lucrece* with *Hamlet*: "His Lucrece, & his tragedie of Hamlet, Prince of Denmarke, haue it in them, to please the wiser sort."[7] The poem was indeed popular in its time, and went through six editions before Shakespeare's death.

What most of us mean now by Shakespeare's poetry is his sonnets, and these, unlike *Venus and Adonis* and *The Rape of Lucrece* are so much "not of an age, but for all time" that critical exploration of their meaning and biographical speculation as to their relationship with the facts of Shakespeare's own life is as vigorous and lively as it ever was. The reasons for the continuing popularity of the sonnets are simple ones. First, obviously, their poetic quality, unlike that of Shakespeare's two long poems, is such that their author would have been celebrated as a great poet had he never written anything else. Then there is the fact that the sonnet form, although it was as much the darling of its age as the Ovidian narrative, is one that has survived, whereas the brief epic and the complaint have long since become museum pieces.

Largely because of Shakespeare's own achievement, we have come to look on the sonnet sequence as an autobiographical form, one that concerns itself with the facts of the poet's mental and spiritual life if not always of his daily life. And since Shakespeare's sonnets seem to afford us both kinds of insight, in an especially cryptic and tantalizing form, we are all the more fascinated by them. Although Wordsworth's bold assertion that in them Shakespeare unlocked his heart has been strongly and frequently dismissed, the faint hope of somehow identifying for all time these mysterious figures, "The fair friend," "The dark lady,"

7. Gabriel Harvey, quoted in E.K. Chambers, *William Shakespeare*, ii, 197.

and "The rival poet" still inspires earnest searches. This interest in Shakespeare's life is surely quite legitimate, but in this instance it is especially necessary not to allow it a disproportionate significance; what really matters most about the sonnets is that in them we have some of the world's greatest and most individual love poetry.

In direct opposition to this autobiographical view of the sonnets is the insistence by some that Shakespeare's sonnets all derive from models. Undoubtedly Shakespeare did make use of themes and ideas that had become established in sonnet writing by Petrarch and his followers, especially by the French poets of the Pléiade such as Ronsard, as well as in the work of English sonneteers. For instance, there are many parallels with sonnets from Daniel's *Delia*, especially those dealing with the theme of immortality through verse, and Sonnet 132 is closely modeled on Sidney's *Astrophel and Stella*, Sonnet 7. As with his narrative poems, Shakespeare was setting out to write a sequence in a popular style of his day. But this agreed, there is no doubt that the originality of the sequence is immensely more significant than its debt to other poets.

The sonnets were published in 1609 by Thomas Thorpe in a text that was probably issued without Shakespeare's supervision, since he did not sign the dedication. At one time it was thought a particularly corrupt text, full of misprints and errors of punctuation; modern editors are more inclined to accept the view of H.E. Rollins, editor of the New Variorum edition of 1944 that it is "an early seventeenth century book printed in the normal early-seventeenth century style," unlike the narrative poems, which were unusually well printed, and that the punctuation is free, ambiguous, and rhetorical rather than logical, in the Elizabethan manner. In view of the immense immediate success of Shakespeare's earlier poems, *Venus and Adonis* and *The Rape of Lucrece*, brought out at a time when he was still young as a dramatist, it is very surprising that the publication of the sonnets, to us so superior poetically, seems to have passed relatively unnoticed, especially since Shakespeare was by then accepted as the foremost playwright of his day. No other edition appeared in his lifetime, and there were fewer printed allusions to the sonnets after 1609 than before. A second edition appeared in 1639 (dated 1640), put out by an unscrupulous publisher, John Benson, entitled *Poems written by William Shakespeare*, and containing 146 of the sonnets, *The Lover's Complaint* (a lament by a betrayed girl that was included in the 1609 edition though not now generally accepted to be by Shakespeare), a miscellany called *The Passionate Pilgrim* (first published in 1599 and containing Shakespeare's sonnets 138 and 144), and various poems by other authors. Benson rearranged the original order of the 1609 edition, ran some of the sonnets together in twos or threes as a single poem, added a heading or title to each group, and made certain verbal changes, so that sonnets originally addressed to a man read as if they had been written to a woman. Altogether, it seems as if he wished to conceal the fact that an earlier edition had ever been published, something it would surely not have been possible to do had that earlier edition been well known. One modern editor[8] suggests that the 1609 edition had been withdrawn or suppressed soon after publication on account of the impropriety of the relationship between the poet and the "fair friend." In the late eighteenth century, after Thorpe's 1609 text with its masculine pronouns had begun to regain its primacy over Benson's, hitherto regarded as the most authoritative, biographical speculation on the sonnets began, and from the start critics were uneasy about the possibility of a homosexual element. Coleridge asserted that "the Sonnets could only come from a man deeply in love, and in love with a woman," and that in all Shakespeare's work there is "not even an allusion to that very worst of all possible vices."[9] Even a twentieth-century editor such as C. Knox Pooler, of the Arden Edition, who would like to reject the bawdy punning Sonnet 20 ("A woman's face with nature's own hand painted"), insists that the poet's feeling for the beautiful youth is not what it seems

> The warmth of tone may be ascribed to the extravagance of metaphor common at a time when love, loyalty, and friendship were often dressed alike. It is not strange that a poet with his singing robes about him should use words strictly appropriate to an emotion different from his own and higher either in regard to the intensity of the feeling or the dignity of its object.[10]

The possibility of the first edition having been suppressed is

8. Martin Seymour-Smith, *Shakespeare's Sonnets*, London, 1963.
9. Quoted in Martin Seymour-Smith, 28–9.
10. C. Knox Pooler, *The Sonnets*, Arden Edition, London, 3rd ed., 1943, xxxiv.

only one of the problems of the sonnets on which critics have exercised themselves. The question of when the poems were written is another. Francis Meres in *Palladis Tamia* of 1598 mentions that Shakespeare was known for his "sugred sonnets among his private friends." The epithet is very appropriate to some of the sonnets we know, for instance sonnets 1 to 19, though there are many more to which it does not apply at all, and it seems quite likely that Shakespeare may have circulated part of his work in manuscript, as other sonneteers such as Sidney had done before publication. Two of the sonnets that are definitely not "sugred" (numbers 138 and 144) were published, in versions that may well represent earlier drafts, in 1599 in *The Passionate Pilgrim*. These facts say nothing for certain of the bulk of the sonnets, except that Shakespeare could write in the manner of 138 and 144, often thought of as "late" or "mature" in style, in the 1590's. We know that he was interested in the sonnet form in 1594–5, for sonnets are included in *Love's Labour's Lost* and *Romeo and Juliet*, and this was a time when many writers were publishing sonnet sequences. Sidney's *Astrophel and Stella* (written about 1582) came into print in 1591, and very soon sequences appeared by Constable, Daniel, Barnaby Barnes, Drayton, Richard Barnes, and Spenser. Some of these had been circulated in manuscript in the 1580's, and some critics, particularly Leslie Hotson,[11] would place Shakespeare's sonnets in that decade. In general, it is thought that they were written in the mid-1590's, between 1592/3 and 1596, though E.K. Chambers believes that Shakespeare continued to write them up to 1599. Some internal evidence is available, but unfortunately it is very ambiguous. Sonnet 107, the most important in this connection, contains lines that point distinctly to outside events:

> The mortall Moone hath her eclipse indur'de,
> And the sad Augurs mock their owne presage,
> Incertenties now crowne them-selues assur'de,
> And peace proclaims oliues of endlesse age.[12]

But the moon and her eclipse can be variously interpreted according to whether the sonnets are deemed to be early or late; they

11. J.L. Hotson, *Shakespeare's Sonnets*, dated London, 1949, and *Mr. W.H.*, London, 1964.
12. All quotations from the sonnets are taken from the Quarto text of 1609.

may refer to the crescent-shaped Spanish armada that appeared in the English channel in 1588 and was shattered by the English heavy guns and finally routed by a violent gale;[13] to the Queen's "climacteric" year 1595–1596,[14] the sixty-third year of her life, according to popular astrology an especially dangerous time since it represented the mystic numbers 7 and 9 in conjunction; to her illness in 1599;[15] or to either her death or Southampton's release from captivity in 1603. Clues for dating have also been extracted from other sonnets, for instance from the "pyramyds buylt vp with newer might" of Sonnet 123 and the reference to "arte made tung-tide by authoritie" on Sonnet 66, but they can be made to suit almost any convenient year between 1588 and 1609.

The question of dating is inevitably linked with biographical theories of the sonnets. If it is to be assumed that the sonnets give a true account of Shakespeare's relationships with a beautiful youth and a dark mistress at a certain time of his life—a theory that is very far from proven—then the evidence from references to events must be consistent with the facts of the lives of these people. For instance, of the two major candidates for the youth, the Earl of Southampton and the Earl of Pembroke, one was sixteen in 1590, the other ten. One candidate, William Hatcliffe, a student at the Inns of Court, was chosen to suit a composition date of 1587–1589 when he was in his late teens and four years younger than Shakespeare. It is usually taken for granted that the friend of the sonnets is the same person as "Mr. W.H." to whom they were dedicated, but this need not be the case; for one thing, the dedication is signed not by Shakespeare himself, as would have been normal, but by the publisher Thomas Thorpe, and for another the "onlie begetter" may have been the man who obtained the manu-script for the publisher rather than the man who inspired its con-tents. Perhaps, after all, "Mr. W.H." was simply a friend of Thorpe's whom the publisher wished to thank for providing what he hoped, wrongly as it turned out, would be the material for a profitable publication. This is indeed possible, and men such as William Harvey, the third husband of Southampton's mother, or William Hall, a printer, have been proposed. Nonetheless, search-ers after the identity of the friend have generally been guided by the initials "W.H." Oscar Wilde thought he may have been an

13. J.L. Hotson, *Mr. W.H.*, 75–8.
14. G.B. Harrison, ed., *Shakespeare's Sonnets*, Harmondsworth, Mid-dlesex, 1938.
15. E.K. Chambers, *William Shakespeare*, i, 564.

actor called William Hughes, and his friend, Lord Alfred Douglas, found an Elizabethan actor to suit, but could supply very few details about him. Samuel Butler, whose edition of the sonnets appeared in 1899, proposed a sailor of the same name. A line from Sonnet 20, "A man in hew all *Hews* in his controwling" was taken as the basis for the idea that the friend's surname was Hughes. Other suggestions have ranged from William Hathaway, Shakespeare's brother-in-law, to "William Himself."

The Earl of Southampton, originally proposed by Nathan Drake in *Shakespeare and his times* (1817), remains the most popular candidate, although his initials were H.W. and not W.H., and it would have been most improper for so high-ranking a figure to be addressed as "Mr." He had been Shakespeare's patron for *Venus and Adonis* and *The Rape of Lucrece*, and it is thought that the language of Sonnet 78 ("So oft I have invok'd thee for my Muse") suggests that the friend was also Shakespeare's patron, although it could be interpreted to mean simply that the young man had inspired many poems. Southampton was of much higher rank than Shakespeare, as several sonnets suggest the friend was. He was also a handsome man and much painted. A Hilliard miniature of him done in the 1590's shows a very aristocratic youth with long hair curling over one shoulder.

Southampton married Elizabeth Vernon in 1598, when she became pregnant; she was one of the Queen's maids of honor. He had been in love with her for several years, but the Queen had opposed the match and was outraged when the marriage took place. His own mother had similar feelings. These facts are not consistent with the tenor of the first seventeen sonnets, in which the friend, who was evidently very reluctant, is strongly urged to marry. But in 1594 Southampton paid out a large sum to be released from a promise he had once made to marry Lady Elizabeth Vere, the granddaughter of the powerful Lord Burghley. Burghley, whose ward Southampton was, had pressed the match for several years, but Southampton was at that time totally uninterested, and wanted nothing more than to serve the gallant Earl of Essex in France. Perhaps this was the situation reflected in these early sonnets.

The second candidate is another young man of high rank, also a patron of poets, William Herbert, Earl of Pembroke, who was put forward a little later than Southampton. His initials are W.H., but again he would hardly have been referred to as "Mr." Pembroke and his brother, the Earl of Montgomery, were chosen as dedicatees of the First Folio when it was published in 1623, after Shakespeare's death, although Southampton was alive at the time. Shakespeare might have become acquainted with the Herbert family if, as is possible, he was writing in 1592–1593 for the company of which William Herbert's father was patron. The young Herbert retreated twice from marriage plans made for him by his family—with Lady Carey, in 1595, and with Lady Bridget Vere in 1598. If he is regarded as a likely "friend" then the earlier date is the more suitable for the composition of the first 17 sonnets, since Lady Bridget was only 13 in 1598 and rather young to provide the heir so strongly urged in these sonnets. Elizabeth Carey's grandfather, Lord Hunsdon, was the Lord Chamberlain and patron of the company for whom Shakespeare was working in 1595; E.K. Chambers conjectures that Shakespeare might have been hired by Lord Hunsdon to urge William Herbert toward the match. In 1598 Herbert came to live in London and acquired a scandalous reputation; in 1601 Mary Fitton, one of the Queen's maids of honor, became pregnant by him, but he refused to marry her and was briefly imprisoned in the Fleet in consequence. Mary Fitton has been strongly put forward as the Dark Lady, but she was not married, as Shakespeare's Dark Mistress clearly was, at that time, and her portraits show her with light brown hair and grey eyes.

Shakespeare offers few details about the Dark Lady. According to the sonnets, she was unfaithful to her husband with both the poet and his friend, and with many others besides. In an age that valued pale-skinned blondes she was conspicuous for her dark coloring and her "raven black" eyes. She could play a musical instrument. This is all that Shakespeare tells us, except for the feelings that she arouses in him and the way she treats him. Even so, elaborate theories have been constructed as to her identity, as that she was a black prostitute, or more specifically Luce Morgan, who had been a gentlewoman at Elizabeth's court in the 1580's, but through unknown circumstances fell from grace by 1595 and became well-known as "Black Luce," the keeper of a brothel in Clerkenwell. If we do not like to imagine the Dark Lady as a mere abstraction, a deliberately designed antidote to the fair and virtuous ladies of other sonnet sequences, then it may be best to see her as a composite, whose sensuality and infidelity epitomized for Shakespeare all the bitterness of sexual experience without love and all the anguish of sexual guilt; the harshness with which he sometimes describes her is not too far from the sexual loathing of *Timon of Athens* and *King Lear*.

The last "character" of the sonnets, the rival poet of numbers 78–86, depends for his identity on the dating and the identity of the friend. Only if the sonnets were written very early could Marlowe have been intended, for he died in 1593. Daniel, Drayton, and Spenser have been proposed, but Chapman is usually regarded as the most serious possibility, although he is not known to have dedicated anything Elizabethan to either Southampton or Herbert or any "Mr. W.H." He had, undeniably, some professional connections with Shakespeare; his poem *The Shadow of Night*, published in 1594, almost certainly contains some references to *Venus and Adonis*, the popular success of which he may well have envied, and Shakespeare's early comedy, *Love's Labour's Lost*, written shortly afterwards, echoes the poem and probably contains some satire of Chapman and his pedantry in the character of Holofernes. The humility with which Shakespeare writes of his rival in sonnets 80 and 86, calling him "a better spirit" and speaking of the "proud full saile of his great verse" in contrast with his own "sawsie barke" and "worthlesse bote" might have been induced by the recognition that, although it had more acclaim, *Venus and Adonis* was an inferior poem to Chapman's continuation of the dead Marlowe's *Hero and Leander*. Chapman belonged to a coterie that included Raleigh, Marlowe, and Harriot, the astronomer, and was suspected of atheism and occult practices. The obscure references in Sonnet 86 to "his spirit, by spirits taught to write" and "his compiers by night / Giuing him ayde" have been thought to allude to the activities of this circle.

A last element in the puzzle of the sonnets is the poem *Willobie his Avisa*, published in 1594. Ostensibly, it is a moral poem, describing the many unsuccessful attempts on the chastity of a lady called Avisa, but it seems to have had some extra significance, because in 1599 it was officially suppressed; it may well be a mockery rather than a serious poem, and C.S. Lewis thinks very plausibly that it was a "scandalous *roman à clef*."[16] One of Avisa's suitors is called H.W.–Henry Willobie, the supposed author–who goes for advice to his "familiar friend" W.S. on how to seduce Avisa. W.S. "who had not long before tryed the curtesy of the like passion" gives H.W. the benefit of his wisdom, but it meets with no success. Prefatory verses allude to Shakespeare's *Lucrece*, and W.S. is made to quote a couplet that Shakespeare

---

16. C.S. Lewis, 466.

uses in *1 Henry VI* (V.iii.78), *Titus Adronicus* (II.i.83) and *Richard III* (I.ii.229):

> She is no Saynt, She is no Nonne,
> I think in tyme she may be wonne.

"W.S." has often been linked with Shakespeare, and perhaps there is some allusion to his personal affairs here; less probably, "H.W." has been reversed into "Mr. W.H." and seen as the friend, with the chaste Avisa as the wanton Dark Lady. But nothing can be said for certain. *Willobie his Avisa* creates more difficulties than it solves. Perhaps, as has been suggested, it was a composite poem put out by Raleigh, Chapman, and their circle, against Shakespeare, Southampton, and *The Rape of Lucrece*; if so, it is not likely to have had any direct connection with the sonnets.

There is no evidence that the order of the sonnets as we have them is the order that Shakespeare intended. In the second edition, Benson partly reordered them, and since then there have been attempts, based on several different principles, to rearrange them. Sir Denys Gray in 1925 produced an arrangement based on a theory of rhyme links: Sonnet 20, the first of his sequence, contains the rhyme-word "pleasure," and so it is followed by sonnet 91, which includes the same word as a rhyme; 91 is linked to 25 by "boast," 25 to 31 by "buried" and "eye", and so on. C. Tucker Brooke in his edition of 1936 based his sequence on the idea that the sonnets had originally been written in groups of from two to five, each group on a single sheet of paper, and that the first publisher, Thorpe, had muddled the separate sheets. But the familiar order has its merits; there are groups of sonnets that obviously belong together, such as 1–20, 33–36, 40–42, and 78–86, and a certain story can be charted, although it is obvious that the sonnets were not intended to be read as if they were a novel. Of the 154 sonnets, the first 126 are addressed to a man, and the next 26 with the exception of 146 ("Poore soule the center of my sinfull earth") to a woman. The last two sonnets are thought to be versions of a poem by Marianus from the Greek Anthology, and have no connection with the rest.

Sonnets 1–17 urge the young man to marry and beget a son; a child, it is argued, is the only real way of preserving oneself despite the ravages of time, and the self-contained life is of value only to itself. The tone of these poems is a formal one; the ideas are metaphorical rather than real. Shakespeare's main theme is the familiar one of time and beauty, expressed here in conventional images of the sun rising lustily but setting feebly, time leading summer on to the destruction of winter, harvested corn, and bare trees, relating the course of human life to the impersonal processes of nature. A second idea enters at Sonnet 15 with the theme of the poet's power to immortalize the youth in his verse, and this notion recurs more powerfully later in the sequence. The poet becomes increasingly involved in the youth's beauty; it is difficult to resist the idea that we can see the man gradually falling in love. In Sonnet 13 he calls the boy "deare my loue," but addresses him with the more formal of the second-person pronouns, "you." The startling adoration of 18 ("Shall I compare thee to a Summers day?") is passionate but not intimate; but the possessive quality of 21 and 22 suggests a definite development of the relationship:

> O therefore loue be of thy selfe so wary,
> As I not for my selfe, but for thee will,
> Bearing thy heart which I will keepe so chary
> As tender nurse her babe from faring ill. (22)

Sonnets 21–39 explore various aspects of the experience of being in love. The poet is speechless and humble in the presence of the beloved; he feels intensely conscious of his own worthlessness, but the thought of the youth's love is enough to banish all his misfortunes. The youth is not blameless, and sometimes his failings hurt and bitterly deceive the poet, but the poet's devotion excuses all faults in him. This tone of extreme self-abnegation persists throughout the series addressed to the boy; the poet asks nothing of the boy, but offers him everything, even his mistress:

> Take all my loues, my loue, yea take them all,
> What hast thou then more then thou hadst before? (40)

Sonnets 40–42 hint at the intrusion of the Dark Lady in the lives of the two men; for the poet, the loss of his mistress is much less significant than the alienation of his friend's affection:

> That thou hast her it is not all my griefe,
> And yet it may be said I lou'd her deerely,
> That she hath thee is of my wayling cheefe,
> A losse in loue that touches me more neerely. (42)

His love has power to render all the friend's failings immaterial, even to purify him; on the other hand, the friend's love for him, or, more accurately, for his experience of loving, more than compensates for any lack of worldly fortune or happiness.

It is impossible to trace any continuing "story" in the remaining part of this sequence. At one point (sonnets 67–70) the youth is accused again of an unspecified sexual fault—"Thou dost common grow" (69)—but this may be merely the slander that attaches most readily to the beautiful and conspicuous, although the poet later warns him against misusing his beauty and charm as a façade for corruption (sonnets 92–96). At another point (sonnets 78–86) the youth shows favor to a rival poet, whom Shakespeare fears is of superior talent and therefore more fitted for the youth's affections. In sonnets 92–98 the poet records an absence from the youth that made spring seem like winter. It has been thought, in fact, that there is a break in the sequence at 96; 97, 98, and 99 form a group on their own, perhaps misplaced from an earlier point in the series, and a new series seems to start at 100 and continue until 115; the remaining sonnets to the youth, 116 to 126, seem to be a very miscellaneous collection. In Sonnet 104 Shakespeare refers to the fact that three years have passed since the two were first acquainted, although the youth looks as beautiful as he ever did; if Shakespeare was writing the sonnets over a long period, as seems likely, and the sonnets were not prepared by him as a coherent sequence for the press, then breaks in the sense and mood of the sequence are to be expected.

While the main emphasis of this part of the series is on the celebration of the poet's self-denying and not unreciprocated love for the young man, and in general of the power of love for good, there are many indications of the disillusionment and clear-eyed self-appraisal more commonly associated with the Dark Lady sonnets. The poet is disgusted with himself and disillusioned with the hypocrisy and injustice of the world in which he lives (Sonnet 66); he envies the talent of a rival, and feels that his own verse is hackneyed and lacking in inspiration. In Sonnet 76 there seems to be a discrepancy in feeling between the octave, in which the poet expresses his distaste for the style that has become associated with his name, and the sestet. The octave begins with extreme disillusion:

Why is my verse so barren of new pride?
So far from variation or quicke change?

Why with the time do I not glance aside
To new found methods, and to compounds strange? (76)

In comparison, the feeling of the sestet, which excuses the poet's
lack of invention by the claim that his love, his main subject, never
changes, seems artificial and inappropriate:

O know sweet loue I alwaies write of you,
And you and loue are still my argument:
So all my best is dressing old words new
Spending againe what is already spent. (76)

In sonnets 110–111 he disparages his life as an actor; he feels
himself coarsened and intrinsically changed by the degrading way
of life to which he has become accustomed:

Thence comes it that my name receiues a brand,
And almost thence my nature is subdu'd
To what it workes in, like the Dyers hand. (111)

Some sonnets (112, 121) allude to an unspecified scandal that has
attached itself to his name; sonnet 121 in particular can be read
as a defiant stance against the public condemnation of his morality:

For why should others false adulterat eyes
Give salutation to my sportiue blood?
Or on my frailties why are frailer spies;
Which in their wils connt bad what I think good?
Noe, I am that I am, and they that leuell
At my abuses, reckon vp their owne. (121)

The young man's morality, too, comes into question in a number of sonnets, and Shakespeare's attitude to it is complex. On
several occasions the youth commits "sensual faults" (35) with
others; Shakespeare feels not only personally betrayed (33, 34, 35)
but also aware of the loss of perfection entailed in the youth's
failings. One theme of the complex Sonnet 94 is that the most
terrible corruption is that of those who were once the best:

Lillies that fester, smell far worse than weeds. (94)

He himself takes on a kind of complicity in the youth's betrayal by
condoning the sins:

All men make faults, and euen I in this,
Authorizing thy trespas with compare,
My selfe corrupting saluing thy amisse,
Excusing their sins more then their sins are. (35)

He sees that the analogies with which he has sought to excuse his
friend ("Roses haue thornes, and siluer fountaines mud"—35) are
false and delusory; he has succeeded only in deceiving himself. He
tries to idealize the friend, while continuing to be aware of the
friend's infidelities (41, 67, 70, 91, 92); the conflict is not so much
between appearance and reality as in the poet's effort to maintain
the ideal despite the real. In Sonnet 93 the poet explicitly compares
himself with a deceived husband, aware not just of his beloved's
treachery, but also of his own self-abasement. Sonnet 96, "Some
say thy fault is youth," a bitter reflection on the power of the
youth's beauty to deceive observers into believing him morally
pure, ends, ironically, with the same couplet as sonnet 36, a self-
denying poem on the poet's feeling that his own worthlessness
may be lessened from contact with his noble friend:

But doe not so, I loue thee in such sort
As thou being mine, mine is thy good report.[17]

The sonnets in which Shakespeare calls himself his friend's "slave"
(57, 58) contain some self-abasement, but there is also the bitter
assertion that despite the friend's unfaithfulness Shakespeare will
act, like a fool, the part of the faithful servant; the couplet of 57
plays ironically on the word "will," meaning both the poet's name
and the friend's sexual appetite:

So true a foole is loue, that in your Will,
(Though you doe any thing) he thinkes no ill. (57)

The ways in which Shakespeare argues himself into believing
the friend still worthy of his love are used again in the Dark Lady
sonnets (127–152), although the relationship here is a very different
one. Whereas many of the sonnets to the youth adopt the conventions and imagery of courtly love—the beloved as a rose or an

---

17. The repetition has been held to be a printer's error, but equally
well it may be an instance of irony.

angel, beautiful as Helen of Troy, the love born of suffering yet
capable of redeeming and refining the lover and conferring all
manner of comfort and joy—the sonnets to the lady deliberately
repudiate all the erotic attitudes that were common in courtly
Elizabethan love poetry. The lady is not remote and unattainable;
she readily sleeps with the poet and with others besides. He calls
her a "baye where all men ride" and "the wide world's common
place" (137). The feeling he has for her, which G. Wilson Knight
calls "finer than lust and cruder than love,"[18] is not one that re-
deems or refines; it makes him helpless and dependent in a way
that he cannot justify, as he could with the friend, by recourse to
her beauty or nobility. She mocks his devotion without compassion:

> Love is my sinne, and thy deare vertue hate,
> Hate of my sinne, grounded on sinfull louing. (142)

But her lack of response to him comes not from commitment to
chastity but from surrender to lust. In Sonnet 135 Shakespeare
uses his own name, Will, which was perhaps also a name or nickname of the friend, to pun bawdily on the lady's vast sexual
appetite (will):

> Who euer hath her wish, thou hast thy *Will*,
> And *Will* too boote, and *Will* in ouer-plus,
> More than enough am I that vexe thee still,
> To thy sweet will making addition thus. (135)

His attitudes range from the semi-comic helpless misery of Sonnet
143, in which he describes himself as a baby who cries to win
his mother's attention, to the violent self-hatred of 137:

> Thov blinde foole loue, what doost thou to mine eyes,
> That they behold and see not what they see:
> They know what beautie is, see where it lyes,
> Yet what the best is, take the worst to be. (137)

As in the sonnets to the young man, much of the complexity
comes from the division within the poet's own personality, between the self that begs to be deceived by kind looks and com-

---

18. G. Wilson Knight, *The Mutual Flame*, London, 1955, 15.

passion (139, 140), and the self that recognizes and despises such equivocation (137, 147, 148). He uses images of blindness, fever, and madness and resorts frequently to the device of antithesis and its various forms—paradox, oxymoron, and contraries—to convey the quality of the feeling that enslaves him. In sonnets 137 and 138 the "blinde foole loue" has destroyed both the true experience of sight and the inner understanding; the poet's faculties are at war within him:

> Why should my heart thinke that a seuerall plot,
> Which my heart knowes the wide world's common place?
> Or mine eyes seeing this, say this is not,
> To put faire truth vpon so foule a face? (137)

In 137 the tone of cold and bitter self-awareness contrasts with the bewilderment described; he says he has lost all ability to judge or discriminate, but he knows enough to be able to explain this. In the less passionate 138 the poet accepts as a solution the paradoxical situation that is created by each partner encouraging the other in an act of self-deception; each will pretend to believe the other's lies in order to appear more desirable, she that she might be thought faithful, he that he might seem young. The punning couplet summarizes this cynical relationship:

> Therefore I lye with her, and she with me,
> And in our faults by lyes we flattered be. (138)

It is hard to see how this part of the sequence can be regarded entirely as a creation of the poetic imagination without recourse to the facts of the poet's life. Some of the sonnets, such as 133, 134, and 144, that relate to the triangular relationship between the poet, the lady, and the friend seem essentially grounded in particular experience. Other of the sonnets to the lady could conceivably be literary inventions designed to exploit, in this instance by counteracting, current poetic conventions. Sonnet 130, "My Mistres eyes," reads like a deliberate parody of the traditional eulogy of the golden-haired mistress, but of course it becomes very much more than this in its context. Sonnet 132 ("Thine eies I loue"), ironically following this disclaimer of traditional methods, praises the lady's black eyes in a manner borrowed "quite shamelessly"[19]

19. M.C. Bradbrook, *Shakespeare and Elizabethan Poetry*, London, 1951, 146.

from Sidney, *Astropel and Stella*, Sonnet 7, which praises Stella
in a similar manner. This need not mean, of course, that Shakespeare didn't have a mistress with dark coloring, but it shows that
when we read Shakespeare's sonnets we need to preserve a bal-
ance between our ideas of poetic originality and our sense of
literary history.

The most bitter sonnet of the sequence, 129 ("Th' expence of
spirit in a waste of shame") is a general poem that is not thought
to be related directly to the poet's own experience or to the Dark
Lady. It may be based on a passage from a rhetorical handbook.[20]
Like its antithesis, 116 ("Let me not to the marriage of true
mindes") it partly relates to the surrounding sonnets, although its
tone is a kind of distillation of that part of the series. Sonnets 127–
152 anatomize lust; Sonnet 129 defines it. Like so many of the best
and most completely realized sonnets, such as 18, 55, 60, 73, 116,
and 146, it is not a personal sonnet dealing with an individual
emotion or situation; it does not present Shakespeare's moods
and experiences for us to examine and wonder at, but instead it
turns directly to us and shows us ourselves. At the same time, it is
a highly complex and rhetorical composition, where syntax, sound,
and rhythm combine to emphasize the paradoxes that are at the
heart of the experience of lust.

The sonnets reveal more of Shakespeare's sensibility than
anything else he wrote in the 1590's, and perhaps reveal it more
directly than anything else he wrote; this is an important reason
for the high value that is set on them. Nonetheless, it should not
be forgotten that the revelation of that sensibility would not have
been made without the command of poetic technique that the
sonnets display. John Benson, in the preface to the 1640 text, described them in lines borrowed without acknowledgment from
another poet's testimonial, as "seren, cleere and eligantly plaine,
such gentle straines as shall recreate and not perplexe your braine,
no cloudy stuffe to puzzell intellect."[21] But it is now obvious that
Benson had misperceived Shakespeare's work: the richness and
complexity of thought in the sonnets is matched by their technique.
"The sonnet's scanty plot of ground" provided ampler space for
Shakespeare to display his genius than the apparently extensive

20. D.L. Peterson,*The English Lyric from Wyatt to Donne*, Princeton,
1967, pp. 227–31, suggests that the source may be Thomas Wilson's
Arte of Rhetorique.
21. Quoted in H. Smith, *Elizabethan Poetry*, University of Michigan
Press, 1968, 176.

area of the Ovidian narrative. There will be much in all of his poetry—particularly in the themes and images of the sonnets—to remind us of his plays; but the best of the sonnets contain for many the quintessential Shakespeare.

A SELECTED BIBLIOGRAPHY

This bibliography, which has been compiled with the needs of students in mind, is divided into the following sections:

1. Editions of Shakespeare's Works
2. Reference Books
3. Background Reading
4. Life and Art
5. Theatres and Stagecraft

1. Editions of Shakespeare's Works

Alexander, P., ed. *The Complete Works*. Tudor Edition. Collins: 1954. (Convenient, well-edited, single-volume Shakespeare with glossary, but no notes.)

Brockbank, P., general editor. *The New Cambridge Shakespeare*. Cambridge University Press: 1984– . (Only a few volumes published so far. Separately edited volumes with illustrations, notes, and appendices. Particular attention is paid to the plays as realized on stage, and to their social and cultural settings.)

Brooks, H.F., Jenkins, H., and Morris B., eds., *The Arden Shakespeare*. Methuen: 1955– . (Individual volumes, separately edited, with very full scholarly notes and substantial introductions, particularly in those more recently produced.)

Evans, G. Blakemore, textual editor, *The Riverside Shakespeare*. Houghton Mifflin: 1974. (Contains illustrations, excellent brief introductions to each play, footnotes, and useful appendices.)

Spencer, T.J.B., general editor, and Wells, S., associate editor. *The New Penguin Shakespeare*. Penguin: 1971– . (Individual volumes, separately edited, with helpful notes and introductions.)

Wells, S., general editor. *The Oxford Shakespeare*. Oxford University Press: 1982– . (Individual volumes, separately edited, of which only a few have yet appeared. Good notes, introductions, and glossaries.)

Wells, S. and Taylor, G. general editors. *William Shakespeare: The Complete Works*. Oxford University Press: 1986; compact edn., 1988. (Incorporates new theories about Shakespeare's texts, and arranges the plays in hypothetical order of composition.)

Wells, S., Taylor, G., with J. Jowett and W. Montgomery. *William Shakespeare: A Textual Companion*. Oxford University Press: 1987.

2. Reference Books

Bergeron, D.M. *Shakespeare. A Study and Research Guide*. Macmillan: 1975. (A handy, practical guide to the study of Shakespeare, designed for the student or general reader.)

McManaway, J.G. and Roberts, J.A. *A Selective Bibliography of Shakespeare. Editions, Textual Studies, Commentary*. The Folger Shakespeare Library: 1975. (A bibliography of 4,500 entries, mostly of books and articles published since 1930. Designed for the research student or scholar.)

Onions, C.T. *A Shakespeare Glossary*, revised and enlarged by R.D. Eagleson. Oxford University Press: 1986. (A dictionary of Shakespearian language.)

Partridge, E. *Shakespeare's Bawdry: A Literal and Psychological Essay and a Comprehensive Glossary*. Routledge: 1947, revised and enlarged, 1968. (Informative glossary of Shakespeare's extensive sexual vocabulary.)

Rubinstein, F. *A Dictionary of Shakespeare's Sexual Puns and their Significance*. 2nd ed. Macmillan: 1989. (More attentive to wordplay than Partridge, but sometimes very speculative.)

Spevack, M. *A Complete and Systematic Concordance to the Works of Shakespeare*, 9 vols. Olms: 1968–80. (Complete computerised concordance.)

Spevack, M. *The Harvard Concordance to Shakespeare*. Belknap Press of Harvard University Press: 1973. (The standard one-volume concordance).

Wells, S. ed. *Shakespeare: A Bibliographical Guide*, new edition. Clarendon Press: 1990. (Selective and up-to-date guide to the best scholarship and criticism in all major areas of Shakespeare study.)

3. Background Reading

Bradbrook, M.C. *The Growth and Structure of Elizabethan Comedy*. Chatto and Windus: 1955; Peregrine Books: 1963. (A study of the development of Elizabethan comedy from medieval origins to about 1610, including sections on Shakespeare.)

Bradbrook, M.C. *Themes and Conventions of Elizabethan Tragedy*. Cambridge University Press: 1935; paperback edn.: 1960. (A study of Elizabethan tragedy with special emphasis on conventions of acting and characterisation, and separate chapters on Marlowe, Tourneur, Webster, and Middleton.)

Cohen, W. *Drama of a Nation: Public Theater in Renaissance England and Spain*. Cornell University Press: 1985. (Densely written comparative study of drama in the political context of an absolutist state.)

Craig, H. *The Enchanted Glass: The Elizabethan Mind in Literature*, 1936. Reissued Basil Blackwell: 1950. (Detailed account of the intellectual environment of Shakespeare and his contemporaries as reflected in literature.)

Cruttwell, P. *The Shakespearean Moment and its Place in the Poetry of the Seventeenth Century*. Chatto and Windus: 1954. (Stimulating study of intellectual changes in the 1590s, and their repercussions on the literature of the seventeenth century.)

Doran, M. *Endeavours of Art: A Study of Form in Elizabethan Drama*. University of Wisconsin Press: 1954. (Wide-ranging and scholarly study of form and genre in Elizabethan drama with useful material on the theoretical background.)

Farnham, W. *The Medieval Heritage of Elizabethan Tragedy*. Reprinted Basil Blackwell: 1956. (A study of the medieval philosophical and dramatic background to Elizabethan tragedy.)

Haydn, H. *The Counter-Renaissance*. Charles Scribner's Sons: 1950. (Interesting account of sceptical thought in the Renaissance.)

Jardine, L. *Still Harping on Daughters: Women and Drama in the Age of Shakespeare*.

Harvester Press: 1983. (Carefully researched studies of separate aspects of the presentation of women in Elizabethan drama, with close attention to the socio-historical background.)

Lanham, R.A. *The Motives of Eloquence. Literary Rhetoric in the Renaissance.* Yale University Press: 1976. (Provocative study of the rhetoric of self-presentation in Renaissance literature, with chapters on *Hamlet* and *Venus and Adonis*.)

Levor, J.W. *The Tragedy of State. A Study of Jacobean Drama*, new edition. Methuen: 1987. (Pioneering account of Jacobean drama in the context of contemporary political issues.)

Lovejoy, A.O. *The Great Chain of Being.* Harvard University Press: 1936. (Seminal study of the philosophical notion of the hierarchical structure of the universe in Renaissance literature.)

Smith, H.D. *Elizabethan Poetry: A Study in Conventions, Meaning, and Expression.* Harvard University Press: 1952. (Detailed account of form, genre and convention in Elizabethan poetry including Shakespeare, whose sonnets and narrative poems are helpfully located in a contemporary context.)

Welsford, E. *The Fool: His Social and Literary History.* Faber and Faber: 1935. (Well-documented account of origins of the Fool in English and European literature and folk-lore.)

Wiles, D. *Shakespeare's Clown, Actor and Text in the Elizabethan Playhouse.* Cambridge University Press: 1987. (Illuminating account of Shakespeare's clown roles in relation to traditions of performance.)

Woodbridge, L. *Women and the English Renaissance. Literature and the Nature of Womankind, 1540–1620.* Harvester: 1984. (Wide-ranging exploration of controversies about the literary representation of gender.)

Wright, L.B. *Middle Class Culture in Elizabethan England.* University of North Carolina Press: 1935. (Extensive survey of minor literature of Shakespeare's day, useful for any study of the social background to the drama.)

4. Life and Art

Adamson, J. *Othello as Tragedy: Some Problems of Judgment and Feeling.* Cambridge University Press, paperback edn.: 1980. (Examines emotional and moral qualities of the play with a view to reinstating it as a great and complex tragedy.)

Adelman, J. *The Common Liar: An Essay on 'Antony and Cleopatra'.* Yale University Press: 1973. (Important account of identity and selfhood in the play.)

Armstrong, W. ed. *Shakespeare's Histories: An Anthology of Modern Criticism.* Penguin Shakespeare Library, Penguin Books: 1972. (Convenient anthology of essays and extracts from books.)

Auden, W.H. *The Dyer's Hand and other essays.* Faber and Faber: 1963. (Includes brilliant essays on Falstaff, *The Merchant of Venice*, Iago, and music in Shakespeare.)

Baldwin, T.W. *William Shakespeare's Small Latine and Lesse Greeke*, 2 vols. University of Illinois Press: 1944. (Long scholarly account of education in Shakespeare's day with detailed discussion of school curricula.)

Barber, C.L. *Shakespeare's Festive Comedy: A Study of Dramatic Form and its Relation to Social Custom.* Princeton University Press: 1972. (Influential book relating Shakespeare's comedy to a background of popular native festivity.)

Berry, E. *Shakespeare's Comic Rites*. Cambridge University Press: 1984. (Relates the comedies to anthropological theory and the rites of passage from adolescence to maturity in Elizabethan social practice.)

Bethell, S.L. *The Winter's Tale: A Study*. Staples Press: 1947. (A Christian interpretation of the play which pays close attention to stage presentation.)

Blake, N.F. *Shakespeare's Language. An Introduction*. The Macmillan Press: 1983. (Clearly written introductory account of the Elizabethan aspects of Shakespeare's language.)

Booth, S. *An Essay on Shakespeare's Sonnets*. Yale University Press: 1969. (Close and detailed analysis of language and structure.)

Bradbrook, M.C. *The Living Monument: Shakespeare and the Theatre of his Time*. Cambridge University Press, paperback edn.: 1976. (An account of the sociology of Shakespeare's theatre, and of the Jacobean elements in his art in this context. Especially interesting on Shakespeare's relation to Jonson.)

Bradbrook, M.C. *Shakespeare and Elizabethan Poetry*. Cambridge University Press, paperback edn.: 1976. (Study of Shakespeare's art focussed on his non-dramatic poetry in relation to the poetry of contemporaries.)

Bradley, A.C. *Shakespearian Tragedy*, 1904. Macmillan Student Editions, reprinted: 1985. (Immensely influential account of Shakespearian tragedy, focussing especially on the characters of the tragic heroes.)

Bradley, A.C. *Oxford Lectures on Poetry*. Macmillan: 1909, 1950. (Includes essays on *Antony and Cleopatra* and the famous 'The Rejection of Falstaff'.)

Brooke, N. *Shakespeare's Early Tragedies*. Methuen: 1968. (Excellent accounts of *Titus Andronicus, Richard III, Richard II*, and *Romeo and Juliet*.)

Brown, J.R. *Shakespeare's Plays in Performance*. Penguin Shakespeare Library. Penguin Books: 1969. (A study both practical and theoretical of Shakespeare's plays as stage pieces, with a discussion of some specific productions.)

Bullough, G. ed. *Narrative and Dramatic Sources of Shakespeare*, 7 vols. Routledge and Kegan Paul: 1957. (Immensely useful work, containing substantial accounts of Shakespeare's treatment of his source-material in each play, as well as extensive extracts from sources and analogues.)

Carroll, W.C. *The Great Feast of Language in 'Love's Labour's Lost'*. Princeton University Press: 1976. (Study of language, wit, and comic art.)

Chambers, Sir E.K. *William Shakespeare: A Study of Facts and Problems*, 2 vols. The Clarendon Press: 1930. (The most thorough and scholarly account of Shakespeare's life and theatrical career, abridged by C. Williams as *A Short Life of Shakespeare with the Sources*, The Clarendon Press, 1933.)

Champion, L.S. *Perspective in Shakespeare's English Histories*. University of Georgia Press: 1980. (Account of both tetralogies, discussing the dramatic creation of various perspectives from which to evaluate the action of the plays.)

Charlton, H.B. *Shakespearian Comedy*, Methuen: 1938, reprinted 1984. (Early, influential attempt to define the specifically Shakespearian aspects of his comedies.)

Charney, M. *Shakespeare's Roman Plays: The Function of Imagery in the Drama*. Harvard Press: 1961. (A study of both visual and verbal imagery.)

——. *Style in 'Hamlet'*. Oxford University Press: 1969. (Lively study, stressing the theatrical aspects of the play.)

Clemen, W.H. *A Commentary on Shakespeare's 'Richard III'*. Methuen: 1968. (Detailed, scene-by-scene account of the play with attention both to patterns of language and to stage presentation.)

——. *The Development of Shakespeare's Imagery*. 2nd edn. Methuen, University Paperback edn.: 1977. (A consideration of the dramatic function of imagery in the plays.)

Coleridge, S.T. *Coleridge's Shakespearian Criticism*, ed. T.M. Raysor, 2 vols. Revised edition, Everyman's Library. J M Dent: 1960. (Useful collection of Coleridge's imaginative and brilliant Shakespeare criticism.)

Curry, W.C. *Shakespeare's Philosophical Patterns*. Louisiana State University Press, 2nd edn.: 1959. (Useful study of the religious and philosophical background to Shakespeare, including useful material on witchcraft and demonology, ghosts, spirits, etc.)

Danby, J.F. *Shakespeare's Doctrine of Nature*. Faber and Faber, paperback edn.: 1975. (A study of the radically contrasting ideas of nature in Shakespeare's time, especially illuminating on *King Lear*.)

Dollimore, J. and Sinfield, A., eds. *Political Shakespeare. New Essays in Cultural Materialism*. Manchester University Press: 1985. (Influential collection of essays by different authors, demonstrating a variety of political readings of Shakespeare.)

Dusinberre, J. *Shakespeare and the Nature of Women*. Macmillan Press, paperback edn.: 1979. (Detailed study tracing feminine sympathies in Shakespeare's presentation of women.)

Elam, K. *Shakespeare's Universe of Discourse: Language games in the Comedies*. Cambridge University Press: 1984. (Detailed account of dramatic rhetoric, particularly in *Love's Labour's Lost*, in a context of modern linguistics.)

Eliot, T.S. *Selected Essays*. Faber and Faber: 1932. (Contains his famous essay on *Hamlet* and an influential view of *Othello* in 'Shakespeare and the Stoicism of Seneca'.)

Ellis-fermor, U. *The Frontiers of Drama*. Methuen, 1946: 1964. (Contains useful essays on imagery in drama and on *Troilus and Cressida*.)

Evans, B. *Shakespeare's Comedies*. The Clarendon Press: 1960, 1967. (Study of Shakespeare's comic technique in terms of the different degrees of understanding of the action possessed by individual characters and its dramatic significance.)

Farnham, W. *Shakespeare's Tragic Frontier*. 2nd edn. Basil Blackwell: 1973. (A study of the later tragedies, with a stress on the mixed moral nature of the protagonists.)

Felperin, H. *Shakespearian Romance*. Princeton University Press: 1972. (Stimulating study of *Pericles, Cymbeline, The Winter's Tale*, and *The Tempest*, especially interesting on their structure.)

Frye, N. *A Natural Perspective: The Development of Shakespearian Comedy and Romance*. Columbia University Press: 1965. (Highly influential account of the genres of comedy and romance as practised by Shakespeare. Theoretical but very stimulating.)

Granville-Barker, H. *Prefaces to Shakespeare*, 6 vols. Batsford: 1971–74. (A series of introductory essays, stressing practical aspects of Shakespeare's stagecraft.)

Greenblatt, S. *Shakespearean Negotiations: The Circulation of Social Energy in Renaissance England*. Clarendon Press: 1988. (Important essays by one of the foremost new historicist critics.)

Harbage, H. *Shakespeare and the Rival Traditions*. Macmillan (New York): 1952. (Argues for a split between public and private theatres in Shakespeare's day which devitalized the private theatre plays.)

Heilman, R.B. *This Great Stage: Image and Structure in 'King Lear'*. Louisiana

State University Press: 1948. (Account of language and poetic structure in the play.)

Heilman, R.B. *Magic in the Web: Action and Language in 'Othello'*. University of Kentucky Press: 1956. (Account of language and poetic structures in the play, especially illuminating about Iago.)

Honigmann, E.A. *Shakespeare: The 'Lost Years'*. Manchester University Press: 1985. (Makes a case for Shakespeare's Roman Catholic background.)

James, D.G. *The Dream of Prospero*. The Clarendon Press: 1967. (An account of *The Tempest* with a useful chapter on Shakespeare's use of contemporary literature of colonization.)

Jenkins, H. *The Structural Problem in Shakespeare's 'Henry the Fourth'*. Methuen: 1956. (Carefully argued theory of the relationship between Parts I and II of *Henry IV*.)

Johnson, S. *On Shakespeare*, ed. W.K. Wimsatt. Hill and Wang: 1960. (Convenient small anthology of Dr. Johnson's much-quoted remarks about Shakespeare.)

Jones, Emrys. *The Origins of Shakespeare*. Oxford University Press: 1977. (A study of Shakespeare's early histories in the light of their origins in medieval and humanist thought.)

——. *Scenic Form in Shakespeare*. Oxford University Paperback. Reissued (with corrections): 1985. (Treats the conception and realization of the scene as a unit and as part of a sequence.)

Jones, Ernest. *Hamlet and Oedipus*. Victor Gollancz: 1949. (Study of Hamlet in terms of Freudian theory.)

Knight, G. Wilson. *The Imperial Theme*. Methuen University Paperback: reprinted 1985. (Influential study of kingship in Shakespeare.)

——. *The Shakespearian Tempest*. Oxford University Press: 1932, 1960. (An analysis of Shakespeare's dramatic use of tempest imagery throughout his work.)

——. *The Sovereign Flower*. Methuen: 1958. (A study of Shakespeare as the poet of royalism, containing indexes to occurrences of major themes throughout his work.)

——. *The Wheel of Fire*. Methuen University Paperback: 1983. (Study of Shakespeare's major tragedies in terms of imagery and symbolic themes. Important chapter on *King Lear*.)

Knights, L.C. *Some Shakespearean Themes*. Chatto and Windus: 1959. (Treats the development of Shakespeare's thought on such all-pervasive themes as time, appearance and reality, and nature.)

Leavis, F.R. *The Common Pursuit*. 1952. Hogarth Press paperback: reissued 1984.) (Contains his well-known essay on *Othello* 'The Diabolic Intellect and the Noble Hero'.)

Lawlor, J.J. *The Tragic Sense in Shakespeare*. Harcourt, Brace: 1960. (Includes treatment of plays other than the tragedies; useful on *Henry IV*.)

Leech, C. *'Twelfth Night' and Shakespearian Comedy*. University of Toronto Press: 1965. (Three lectures in the nature of Shakespearian comedy, including discussion of *Troilus and Cressida* and *The Winter's Tale*.)

Leggatt, A. *Shakespeare's Comedy of Love*. Methuen: 1974. (Account of romantic and moral themes in Shakespeare's great comedies.)

Leishman, J.B. *Themes and Variations in Shakespeare's Sonnets*. Hutchinson: 2nd edn. reprinted 1967. (Discusses Shakespeare's treatment of the major themes of Love, Beauty, and Time, and relates it to the work of other poets.)

Lenz, C., Greene, G., and Neely, C., eds. *The Woman's Part: Feminist Criticism of Shakespeare.* University of Illinois Press: 1980. (Useful collection of articles, mostly by American feminists, on issues of gender in Shakespeare.)

Lever, J.W. *The Elizabethan Love Sonnet*, 2nd edn. Methuen: 1966. (Considers major Elizabethan sonnet-writers including Shakespeare, and explores the influence on them of other poets, especially Petrarch.)

Long, M. *The Unnatural Scene: A Study in Shakespearian Tragedy.* Methuen: 1976. (Considers the tragedies in relation to the social worlds in which they are set.)

MacCallum, M.W. *Shakespeare's Roman Plays and their Background.* 1910. Macmillan: new edition 1967. (A full and useful account of the Roman plays in relation to their sources in Plutarch.)

Mahood, M.M. *Shakespeare's Wordplay.* Methuen: 1957. (Stimulating study of punning, innuendo, etc. in the plays and poems.)

Muir, K. *The Sources of Shakespeare's Plays.* Methuen: 1977. (A study of the relationship between Shakespeare's reading and his plays, which illuminates his working methods.)

Nevo, R. *Comic Transformations in Shakespeare.* Methuen: 1980. (Stimulating study of the comedies, especially on themes of metamorphosis and identity.)

Parker, P. and Hartman, G., eds. *Shakespeare and the Question of Theory.* Methuen Press: 1985. (Represents a wide range of theoretical approaches. See esp. N.J. Vickers on *The Rape of Lucrece.*)

Patterson, A. *Shakespeare and the Popular Voice.* Blackwell: 1989. (Provocative accounts of seven plays which challenge the view of Shakespeare as conservative and undemocratic.)

Paul, H.N. *The Royal Play of 'Macbeth'.* Macmillan (New York): 1950. (A study of the play's contemporary background and its connections with King James I.)

Proser, M.N. *The Heroic Image in Five Shakespearian Tragedies.* Princeton University Press: 1965. (An analysis of the relationship between the hero's self-image and his true nature.)

Prosser, E. *Hamlet and Revenge.* Stanford University Press: 1972. (A study of Shakespeare's treatment of the dramatic and ethical aspects of revenge.)

Reese, M.M. *The Cease of Majesty: A Study of Shakespeare's History Plays.* E. Arnold: 1961. (Basic account of the history plays and their relation to Tudor political thought.)

——. *Shakespeare: His World and His Work.* St. Martin's Press: 1953. (Useful study of Shakespeare's life and achievement.)

Righter, A. *Shakespeare and the Idea of the Play.* Chatto and Windus: 1962. (Fascinating study of the conceptions of the actor and the play as expressed within Shakespeare's work.)

Rosenberg, M. *The Masks of Othello.* University of California Press: 1981. (An account of stage interpretations of *Othello.*)

Salingar, L. *Shakespeare and the Traditions of Comedy.* Cambridge University Press, Paperback edn.: 1976. (Detailed account of the comedies in relation to their background in European comic literature.)

Schoenbaum, S. *Shakespeare's Lives.* Oxford University Press: 1970. (Comprehensive and fascinating history of Shakespeare biography, including discussion of legends and apocryphal material, as well as formal biographies.)

Slater, A.P. *Shakespeare the Director.* Harvester Press, paperback edn.: 1984.

(Illuminating study of internalized stage-directions within Shakespeare's plays.)

Spencer, T. *Shakespeare and the Nature of Man*. Macmillan (New York): 1942, 2nd edn., 1958. (A lucid account of Shakespeare's plays in relation to their framework of religious and philosophical belief.)

Spenser, T.J.B. ed. *Shakespeare's Plutarch*. Penguin Shakespeare Library, Penguin Books: 1968. (Anthology of extracts from Plutarch's *Lives* on which Shakespeare based his plays.)

Spivack, B. *Shakespeare and the Allegory of Evil*. Oxford University Press: 1959. (A consideration of the relation of Shakespeare's villains to the Medieval figure of the Vice.)

Stauffer, P.A. *Shakespeare's World of Images: The Development of his Moral Ideas*. Norton: 1949. (An analysis of Shakespeare's moral ideas in relation to his conception of the imagination.)

Taylor, G. and Warren, M., eds. *The Division of the Kingdoms*. Clarendon Press: 1986. (Theories as to the nature and relationships of the Quarto and Folio texts of *King Lear*. A major addition to the new bibliography.)

Tillyard, E.M.W. *Shakespeare's Last Plays*. Athlone Press: paperback edn., 1983. (A study of the romances as the last regenerative phase of Shakespeare's tragic cycle.)

——. *Shakespeare's History Plays*. Penguin Books: 1962. (An interesting book, arguing for the history plays as vehicles of Tudor political propaganda.)

——. *Shakespeare's Problem Plays*. Penguin Books: 1965. (Includes *Hamlet* with *Troilus and Cressida, All's Well That Ends Well* and *Measure for Measure* in an account of plays united by concern with abstract speculation and interest in details of human nature.)

Traversi, D. *Shakespeare: From 'Richard II' to 'Henry V'*. Hollis: 1958. (Systematic play-by-play study of the second tetralogy as a coherent sequence.)

——. *Shakespeare: The Last Phase*. Hollis: 1965, 1973. (Relates the last plays to the great tragedies, and discusses them as poetic drama.)

——. *Shakespeare: The Roman Plays*. Hollis: 1963. (A general study of the Roman plays showing them to be a new growth of Shakespeare's tragic vision.)

Vickers, B. *The Artistry of Shakespeare's Prose*. Methuen: 1968. (Detailed, illuminating account of Shakespeare's uses of prose speech.)

Weimann, R. *Shakespeare and the Popular Tradition in the Theatre*. ed. R. Schwartz. Johns Hopkins University Press: 1978. (Wide-ranging study of the disparate sources in popular art that went to form Shakespeare's drama, written from a Marxist perspective.)

Wilders, J. *The Lost Garden: A View of Shakespeare's English and Roman History Plays*. Macmillan: 1978. (Thoughtful account of the history plays, which is critical of the view of them as propaganda.)

Wilson, J.D. *What Happens in Hamlet*. Cambridge University Press: 1935, reprinted 1984. (Provocative and stimulating study, stressing the play in performance.)

Young, D. *The Heart's Forest. A Study of Shakespeare's Pastoral Plays*. Yale University Press: 1972. (Discusses Renaissance pastoral, and ideas of art and nature, in relation to a range of plays including *As You Like It, King Lear, The Winter's Tale*, and *The Tempest*.)

5. Theatres and Stagecraft

Bentley, G.E. *The Jacobean and Caroline Stages*, 7 vols. The Clarendon Press: 1941–68. (Massive work of scholarship and reference, a mine of facts and information on playhouse buildings, theatre companies, players and playwrights, performances, etc.)

Bentley, G.E. *The Profession of Dramatist in Shakespeare's Time, 1590–1642*. Princeton University Press: 1917. (Closely documented study of the professional circumstances of Shakespeare and his fellow playwrights.)

Bradbrook, M.C. *The Rise of the Common Player*. Chatto and Windus: 1962; Cambridge University Press, paperback: 1979. (Study of the actor and society in Elizabethan times.)

Chambers, E.K. *The Elizabethan Stage*, 4 vols. The Clarendon Press: 1923. (Like Bentley's *The Jacobean and Caroline Stage*, a huge work of scholarship, still the authority on its subject.)

Cook, A.J. *The Privileged Playgoer of Shakespeare's London* (1576–1642). Princeton University Press: 1982. (Exhaustively documented study of Elizabethan playgoers, arguing that they represented a privileged elite in their society.)

Eccles, C. *The Rose Theatre*. Routledge: 1990. (Account of the history and significance of this theatre in the light of recent archaeological finds.)

Gurr, A. *Playgoing in Shakespeare's London*. Cambridge University Press: 1987. (Important study of audiences and tastes.)

Gurr, A. *The Shakespearian Stage, 1574–1642*. 2nd edn. Cambridge University Press: 1980. (A redaction of the multi-volume works by Chambers and Bentley, and a lucid summary of accepted facts and modern scholarly opinion on players, playhouses, staging, audiences, etc., in the period.)

Hattaway, M. *Elizabethan Popular Theatre Plays in Performance*. Theatre Production Studies. Routledge and Kegan Paul: 1982. (Contains a detailed account of Elizabethan theatre practice in general, and a useful chapter on *Titus Andronicus*.)

Hodges, C.W. *The Globe Restored*. 2nd edn. Oxford University Press: 1968. (Handsomely illustrated account of Hodge's theory of the Globe theatre's structure and origins.)

King, T.J. *Shakespearean Staging 1599–1642*. Harvard University Press: 1971. (Comprehensive, authoritative account of stage structures and staging in this period.)

Orrell, J. *The Human Stage. English Theatre Design, 1567–1640*. Cambridge University Press: 1988. (Sees theatre of the period as embodying the architectural principles of the age of humanism.)

Styan, J.L. *Shakespeare's Stagecraft*. Cambridge University Press: 1967. (Practical guide to Shakespeare's stage practice, focussing on plays in the theatre.)

Thomson, P. *Shakespeare's Theatre*. Theatre Production Studies. Routledge and Kegan Paul: 1983. (Account of playhouse practice and play production at the Globe theatre 1599–1608, with chapters on *Twelfth Night*, *Hamlet*, and *Macbeth*.)

Wickham, G.W.G. *Early English Stages 1300–1600*, Vol. 2, Parts 1 and 2. Routledge and Kegan Paul: 1963, 1972. (A very fully documented account, with some illustrations, of stages and stage practice, their history and development, in this period.)

Aaron. In *Titus Andronicus*, the Moorish lover of the Gothic queen, Tamora. He arranges the elaborate murders of Bassianus, Quintus, and Martius, and the mutilation of Titus and Lavinia. He is ruthlessly punished by Lucius, the new emperor, for his treachery and cruelty on behalf of Tamora against Titus's family. His devotion to evil-doing recalls Barabas in Marlowe's *The Jew of Malta*.

Abergavenny, Lord. In *Henry VIII*, a baron who adheres to Buckingham's cause against Wolsey and is sent to the Tower with Buckingham.

Abhorson. In *Measure for Measure*, an executioner who thinks of his job as a "mystery" (i.e., a skilled craft).

Abigail. In Christopher Marlowe's play *The Jew of Malta*, the daughter of Barabas. The dialogue between father and daughter is in some ways very close to that between Shylock and Jessica in *Merchant of Venice*.

Abram. In *Romeo and Juliet*, a servant of Montague.

Achilles. In *Troilus and Cressida*, a Greek commander who is aroused from his moody inactivity in the war by the death in battle of his friend Patroclus. To avenge his friend, Achilles attacks Hector (who is resting unarmed) and then orders his Myrmidons to murder Hector.

Adam. In *As You Like It*, the old servant who faithfully follows the exiled Orlando, leaving the service of Orlando's elder brother, Oliver. There is a late tradition, based on a statement (1750) of William Oldys, that Shakespeare himself acted this part.

Adam Cupid. In *Romeo and Juliet*, a nickname of Cupid.

Admiral's Men. See **Lord Admiral's Men.**

Adrian. In *Coriolanus*, a Volscian.

Adrian. In *The Tempest*, a lord who attends Alonso and is shipwrecked with him.

Adriana. In *The Comedy of Errors*, the wife of Antipholus of Ephesus. She confuses her husband with his twin, Antipholus of Syracuse.

Aegeon. In *The Comedy of Errors*, a merchant of Syracuse, husband of Aemilia, and the father of the Antipholus twins.

Aemilia. In *The Comedy of Erorrs*, the wife of Aegeon and mother of the Antipholus twins. When she is separated from her family she becomes an abbess at the convent of Ephesus, where she later harbors Antipholus of Syracuse when he is thought to be a lunatic.

Aemilius. In *Titus Andronicus*, a Roman who asks Titus's brother Marcus to present Lucius as emperor in the final scene.

Aeneas. In *Troilus and Cressida*, a Trojan commander who informs Troilus of the exchange of Cressida for the Trojan warrior Antenor, a prisoner of the Greeks.

Aetion. A character in Spenser's *Colin Clout's Come Home Again*, thought by some critics to represent Shakespeare.

Agamemnon. In *Troilus and Cressida*, the Greek general. He opens the discussion with Nestor, Ulysses, and Menelaus on the ill fortunes of the Greeks in the war with Troy (I.iii), and is present in many of the following scenes.

Agincourt. A village in N France, near which the English bowmen under Henry V defeated (1415) a very much larger force of heavily armed French knights. This battle forms the background of some of the principal scenes in *Henry V*.

Agrippa. In *Antony and Cleopatra*, a friend of Octavius who suggests that Antony marry Octavia, the sister of Octavius.

Aguecheek, Sir Andrew. In *Twelfth Night*, a timid, silly, but amusing country squire. He is the friend of Sir Toby Belch.

Ajax. In *Troilus and Cressida*, a Greek commander who is praised beyond his worth by the other leaders in order that Achilles, who has refused to go to battle, will become indignant and return to the wars. Alexander, Cressida's servingman, compares him to the lion, the bear, and the elephant, says that he has every virtue and every vice, and that he is "all eyes and no sight" (I.ii).

Alarbus. In *Titus Andronicus*, the eldest son of Tamora. When he is sacrificed by the sons of Titus, Tamora is provided with the motive for her acts of cruel and bloody vengeance.

Albany, Duke of. In *King Lear*, the husband of Goneril, Lear's eldest daughter. At first he is apparently a nonentity, but the play reveals him as an honorable and kind man who accuses Goneril and Regan of being unnatural in their treatment of Lear. At the death of Lear, the kingdom becomes his.

Alcibiades. In *Timon of Athens*, an Athenian captain who is banished for speaking hotly before the Senate when its members refuse to pardon one of his friends. Timon aids him toward the capture of Athens and thus they get revenge on their common enemy.

Alençon, Duke of. In *Henry V*, a French noble, the father of the Duke of Alençon in *1 Henry VI*, who is mentioned as having been killed in battle by Henry. Henry gives William's glove to Fluellen, saying it is Alençon's, in order to be amused by the two men challenging and attacking each other.

Alençon, Duke of.   In *1 Henry VI*, a French nobleman who speaks contemptuously of Englishmen's habits, but admires their bravery in battle; he also praises Joan of Arc.

Alexander.   In *Trolius and Cressida*, a servant of Cressida.

Alexas.   In *Antony and Cleopatra*, an attendant of Cleopatra who, as Enobarbus relates, deserts Antony, only to be hanged by Octavius.

Alice.   In *Henry V*, a lady in attendance on Princess Katherine. She gives the Princess a lesson in English (III.iv.).

Aliena.   In *As You Like It*, the name assumed by Celia when, disguised as a shepherdess, she follows Rosalind.

Alinda.   A character in Lodge's *Rosalynde*, the source of *As You Like it*. She corresponds to Celia.

Alleyn, Edward.   [Also **Alleyne**; called **Ned Allen.**] b. at London, Sept. 1, 1566; d. Nov. 25, 1626. An English actor; son-in-law of Philip Henslowe and later, by a second marriage, of John Donne. He was the founder (1613) and director (1619–26) of Dulwich College (the College of God's Gift), at London. Rated by Jonson, Nash, and others as the foremost actor, especially of tragedy, of his time, he was a member of the Earl of Worcester's Men (1586 *et seq.*), head of the Lord Admiral's (Earl of Nottingham's) Men (c1592), and owner-manager, with Henslowe, of various London theatres, including the Rose and the Fortune (built in 1600), and of a bearbaiting house at Paris Garden (1594–1626). He played leads in Marlowe's *Jew of Malta*, *Tamburlaine*, and *Doctor Faustus* and it is thought that his acting mannerisms are parodied by Shakespeare in the character of Pistol in *2 Henry IV*. His last known appearance was at a reception address to James I (c1604).

All's Well That Ends Well.   A comedy by Shakespeare, played as early as c1596. Portions of this play were written not later than 1593, but the play as we have it was probably written in large part in the period 1602–04. It was first printed in the folio of 1623. The only known source for the plot is the story of Giletta of Narbone from Boccaccio's *Decameron* (Day 3 Story 9), which Shakespeare probably knew in the translation by William Painter in *The Palace of Pleasure* (1566–67, 1575). Giletta, unlike Shakespeare's heroine Helena, is a rich heiress who has refused many suitors; otherwise her situation is very similar. She too wins the right to choose a husband after curing the King of a mysterious illness, is rejected by the man she chooses, and finally wins him after performing the seemingly impossible task of conceiving a son by him and gaining possession of a ring from his finger in his absence. Shakespeare alters Boccaccio's story chiefly by adding the characters of the Countess, Bertram's mother, and Lafew, the old courtier, whose support of Helena helps to make her a more sympathetic character, and also Parolles, the boastful coward, whose relationship with Bertram explains and partly excuses the young man's failings, while his own exposure parallels Bertram's painful self-discovery. In Boccaccio and Painter, the King is unwilling for the heroine to marry the man of her choice because he is of higher rank than she; Shakespeare not only widens the social gulf between Helena and Bertram but also gives the King a significant speech on the worth of true virtue over high birth, an important theme in the play.

Dramatis Personae

King of France
Duke of Florence
Bertram, Count of Rossillion
Lafew, *an old Lord*
Parolles, *a follower of Bertram*
Steward to the Countess of
   Rossillion
Clown, in her household
A Page

Countess of Rossillion, *mother of Bertram*
Helena, *a gentlewoman protected by the Countess*
A Widow of Florence
Diana, *daughter of the widow*
Violenta, *Friend of the Widow*
Mariana, *Friend of the Widow*
Lords, Officers, Soldiers

The Story. Helena, the daughter of a famous physician, Gerard de Narbon, cures the King of France of a supposedly incurable disease and as a reward asks that Bertram, the young Count of Rossillion, marry her. This Bertram does reluctantly, and leaves immediately for the wars, at the suggestion of the coward and braggart Parolles, one of Shakespeare's most amusing comic characters. Bertram sends a message to Helena that "When thou canst get the ring upon my finger which never shall come off, and show me a child begotten of thy body that I am father to, then call me husband" (III.ii). Passing through Florence on a pilgrimage, Helena discovers that Bertram is engaged in dalliance with Diana, the daughter of her hostess. She arranges to have Bertram informed that she (Helena) is dead, and to replace Diana in bed. Bertram gets her with child and she exchanges her ring (which the King had given her) for Bertram's. When Bertram returns home, the King notices the ring and accuses Bertram of killing Helena. Helena arrives in time to explain and to demand that Bertram accept her as his wife now that the conditions in his letter have been met.

Alonzo. In *The Tempest*, the King of Naples, who has helped Antonio to usurp Prospero's dukedom. On a return voyage from Tunis he is shipwrecked on Prospero's island and is made to repent his action. His son, Ferdinand, marries Miranda.

Amiens. In *As You Like It*, one of the lords attending the banished father of Rosalind. His cheerfulness is a foil to the melancholy cynicism of the other lord, Jaques. It is Amiens who sings the well-known "Under the greenwood tree" (II.v) and "Blow, blow, thou winter wind" (II.vii).

Andromache. In *Troilus and Cressida,* the wife of Hector. She, the prophetess Cassandra, and Hector's father Priam, the King of Troy, plead with Hector not to go into battle, because they feel certain that he will be killed, as he is.

Angelo. In *The Comedy of Errors,* a goldsmith.

Angelo. In *Measure for Measure,* the Duke's deputy who is granted full administrative powers in Vienna when the Duke pretends to leave. He condemns Claudio to death for unchastity, but agrees to pardon him if his sister, Isabella, will yield herself to him (Angelo). When the Duke resumes his own guise, Angelo is punished and is forced to marry Mariana (to whom he had been engaged).

Angus. In *Macbeth,* a Scottish thane who eventually supports Malcolm against Macbeth.

Anne, Lady. In *Richard III,* the historical Anne Neville, daughter of Warwick "the Kingmaker" and widow of Edward, Prince of Wales. She curses Richard for the murder of her husband, but she is won over by his rhetoric and his curious fascination and marries him. Later, Richard has her put away when he plans to marry Elizabeth, and she dies under unexplained circumstances. Her ghost appears to Richard before the battle of Bosworth.

Antenor. In *Troilus and Cressida,* a Trojan commander who is captured by the Greeks and exchanged for Cressida.

Antigonus. In *The Winter's Tale,* a lord of Sicilia and husband of Paulina. He is sent by Leontes to abandon Perdita in a "desert place" (II.iii), takes her to the "seacoast of Bohemia" (III.iii) and there is killed by a bear.

Antiochus. In *Pericles,* the King of Antioch. He tries to poison Pericles, who has discovered his incestuous relationship with his daughter. Fire from heaven finally destroys him.

Antipholus of Ephesus and **Antipholus of Syracuse.** In *The Comedy of Errors,* twin brothers, the first of a violent and the latter of a mild nature. They are the sons of Aegeon, a merchant of Syracuse, and his wife, Aemilia. Their identical appearance and opposite natures furnish the plot complications, as each is mistaken for the other.

Antonio. In *The Merchant of Venice,* the princely merchant who gives the play its name. He is of a sensitive, melancholy nature, with a presentiment of evil and danger. Being obliged to borrow money from Shylock to meet the needs of Bassanio, his friend, he is induced to sign a bond agreeing to forfeit a pound of flesh if he does not repay the money within a specified time.

Not being able to pay, he nearly loses his life to satisfy the demands of Shylock, but is saved by Portia who, disguised as a lawyer, points out to Shylock the impossibility of taking the flesh—his legal right—without spilling a drop of blood—a criminal act.

Antonio. In *Much Ado About Nothing,* the aged brother of Leonato, Governor of Messina. When Leonato's daughter Hero has her reputation impugned by Claudio, he tries to comfort Leonato and himself challenges Claudio.

Antonio. In *The Tempest,* the usurping Duke of Milan, and Prospero's brother, who is wrecked on the island where Prospero landed twelve years before. By Prospero's use of magic he is made to repent, and restores the dukedom to its rightful ruler.

Antonio. In *Twelfth Night,* a sea captain devoted to Sebastian. He lends his purse to Sebastian and later (upon arriving in Illyria) mistakes Viola for Sebastian. Upon being arrested by the officers of Duke Orsino for fighting in defense of the supposed Sebastian, he demands the purse from her.

Antonio. In *Two Gentlemen of Verona,* the father of Proteus.

Antonio. The chief male character of John Marston's double tragedy, *Antonio and Mellida* and *Antonio's Revenge.* In the course of the action comprising the second part, the ghost of Antonio's father appears twice in a fashion quite similar to that of Hamlet's father in *Hamlet.*

Antony. In *Antony and Cleopatra,* the hero. See also **Mark Antony.**

Antony and Cleopatra. [Full title, **The Tragedy of Antony and Cleopatra.**] A tragedy by Shakespeare, written and produced c1607, entered on the Stationers' Register in 1608 and printed in 1623. The main source was North's translation of the life of Antony from Plutarch's *Lives of the Noble Grecians and Romans,* which Shakespeare followed very closely, even in places that might seem unlikely, as for instance Enobarbus's famous speech about Cleopatra on the river Cydnus. As well as following North's wording, he also made some use of almost every incident in Plutarch's account of Antony's later years, except for the long Parthian campaign that is merely alluded to in III.i. The Antony of Plutarch is crueller and coarser than Shakespeare's character, but in other respects the characterization of the protagonists is very similar in the two accounts. Shakespeare's one addition is the character of Enobarbus, which he created from a few sentences in Plutarch. In the later scenes of the play the time sequence is shortened; in particular, Shakespeare leaves no interval between the battle of Actium and the events that follow it, whereas in Plutarch there is a long space of time between Antony's defeat and his embassy to Caesar.

Hints for Caesar's character may have come from Simon Gou-
lart's *Life of Octavius Caesar Augustus*, which was published in
North's translation in the 1603 edition of Plutarch, although this
added nothing to the account of the life of Antony. Shakespeare
supplemented Plutarch's account of the military background
with *The Roman Civil Wars* of Appian of Alexandria, Book V,
in a translation of 1578; this gave details of the wars of Fulvia,
Lucius Antonius (Antony's brother), and Pompey. The story of
Antony and Cleopatra appealed to the Renaissance, and there
were several dramatic versions of it. Some verbal echoes suggest
that Shakespeare may have consulted the Countess of Pembroke's translation of Garnier's *Marc Antoine* (1592), a moral
play with a simple, sincere Cleopatra. It is more likely that he
used Samuel Daniel's play *Cleopatra*, which was first published
in 1594 and considerably remodeled before its reappearance in
1607 after Daniel had seen another stage version, possibly the
Countess of Pembroke's *The Tragedie of Antonie*, less possibly
Antony and Cleopatra. Daniel's play and Shakespeare's share
certain features not found elsewhere, for instance Cleopatra's
fear of Octavia's scorn as one of the motives for her actions
after Antony's death, and the reminiscence of Cydnus as Cleopatra prepares for death. Shakespeare may also have used
Daniel's poem "A Letter from Octavia to Marcus Antonius,"
which was published in his *Poeticall Essayes* (1599). The subject
was used by John Dryden in *All for Love* (1678), and by John
Fletcher and Philip Massinger in *The False One*, but the character
of Mark Antony is incomparably stronger in Shakespeare's play
than in the others. Dryden makes him a weak voluptuary entirely
given up to his passion for Cleopatra, whereas Shakespeare
shows him as brave and noble. However, Dryden's play was
acted more often than Shakespeare's for a century. It was not
until 1849 that the Shakespeare play was produced in its original
form, being mixed with scenes from Dryden until that time. The
play is noted for its rich imagery, and J. Middleton Murry has
pointed out the close relationship between these images and what
he regards as the theme of the play, a powerful exposition of the
beauty and strength of love. Many critics, however, have seen
the play as an account of Antony's loss of honor and moral
destruction at the hands of Cleopatra.

Dramatis Personae

Mark Antony, *Triumvir*	Taurus, *Lieutenant-General*
Octavius Caesar, *Triumvir*	Canidius, *Lieutenant-General*
M. Aemilius Lepidus,	Silius, *Officer*
Triumvir	Euphronius, *Ambassador*
Sextus Pompeius (Pompey)	Alexas, *Attendant on Cleopatra*

Enobarbus, *Friend of Antony*
Ventidius, *Friend of Antony*
Eros, *Friend of Antony*
Scarus, *Friend of Antony*
Dercetas, *Friend of Antony*
Demetrius, *Friend of Antony*
Philo, *Friend of Antony*
Maecenas, *Friend of Caesar*
Agrippa, *Friend of Caesar*
Dolabella, *Friend of Caesar*
Proculeius, *Friend of Caesar*
Thyreus, *Friend of Caesar*
Gallus, *Friend of Caesar*
Menas, *Friend of Pompey*
Menecrates, *Friend of Pompey*
Varrius, *Friend of Pompey*

Mardian, *Attendant on Cleopatra*
Seleucus, *Attendant on Cleopatra*
Diomedes, *Attendant on Cleopatra*
A Soothsayer
A Clown
Cleopatra, Queen of Egypt
Octavia, *Sister to Caesar and Wife to Antony*
Charmian, *Attendant on Cleopatra*
Iras, *Attendant on Cleopatra*
Officers, Soldiers, Messengers, and other Attendants

The Story. In Alexandria, Antony luxuriates in the love of Cleopatra and the sybaritic life of the Egyptian court, but hearing of the death of his wife Fulvia and Pompey's uprising, he reluctantly departs for Rome. There he quarrels with Octavius, one of the Triumvirate with Lepidus and Antony, and in order to heal the breach between them Antony agrees to marry Octavius's sister, Octavia. Cleopatra, meanwhile, longs for Antony, and when the news of his marriage reaches her she almost kills the messenger in jealous wrath. In Rome, the antagonism between the two men resumes, and unable to stay away from Cleopatra longer, Antony returns to Egypt. Octavius imprisons Lepidus, renews the war against Pompey, and begins a campaign against Antony. In Egypt, Octavius challenges Antony to a sea battle and Antony accepts, although his forces would have proved superior on land. During the battle at Actium, Cleopatra suddenly orders her fleet to retreat and Antony follows, thus losing both the battle and his honor. He tries to make peace with Octavius, requesting to be allowed to live in Rome, but Octavius refuses and sends a messenger to try to persuade Cleopatra to renounce Antony. Relations are tense between the two lovers, and as Antony's followers, including his friend Enobarbus, desert him, doom seems imminent. Antony sends his friend's belongings after him, and Enobarbus, doubly stricken by his own betrayal in the face of this magnanimity on the part of Antony, dies of a broken heart. A land battle commences, but once more Cleopatra's retreat decides the victory in favor of Octavius. Antony determines to kill Cleopatra for her supposed treachery, and she, in terror, flees to her tomb and sends word to Antony that she has killed herself. Antony, believing the news, falls on his own sword, but lives long enough to be carried to Cleopatra, and the two reaffirm their eternal love. Cleopatra thereupon procures her own death with the bite of an asp.

Apemantus.   In *Timon of Athens*, a cynical and churlish philosopher who warns Timon about his false friends. When Timon becomes a recluse, and even more misanthropic, he drives even Apemantus away from his cave.

Archibald, Earl of Douglas.   See **Douglas, Archibald,** (4th) **Earl of.**

Archidamus. In *The Winter's Tale*, a Bohemian lord.

Arcite.   In *The Two Noble Kinsmen*, one of the principal characters, the cousin of Palamon.

Arden, Forest of.   An English forest that in former times extended through Warwickshire and other midland counties of England. Many scholars of Shakespeare have held that the Forest of Arden of *As You Like It* was the Forest of Ardennes in French Flanders. But it is likely from the allusions to Robin Hood and the bits of description that it is the English forest that Shakespeare meant, though some of the characters have French names.

Arden of Feversham, Tragedy of Mr.   A tragedy first printed (anonymously) in 1592, sometimes attributed to Shakespeare, and dramatized from Raphael Holinshed's account of the murder of a leading citizen of Feversham in Kent in 1551. The play offers a vivid and fairly realistic picture of English middle-class life of the time. The plot, which has the wife Alice and her paramour Masby (or Mosbie) murdering her husband Arden, suggests Clytemnestra and Aegisthus in the *Agamemnon* of Aeschylus. According to Frederick Gard Fleay, who dates it 1585, there is some ground for attributing it to Thomas Kyd. Ludwig Tieck translated it into German as Shakespeare's work.

Ariel.   "An airy spirit" in *The Tempest*, employed by Prospero. Ariel has been imprisoned by the witch, Sycorax, in a cloven pine, from which Prospero frees him on promise that he assist his plans, which Ariel does with the utmost ingenuity and good will. At the close of the play, after Ariel presents a charming masque before the lovers, Ferdinand and Miranda, Prospero dismisses him. The well-known lyrics "Come unto these yellow sands" (I.ii), "Full fathom five" (I.ii), and "Where the bee sucks" (V.i), are sung by Ariel.

Armado, Don Adriano de.   In *Love's Labour's Lost*, a fantastical Spaniard who speaks with elaborate language and contends with Costard for Jaquenetta. He is a satire of the popular literary figure of the melancholy lover and is thought by some scholars to caricature Sir Walter Raleigh.

Arne, Thomas Augustine.   b. at London, March 12, 1710; d.

there, March 5, 1778. An English composer of songs, especially
for Shakespearean plays, and of oratorios and operas. He wrote
music for "Under the Greenwood Tree" and other songs in *As
You Like It* and for "Where the Bee Sucks," among others, from
The Tempest.

Arragon, Prince of. In *The Merchant of Venice*, the second of
Portia's suitors. He chooses the silver casket as the one containing her portrait; it doesn't and he thus fails to win her.

Arragon, Prince of. See **Pedro, Don.**

Artemidorus. In *Julius Caesar*, a teacher of rhetoric who tries
to save Caesar by a note of warning. However, Caesar refuses
to read the note.

Artesius. In *The Two Noble Kinsmen*, an Athenian captain.

Arthur, Duke of Britain. In *King John*, the historical Arthur
of Brittany, son of Constance of Brittany and (posthumously) of
Geoffrey Plantagenet, John's elder brother. Arthur should therefore have been king, but John was chosen by the Great Council.
Arthur serves as a rallying point for the discontented English
nobles and John orders him put to death. Spared by the chamberlain, Hubert de Burgh, Arthur escapes, but in doing so falls
to his death in such a way as to make it appear that murder has
been committed.

Arthur's Show. A representation, principally an exhibition of
archery, by fifty-eight city worthies who called themselves by
the names of the Knights of the Round Table, referred to in
Shakespeare's *2 Henry IV*.

Arviragus. In *Cymbeline*, the son of Cymbeline, brought up as
Cadwal, the son of Belarius, a banished lord, who is disguised as
Morgan.

As You Like It. A comedy by Shakespeare. Some scholars believe it was produced in 1599, but no copy of it is known to
exist earlier than the folio of 1623. During the 18th century it
was frequently performed, such actors as Macklin, Kitty Clive,
Peg Woffington, Charles Kean, and Mrs. Siddons taking principal roles. The play was based on the prose romance *Rosalynde*
by Thomas Lodge, published in 1590. Lodge's tale derived from
a medieval poem, the *Tale of Gamelyn*, once attributed to
Chaucer, which contained the basic situation of the three
brothers, the youngest hated by the eldest and forced into exile
in the forest where he lived with a band of outlaws until restored
to his rightful position. There are a few resemblances of detail
between *As You Like It* and the *Tale of Gamelyn* that are not
found in *Rosalynde*, and it has been argued that Shakespeare
did know the unpublished poem. He followed *Rosalynde* quite
closely, both in detail and in general conception, though he did
make certain alterations. The names of almost all Lodge's

characters, with the exception of the heroine's, are changed and made less exotic; the brothers Oliver, Jaques, and Orlando were Saladyne, Fernadyne, and Rosader in Lodge, Celia's name was Alinda, and Duke Frederick was King Torismund. Lodge's forest of Arden was theoretically in the Ardennes in France, but like Shakespeare's more Anglicized setting it was basically an Arcadia with no relation to a real forest anywhere. Shakespeare added the characters of Le Beau, Touchstone, and the melancholy Jaques, who give to the play a satirical tone lacking in *Rosa-lynde*, and also Audrey and William, whose earthy reality forms a contrast with the pastoralism and artifice of the shepherdess Phebe and her lover Silvius. Some of Shakespeare's alterations were made in the interests of symmetry; for instance, Celia's father, the usurping Duke, is made brother to Rosalind's father, the rightful Duke, so that a parallel is formed with the brothers Oliver and Orlando, where again one is mistreated and deprived of his rights by the other. Shakespeare takes over Lodge's theme of the opposition between court and country, nature and artifice, but whereas Lodge's romance is basically a study of the escape from cruel society to an idyllic pastoral world, Shake-speare's play treats the pastoral world more critically in its consideration of true and false attitudes toward love. Shake-speare may also have used the anonymous play *Sir Clyomon and Sir Clamydes*, written 1570–90, for the characterization of Corin and the treatment of "real" country life as opposed to the pas-toral version of it.

Dramatis Personae

Duke Senior
Frederick, *his brother, usurper*
  of his dominions
Amiens, *Lord attending Duke*
Jaques, *Lord Attending Duke*
Le Beau, *a Courtier*
Charles, *a Wrestler*
Oliver, *Son of de Boys*
Jaques, *Son of de Boys*
Orlando, *Son of de Boys*
Adam, *Oliver's Servant*
Dennis, *Oliver's Servant*
Touchstone, *a Clown*

Sir Oliver Martext, *a Vicar*
Corin, *Shepherd*
Silvius, *Shepherd*
William, *in love with Audrey*
A person presenting Hymen
Rosalind, *Daughter of the Duke*
Celia, *Daughter of Frederick*
Phebe, *a Shepherdess*
Audrey, *a Country Wench*
Lords, Pages, Foresters, and
  Attendants

The Story. Orlando, the son of the late Rowland de Boys, objects to cruel treatment by his brother, Oliver, in whose charge he has been left, whereupon Oliver plans that Orlando will be killed during a wrestling match sponsored by Frederick, usurper of the dukedom of his elder brother, the Duke Senior. The latter has had to flee with his followers, including the melancholy Jaques, to the Forest of Arden, leaving behind his daughter Rosalind with her cousin and friend, Celia, the daughter of Frederick. During the wrestling match, Orlando and Rosalind fall in love, and when Orlando defeats his opponent he escapes from Oliver to the Forest of Arden, accompanied by the old family servant, Adam. There they fall in with the banished Duke and his attendants. Frederick, meanwhile, banishes Rosalind. She disguises herself as a boy, calling herself Ganymede, and with Celia (posing as Aliena, sister of the supposed boy Ganymede) also seeks refuge in the Forest of Arden. Their jester Touchstone goes with them. There Rosalind meets Orlando, who, thinking she is the boy Ganymede, accepts her suggestion that he should court her as if she were his beloved Rosalind. Oliver arrives in pursuit of Orlando, but is saved from a lion and, repentant, falls in love with Celia. Ganymede promises Orlando that by magic Rosalind will appear in time for the wedding the following day, and at that time Rosalind reveals herself. These two couples, plus two more (Audrey and Touchstone, Phebe and Silvius), are gathered for the ceremonies, when Orlando's second brother, Jaques de Boys, arrives with the news that Frederick has left for a monastery and restored the dukedom to his elder brother.

Athens, Duke of. See *Theseus.*

Aubrey, John. b. in Wiltshire, England, 1626; d. at Oxford, in June, 1697. An English antiquary. Reduced to poverty by various lawsuits and amorous adventures, he was commissioned (1671) to make surveys of antiquities, which he described in *Perambulation of Surrey* and other manuscripts published after his death. Supported mainly by wealthy friends, he collected anecdotes of such notables as Francis Bacon, John Milton, William Shakespeare, Thomas Hobbes, and Sir Walter Raleigh, which he contributed to the historian Anthony à Wood, as *Minutes of Lives* (first published separately in 1813; called *Brief Lives* in 20th-century editions), for his *Athenae Oxonienses* (1690). Author also of *Miscellanies* (1696), a collection of ghost stories and dreams.

Audrey. In *As You Like It*, an awkward country girl. Touchstone discovers her in the Forest of Arden and eventually marries her.

Aufidius, Tullius. In *Coriolanus*, the general of the Volscians. He accepts the offer of his old enemy, Coriolanus, who has been banished from Rome, to lead the Volscian army against Rome. When Coriolanus spares Rome, the Volscians kill him.

Aumerle, Duke of. See under **York, (2nd) Duke of.**

Austria, Duke of. [Also, **Lymoges**.] In *King John*, an ally of Philip and the Dauphin, supposed to have killed Richard I (the Lion-Hearted). The Bastard, Philip Faulconbridge, kills him in battle (III.ii).

Autolycus. In *The Winter's Tale*, a witty thieving peddler, a "snapper up of unconsidered trifles" (IV.iii). He uses the kind of trickery described in the cony-catching pamphlets of Greene and Dekker to deceive the innocent Clown, and the simple Bohemian country folk. He sings the song, "When daffodils begin to peer" (IV.iii).

Auvergne, Countess of. In *1 Henry VI*, a French noblewoman. She tries but fails to trap Talbot. He shows her that his power lies in his army, not himself.

Avisa. [Full title, *Willobie his Avisa, or the True Picture of a Modest Maid and of a Chast and Constant Wife.*] A poem by an English writer named Henry Willoughby (or Willobie). It was first printed in 1594, and prefixed to the second edition in 1596 are some verses that allude to Shakespeare's *Rape of Lucrece*. This is the earliest known work to make printed mention of Shakespeare's name.

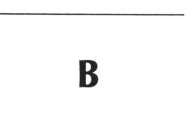

B

Bagot. In *Richard II*, a parasitic follower of King Richard. He is imprisoned after Richard's deposition and informs against Aumerle.

Balthasar. In *The Merchant of Venice*, a servant of Portia. The name is assumed by Portia in her guise as a lawyer.

Balthasar. In *Much Ado About Nothing*, a servant of Don Pedro. He sings the song "Sigh no more, ladies" (II.iii).

Balthasar. In *Romeo and Juliet*, Romeo's servant who bears the word to Romeo in Mantua of Juliet's supposed death and returns with him to Verona. When Romeo enters the tomb, he threatens Balthasar with death if he follows or watches.

Balthazar. [Also, **Balthasar**.] In *The Comedy of Errors* (III.i), a merchant who is accompanying Antipholus of Ephesus to dinner when the latter's wife has locked him out. He convinces Antipholus that to break down the door would reflect on the character of his wife.

Bankside. The south bank of the Thames between the Black-friars and Waterloo bridges, London. In the time of the Tudors it consisted of a single row of houses, built on a dike, or levee, higher both than the river at high tide and the ground behind the bank. At one end of "Bank Side" (as it was then spelled) stood the Clink Prison, Winchester House, and Saint Mary Overies Church. Numerous theatres were located in this district, including the Globe (a little to the W of the Clink and behind the houses), the Swan, the Rose, and the Hope.

Banquo. In *Macbeth*, the Thane of Lochaber. He is a general in the king's army, with the same rank as Macbeth, but he does not share either Macbeth's ambition or his moral weakness. Macbeth has him murdered because the witches prophesy that his offspring shall be kings, and his ghost appears at Macbeth's banquet to taunt and horrify the murderer. Although Holinshed mentions him, Banquo is not a historical figure, but was included as a compliment to King James I, before whom the play was first performed.

Baptista Minola. In *The Taming of the Shrew*, a rich gentleman of Padua, the father of Katherina (the "Shrew") and the gentle Bianca. He will not allow the latter to wed until Katherina has a husband.

Barbason. A fiend referred to in *Henry V* (II.i) and *The Merry Wives of Windsor* (II.ii).

Bardolph. In *1* and *2 Henry IV*, a sharper and hanger-on, one of Falstaff's dissolute and amusing companions, called the "Knight of the Burning Lamp" by Falstaff on account of his red face. He is characterized also in *Henry V* "white livered and red-faced, by means whereof a' faces it out and fights not" (III.ii). As a military man his exploits in *Henry V* are limited to robbing a church, on account of which he is hanged, unjustly as Pistol sees it. In *The Merry Wives of Windsor*, he is a tapster (bartender) at the Garter Inn, having been cast off by Falstaff.

Bardolph, Lord. In *2 Henry IV*, a supporter of Northumberland who brings false news of Hotspur's victory over Prince Hal at Shrewsbury. He discusses the uprising with Archbishop Scroop, and Lords Hastings and Mowbray, and later (IV.iv) news is brought to the King that he has been defeated with Northumberland.

Barnardine. In *Measure for Measure*, a savage and sullen prisoner who torpidly "apprehends death no more dreadfully but as a drunken sleep." He is ordered executed by the Duke of Vienna in place of Claudio, whose execution has been ordered by the Duke's deputy Angelo (Barnardine refuses, however, to die on that particular day and eventually is pardoned).

Bartholomew pig.   Pork sold at Bartholomew Fair (formerly held at Smithfield, London). The epithet "little tidy Bartholomew boar-pig" is applied endearingly to Falstaff by Doll Tearsheet in *2 Henry IV* (II.iv).

Basilisco.   A boastful character in the old play *Soliman and Perseda*, by Thomas Kyd, referred to in Shakespeare's *King John*.

Bassanio.   In *The Merchant of Venice*, a Venetian nobleman, the friend of Antonio, and Portia's successful suitor. It is on Bassanio's account that Antonio obligates himself to Shylock, since Bassanio needs money to woo Portia.

Basset.   In *1 Henry VI*, a supporter of the Lancastrian (or Red Rose) faction, who quarrels with Vernon, who is on the Yorkist (or White Rose) side.

Bassianus.   In *Titus Andronicus*, a brother of Saturninus and son of the late emperor of Rome. He marries Lavinia, but is murdered by Tamora's sons.

Bastard of Orleans.   In *1 Henry VI*, the historical Jean Dunois, bastard son of Louis Duc d'Orléans. Persuaded that Joan of Arc may be able to save France from the English, he arranges a meeting between her and the Dauphin (I.ii).

Bates, John.   In *Henry V*, an English soldier who talks with the disguised King before the battle of Agincourt. Although wishing he were at home in England, he determines to fight bravely for the King and adjures his friend, Williams, to stop arguing with another Englishman (the disguised King) since they all will be fighting the French soon.

Bawd.   In *Pericles*, the wife of the Pander who keeps the brothel in Mytilene.

Beatrice.   In *Much Ado About Nothing*, the gay and wayward niece of Leonato, and rebellious lover of Benedick. She is a person of intrigue, gaiety, and wit. Her affair with Benedick is actually a subplot, but her character overshadows those in the main action, particularly in the scene (IV.i) where, having previously revealed her love for him to the audience, she encounters Benedick and they admit their love for each other in some of the play's best lines. She is the only one to recognize at once the falseness of Claudio's accusation of Hero, and she tests Benedick's love by demanding that he challenge Claudio to a duel.

Beaufort.   The family name of a number of historical figures who appear in Shakespeare's plays.

Beaufort, John.   See under **Somerset, Earl of.**

Beaufort, Henry.   See under **Winchester, Bishop of.**

Beaufort, Thomas.   See under *Exeter, Duke of.*

Beaumont.   In *Henry V,* a French lord.

Bedford, Duke of.   See under *Lancaster, Prince John of.*

Belarius.   In *Cymbeline,* a banished lord disguised under the name of Morgan. He steals Arviragus and Guiderius, Cymbeline's sons, out of revenge, passing them off under false names as his own sons. When Cymbeline is made prisoner by the Roman general, Belarius comes to his rescue, is reconciled, and restores the princes.

Belch, Sir Toby.   In *Twelfth Night,* the uncle of Olivia. He is a roistering knight, fond of drinking and singing. In his enjoyment of Maria's plot against Malvolio, he decides to marry her.

Bellaria.   The wife of Pandosto in Robert Green's *Pandosto.* She is the character on which Hermione in Shakespeare's *Winter's Tale* is based.

Bellario, Doctor.   In *The Merchant of Venice,* an erudite lawyer of Padua, as whose substitute Portia appears in the trial scene. He makes no stage appearance.

Belmont.   In *The Merchant of Venice,* Portia's estate.

Benedick.   In *Much Ado About Nothing,* a young gentleman of Padua, of inexhaustible humor, wit, and raillery, a ridiculer of love. He engages in witty verbal duelling with Beatrice, adopting the pose of a confirmed bachelor, but is easily maneuvered by Claudio and Don Pedro into falling in love with her. He proves his love by agreeing to fight Claudio, formerly his friend.

Benfield, Robert.   English actor. He is listed in the First Folio (1623) of Shakespeare's plays as a principal actor, and probably joined the King's Men as a shareholder in 1614.

Benvolio.   In *Romeo and Juliet,* a friend of Romeo and nephew of Montague. His actions contribute to the tragic outcome of the play, for it is his fight with Tybalt in the opening scene that leads to the decree that street brawling is a capital offense, and it is he who persuades Romeo to attend Capulet's ball, where Romeo meets Juliet. He is present at Mercutio's death and at the time of Romeo's revenge against Tybalt for this.

Bergomask.   A dance parodying what the people of Elizabethan England considered the ridiculous antics of the peasants of Bergamo, an Italian province formerly in the state of Venice. In *A Midsummer Night's Dream,* Bottom asks the audience if they would like "to hear a Bergomask" instead of the Epilogue (V.i).

Berkeley.   In *Richard III,* a gentleman attendant on the Lady Anne.

Berkeley, Lord.   In *Richard II,* a minor character who appears once to ask Bolingbroke why he has returned, armed, to England.

Bermoothes.   An old name for Bermuda. It is the name of the island in *The Tempest.*

Bernardo.   In *Hamlet*, a Danish officer. It is he, with Marcellus, who first sees the murdered king's Ghost.

Berowne.   (Also, **Biron**). In *Love's Labour's Lost*, one of the three lords attending the King of Navarre at his rural academy. In order to get wisdom they swear to study at the academy for three years and to avoid the sight of women. Berowne is a somewhat unwilling partner to the agreement because he realizes the folly of it. Shortly after the Princess of France and her ladies, including the volatile Rosaline, appear on the scene, each of the lords and the King find that the vow has been broken by their falling in love. As the others play the part of ridiculously affected wooers, Berowne himself confesses the powers of Rosaline in a speech about the torments of love (IV.iii).

Bertram.   In *All's Well That Ends Well*, the young Count of Rossillion, who is loved by Helena and forced to marry her. He refuses to treat her as his wife unless she fulfills certain apparently impossible conditions; these she meets by means of a ruse, and Bertram agrees (in the event, happily) to live with her.

Bevis, George.   In *2 Henry VI*, a supporter of Jack Cade.

Bezonian.   A name given to a beggar; a mean, low person. According to John Florio a *bisogno* was "a new leuied souldier such as comes needy to the war." Randle Cotgrave defines *bisongne* as "a filthie knave, or clowne, a raskall, a bisonian, basehumoured scoundrel." Its original sense is a raw recruit; hence, as a term of contempt, a beggar, a needy person. The word is used in *2 Henry IV* and derives from the Italian noun *bisogno* (need).

Bianca.   In *Othello*, a woman of Cyprus and the mistress of Cassio. Cassio has no affection for her, but she is loyal and devoted to him.

Bianca.   In *The Taming of the Shrew*, the gentle sister of Katherina (the "Shrew"). She is wooed by Hortensio and Gremio, but is won by Lucentio.

Bigot, Lord.   In *King John*, a noble who joins the French after Arthur's death but later returns to England.

Biondello.   In *The Taming of the Shrew*, a servant to Lucentio.

Birnam Wood.   In *Macbeth*, a forest near Dunsinane, the seat of the Scottish kings. The witches prophesy that Macbeth will not be vanquished until Birnam Wood shall come to Dunsinane Hill against him. The prophecy is fulfilled when Macduff's army takes branches from the woods for concealment as they march against Macbeth.

Blackfriars Theatre.   A private playhouse in use from 1576 to 1584, and reopened in 1596, formed from a Dominican priory originally built in 1275. One portion of this priory passed to the Master of the Revels, after the suppression of the monasteries in 1538, then to Sir William More in 1559. This part of the priory was a series of two-story buildings along the west side of the cloisters. A chamber in the priory 125 feet by 25 feet was leased in 1576 to Richard Farrant, Master of the Children of the Chapel, for public performances by the Children preceding their Court appearances. After Farrant's death the performances continued under William Hunnis and Henry Evans. The Children of the Chapel and of Paul's performed Lyly's plays there (1582–84). More recovered the chamber in 1584. The second theatre was formed from buildings bought by James Burbage in 1596. A hall 66 feet by 46 feet, it had a stage, galleries, and seats. It was leased (1600) to Henry Evans and Nathaniel Giles for performances by the Children of the Chapel, who were not competing with adult companies. The King's Men obtained the theatre in 1608 when a syndicate was formed of Richard Burbage, Cuthbert Burbage, Shakespeare, Heming, Condell, Sly, and Thomas Evans. Since it was an enclosed theatre with somewhat different arrangements from the public playhouses, the style of acting was different. Shakespeare's romantic comedies with their masques and scenic requirements were written for this theatre or ones like it, and musical background, as in the plays of Marston, was often used. The theatre was also well suited to the exotic setting of Beaumont and Fletcher's tragedies. The building was torn down in 1655.

Blanch of Spain.　　In *King John*, the historical Blanche of Castile, daughter of the King of Castile and the niece of John. She is married to the French Dauphin to seal the truce between John and the French, but her loyalties are soon strained when Pandulph excommunicates John and the French fight him. She follows the Dauphin.

Blunt.　　In *2 Henry IV*, an officer in the royal army who is ordered by John to Lancaster to guard the rebel, Colevile (IV.iii).

Blunt, Sir James.　　In *Richard III*, a supporter of Richmond.

Blunt, Sir Walter.　　In *1 Henry IV*, the historical Sir Walter Blount, a supporter of King Henry. He acts as intermediary between the King and the rebels before the battle of Shrewsbury. Later Douglas kills him thinking he is King Henry.

Boar's Head.　　A tavern in Eastcheap, London, celebrated by Shakespeare as the scene of Falstaff's carousals in *1* and *2 Henry IV*. The tavern is not explicitly mentioned in the original text, but is inferred from remarks made by Falstaff and others. It was destroyed in the great fire of London (September, 1666), afterward rebuilt, and again demolished to make room for one of the approaches to London Bridge.

Boar's Head Theatre.　　The innyard of the Boar's Head Inn, east of Aldgate, where, from the late 1550's on, plays were enacted.

Bohan.   A cynical humorist in an interlude from Robert Greene's comedy *James IV*, who perhaps inspired Shakespeare's Jaques in *As You Like It*.

Bohemia, seacoast of.   In *The Winter's Tale*, the place where Antigonus abandons Perdita. Since Bohemia (now part of Czechoslovakia) has no coast, this has been often cited as an example of a mistake on Shakespeare's part. In view of the generally unrealistic nature of the play itself, however, it is quite likely that this is a deliberate confusion.

Bolingbroke, Henry.   In *Richard II*, the usurper of the throne; in *1* and *2 Henry IV*, the King of England (i.e., Henry IV himself). He is the Duke of Hereford, son of John of Gaunt, and, after the latter's death, Duke of Lancaster. In *Richard II*, Bolingbroke, a practical and ambitious man, replaces the weak, poetic, and much more charming Richard on the throne. In *1 Henry IV*, he is a less dynamic personality. Factions around the kingdom are in rebellion, and he grieves for his wild son, Prince Hal, wishing him more like the brave and chivalrous Hotspur. In *2 Henry IV*, he has become yet more weary and anxious about the fate of his kingdom, which he got through violence and has kept only at the price of constant vigilance. He recognizes his insecurity as the price of his usurpation.

Bolingbroke, Roger.   In *2 Henry VI*, a conjurer. He summons a prophetic spirit for Eleanor, Duchess of Gloucester, who aspires to the throne. York discovers them and arrests them as traitors.

Bona.   In *3 Henry VI*, the sister of the Queen of France who has agreed to marry Edward IV at Warwick's suggestion but finds that he has taken Lady Grey instead. She urges King Lewis (Louis) to support Margaret in her fight against Edward and is joined by Warwick, who has been made a fool by the secret marriage.

Borachio.   In *Much Ado About Nothing*, a follower of Don John. He has the incriminating conversation with Margaret (who pretends to be Hero) that persuades Claudio of Hero's infidelity. He is arrested and confesses the scheme under Dogberry's cross-examination. The name also is used by other Elizabethan dramatists for a drunkard, alluding to the Spanish word for a large leather bag used for wine.

Bottom, Nick.   In *A Midsummer Night's Dream*, an Athenian weaver who plays the part of Pyramus in the interpolated play. He is ambitious and enthusiastic, and in his eagerness wants to take all the parts in the play. While rehearsing the play in the forest, he has an ass's head put on him by Puck. In this guise he meets Titania; she has been put under a spell by Oberon to love the first person she sees on waking; when this is Bottom with his ass's head, she is deluded into thinking him beautiful, until Oberon releases her from the magic. He is the only one of the mortal characters to see the fairies, and seems to represent a kind of wise fool.

Bottom the Weaver, The Merry Conceited Humours of. Farce made from the comic scenes of *A Midsummer Night's Dream*, published in 1672, atributed to Robert Cox, a comedian of the time of Charles I of England.

Boult.   In *Pericles*, a servant to the Pander in Mytilene.

Bourbon, Duke of.   In *Henry V*, a leader in the French army who is captured at Agincourt after urging on the French forces to the attack.

Bourchier, Cardinal.   In *Richard III*, the Archbishop of Canterbury. Gloucester persuades him to take the young Duke of York from his mother, Queen Elizabeth, so that Gloucester can imprison him, with his brother Edward, Prince of Wales, in the Tower, on the pretext that they there await the coronation.

Boyet.   In *Love's Labour's Lost*, a mocking, mirthful lord attending on the Princess of France. He informs the Princess and her ladies that the Muscovite masquers are the King of Navarre and his lords.

Brabantio.   In *Othello*, a Venetian senator, father of Desdemona. He violently denounces Othello for his marriage with the latter.

Brakenbury, Sir Robert.   In *Richard III*, the Lieutenant of the Tower who surrenders Clarence to the two murderers sent by Gloucester. He presumably surrenders the two young Princes later to Tyrrel.

Brandon.   In *Henry VIII*, an officer who arrives with the sergeant-at-arms to arrest Buckingham and Abergavenny on charges of high treason.

Brandon, Sir William.   In *Richard III*, a follower of the Earl of Richmond. He is the father of Charles Brandon, Duke of Suffolk, who appears in *Henry VIII*.

Broke or Brooke, Arthur.   An English translator, d. 1563, who wrote *The Tragicall Historye of Romeus and Iulieit* (1562), one of the first English versions of that famous tragedy of love. This is probably the version used by Shakespeare as the source for the plot of his *Romeo and Juliet*. Broke translated freely from the French version of Matteo Bandello's Italian version of the story, published in the *Histoires tragiques* (Paris, 1559).

Brook, Master.   In *The Merry Wives of Windsor*, the name assumed by Ford for the purpose of fooling Falstaff, who is seeking an affair with Ford's wife. Falstaff, all unaware of Brook's true identity, boasts to him of progress in his pursuit of Mistress Ford.

Brutus, Decius.   In *Julius Caesar*, one of the conspirators who succeeds in bringing Caesar to the Capitol by interpreting Calphurnia's dreams in a hopeful fashion. This is probably the historical Decimus Junius Brutus, who was put to death by Antony in 43 B.C.

Brutus, Junius.   In *Coriolanus*, a tribune who, together with Sicinius, so arouses the Romans against Coriolanus that the latter is banished. Upon Coriolanus's return with the Volscian army, they deny responsibility and ask Menenius to stop his advance.

Brutus, Marcus.   In *Julius Caesar*, the historical Marcus Junius Brutus, the chief assassin. The conspirators appeal to his love of Rome and its traditional freedoms in order to obtain his aid in their plot against Caesar as the embodiment of tyranny. Brutus is Caesar's friend, and at the assassination his presence calls forth the shocked "*Et tu Brute*, Then die Caesar" from the fallen Caesar (III.i). Brutus is a man of scrupulous honor, who falls because of an inability to understand the practical aspects of politics and war and a lack of awareness of his own weakness. In spite of Cassius's warning, he permits Antony to make his inflammatory address to the people over Caesar's body; he nearly alienates Cassius by censuring his levy of funds from their supporters; and finally he loses the struggle with Antony and Octavius by choosing to fight on the plains of Philippi instead of withdrawing as Cassius advises. When the battle is lost, he kills himself.

Bryan, George.   fl. c1586–1598. English actor. He is listed as a principal actor in the First Folio (1623) of Shakespeare's plays and was probably an original member of the Lord Chamberlain's Men (formed 1594).

Buckingham, Duke of.   In *2 Henry VI*, the historical Humphrey Stafford, one of the nobles who cause Gloucester's downfall. He persuades the followers of the rebel, Jack Cade, to disperse and later supports Henry in the war with the Yorkists. In *3 Henry VI*, his death is reported at the battle of St. Albans (1455); Shakespeare was compressing history to fit his play, since the historical personage was killed at Northampton in 1460.

Buckingham, (2nd) Duke of.   In *Richard III*, the historical Henry Stafford, the accomplice of Richard (Gloucester) in his conspiracy and crime. Buckingham arrests the relatives (Rivers, Grey, and Dorset) of Edward IV's widow, and then helps to betray the unsuspecting Hastings on a trumped-up charge of conspiring in witchcraft against Richard. He then stages for the citizens of London the spectacle of Richard studying piously in the company of clergymen and refusing the kingship that Buckingham would thrust upon him. This obtains the throne for Richard, but Richard further demands that he kill the two sons of Edward IV, the Princes in the Tower. At this, Buckingham at last has scruples, and thus becomes useless to Richard. His request for some property is refused by Richard, and he goes with foreboding to join Richmond's army but is put to death before reaching it. His ghost appears to Richard on the night before the battle of Bosworth warning him of impending doom.

Buckingham, (3rd) **Duke of.** In *Henry VIII,* the historical Edward Stafford, son of the Buckingham who was executed by Richard III. He is an enemy of Wolsey, whom he sees as dangerous to England. Arrested by Wolsey on a charge of threatening Henry's life, he defends himself at the place of execution (in a speech probably written by Fletcher).

Bullcalf, Peter. In *2 Henry IV,* a recruit.

Bullen, Anne. In *Henry VIII,* the historical Anne Boleyn, second wife of the King and former lady-in-waiting of Katherine, his first wife. Wolsey's downfall is brought about by the discovery of his plan to prevent the King from divorcing Katherine and marrying Anne. She is the mother of Elizabeth.

Burbage, Cuthbert. c1566–1636. English theatre manager. He was the elder son of James Burbage and the brother of Richard Burbage, the actor, with whom he built the Globe Theatre. He held interests in several theatres, and developed the "stock company" system, in which shareholders owned a part of the company.

Burbage, James. d. 1597. An English actor and the first builder of a theatre in England; father of Richard and Cuthbert Burbage. He was originally a joiner. In the period 1576–77 he erected the first English building specially intended for plays. It was "between Finsbury Fields and the public road from Bishopsgate and Shoreditch," in what is now part of London. It was of wood, and was called "The Theatre." The material was removed to the Bankside in 1598 and was rebuilt as the Globe theatre. The Curtain theatre was put up near The Theatre soon after the latter was opened, and Burbage was instrumental in the conversion of a large house at Blackfriars Theatre, probably in November 1596.

Burbage, Richard. b. c1567; d. 1619. An English actor; son of James Burbage. With his brother Cuthbert he was proprietor of The Theatre and later of the Globe, as well as of the Blackfriars Theatre. He already had some acting experience when he joined with Shakespeare and others in forming the Lord Chamberlain's Men in 1594, but he went on to make his fame as an actor with this company (which became the King's Men in 1603). He apparently played the leading parts in most of the plays pro-

duced by this company, and seems to have been the original
Hamlet, Lear, and Othello as well as playing the heroes in many
other of Shakespeare's plays. It is thought that his ability and
style of acting had some influence on the kinds of heroes Shakespeare created for his plays. Burbage excelled in tragedy and
was held in high esteem by authors as well as by the public; he
was sometimes even introduced into plays in his own proper
person. Besides his fame as an actor he was known as a painter
and is traditionally held to be the painter of one of the extant
Shakespeare portraits. At his death, many poems and tributes
were written in his memory.

Burgundy, Duke of. In *Henry V*, the French noble who arranges the terms of peace between the French and the English.
In a long, elaborate speech (V.ii) he compares war-torn France
to a dying and uncared-for garden. In *1 Henry VI*, he fights at
first on the English side, but in a speech much like his own in
Henry V, Joan of Arc persuades him to return to the French
(III.iii).

Burgundy, Duke of. In *King Lear*, a rival of the King of
France for the hand of Cordelia. He refuses to marry her when
she is left without a dowry.

Bushy. In *Richard II*, a follower of the King.

Butts, Doctor. In *Henry VIII*, the King's physician, the historical Sir William Butts.

C

cacodemon. In *Richard III*, an evil spirit mentioned by Margaret.
She calls Gloucester "Thou cacodemon!" (I.iii).

Cade, Jack. In *2 Henry VI*, the rebel leader, the historical John
Cade. York, planning to usurp the throne, encourages Cade to
stir up a rebellion in England. Cade assumes the name Mortimer
and claims the throne himself. He captures London Bridge, but
his followers desert him; he flees and is killed by Alexander
Iden.

Cadwal. In *Cymbeline*, the name under which Arviragus is raised from infancy. As Cadwal, Arviragus believes himself to be the son of Morgan (who is actually Belarius).

Caesar, Julius. In *Julius Caesar*, the dictator of Rome, whom the conspirators, led by Brutus and Cassius, assassinate (on the part of Brutus solely, and on the part of Cassius at least partly, for fear that he would abridge the traditional Roman freedoms). Shakespeare's presentation of him is ambiguous: he is a noble man but also an egoist, over-insistent on his personal integrity and fearlessness. He is arrogant, yet also physically weak, superstitious, yet acute in his understanding of men.

cain-coloured. Yellowish red, the supposed color of Cain's hair. In *The Merry Wives of Windsor* Shakespeare refers to a "cain-coloured beard" (I.iv).

Caithness. In *Macbeth*, a Scottish thane.

Caius. In *King Lear*, the assumed name of Kent.

Caius. In *Titus Andronicus*, a kinsman of Titus.

Caius, Dr. In *The Merry Wives of Windsor*, a French doctor in love with Anne Page. Despite an arrangement with Mistress Page to carry off Anne and marry her, he loses her through a substitution arranged by Fenton and the Host of the Garter Inn.

Caius Lucius. See *Lucius, Caius*.

Caius Marcius. See *Coriolanus*.

Calchas. In *Troilus and Cressida*, a Trojan priest who becomes a traitor to his native city and joins the Greeks. He requests that his daughter Cressida (whom he has left in Troy) be exchanged for Antenor, a Trojan held prisoner by the Greeks. He does not object to Diomedes's seduction of his daughter.

Caliban. In *The Tempest*, a deformed and repulsive slave. The son of the witch Sycorax, who ruled the island before Prospero's shipwreck on it, he becomes a reluctant captive to Prospero's magic powers. He grumbles at his lot and wishes to break free, allying himself with Stephano and Trinculo for that purpose. After Prospero's rescue, Caliban is left the sole inhabitant of the island.

Calipolis. In George Peele's play *The Battle of Alcazar*, the wife of Muly Mahamet. During a famine her husband presents her with a bit of meat, stolen from a lioness, on his bloody sword, with these words: "Feed then and faint not, fair Calipolis." Pistol ridicules this line in *2 Henry IV* (II.iv).

Calphurnia. In *Julius Caesar*, the historical Calpurnia, wife of Caesar. She is fearful for her husband's safety because of dreams she has had and tries to persuade him not to go to the Capitol.

Cambridge, Earl of. In *Henry V*, the historical Richard, Earl of Cambridge, a conspirator who plots with Scroop and Grey to murder the King. The plot is discovered and the King hands them death warrants in place of the expected commissions for his French campaign. In *Richard II*, he is a son of the Duke of York and brother of Aumerle. His son is the York appearing in *1, 2*, and *3 Henry VI*.

Camillo.   In *The Winter's Tale*, a Sicilian noble. He saves Polixenes and induces Leontes to protect Florizel and Perdita.

Campeius, Cardinal.   In *Henry VIII*, a papal legate who, with Wolsey, considers the question of the King's divorce from Katherine.

Canidius.   In *Antony and Cleopatra*, the chief lieutenant of Antony. He withholds his forces from the sea battle and, when he sees that Antony is losing, joins Octavius.

Canterbury, Archbishop of.   In *Henry V*, a counsellor to the King who, in hopes that a war with France will deter the King from confiscating church property, proves at length that the old Salic Law, forbidding the succession of women and the'r decendants to the throne, would not apply to France, and that Henry's genealogy entitles him to claim French lands.

Canterbury, Archbishop of.   See under **Bourchier, Cardinal,** and under **Cranmer.**

Caphis.   In *Timon of Athens*, a servant of one of Timon's creditors.

Capucius.   In *Henry VIII*, an ambassador from Charles V to the dying Katherine.

Capulet.   In *Romeo and Juliet*, a coarse, jovial old man with a passionate temper, the father of Juliet. Ignorant of her marriage to Romeo, he insists that she take Paris as her husband.

Capulet, Lady.   In *Romeo and Juliet*, Juliet's mother. She urges her daughter to marry Paris and, in an elaborate figure of speech, likens him to a beautiful book (I.iii).

Cardenio, The History of.   A play of this name was entered on the Stationers' Register in 1653 as by John Fletcher and Shakespeare. It is based on a story in *Don Quixote* of Cardenio, who has been driven mad by the loss of his love, Lucinda. He has intervals of sanity and recovers completely when Lucinda is restored to him. Scholars are not certain beyond any possible doubt that Shakespeare did not have a hand in the play, but it seemed probable to Lounsbury in *The First Editors of Shakespeare* that Lewis Theobald, the Shakespeare scholar who published it in 1728 as *The Double Falsehood*, was the real author of that version, even though Theobald claimed it was "written originally by W. Shakespeare, and now revised and adapted to the stage by Mr. Theobald."

Carlisle, Bishop of.   In *Richard II*, a loyal supporter of Richard. He strenuously protests Bolingbroke's ascension to the throne and direly predicts that "The blood of English shall manure the ground and future ages groan for this foul act" (IV.i.). He is arrested for treason, but pardoned by Bolingbroke.

Casca. In *Julius Caesar*, a conspirator against Caesar. Described as "a blunt fellow" of "quick mettle," his belief that Caesar has overstepped himself makes him willing to assist in the assassination. He plays no further part in the play after that event.

Cassandra. In *Troilus and Cressida*, a prophetess, daughter of King Priam of Troy, who foretells Troy's destruction and Hector's death.

Cassibelan. In *Cymbeline*, the historical Cassivellaunus, a British prince captured by Caesar, mentioned in the play.

Cassio, Michael. In *Othello*, a lieutenant of Othello. A somewhat weak but honorable man, he becomes, by the devices of Iago, the innocent object of Othello's jealousy.

Cassius. In *Julius Caesar*, the historical Gaius Cassius Longinus, one of the chief members of the conspiracy against Caesar, motivated partly by fear of the threat to Rome's traditional freedoms, but also by jealousy and a kind of hero worship of Brutus. He is an extremely realistic man, but his reverence for Brutus causes him to accede to his friend's wishes even when this is ill-advised, as in allowing Antony to make a funeral oration. After the Battle of Philippi, believing that Brutus has already been captured, he kills himself. It is he whom Caesar describes as having "a lean and hungry look, / He thinks too much" (I.ii).

Cataian. A Cathaian or inhabitant of Cathay (China). The word was used by the Elizabethans (in reference to the supposed thieving habits of the Chinese) for a "sharper." Shakespeare uses the term in *The Merry Wives of Windsor*.

Catesby, Sir William. In *Richard III*, a follower of Richard.

Catherine and Petruchio. A play condensed and adapted from *The Taming of the Shrew* by David Garrick, produced in 1756.

Cato, Young. In *Julius Caesar*, a friend of Brutus and Cassius who appears briefly at the Battle of Philippi.

Cawdor, Thane of. In *Macbeth*, a prosperous gentleman whose rank was promised to Macbeth by the witches. No sooner had the prophecy been made than Macbeth learned that Cawdor was to be executed by order of Duncan for treason. He dies nobly—"nothing in his life became him like the leaving it" (I.iv) —and Macbeth succeeds to his rank. It has sometimes been said that the Thane's behavior corresponds in almost every circumstance with that of the unfortunate Earl of Essex beheaded by Queen Elizabeth. The Thane of Cawdor does not appear on the stage at all.

Celia. In *As You Like It*, the cousin and devoted friend of

Rosalind, and daughter of Frederick, the usurping duke. She is the companion of Rosalind in the Forest of Arden, in the disguise of Aliena, a shepherdess. She falls in love with and marries Oliver, older brother to Orlando.

Ceres. In *The Tempest*, a spirit summoned by Prospero to celebrate the vows of Ferdinand and Miranda. She also addresses her blessings to the audience (probably referring to the Elector Palatine and Princess Elizabeth, before whom the play was first given).

Cerimon. In *Pericles*, a lord of Ephesus who revives Thaisa. He sends her to the temple of Diana, where she becomes one of the vestals.

Cesario. In *Twelfth Night*, the name Viola takes when in disguise.

Chamberlain. In *1 Henry IV*, an attendant at the inn of Rochester who tells Gadshill about some wealthy guests and is promised a share in the plunder.

Chamberlain, Lord. See **Lord Chamberlain.**

Chamberlain's Men. See **Lord Chamberlain's Men.**

Chancellor, Lord. See **Lord Chancellor.**

Chapman, George. b. near Hitchin, Hertfordshire, England, c1559; buried at London, in the parish of St. Giles-in-the-Fields, May 12, 1634. An English poet and dramatist, chiefly celebrated for his translation of Homer. He is said to have studied at Oxford and afterward at Cambridge. He lived, according to report, in straitened circumstances, but was intimate with Ben Jonson, John Fletcher, and other prominent figures of the time. Among his dramatic works are *The Blind Beggar of Alexandria* (produced in 1595, printed in 1598), *All Fools* (produced c1598, printed in 1605), *An Humorous Day's Mirth* (printed in 1599), *Eastward Ho!* with Jonson and John Marston (printed 1605), which, because of its satire on the Scottish nobility surrounding James I, caused the authors' imprisonment, *The Gentleman-Usher* (printed 1606), *Monsieur d'Olive* (printed 1606), *Bussy d'Ambois* (printed 1607), *May Day* (produced c1600, printed in 1611), *The Revenge of Bussy d'Ambois* (printed 1613), *The Conspiracy and Tragedy of Charles, Duke of Byron* (printed 1608; a play in two parts), *The Widow's Tears* (printed 1612), *Caesar and Pompey* (printed 1631), and *Chabot, Admiral of France*, with James Shirley (printed 1639). He completed Marlowe's fragment of *Hero and Leander* in 1598. The first part of his translation of the *Iliad* was published in 1598; the whole was not issued before 1609 (entered on the Stationers' Register in 1611). The translation of the *Odyssey* was entered on the Stationers' Register in 1614. Finally, the *Iliad* and *Odyssey* were issued together with the date 1616 on Chapman's portrait prefixed. He translated also the Homeric hymns, Petrarch, Musaeus, Hesiod, and Juvenal. He is thought by some Shakespeare scholars to be the "rival poet" referred to in Shakespeare's sonnets.

Charles.   In *As You Like It*, a wrestler hired by Duke Frederick and defeated by Orlando.

Charles VI.   In *Henry V*, the King of France. He makes the Treaty of Troyes whereby his daughter Katherine is to marry Henry and the latter to inherit France after his death. This follows an episode in the life of the real Charles (1368–1422).

Charles, the Dauphin.   In *1 Henry VI*, the son of Charles VI (historically not, as Shakespeare makes him, the Dauphin). When Joan of Arc arrives to request troops, she impresses him with her prowess by overcoming him in a duel and he falls in love with her. He attributes the French victories to her, and when she is captured, he becomes viceroy under Henry.

Charmian.   In *Antony and Cleopatra*, Cleopatra's favorite waiting-woman. She kills herself after Cleopatra's death.

Chatillon.   In *King John*, an ambassador from France sent by Philip to demand that John give up the throne to Arthur.

Chettle, Henry.   b. c1560; d. c1607. An English dramatist and pamphleteer, son of a dyer of London, and a stationer by trade. He was in a printing partnership from 1589 to 1591, but after that no book of his publication has been found. However, Nash's *Strange News* (1592) and *Terrors of the Night* (1594) came from the press of a former associate of Chettle's and a letter by Chettle printed in another Nash work refers to himself as "old compositor." He was the author or joint author of a large number of plays. *The Tragedy of Hoffman* (1602) is the only play now extant that is attributed to Chettle. By 1598 he was writing for the stage, and is mentioned by Francis Meres in his *Palladis Tamia* (1598) as "best for Comedy among us." In the period from 1598 to 1603 he collaborated on about forty-eight plays. He is also remembered for editing *Greene's Groatsworth of Wit*, for his pamphlet, *Kind-Hart's Dream* (1592), and for his eulogy on Queen Elizabeth, *England's Mourning Garment* (1603).

Chief Justice.   See **Lord Chief Justice**.

Children of the Chapel.   [Also, at various times: **Children of the Revels, Children of Blackfriars, Children of the Queen's Revels.**] An Elizabethan and Jacobean company of child actors, comprising the choir boys of the Chapel (or Chapel Royal), a part of the royal household that presented interludes with adult actors in the early sixteenth century. William Cornish was Master of the Children from 1509 until 1523 and actually formed the acting company. The company continued during the rest of the century under such masters as Edwards, Farrant,

Hunnis, and Giles, and played, at various times, at the Blackfriars Theatre. The Children of the Chapel, and a similar group, Paul's Boys, competed with adult companies, and are disparaged by Hamlet in the "player scene" (II.i). A number of the King's Men were once child actors with this company. The children's company lost favor at Court, became the Children of the Revels, and finally, in 1606, the Children of Blackfriars. In 1608, they left Blackfriars Theatre and moved to Whitefriars, where they remained until 1610, when they again came under royal patronage, as the Children of the Queen's Revels. When Nathan Field left them about 1616, the company fell into obscurity.

Child Rowland. In *King Lear*, Edgar utters snatches from old ballads, one being "Child Rowland to the dark tower came" (III. iv). The words come from an old Scottish ballad wherein a young man rescues his sister from an elf's castle ("child" or "childe" means a squire or young lord who has not yet won his knightly spurs).

Chiron. In *Titus Andronicus*, a son of Tamora. He and his brother Demetrius are guilty of various wicked crimes; Titus kills both by cutting their throats and then bakes them in a pie to serve to their mother.

Chronicles of England, Scotland, and Ireland, The. [Called *Holinsheds' Chronicles.*] A prose historical work (published 1577, in two folio volumes, and a second edition in three volumes in 1587) by Raphael Holinshed, with the assistance of William Harrison, Richard Stanyhurst, Edward Campion and others. The literary importance of the work is due partly to the fact that Shakespeare drew much from it for his *Cymbeline*, *Richard II*, *Richard III*, and all his *Henry* (IV, V, VI, VIII) plays.

Cicero. In *Julius Caesar*, Roman senator who is not asked to join the conspiracy.

Cimber, Metellus. In *Julius Caesar*, one of the conspirators. His suit to Caesar (to recall his brother, Publius, from banishment) is the pretext for the gathering of the conspirators around Caesar to assassinate him.

Cinna. In *Julius Caesar*, the historical Gaius Helvius Cinna, a poet. He is mistaken for the other Cinna and is mobbed and murdered.

Cinna. In *Julius Caesar*, the historical Lucius Cornelius Cinna (the younger), one of the conspirators against Caesar. He places tracts so that Brutus will find them and join in the conspiracy.

Clarence, George, Duke of. In *3 Henry VI*, the historical George Plantagenet, brother of Edward IV, who creates him Duke of Clarence. He deserts the King in anger at his marriage with Lady Grey, but rejoins him later. In *Richard III*, he is imprisoned by Edward IV and ordered to his death. The reprieve that the Queen has persuaded Edward to give him is intercepted by Gloucester (Richard) and he is murdered.

Clarence, Thomas of. In *2 Henry IV*, the Duke of Clarence, second son of the King and brother of Prince Hal. The King asks Clarence to advise Hal and keep him from his wild companions when he becomes king. In *Henry V*, he is asked by Henry to help arrange the peace terms with the French King (V.ii).

Claudio. In *Measure for Measure*, the brother of Isabella, condemned to death for seducing Juliet. Through Isabella, Angelo offers him his life, in exchange for Isabella becoming his (Angelo's) mistress. In a dramatic scene Claudio begs Isabella to yield to Angelo's wishes, but is refused. Later his death is ordered by Angelo, but the Provost of the prison prevents the execution.

Claudio. In *Much Ado About Nothing*, a young Florentine in love with Hero. He falls too easily into belief in Hero's dishonor, but becomes convinced of her virtue and is finally married to her.

Claudius. In *Hamlet*, the King of Denmark and uncle of Hamlet. He is a competent ruler, but a cunning and unscrupulous man who does not hesitate to employ treachery and murder to realize his ambitions. When his attempt to get rid of Hamlet by sending him to England fails, he contrives a duel between Hamlet and Laertes in which Laertes is to fence with a poisoned and unbaited foil. Hamlet, stabbed and dying, kills Claudius in the final scene with the same poisoned foil.

Claudius. In *Julius Caesar*, a servant of Brutus.

Cleomenes. In *The Winter's Tale*, a Sicilian noble who, with Dion, is sent by Leontes to the oracle at Delphi to ask if Hermione is chaste. They return with an affirmative answer.

Cleon. In *Pericles*, the governor of Tharsus (Tarsus) who is burned to death to avenge the supposed murder of Marina.

Cleopatra. In *Antony and Cleopatra*, the heroine, a paradoxical and fascinating character, of whom Enobarbus says: "Age cannot wither her, nor custom stale her infinite variety" (II.ii). She is a woman of constantly changing moods who enrages Antony but still enslaves him. At several crucial points in the play the motives for her actions appear ambiguous, and even at the moment of her death she seems as anxious to outwit Caesar as to be reunited with Antony. Her character seems deliberately composed of opposing qualities: sensual yet spiritual, fearful of pain and humiliation yet ready to undergo suicide, she is part whore, part queen, and quintessential woman.

Clerk of Chatham. In *2 Henry VI*, a clerk, assaulted by the mob led by Jack Cade because he can read and write.

Clifford, Lord. In *2 Henry VI*, a Lancastrian and supporter of the King's party. With Buckingham, he persuades the rebellious mob to desert their leader Cade. He is killed by York at the battle of St. Albans.

Clifford, Lord. In *2 Henry VI*, Young Clifford, the son of the elder Lord Clifford. In *3 Henry VI*, he is a member of the Lancastrian faction and stabs York at the battle of Wakefield, after first killing York's son, Rutland, both deeds having been done to avenge his father's death (I.iii, iv). He himself is wounded in battle at Towton and dies despairing of the Lancastrian cause (II.vi).

Clitus. In *Julius Caesar*, a servant of Brutus.

Cloten. In *Cymbeline*, the queen's son by a former husband. He is rejected by Imogen. In the first part of the play (in a revised version) he is a foolish and malicious braggart; but in the fourth act, which belongs to an earlier version, he not deficient in manliness.

Clown. In *The Winter's Tale*, a rustic countryman, the son of the Old Shepherd. He reports the death of Antigonus (III.iii) and later is forced to go to Sicilia, where he gives himself the airs of a gentleman.

Clowns. In *Hamlet*, the two Grave-diggers who are jesting and singing when Hamlet comes upon them as they dig Ophelia's grave (V.i). Their rough comedy provides a sharp contrast to the sensitive Hamlet's remarks about life and death. There are also unnamed clowns making brief appearances in *Othello, Titus Andronicus* and *Antony and Cleopatra*. Other characters, such as Touchstone, Feste, and Lavatch, are identified in the Dramatis Personae as clowns, but display a superior, more sophisticated type of humor, quite unlike the buffoonery of most of the clowns. See also under *Fool*.

Cobbler of Preston, The. A musical farce by Charles Johnson, founded on the adventures of Christopher Sly in *The Taming of the Shrew* but using incidents also from *The Merry Wives of Windsor*. It was first acted in 1716, and altered and produced with music in 1817. Another, more popular, version was produced by Christopher Bullock at about the same time.

Cobweb. A fairy in *A Midsummer Night's Dream*.

Colevile, Sir John. In *2 Henry IV*, a "famous rebel" who yields to Falstaff in Gaultree Forest and is sent to his execution at York.

Comedy of Errors, The. A play by Shakespeare, first acted at Gray's Inn, in London, on Dec. 28, 1594. It is known certainly to have been one of the playwright's earliest works (most modern scholars believe 1592 or 1593 to be the years that may most probably be assigned to it, although neither 1591 nor 1594 can definitely be ruled out); some older reference works have suggested that its title was at one time simply *Errors*. It may be the play listed by Francis Meres in his *Palladis Tamia* as *Love's Labour's Won*. The main plot is taken from Plautus's comedy, the *Menaechmi*, a play much edited and adapted in the Renaissance, in which the action is based on the confusions between identical twin brothers. One brother arranges to dine with a courtesan but the other turns up instead; the wife of the first brother is informed and becomes outraged, but finally all is explained. Shakespeare enlarged this very short play with material from another of Plautus's comedies, *Amphitruo*, in which the god Jupiter disguises himself as Amphitruo and takes his place in his wife's bed, while the god Mercury adds to the confusion by disguising himself as Amphitruo's slave Sosia. Shakespeare added the notion of identical twin slaves to the plot of *Menaechmi*, thereby immensely increasing the opportunities for confusion, and developed more fully the situation of one spouse being excluded while a double dines with the other. He also changed the characterization of the wife, who in Plautus is a very cynically treated shrew, making her more important in the play and also more sympathetic, gave her a sister, Luciana, as a bride for the other brother, and considerably deepened the treatment of marriage. He added the non-farcical story of his twin's father, Aegeon, doomed to death for no fault of his own, and his moving recovery of his lost wife Aemilia in a scene that probably derives from a version of the story of Apollonius of Tyre, retold by John Gower in *Confessio Amantis*. He changed the setting from Epidamnum to Ephesus, partly perhaps because Ephesus figures strongly in the Apollonius of Tyre story but also, it is thought, because of St. Paul's visit to Ephesus described in *Acts XIX* as a city of exorcists, evil spirits, and strange arts; in the *Epistle to the Ephesians* St. Paul urges the people to seek marital unity, and talks of the relationships between children and parents, masters and servants, all of these important ideas in *The Comedy of Errors*. The suggestion that Shakespeare's chief source was actually *The Historie of Error*, acted by the boys of Saint Paul's chapel on Jan. 1, 1577, is now discounted by virtually all scholars of Shakespeare: the derivation from Plautus seems not only likely beyond reasonable doubt, but also casts an interesting light on the actual meaning of Ben Jonson's much-quoted statement that his friend Shakespeare had "small Latin and less Greek." In view of the fact that no English translation of the *Menaechmi* is known to have been published before 1594 (and of the *Amphitruo* for about a hundred years after that), it would appear that Shakespeare must have worked from Latin sources available at the time (indeed, there is much internal evidence that Shakespeare was influenced by Latin turns of phrase, although his use of the Latin was at no point close to translation). However, if the play was written in 1593, Shakespeare may have seen Warner's translation of the *Menaechmi* in manuscript.

Dramatis Personae

Solinus, Duke of Ephesus

Aegeon, *a Merchant of Syracuse*

Antipholus of Ephesus, *son of Aegeon and Aemilia, twin of:*

Antipholus of Syracuse

Dronio of Ephesus, *twin of:*

Dromio of Syracuse, *attendants of the two Antipholuses*

Balthazar, *a Merchant*

Angelo, *a Goldsmith*

A Merchant, *Friend to Antipholus of Syracuse*

A Merchant *trading with Angelo*

Pinch, *a Schoolmaster*

Aemilia, *Wife to Aegeon, an Abbess at Ephesus*

Adriana, *Wife to Antipholus of Ephesus*

Luciana, *her Sister*

Luce, *Servant to Adriana*

A Courtesan

Jailers, Officers, *and other Attendants*

The Story. Aegeon, a Syracusan merchant, had been shipwrecked with his wife, Aemilia, their twin sons, both named Antipholus, and twin slaves, both named Dromio. One of each pair of twins remained with Aegeon, but the others disappeared with Aemilia. At eighteen, one of the twins, Antipholus of Syracuse, had been allowed by his father to go and search for his lost twin brother. When he did not return in five years, his father set out in search of him. The action of the play commences when Aegeon is arrested at Ephesus and sentenced to death because of the enmity between that city and Syracuse. His story moves Solinus, the Duke of Ephesus, to allow him until nightfall to obtain his ransom money. Meanwhile, Antipholus of Syracuse has arrived in Ephesus where, unknown to him, live his brother and his brother's wife Adriana, and their Dromio. From this situation arise the complications—the comedy of errors—because everyone confuses the two sets of twins, including themselves. Antipholus of Syracuse beats Dromio of Ephesus for insisting he go home to dinner; Antipholus of Syracuse does, however, dine at Adriana's house, from which the Ephesian twin is locked out, Adriana believing her husband to be within; Antipholus of Ephesus is arrested for not paying for a gold chain that was mistakenly given to Antipholus of Syracuse. Everyone is convinced of the insanity of the others. At length, the Syracusans take refuge in an abbey. When Aegeon is led to his execution the Ephesian twins arrive to demand justice from the Duke. They, of course, do not recognize Aegeon; they deny receiving the gold chain; and after considerable more confusion, the abbess arrives with the Syracusans. With the presence of everyone, the errors are solved, and the pardoned Aegeon discovers the abbess to be his lost wife.

Comical Gallant: or, The Amours of Sir John Falstaffe, The. An adaptation of *The Merry Wives of Windsor* by John Dennis, played in 1702.

Cominius. In *Coriolanus,* a Roman general. He tries to persuade the people of Rome not to banish Coriolanus, and later, when Coriolanus has joined the Volscian forces, undertakes to persuade him to spare Rome.

Condell, Henry. [Also, **Cundell.**] d. at Fulham, England, in December, 1627. An English actor, and editor with Heming of the First Folio edition of Shapespeare's plays. He was a member of the Lord Chamberlain's Men, to which Shakespeare was also admitted, probably in 1594. A share of the company was given him in 1604 and in 1608 he, along with Shakespeare, received a share in the Blackfriars Theatre owned by the Burbages. He is mentioned in Shakespeare's will. By 1612 he had acquired a portion also of the Globe Theatre.

Conrade. In *Much Ado About Nothing,* a follower of Don John, the bastard brother of Don Pedro.

Constable, Henry. b. at Newark, Nottinghamshire, England, 1562; d. at Liége, Belgium, October 9, 1613. An English poet. He was graduated at Cambridge (St. John's College) in 1580, became a Roman Catholic, and for the greater part of his later life resided at Paris, occupied with political affairs and especially with schemes for promoting the interests of Catholicism. In 1603 he went to London and was for a short time confined in the Tower. He published in 1592 a collection of twenty-three sonnets entitled *Diana the Praises of his Mistress in certaine sweete Sonnets by H.C.*

Constable of France. In *Henry V,* one of the chief French lords and military leaders. He is killed at Agincourt.

Constance. In *King John,* the mother of Arthur, Duke of Britain (Brittany).

Cooke, Alexander. fl. 1603–13. An English actor. He is listed in the First Folio edition of Shakespeare's works (1623) and was a member of the Lord Chamberlain's Men. He presumably appeared in their plays until 1613. It is known that he played the principal tragic role in Jonson's *Sejanus.*

Corambis. The name of Polonius in the first quarto *Hamlet* (1603).

Cordelia. In *King Lear,* the youngest daughter of Lear. She offends him by the seeming coolness of her protestations of love for him, and he disinherits her, not realizing that she really loves him deeply but will not stoop to flattery in order to prove it. When he is ill-treated, maddened, and turned out by his elder daughters, to whom he has given everything, she comes with an army to oust them. She is taken captive, however, and is killed in prison. Lear, in a last outburst, kills the slave who hanged her and dies holding her body.

Corin. In *As You Like It,* a shepherd.

Corinthian. A gay fellow, or sport; used in *1 Henry IV.*

Coriolanus. In *Coriolanus,* the name given to Caius Marcius. He is a stiff-necked Roman soldier aristocrat, arrogant and contemptuous of the common people; his insistence on his personal integrity and his inability to make compromises bring about his downfall.

Coriolanus. [Full title, **The Tragedy of Coriolanus.**] Tragedy by Shakespeare, written 1607–08. The principal source for the play was Plutarch's *Life of Caius Marcius Coriolanus,* which Shakespeare read in North's translation of Plutarch's *Lives* (1579), probably supplemented by Livy's history *Ab Urbe Condita,* translated by Philemon Holland in 1600, and L. Annaeus Florus's *Epitome* of Livy. As usual when using North's Plutarch, Shakespeare modified some parts extensively but elsewhere followed North's wording very closely. Events are telescoped and rearranged, but the scene of Coriolanus's attack on the tribunes and the distribution of free corn (III.i), his speech introducing himself to Aufidius (IV.i), and Volumnia's appeal to her son (V.iii) are adapted directly from North's prose with very few changes. Shakespeare's purpose was not only to recreate the characters of Coriolanus and his associates, but also to interpret the political situation in Rome in terms appropriate to England of 1607–08, when there had recently been uprisings by the poor against farmers and landlords on account of the scarcity of food and the high prices. In the play he minimizes the genuine grievances of the plebeians and emphasizes from the start the enmity between them and Coriolanus, which in Plutarch does not begin to be important until a third of the way through the narrative. Shakespeare also makes Coriolanus, after his banishment, long to destroy Rome completely, whereas in Plutarch he wants only to harm the common people. Menenius and Volumnia are considerably developed from Plutarch. Menenius, as mediator, peacemaker, and admirer of Coriolanus, helps to make Coriolanus a more sympathetic character; Volumnia's influence on her son is evident from the citizen's talk in Act I, Scene 1, and her first appearance before her embassy of peace. Her unnatural glorification of bloodshed and military glory is Shakespeare's invention. Several sources for Menenius's fable of the belly and the members (I.i.) have been suggested; in particular, Shakespeare seems to have used the versions in William Camden's

Remaines of a greater worke concerning Britaine (1605), and a pamphlet by William Averell called *A Meruailous Combat of Contrarieties* (1588). The play was printed in the 1623 folio, but the date of its first performance is not recorded. In 1705 John Dennis produced a play founded on *Coriolanus,* which he called *The Invader of His Country, or the Fatal Resentment,* and two decades earlier Nahum Tate had adapted the Shakespeare play for political purposes with the additional title, *The Ingratitude of a Commonwealth* (1682).

Dramatis Personae

Caius Marcius, *afterwards*	*A Citizen of Antium*
Caius Marcius Coriolanus	*Two Volscian Guards*
Titus Lartius	Volumnia, *Mother of Coriolanus*
Cominius	Virgilia, *Wife of Coriolanus*
Menenius Agrippa	Valeria, *Friend to Virgilia*
Sicinius Velutus	*Gentlewoman, attending on*
Junius Brutus	*Virgilia*
Young Marcius	*Roman and Volscian Senators,*
A Roman Herald	*Patricians, Aediles, Lictors,*
Tullius Aufidius	*Soldiers, Citizens, Messengers,*
Lieutenant to Aufidius	*Servants to Aufidius, and*
Conspirators with Aufidius	*other Attendants.*

The Story. Caius Marcius, having heroically captured the Volscian city, Corioli, returns to Rome and is given the surname Coriolanus in honor of his great accomplishments. The Senate offers him the consulship, but he must first, according to custom, appear before the people of Rome, show them his wounds, and humbly ask for their support. Despite his contempt, as a Roman soldier of good family, for the rabble, he does this, and the people agree to vote for him. However, two tribunes, Sicinius and Brutus, convince the mob that Coriolanus would rule as a tyrant, and the fickle people of Rome reverse their decision. Coriolanus's outspoken rage at their behavior infuriates the crowd and they attack him. Once more, at the persuasion of his friend Menenius, and particularly of his mother, Volumnia, he approaches the people, willing to conceal his contempt for them. But because of the accusations of the tribunes, he again loses his temper and this time is banished from Rome. Bent on revenge, he offers his services as leader of the Volscian army to his old enemy, Tullius Aufidius. Under the leadership of Coriolanus the Volscians successfully advance on Rome. His old friends, Menenius and Cominius, meet him outside the gates and plead with him to spare the city. He is deaf to all entreaties until his wife Virgilia, his young son, and his mother plead with

him. He returns to the Volscians and tells them that he will not
capture Rome, but has arranged a treaty favorable to the Volscians. Aufidius, already jealous of Coriolanus's military talent
and popularity, calls him a traitor, and with the angry support
of the commoners of Corioli, Aufidius's followers stab him.

Cornelius. In *Cymbeline*, a physician. He recognizes the
Queen's evil designs and gives her, not the poison she intends
to use, but a sleep drug and thus saves Imogen's life.

Cornelius. In *Hamlet*, a courtier. He and Voltimand are sent
on an embassy to Norway by Claudius.

Cornwall, Duke of. In *King Lear*, the husband of Regan; a
cruel and ambitious man, inflexible in his decisions. He puts out
Gloucester's eyes and is then killed by one of his servants.

Costard. In *Love's Labour's Lost*, a clownish peasant who tries
to be a learned wit. Into his mouth Shakespeare puts such mani-
fest idiocies as the word "honorificabilitudinitatibus" (V.i) or
has him speak of the "contempts" of a letter. He acts as messenger from Berowne to Rosaline and from Armado to Jaquenetta, confusing the two letters.

Court, Alexander. In *Henry V*, a soldier in the King's army.

Cowley, Richard. d. 1619. English actor, listed as a principal
actor in the First Folio (1623) of Shakespeare's plays. He is
believed to have been an original member of the Lord Chamberlain's Men (formed 1594).

Crab. In *Two Gentlemen of Verona*, the dog of Launce.

Cranmer. In *Henry VIII*, the historical Thomas Cranmer, Archbishop of Canterbury. He obtains the divorce of Henry from
Katherine and remains a favorite of the King, although nobles
try to convict him of heresy. The King names him godfather of
Princess Elizabeth, and at her christening Cranmer predicts the
glory she will bring England as Queen.

Cressida or **Cressid.** Daughter of the Trojan priest Calchas,
whose supposed infidelities have made her name a byword for
female faithlessness. Shakespeare presents her as a weak-willed
and basically frivolous girl who delights in her power over men.
Her behavior in the Greek camp confirms Ulysses' judgment of
her as a "daughter of the game" (IV.v., *Troilus and Cressida*).

Cromwell. In *Henry VIII*, one of Wolsey's servants. He is the
audience for Wolsey's speech bidding farewell to his greatness,
and as secretary of the Council defends Cranmer against Gardiner's attack.

Crosby Hall. [Also, **Crosby Place.**] An ancient house in Bishopsgate Street, London. The site was leased from Alice Ashfield,
prioress of St. Helen's, in 1466 by Sir John Crosby, a grocer and
lord mayor. He built the beautiful Gothic palace. The mansion

covered a large part of what later became Crosby Place or Square. Richard of Gloucester lived there at the death of Edward IV, and there held his levees before his usurpation of the crown. It was afterward bought by Sir Thomas More, who wrote there the *Utopia* and the *Life of Richard III*. Crosby Hall was the central feature of Shakespeare's London. Shakespeare himself had a residence in the neighborhood.

Crosse, Samuel. d. c1605. English actor. He is listed as a principal actor in the First Folio (1623) of Shakespeare's plays and was probably a member of the King's Men (1604).

Cumberland, Prince of. A title formerly bestowed on the successor to the crown of Scotland when succession was declared in the king's lifetime (the crown was originally not hereditary). In *Macbeth* the title is given to Malcolm by his father Duncan.

Cupid. In *Timon of Athens*, a participator in the masque presented to Timon in his home.

Curan. In *King Lear*, a courtier. He may possibly be the "Gentleman" appearing in Act III, Scene 1.

Curio. In *Twelfth Night*, a gentleman in attendance on Orsino, Duke of Illyria.

Curtain, The. A London playhouse established (c1576) in Shoreditch, near Bishopsgate. It is thought that Shakespeare acted here in his own plays as a member of the Lord Chamberlain's Men. It remained open until the accession (1625) of Charles I, after which the drama gave way to exhibitions of athletic feats. It was associated, under James Burbage's management, with The Theatre, which stood nearby. Henry Laneman had an agreement to pool profits from the two theatres with Burbage. It took its name not from any theatrical apparatus but because the land upon which it was built was called Curtain Close.

Curtis. In *The Taming of the Shrew*, a servant. This part was originally described in the Dramatis Personae as that of a servingman (possibly played by Curtis Greville, a Jacobean actor), but it is now played as an old woman, the housekeeper of Petruchio.

Cymbeline. In *Cymbeline*, the King of Britain, dominated by his crafty Queen. After her death he is, according to the prophecy, a "lofty cedar." He treats the defeated Roman forces with clemency and proclaims a generous peace.

Cymbeline. A drama by Shakespeare, produced probably c1610. No main source is known for the whole plot of Cymbeline, but each of the play's three main strands has a different origin. The story of Imogen, her love for the orphan Posthumus Leonatus and his banishment from court, her boorish stepbrother Cloten, the exiled Belarius, a former courtier living in a cave, and the providential intervention of the god Jupiter, all come from an anonymous play called *The Rare Triumphs of Love and Fortune*, published in 1589. The vision scene in *Cymbeline* particularly resembles the intervention of the gods in this play. Shakespeare took the name of the heroine, Princess Fidelia, for the name Imogen assumes in disguise, Fidele, and he used the name of her lover, Hermione, for a female character in *The Winter's Tale*. The play provided Shakespeare with his opening, his pastoral scenes, and his last act. The setting, the early legendary period of British history, seems to derive principally from the additions to *The Mirrour for Magistrates* made by Thomas Blennerhasset and John Higgins, in 1578 and 1587 and to Holinshed's *Chronicles* (2nd ed., 1587), and from "The chronicle of Briton Kings" in Spenser's *The Faerie Queene* (1590), Book II Canto X, although other chronicles and plays available to Shakespeare contained accounts of this period. But *The Mirrour for Magistrates*, Holinshed, and Spenser presented conflicting stories of Cymbeline's reign, and Shakespeare's decision to make Cymbeline rather than one of his sons refuse to pay the Roman tribute seems to have been motivated by dramatic necessity rather than adherence to historical fact. The third element of the plot, the story of Iachimo's wager with Posthumus and his misrepresentation of Imogen's chastity comes from two sources, a story in Boccaccio's *Decameron*, Day 2 Tale 9, which Shakespeare must have read either in the original or in a French translation, or else from an English version of the story called *Frederyke of Jennen* (originally published in 1518 but reprinted in 1560). In both tales the heroine's husband extols her virtue and is challenged by a companion who bets that he can seduce her. The challenger meets the lady and realizes that he cannot win his bet but contrives instead to conceal himself in a chest in a bedroom so that he can observe her asleep. He gathers enough information to convince the husband that he has slept with her; the husband is enraged and tries to kill her, but she escapes and lives in male disguise. Finally, the slanderer is exposed and put to death, and the couple is reunited. The combination of elements from Roman history, Italian Renaissance fabliau, and Elizabethan romantic drama produces a strngely mixed play; but Kenneth Muir (*Shakespeare's Sources*, 1957, p. 240) suggests that the confusion of genres was deliberate, so as to "assist the creation of an imaginary world in which the poet's new symbolic method could have unrestricted scope." The play (which is now generally considered one of Shakespeare's less successful works) resembles Beaumont and Fletcher's *Philaster*, but it is not known which was first. It was first published in the folio of 1623. Thomas D'Urfey in 1682 added to it material designed to please the Restoration taste, and Garrick produced the original again in 1762. Shaw wrote a new fifth act in 1937, and the play as thus amended was produced in that same year.

Dramatis Personae

Cymbeline, King of Britain
Cloten, *Son to the Queen*
Posthumus Leonatus,
  Husband to Imogen
Belarius, *a banished Lord,*
  disguised under the name
  of Morgan
Guiderius
Arviragus
Philario
Iachimo
Caius Lucius
Pisanio
Cornelius
A French Gentleman, *Friend*
  to Philario

A Roman Captain
Two British Captains
Two Lords of Cymbeline's Court
Two Gentlemen of the same
Two Jailers
Queen, *Wife to Cymbeline*
Imogen, *Daughter to Cymbeline*
  by a former Queen
Helen, *a Lady attending on*
  Imogen
Lords, Ladies, Roman Senators,
  Tribunes, a Soothsayer, a
  Dutch Gentleman, a Spanish
  Gentleman, Musicians,
  Officers, Captains, Soldiers,
  Messengers, and other
  Attendants.
Apparitions

The Story. Imogen, the daughter of Cymbeline, King of Britain, has secretly married Posthumus Leonatus, a gentleman at court who is banished when Imogen's stepmother, the Queen (angry that Imogen did not marry her son Cloten), tells the King about the marriage. In Rome, Posthumus brags of the virtue of his wife and makes a wager with Iachimo, a crafty Roman, that Iachimo cannot seduce her. By the terms of the wager, if Iachimo wins Posthumus will give him a diamond ring, which he has as a gift from Imogen. In Britain, Iachimo is scorned by Imogen, but by hiding in a chest in Imogen's room one night he is enabled to describe a fictitious seduction with such a background of detail, backed up by a bracelet that he has stolen, as to convince Posthumus that Imogen has been unfaithful. Posthumus thereupon writes his servant Pisanio instructing him to kill Imogen. Instead, Pisanio disguises Imogen as a page and suggests she flee the court and join the invading Roman forces under Lucius. However, she loses her way and instead of joining the Romans, joins Belarius, a banished nobleman who twenty years before had kidnapped Cymbeline's two sons, Guiderius and Arviragus. The Queen's son, Cloten, dressed in the clothes of Posthumus and in pursuit of Imogen, is killed by Guiderius. The two sons then come upon Imogen, apparently dead, and lay her beside the beheaded Cloten, whom Imogen mistakes for her husband when she revives. Finally, Lucius finds her and accepts her in his entourage as a page, but the Romans, with Iachimo, are defeated and taken prisoners as a result of the heroic fighting of Belarius, Cymbeline's two sons, and Posthumus (who has meanwhile returned to Britain). Imogen (still in the guise of a page) is granted a favor by the King and demands to know how Iachimo obtained the diamond ring. When he explains, and her identity is revealed, she is happily reunited with Posthumus. The King also discovers his sons and makes peace with the Romans.

D

Daniel, Samuel. b. near Taunton, Somersetshire, England, 1562; d. at Beckington, Wiltshire, England, Oct. 14, 1619. An English poet and dramatist. He was educated at Oxford and was for a time tutor to William Herbert, a nephew of Sir Philip Sidney. In 1592 he issued a volume containing *Delia*, one of the first of the Elizabethan sonnet sequences and his best known work, and *The Complaint of Rosamond*, a narrative poem. *Cleopatra* (1594) was an attempt at Senecan tragedy, as was *Philotas* (1605). His poem *Musophilis, or A General Defence of Learning* (1599) upholds poetry as part of the background of the courtier or the warrior. He wrote a *Defense of Rime* (1603) in answer to Thomas Campion's attack on English rhyme in *Observations on the Art of English Poesie* (1602). In 1595 he issued *The Civil Warres between the Two Houses of Lancaster and York* in four books, a verse history expanded in 1609 to eight books but even then left still incomplete. Between 1612 and 1617 he wrote a prose history of England. He is said to have been poet laureate for a short period in 1599, but to have resigned the post in Ben Jonson's favor. He was appointed (1603) master of the revels, and between 1604 and 1615 (when he seems to have retired to his Wiltshire farm) he worked at turning out court masques.

Dardanius. In *Julius Caesar*, one of the servants of Brutus. He refuses his master's request to kill him.

Dark Lady. The subject of Shakespeare's later sonnets (127 *et* *seq.*), a woman variously thought to be an abstract antithesis of the conventions of courtly Elizabethan sonnets, a composite image of sensuality, infidelity, and the bitterness of loveless sexual experience, or an actual person with whom Shakespeare was involved. The speculation concerning this third possibility has produced a number of suggested identities, including both women of the court and of London. At various times scholars have proposed Mary Fitton (a maid of honor to Queen Elizabeth and mistress of William Herbert, Earl of Pembroke), Penelope Devereux, Lady Rich, the Avisa of *Willobie his Avisa*, Luce Morgan (a gentlewoman of Elizabeth's court who fell from favor and became a brothel keeper), and others, including a recent suggestion by A.L. Rowse that she was Emilia Bassano, of a family of court musicians. The sonnets provide few clues to her possible identity: she had dark coloring and black eyes, she played a musical instrument, and she was married but unfaithful. See the essay "Shakespeare's Major Poetry."

Dauphin, Charles the. See *Charles, the Dauphin.*

Dauphin, Lewis the. See *Lewis, the Dauphin.*

Davy. In *2 Henry IV*, a servant of Shallow. He asks his master to judge his friend leniently because "an honest man is able to speak for himself when a knave is not" (V.i).

Deiphobus. In *Trolius and Cressida*, a son of King Priam of Troy.

Dekker, Thomas. [Also, **Decker.**] b. at London, c1572; d. at Clerkenwell (now part of London), Aug. 25, 1632. An English dramatist, at various times a collaborator of Middleton, Webster, Massinger, Rowley, and others. Little is definitely known of his life. He is first noticed in Henslowe's diary in 1598 as a playwright for the Admiral's Men. In February of that year he was imprisoned in the Counter. Between 1598 and 1602 he wrote eight plays alone and many others in collaboration (the total, according to Chambers, being forty-four plays). In 1601 he wrote *Satiromastix, or the Untrussing of the Humorous Poet* (published 1602), a satirical dramatic attack on Ben Jonson, with whom a quarrel had broken out, before 1600, when Jonson reflected upon him in *Every Man Out of His Humour* and *Cynthia's Revels*. In 1601 Jonson attacked Dekker and Marston vigorously in *The Poetaster*. Dekker appears as Demetrius Fannius, the "dresser of plays about the town here," and is made to accuse the poet Horace of being a plagiarist, although he himself knows little about classical literature. *Satiromastix* (1602) was Dekker's retort, parodying and ridiculing Jonson's style. However, he shared with Jonson the pageant produced (1604) at James I's entry into London for his coronation. From 1613 to 1619 he seems to have been imprisoned in the King's Bench prison because of debt. He had always been close to poverty and was saved by Henslowe on two previous occasions from arrest. He wrote many pamphlets ridiculing the follies of the times; and in the plays written with others he excelled in good shop scenes and those laid in inns, taverns, and suburban pleasure-houses.

Demetrius. In *Antony and Cleopatra*, a friend of Antony.

Demetrius. In *A Midsummer Night's Dream*, a Grecian gentleman in love with Hermia. He is very little distinguished from his friend and rival Lysander.

Demetrius. In *Titus Andronicus*, a son of Tamora, Queen of the Goths, and brother of Chiron.

Dennis. In *As You Like It*, a servant to Oliver.

Denny, Sir Anthony. In *Henry VIII*, a gentleman of the court who appears once (V.i) to present Cranmer to the King.

Derby, Earl of. See **Stanley, Lord.**

Derby's Men. See **Lord Chamberlain's Men.**

Dercetas. In *Antony and Cleopatra*, a friend of Antony who, bearing the sword on which Antony died, informs Octavius of his death.

Desdemona. In *Othello*, the wife of Othello the Moor, and the daughter of Brabantio, a Venetian senator. Othello smothers her in an outburst of rage produced by a belief in her unfaithfulness, a belief carefully instilled in him by Iago. Shakespeare has heightened the tragedy attendant upon Othello's mistaken feeling by making her a chaste, modest, and wholly devoted wife, who even at the moment of her death is willing to submit to Othello in her love for him. Her very innocence brings about her downfall in that she is completely unable to understand what is happening and hence to defend herself.

Devereux, Robert. [Title, **2nd Earl of Essex.**] b. at Netherwood, Hertfordshire, England, Nov. 19, 1566; beheaded at London, Feb. 25, 1601. An English nobleman; son of Walter Devereux, 1st Earl of Essex of the Devereux line; a favorite of Queen Elizabeth. He was appointed in 1585 general of the horse to the expedition sent under Robert Dudley, 1st Earl of Leicester, his stepfather, to the aid of the States-General in the Netherlands. In 1587 he attended the court of Queen Elizabeth, who at this time began to show him unmistakable signs of attention, emphatically so after the death (1588) of Leicester. He secretly married (1590) the widow of Sir Philip Sidney, Frances Walsingham, daughter of Elizabeth's secretary of state. Despite Elizabeth's great anger when she heard of the marriage, he made his peace with her and became a privy councilor in 1593. He commanded the land forces in the successful raiding expedition against Cádiz in 1596 but failed to win a complete victory or to capture the Spanish treasure ships and was reprimanded by the

Queen. In 1597 he led an expedition against the Azores, where he again failed to accomplish a real victory, permitting the Argentine ships to escape and almost falling into a trap. But Elizabeth made peace with him and he was appointed earl marshal of England in 1597. He became chancellor of Cambridge University in 1598. In 1599 he was appointed lord lieutenant of Ireland, in which post he aroused the Queen's anger by the failure of his operations against the Irish rebels, and by his inability to follow orders from the Queen. He made a truce with Hugh O'Neill, the Earl of Tyrone, leader of the Ulster rebels, and leaving his post without authorization, returned (September, 1599) to England to lay his defense before the Queen in person. He failed to regain his standing at court, was tried and stripped of his offices. He then formed a conspiracy with Charles Blount, Baron Mountjoy, and Henry Wriothesley, 3rd Earl of Southampton, to compel Elizabeth by force of arms to dismiss his enemies in the council, the Cecil faction. On Feb. 8, 1601, he led a group of his retainers through the streets of London, trying to arouse the citizenry to join him; but this half-formed uprising was met with apathy and he returned to his palace, Essex House, where he was captured. He was tried for treason; Francis Bacon, who had consistently attempted to mediate between Essex and Elizabeth, prosecuted the charge virulently. Essex was found guilty and executed on the charge of treason.

Diana. In *All's Well That Ends Well*, the daughter of the Florentine widow with whom Helena lodges. She makes possible the reconciliation of Bertram to Helena by her willingness to permit Helena to take her (Diana's) place in an assignation with Bertram.

Diana. In *Pericles*, the goddess who appears in a dream to Pericles and sends him to the Temple of Diana to find his wife, Thaisa.

Dick the Butcher. In *2 Henry VI*, a butcher of Ashford, follower of Jack Cade.

Diomedes. In *Antony and Cleopatra*, an attendant of Cleopatra.

Diomedes. In *Troilus and Cressida*, a Greek commander who is sent to Troy to conduct Cressida to the Greek camp. She accepts his advances and gives him the love token that Troilus had given her.

Dion. In *The Winter's Tale*, a Sicilian lord who is sent with Cleomenes to the oracle at Delphi.

Dionyza. In *Pericles*, the wife of Cleon. She attempts the murder of Mariana, and with her husband is finally punished by being burned to death.

Dogberry. In *Much Ado About Nothing*, an absurd constable.

Dogberry catches Borachio and Conrade after Borachio has staged a pretended assignation with Hero, and forces the truth from him. But because of Dogberry's inability to speak plainly Leonato fails to understand what has happened, and the result is near tragedy for Hero.

Dolabella.   In *Antony and Cleopatra*, a friend of Octavius who informs Cleopatra that she is to be taken to Rome in triumph.

Don Adriano de Armado.   See *Armado, Don Adriano de.*

Donalbain.   In *Macbeth*, a son of Duncan, king of Scotland. He goes to Ireland after Duncan's murder and does not appear after Act II, Scene 3.

Donne, John.   b. at London, in 1571 or 1572 (1573 according to his friend and biographer Izaak Walton); d. there, March 31, 1631. An English poet and divine, the first and greatest of the metaphysical poets. On his mother's side he was connected with Sir Thomas More and John Heywood. He was brought up as a Roman Catholic, and was educated at Oxford (1584), Cambridge (1587), and Lincoln's Inn (1592). In 1596 and 1597 he took part in the expeditions led by the earl of Essex against Cádiz and the Azores. In 1597 he was appointed secretary to Sir Thomas Egerton, Lord Keeper of the Great Seal, but lost his post in 1601 by his clandestine marriage to Egerton's niece, and was imprisoned (1602) for a time, the marriage being a violation of both common and canon law. After several years spent in fruitless attempts to obtain a position through court favor, his *Pseudo-Martyr* (1610) won him the notice of King James I. James, however, refused to promote him except in the Anglican Church, and at last, in 1615, Donne received Anglican orders. He was appointed successively royal chaplain, reader in divinity at Lincoln's Inn, and finally, in 1621, dean of Saint Paul's. In his later years he was widely regarded as the foremost preacher of his day.

Writings.   Most of Donne's poems circulated in manuscript during his lifetime, and his collected poems were not published until 1633, after his death. His prose works include over 150 sermons, *Ignatius his Conclave* (a satirical attack on the Jesuits), and a small book of *Devotions* (written during a serious illness in 1623), from which Ernest Hemingway took the title *For Whom the Bell Tolls:*

"No man is an island, entire of itself; . . . Therefore never send to know for whom the bell tolls; it tolls for thee."

Donne's reputation stood very high during the seventeenth century, but during the eighteenth and nineteenth centuries, though never completely forgotten, he was little read. His modern reputation owes much to the edition of the *Poems* by H.J.C. Grierson

(1912) and to the influence of the criticism of T.S. Eliot. Donne is best known for his love poems, his sonnet to Death (*Death, be not Proud*), and his *Anniversaries*, two elegies in memory of sixteen-year-old Elizabeth Drury. His poetry is contrary to the courtly Petrarchan tradition established in English by Wyatt and Surrey; his approach is more natural, his attitude towards women often cynical, his writing more abrupt and witty.

Dorcas. In *The Winter's Tale*, a shepherdess.

Doricles. In *The Winter's Tale*, the name assumed by Florizel.

Dorset, Marquess of. In *Richard III*, the historical Thomas Grey, eldest son of Lady Grey (Elizabeth Woodville), who later became Edward's Queen. When Dorset's brother, Lord Grey, and his uncle, Rivers, are executed by Richard, he joins Richmond in Brittany.

Douglas, Archibald, (4th) **Earl of.** In *1 Henry IV*, the historical Archibald Douglas, 4th Earl of Douglas, an ally of Hotspur at Shrewsbury; he almost kills King Henry and is later captured when the rebels flee.

Drayton, Michael. b. at Hartshill, Warwickshire, England, 1563; d. at London, Dec. 23, 1631. An English poet. He is buried in Westminster Abbey, and his epitaph is said to be by Ben Jonson. His chief works are *Idea: the Shepherd's Garland* (1593), a pastoral sequence; *Idea's Mirror* (1594), a sonnet sequence; *Mortimeriados* (1596; this afterward appeared with many alteration as *The Barons' Wars*, 1603); *England's Heroical Epistles* (1597); *Poems, Lyric and Pastoral* (c1606, containing "The Ballad of Agincourt" and "To the Virginian Voyage"); *Poly-Olbion* (1613–22), a description of England both topographical and legendary; *Nimphidia, the Court of Faery* (1627), a light-touched fairy poem; and *The Muses' Elysium* (1630). From 1597 to 1602 he wrote for the theatre, and scholars have found traces of what may be Drayton's writing in some of Shakespeare's plays. There is no doubt that the two playwrights were acquainted, and Drayton, along with Jonson, was present at the "merry meeting" that is traditionally held to have brought on a fever of which Shakespeare died.

Dromio of Ephesus and **Dromio of Syracuse.** In *The Comedy of Errors*, twin brothers, servants respectively of the twins Antipholus of Ephesus and Antipholus of Syracuse. The Dromio of Ephesus is a stupid servant, the Dromio of Syracuse a witty one. In Plautus's *Menaechmi*, from which this play is derived, there is only one servant.

Duke Senior. In *As You Like It*, the father of Rosalind. As his name suggests, he was "the elder duke," and he has no more specific name in the play. He is driven into exile by his brother, Frederick, but is eventually restored when Frederick repents.

Dull. In *Love's Labour's Lost,* a constable who (at Armado's suit) arrests Costard for breaking the King's decree and wooing Jaquenetta.

Dumain. In *Love's Labour's Lost,* one of the three French lords attending the King of Navarre at his rural academy. He falls in love with Katherine. His song to her "On a day—alack the day!" (IV.iii) appears also in *The Passionate Pilgrim.*

Duncan. A king of Scotland. He succeeded to the throne c1034 on the death of his grandfather Malcolm II, and was assassinated near Elgin in 1040 or 1039. In *Macbeth,* he is a gracious, kindly old man, murdered by Macbeth, who looks in horror at the "silver skin laced with golden blood" of the corpse and likens the result of his monstrous deed to "a breach in nature" (II.iii).

Dunsinane. See **Birnam Wood.**

E

Earl of Nottingham's Company. See **Lord Admiral's Men.**

Earl of Pembroke's Men. [Also, **Pembroke's Men.**] An acting company whose patron was Henry Herbert, 2nd Earl of Pembroke. It is possible that Shakespeare was a member of this company before he joined Chamberlain's (1594). See **Herbert, William.**

Ecclestone, William. English actor. He joined the King's Men in 1614, probably as a shareholder, and is listed in the First Folio (1623) of Shakespeare's plays as a principal actor.

Edgar. In *King Lear,* the legitimate son of the Earl of Gloucester. He is banished by Gloucester as the result of a plot contrived by the bastard son, Edmund, and wanders, disguised as a mad beggar, on the heath, where he meets Lear and eventually becomes a guide to the blinded Gloucester. In Edgar, Shakespeare has created a figure of rejected goodness, sanity driven out to live with insanity, and his humility is contrasted with the disloyalty of Goneril and Regan and the cruel ambition of Edmund. In the famous "cliff" scene (IV.vi), Edgar leads the blind Gloucester to what Gloucester believes to be the edge of the cliff and allows the blind man to "fall" so that he may be "saved" from the "fiend" who has led him there, and thus brings Gloucester to an acceptance of his affliction. Edgar is finally left with Albany to restore the kingdom.

Edmund.   In *King Lear*, the bastard son of the Earl of Gloucester. He contrives to have his legitimate brother Edgar banished, so that he can inherit his father's land, and allies himself with Goneril, Regan, and Cornwall against Lear. Like Goneril and Regan, he has no love or respect for his father and he is dedicated to the fulfillment of his selfish ambitions. He intrigues with both Goneril and Regan separately and is finally killed in a duel by Edgar.

Edmund of Langley, Duke of York.   See **York, (1st) Duke of.**

Edmund, Earl of Rutland.   See **Rutland, Edmund, Earl of.**

Edward IV.   See under **Edward, Earl of March.**

Edward V.   See **Edward, Prince of Wales.**

Edward, Earl of March.   In *2 Henry VI*, the eldest son of Richard Plantagenet, Duke of York. In *3 Henry VI*, he shows his father his sword, bloody from the wounds of the Duke of Buckingham (I.i). On the death of his father he becomes Duke of York. He defeats the Lancastrians, is proclaimed king, as Edward IV, and marries Lady Grey. In *Richard III*, ill, he learns that the order for Clarence's death was executed despite his reversal of it (II.i). In the following scene word comes of his death.

Edward, Prince of Wales.   In *3 Henry VI*, the only son of Henry VI. He is disinherited when the Yorkists persuade the King to leave the crown to the heir of York, and is captured at Tewkesbury and killed.

Edward, Prince of Wales.   In *3 Henry VI*, the son of Edward IV. In *Richard III*, he becomes king, as Edward V, on the death of his father, but he and his brother are put in the Tower and murdered by Richard, Duke of Gloucester.

Egeus.   In *A Midsummer Night's Dream*, the father of Hermia.

Eglamour.   In *Two Gentlemen of Verona*, a courtly knight who helps Silvia escape from Milan and from Thurio, whom her father wishes her to marry. Eglamour deserts her when she is captured by a band of outlaws.

Elbow.   In *Measure for Measure*, a constable, comparable but inferior to Dogberry in *Much Ado About Nothing*.

Eleanor, Duchess of Gloucester.   See **Gloucester, Eleanor, Duchess of.**

Elector Palatine's Company.   See **Lord Admiral's Men.**

Elinor, Queen.   In *King John*, the mother of John. She follows him to France and he learns she has died there (IV.ii). She is the historical Eleanor of Aquitaine, first married to Louis VII of France and then to Henry II of England.

Elizabeth. In *Henry VIII*, the future Queen Elizabeth. She is not often referred to by Shakespeare, but in this play her christening forms a kind of climax, as a sign that a better time is in the offing for the English nation:

> This royal infant . . .
> Though in her cradle, yet now promises
> Upon this land a thousand thousand blessings,
> Which time shall bring to ripeness (V.v).

Elizabeth. [Also, **Elizabeth I, Elizabeth Tudor;** sometimes called **The Virgin Queen.**] Queen of England (1558–1603); b. at Greenwich Palace, London, September 7, 1533; d. at Richmond, Surrey, March 24, 1603. The daughter of Henry VIII and Anne Boleyn, to marry whom Henry divorced Catherine of Aragon. Elizabeth was regarded as illegitimate by Catherine's adherents and by Pope Clement VII. Thus her right to the throne was in question throughout the reign, and many plots against her were based on this question of usurpation, although her succession was set by act of Parliament and Henry's will, which established that Henry should be followed by Edward VI (son of Henry's third wife, Jane Seymour), then Mary Tudor (daughter of Catherine of Aragon), and then Elizabeth, and she supported Mary's claim to the throne on the death of Edward VI. Elizabeth was educated by teachers who followed the new Humanism; she was expert in languages, modern as well as Greek and Latin, and was known as an eloquent speaker. Raised a Protestant, she followed a policy of tolerance after her accession. In foreign affairs, she pursued a policy of aggressive resistance to the spread of the power of Spain. Unofficial war was waged constantly by privateers, bringing great fortunes to the royal treasury. During nearly thirty years of her reign England was at peace, until Philip II of Spain resolved to put a stop to English privateer raids on his shipping and to English support of the Dutch rebels. He dispatched the Invincible Armada; but the fleet of the Armada was caught off Calais and destroyed (1588). When Mary, Queen of Scots, fled the wrath of the Scots after becoming embroiled with John Knox and sought refuge in England, Elizabeth kept her in custody for nearly twenty years and then reluctantly approved her execution because of the many plots to rescue Mary and to revive her claims to the thrones of both England and Scotland. Under Elizabeth, English coinage was standardized on a silver basis; a Statute of Artificers, a labor code, was enacted; and the Poor Laws of 1597 made parishes responsible for their own poor and set heavy penalties for vagabondage. The acts of uniformity and of supremacy establishing the Church of England were passed by Parliament; the Archbishop of Canterbury drew up the Thirty Nine articles of convocation and edited a new edition of the Bible known as the "Bishop's Bible." Elizabeth's spinsterhood and the question of the succession were recurring and continuing problems. Several diplomatic marriages were suggested, but she would not risk her hold on the throne by making a foreign marriage, nor could she risk the scandal of a marriage to Robert Dudley, who was perhaps her one real love. Her affair with Robert Devereux, Earl of Essex, toward the end of her life, ended unhappily with his rebellion and execution (1601). Elizabeth died, in 1603, the only English ruler of adult years since the Norman Conquest in 1066 who had not married. She recognized clearly the problem that would face the kingdom at her death and part of her reluctance to order the execution of Mary, Queen of Scots, is traceable to the fact that Mary's son, James VI of Scotland, was the logical successor to the English throne. On Elizabeth's death, he became James I of England.

The four and one half decades of Elizabeth's reign mark probably the most brilliant period in English history. The long period of official peace with other nations built up about Elizabeth a colorful court whose energies were turned to other matters than war, although freebooting and soldiering expeditions by her military captains gave glamour to their names. Elizabeth's captains and advisers, the Cecils, Dudley, the Walsinghams, Raleigh, Hawkins, Drake, the Bacons, while not uniformly successful, were nevertheless instrumental in carrying out her policies. England became in Elizabeth's time a world power, not yet as strong as Spain but soon to surpass her; the English navy grew to be second to none; commerce expanded and colonies were established where such explorers as Frobisher and Drake had gone. Literature reached a golden age in this time, a period marked with Elizabeth's name, although much of the so-called Elizabethan literature (for example much of the body of dramatic literature) dates from the period of the first Stuart kings (1603–1642). Such poets as Spenser, Drayton, and Gascoigne, playwrights like Marlowe, Greene, Lyle, and Shakespeare, essayists, romancers, and critics of the stamp of Raleigh, Bacon, and Sidney make the period incomparable in its brilliance. She was a great patron of literature and of the theatre, and theatrical companies performed at Court at various times throughout her reign. In 1583 she became patron of her own company, the Queen's Men, of which Shakespeare is thought to have become a member for a time about 1587. By 1594, however, the Queen's Men had been generally replaced at Elizabeth's Court by the Admiral's Men and by the new company that Shakespeare had joined, the Chamberlain's Men. From various reports it would seem that Shakespeare's plays were much appreciated by Elizabeth, and it is traditionally held that Shakespeare wrote *The Merry Wives of Windsor* at her request, because she had been especially pleased by the character Falstaff, in *1* and *2 Henry IV*, and wished a play showing him in love. There are few references to Elizabeth in Shakespeare's plays and sonnets, and most of these follow the conventions of flattery to the reigning monarch. Perhaps because of the fame in later ages of Elizabeth and Shakespeare, a number of apocryphal stories have arisen at various times describing encounters between the two—usually hinging upon the ideas of Shakespeare's extemporaneous wit and Elizabeth's admiration of it.

Elizabeth, Queen.   See under **Grey, Lady.**

Elsinore.   English name of Helsingør, a city in Denmark, in which is situated Kronborg Castle, the traditional scene of *Hamlet*.

Ely, Bishop of.   In *Henry V*, a counsellor who supports the Archbishop of Canterbury on the legality of the King's proposed war with France.

Ely, Bishop of.   See also under **Morton, John.**

Emilia.   In *Othello*, the wife of Iago. At the begining of the play, she does not know her husband's nature, and she later helps him by giving him Desdemona's handkerchief. But when she realizes what he has done, she does not hesitate to reveal it, although at the cost of her life.

Emilia.   In *The Winter's Tale*, a lady attendant on Hermione.

Enobarbus.   In *Antony and Cleopatra*, a friend of Antony. He is a blunt, rough-spoken man, but possesses a degree of humorous sagacity. It is he who gives the famous description of Cleopatra in her barge coming down the Cydnus (II.ii), and the fact that Cleopatra's beauty should so deeply move a practical, unromantic man as Enobarbus emphasizes her tremendous power to stir men. Enobarbus deserts Antony, but dies of a heart broken by remorse at his betrayal of his friend when Antony sends his treasure after him.

Ephesians.   A word meaning boon companions; used in *2 Henry IV* and *The Merry Wives of Windsor*.

Ephesus, Duke of.   See **Solinus.**

Ercles.   A variant of Hercules. The term is used by Bottom in *A Midsummer Night's Dream*.

Eros.   In *Antony and Cleopatra*, the freed slave of Antony. He is devoted to Antony, and kills himself with his own sword when ordered by Antony to slay him.

Erpingham, Sir Thomas.   In *Henry V*, one of Henry's officers.

Escalus.   In *Measure for Measure*, an old lord who urges Angelo to deal more leniently with offenders.

Escalus.   In *Romeo and Juliet*, the Prince of Verona. The real Romeo and Juliet supposedly lived during the reign (1301–04) of

Bartolomeo della Scala. "Escalus" is a corruption of della Scala.

Escanes. In *Pericles*, a lord of Tyre who appears with Helicanus, another lord.

Essex, Earl of. In *King John*, a lord in attendance on the King.

Euphronius. In *Antony and Cleopatra*, an ambassador for Antony to Octavius.

Evans, Henry. London theatre manager. He was an early lease-holder in the Blackfriars Theatre. In 1608 the lease was taken over by the King's Men but it is probable that Henry Evans retained a share.

Evans, Sir Hugh. In *The Merry Wives of Windsor*, a ludicrous, officious, and simple-minded Welsh parson. On the evening when Falstaff is being baited, Evans leads the children's revels as Fairy Queen.

Exeter, Duke of. In *Henry V*, the historical Sir Thomas Beaufort, an uncle of the King. He arrests Cambridge, Scroop, and Grey for treason, acts as ambassador to France, and goes with Henry on the French campaign, where he reports the deaths of Suffolk and York after the battle. In *1 Henry VI*, he mourns the death of Henry V, but looks forward to defeating the French under the young King, whose special governor he is (I.i). He plays the part of a peacemaker, but foresees the Wars of the Roses.

Exeter, Duke of. In *3 Henry VI*, the historical Henry Holland, a supporter of King Henry during the Wars of the Roses.

Exton, Sir Pierce of. In *Richard II*, the nobleman who overhears Henry IV's wish for Richard's death and murders Richard in Pomfret Castle. Holinshed reports this, possibly confusing him with Sir Nicholas Exton, who violently opposed Richard in Parliament.

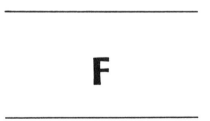

F

Fabian. In *Twelfth Night*, a servant of Olivia. He joins Maria's plot against Malvolio because the latter has brought him into disfavor with Olivia.

Falstaff, Sir John. A celebrated character in Shakespeare's historical plays *1* and *2 Henry IV*, and also in his comedy *The Merry Wives of Windsor*. In the *Henry IV* plays he is a very fat, sensual, and witty old knight; a swindler, drunkard, and good-tempered liar and something of a coward. Morgann in his *Essay on the Dramatic Character of Sir John Falstaff* (1777) argued that Falstaff was not a coward, and proponents of this view have sought to see the "wholeness" of his character, looking upon his flight from Henry and Poins at Gadshill as merely carrying a joke along. He characteristically gets out of this scrape by his quick wit: "Was it for me to kill the heir apparent? But beware instinct, the lion will not touch the true prince. I was a coward upon instinct." It might better be argued that he believed, as he says: "The better part of valour is discretion." He provides a contrast to the heroic, poetic Hotspur, whom Prince Hal parodies (*1 Henry IV*, II.iii), and pretends to have killed Hotspur at Shrewsbury, although actually he played dead until Hal defeated Hotspur. In *2 Henry IV* he is presented more critically and with less sympathy; he emerges as a quick-witted and unscrupulous old man with no sense of responsibility. He deftly insults the Lord Chief Justice with a play on words and ideas, defrauds Mistress Quickly, who is nearly bankrupt with debt, captures Colevile only because Colevile gives himself up, then assumes the airs of a hero and comments satirically on Justice Shallow's administration of justice and his feeble reminiscences of younger days. His character becomes more coarse, and he oversteps the bounds when Hal becomes King (whereupon he is dismissed). In *Henry V*, Pistol comments "his heart is fracted and corroborate" (II.i) giving the impression that Falstaff has died broken-hearted from Henry's ill-treatment. He appears again, according to legend at the request of Queen Elizabeth herself, in *The Merry Wives of Windsor*. It is not the same Sir John, but a debased version of him, a mere buffoon serving as butt for the tricks of others. The first actor of the part is said to have been John Heming.

Fang. In *2 Henry IV*, a sheriff's officer who with Snare tries to arrest Falstaff.

Fastolf, Sir John. In *1 Henry VI*, a cowardly knight who flees from the Battle of Rouen. The historical Fastolf was an English soldier and benefactor of Magdalen College, Oxford. He is supposed by some to be the original of Shakespeare's Sir John Falstaff (*q.v.*) though the evidence is slight: Fastolf was accused of cowardice for his flight (although this did not take place until after Talbot had lost the battle) at Patay. Fastolf was connected with Lollardry.

Faulconbridge, Lady. In *King John*, the widow of Sir Robert Faulconbridge and mother of Robert and Philip Faulconbridge.

She confesses (I.i) to Philip that his father was the late King Richard I (the Lion-Hearted).

Faulconbridge, Philip. [Called **Philip the Bastard.**] In *King John*, the illegitimate son of Richard I (the Lion-Hearted), and the half-brother of Robert Faulconbridge. He follows John in his French wars and is recognized by Queen Elinor as her grandson. He comments with bitter wit upon the politics involved in making peace with France, preferring instead a good open fight (which eventually occurs).

Faulconbridge, Robert. In *King John*, the legitimate younger son of Lady Faulconbridge.

Feeble, Francis. In *2 Henry IV*, one of Falstaff's recruits, characterized by Falstaff as "most forcible Feeble" (III.ii).

Fenton. In *The Merry Wives of Windsor*, a gentleman in love with Anne Page. He intends to marry her for her money alone but is won over to true love by her charms.

Ferdinand. In *The Tempest*, the son of the King of Naples, and lover of Miranda.

Ferdinand, King of Navarre. In *Love's Labour's Lost*, the King of Navarre who wishes to make his court a "little Academe." He, as well as each of his lords, soon breaks his vow to avoid women for three years (he falls in love with the Princess of France shortly after she appears in the play).

Feste. In *Twelfth Night*, Olivia's clown. He takes part in the baiting of Malvolio, pretending to be Sir Topas, who treats Malvolio as a lunatic. He sings the well-known songs "O mistress mine" (II.ii), "Come away, come away, death" (II.iv), and "When that I was a little tiny boy" (V.i).

Fidele. In *Cymbeline*, the name assumed by Imogen, when disguised as a boy.

Field, Nathaniel (or **Nathan**). b. in the parish of St. Giles, Cripplegate, London, 1587; date of death unknown. An English actor and occasional playwright. He is chiefly remembered as the author of *A Woman is a Weathercock* (acted c1609 and printed 1612) and *Amends for Ladies* (acted c1615 and printed in 1618), probably intended with its character of Moll Cutpurse to challenge Dekker and Middleton's very successful *Roaring Girl*, and as the joint author with Massinger of *The Fatal Dowry* (1632). He was the son of John Field, a preacher (and, curiously enough, one of those who censured the stage). He has been widely confused with his brother, who was apprenticed to a stationer (printer) in 1596, and published on his own between 1624 and 1627. Field was impressed by Nathaniel Giles, master of the Children of the Chapel, to serve this company while he was still at St. Paul's Grammar School (c1600). Ben Jonson must have continued his education, since he recorded that Field had read Latin classics with him. Jonson complimented him in *Bartholomew Fair* as an actor, but his work apparently did not spare him financial embarrassment, since Henslowe occasionally had to save him from arrest for debt. In 1615 he joined the King's Men, appearing in *The Loyal Subject* (by Fletcher) and *Bussy D'Ambois* (by Chapman), as well as various other popular plays. In 1619 he apparently left this company, since his name disappears from the livery lists after that year. Of his later life nothing is known save a dubious 1633 entry in the Blackfriars Parish registry.

Finsbury.   An open field area to the north of the City of London and adjacent to Shoreditch (the borough in which The Theatre and The Curtain were located). A shooting field in the early sixteenth century, Finsbury became a resort of the common people and was avoided by people of fashion. It was referred to by both Jonson and Shakespeare (*1 Henry IV*, III.i) in their writings.

Fitzwater, Lord.   In *Richard II*, a nobleman who accuses Aumerle of causing the Duke of Gloucester's death and challenges him to a duel.

Flaminius.   In *Timon of Athens*, a servant to Timon.

Flavius.   In *Julius Caesar*, a tribune of the people. With Marullus, his fellow tribune, he is opposed to the growth of Caesar's power.

Flavius.   In *Timon of Athens*, Timon's steward. Timon ignores his warning of the dangers of reckless spending, and after Timon's ruin, he visits him in his cave. Here Timon first curses him, then calls him "thou singly honest man" (IV.iii) and offers him gold if he will promise to "show charity to none" (IV.iii).

Fleance.   In *Macbeth*, the son of Banquo. He escapes when his father is murdered. Like his father, he has no basis in history (although he has been mentioned in Scottish tradition as an ancestor of the Stuart Kings).

Fletcher, Lawrence.   d. 1608. English actor, member of the King's Men (1603), perhaps as a Groom of the Chamber.

Flibbertigibbet.   A fiend ("of mopping and mowing") named by Edgar in *King Lear* (IV.i). Latimer, in a sermon, used the name "flibbergib" to stand for a chattering or gossiping individual. However, Shakespeare probably derived it from Samuel Harsnett's *Popish Impostures* (1606).

Florence, Duke of.   In *All's Well That Ends Well*, a minor character.

Florizel.   In *The Winter's Tale*, the Prince of Bohemia, in love with Perdita. He is temporarily estranged from his father Polixenes but is reunited with him when they meet at Leontes's court in Sicilia.

Fluellen.   In *Henry V*, a pedantic but courageous Welsh captain.

He expounds the virtues of Roman military life much as one faction of Shakespeare's contemporaries argued the advantages of war according to the mode of the ancients. Shakespeare also uses the incident of Fluellen and the leek (symbol of Wales) to show the tolerance which must be practiced as the price of unity among the English allies.

Flute, Francis.   In *A Midsummer Night's Dream,* a bellows-mender. He plays the part of Thisby (Thisbe) in the interpolated play.

Fool.   In *King Lear,* a companion of Lear in his wanderings on the heath. He acts as the conscience of the King, reminding him continually of his folly in giving away his kingdom, and sits as a judge with Edgar (disguised as Tom o'Bedlam) in the mock trial of Lear's daughters (III.vi). The Fool, like Lear, has a kind of "reason in madness"; his apparent simplicity disguises a shrewd understanding of the cruelty and harshness of the world.

Fool.   In *Timon of Athens,* a servant who arrives with Apemantus and jests with the servants of Timon's creditors (II.ii).

Ford, Master.   In *The Merry Wives of Windsor,* a well-to-do gentleman. He assumes the name of Master Brook and induces Falstaff to confide to him his passion for Mistress Ford and his success in duping Ford, her husband.

Ford, Mistress.   In *The Merry Wives of Windsor,* the wife of Ford. Falstaff writes identical love notes to her and Mistress Page, the "merry wives," and they set about making a fool of him.

Forrest.   In *Richard III,* a murderer (mentioned in IV.iii) hired by Tyrrel to kill the Princes imprisoned in the Tower.

Fortinbras.   In *Hamlet,* the Prince of Norway. He aspires to recover the lands and power lost by his father. On the way to attack Poland, he marches through Denmark, where Hamlet encounters him, Hamlet's reaction being the soliloquy "How all occasions do inform against me" (IV.iv).

Fortune, The.   A public playhouse built at London in 1600. Edward Alleyn had the lease of the site, on Golders Lane; Philip Henslowe, his father-in-law, became his partner in 1601. In 1621 it was burned down but another round building of brick was put up in 1623. This was dismantled in 1649.

Francis.   In *1 Henry IV,* a drawer (bartender) in a tavern, made fun of by Poins and Prine Hal.

Francis, Friar.   In *Much Ado About Nothing,* a friar who suggests to Leonato that he pretend Hero has died of grief, in order to revive Claudio's lost love.

Francisca.   In *Measure for Measure,* a nun.

Francisco.   In *Hamlet,* a soldier who, at the beginning of the play, is relieved from watch by Bernardo.

Francisco. In *The Tempest*, a lord shipwrecked with Alonso.

Frateretto. In *King Lear*, a fiend mentioned by Edgar. The name comes from Samuel Harsnett's *Popish Impostures.*

Frederick, Duke. In *As You Like It*, the usurping brother of the exiled duke.

Froth. In *Measure for Measure*, a tapster and "foolish Gentleman" who is arrested by Elbow (II.i).

G

Gadshill. In *1 Henry IV*, a rascally companion of Falstaff. With Falstaff and others he robs travelers and is in turn robbed by Prince Hal and Poins. He supports Falstaff's lies when Prince Hal questions him about the episode.

Gallus. In *Antony and Cleopatra*, a friend of Octavius.

Ganymede. In *As You Like It*, the name assumed by Rosalind when disguised as a boy.

Gardiner. In *Henry VIII*, the historical Stephen Gardiner. He is secretary to the King, and later becomes Bishop of Winchester and leader of the attack on Cranmer as a heretic.

Gargrave, Sir Thomas. In *1 Henry VI*, an English officer.

Gaunt, John of. See ***John of Gaunt.***

George, Duke of Clarence. See ***Clarence, George, Duke of.***

Gerrold. In *The Two Noble Kinsmen*, a schoolmaster.

Gertrude. In *Hamlet*, the mother of Hamlet, and Queen of Denmark. She is a devoted mother but a weak woman, easily swayed by the unscrupulous Claudius. As Claudius has corrupted her, she dies, appropriately, from poison that he has prepared.

Ghost. In *Hamlet*, the ghost of Hamlet's father, who appears to tell how Claudius poisoned him in his sleep and later to warn Hamlet against killing his mother. It is claimed that Shakespeare himself once acted the part. Ghosts also appear in *Richard III*, *Julius Caesar*, and *Macbeth* and are found in many other

Elizabethan plays, usually with the purpose of prodding the consciences of various characters. According to tradition, ghosts could, if they chose, appear only to a single individual, they must return to the grave at daybreak, and (if they were messengers of the devil) they could not abide light, holy objects, or seasons (like Christmas) that were sacred in character. Although some modern scholars have interpreted these appearances of ghosts as being the Elizabethan equivalent of mental delusions, it is generally held that the Elizabethans found them more than a useful dramatic convention (possibly derived from Senecan revenge tragedy) and also believed in their actual existence.

Gilburne, Samuel. English actor, listed as one of the principal actors, in the First Folio (1623) of Shakespeare's plays. He was probably a member of the King's Men (1605).

Glamis, Thane of. In *Macbeth*, the title that Macbeth holds at the beginning of the play. The Witches show their recognition of him by hailing him "Thane of Glamis." There is in southern Scotland an actual village of Glamis (or Glammis) and a castle associated by tradition with Macbeth.

Glansdale, Sir William. In *1 Henry VI*, an English officer.

Glendower, Owen. In *1 Henry IV*, a Welsh ally of the Percys. His claim to supernatural powers and his boastfulness antagonize Hotspur and the two men exchange heated words (III.i). Glendower is not present at the battle of Shrewsbury.

Globe, the. A celebrated London theatre, built by Richard and Cuthbert Burbage in 1599. When the Theatre in Shoreditch was taken down, the materials were carried to Bankside and used in the erection of the Globe. The Globe was polygonal in shape and open to the sky in the middle; the galleries and probably the stage were covered by a thatched roof. This caught fire as the result of a misfiring of a small cannon during the pageantry of an early production at a performance of *Henry VIII* in 1613, when the whole theatre burnt down. It was rebuilt in 1614, at a cost of £1400, this time with a tiled roof, but was pulled down during the Puritan regime in 1644. Shakespeare was a sharer in the Lord Chamberlain's Men (later the King's Men) who played at this theatre, and it was here that many of his plays were first performed. Excavations in 1989 uncovered a small part of the foundations of the Globe, now largely buried under a Georgian building. This discovery of the remains of a stair-turret confirms the view that admission to the Globe was on a different basis from the other theatres. The excavations fixed the location of the theatre, and demonstrated that its stage was to the south-west. They also testified to the accuracy of Wenceslas Hollar's depiction of the second Globe in his panorama of the 1630s.

Gloucester, Duchess of. In Richard I, the historical Eleanor de Bohun, widow of Thomas of Woodstock, Duke of Gloucester, whose murder (by Mowbray at the command of Richard II) she recalls to Gaunt, with a demand for vengeance.

Gloucester, Earl of.   [Also, **Gloster.**] In *King Lear*, the father of Edgar and Edmund. His story is taken from that of the Prince of Paphlagonia in Sidney's *Arcadia*. His desertion by his bastard son, Edmund, and his willful cruelty to another son, Edgar, correspond on a lower plane to Lear's desertion by his daughters and his harshness to Cordelia. Through his suffering and his blindness, Gloucester comes to realize how he has failed in his duty both to his son Edgar and to all mankind, and like Lear he attains to a fuller understanding of life that would not have been possible to him in his condition of heedless prosperity. He dies finally of mingled grief and joy when Edgar is restored to him.

Gloucester, Eleanor, Duchess of.   In *2 Henry VI*, the historical Eleanor Cobham, wife of Humphrey of Gloucester. She desires to be Queen, engaging in sorcery for this purpose, and is betrayed by Richard, Duke of York. She is banished, after doing penance by walking three days about the street with a taper in her hand. Meeting Gloucester in the street, she chides him for permitting her shame and warns him against Suffolk, York, and Cardinal Beaufort.

Gloucester, Humphrey of.   In *2 Henry IV* and *Henry V*, the youngest son of Henry IV, who plays a minor part as Prince Humphrey of Gloucester and the Duke of Gloucester. In *1 Henry VI*, he is the King's uncle and quarrels with Henry Beaufort, Bishop of Winchester, because he suspects the Beaufort family of seeking to rule England. As the faithful protector of the King and a man who bears his sufferings patiently, he is seen in Shakespeare's *2 Henry VI*, where he is deprived of the Protectorship by the influence of various enemies banded together. Later he is arrested on the false charge of torturing prisoners and purloining army payrolls and is executed.

Gloucester, Richard, Duke of.   In *2* and *3 Henry VI* and *Richard III*, the fourth son of Richard Plantagenet, Duke of York, and later Richard III. In *3 Henry VI*, Margaret refers to him as "that valiant crookback prodigy . . . that with his grumbling voice / Was wont to cheer his dad in mutinies" (I.iv), and he himself has already looked beyond those who are in succession to the throne to the throne itself, which he will get by hewing his way with a bloody axe. After the battle of Tewkesbury he kills the Prince of Wales, murders Henry VI in the Tower, and goes on in *Richard III* to execute all those who stand between him and the throne, experiencing no setbacks until Buckingham's refusal to kill the Princes in the Tower. This murder, eventually perpetrated by Tyrrel, represents the height of Richard's successful villainy, and after it his fortunes decline. Although he is a totally ruthless villain with no pity or feeling for any of his victims, his wit and vitality make him at first curiously attractive; but in the second half of the play he loses his self-confidence, and his repentance comes too late to redeem him from a deservedly wretched death.

Gobbo, Launcelot.   In *The Merchant of Venice*, a whimsical conceited servant. In an involved bit of rationalization (II.ii), he persuades himself that to stay with Shylock, as his conscience bids him, would be to serve the devil; and to run away, as the fiend, who is the devil, bids him, is to obey more friendly counsel. He leaves Shylock and helps Lorenzo escape with Jessica. He is one of Shakespeare's best clowns.

Gobbo, Old.   In *The Merchant of Venice*, the "sand-blind" father of Launcelot Gobbo. Appearing in Act II, Scene 2, with a present for Shylock, he is persuaded by Launcelot to give it to Bassanio, thus aiding Launcelot to enter Bassanio's service.

Goffe, Matthew.   In *2 Henry VI*, a follower of Jack Cade.

Goneril.   In *King Lear*, the eldest daughter of Lear. She despises her honorable husband Albany for his kindness toward Lear, whom she has driven from her house. Planning to put Edmund, whom she loves, in Albany's place by killing the latter, she jealously poisons her sister Regan when she discovers that Regan too loves Edmund. Goneril finally commits suicide.

Gonzago.   In *Hamlet*, the king who is murdered in the interpolated play (and, therefore, in Claudius's eyes, the character representing Hamlet's father). The name of the character is not mentioned in the Dramatis Personae for *Hamlet*.

Gonzalo.   In *The Tempest*, an "honest old counsellor" who gave supplies and books to Prospero and Miranda when they were set adrift. He is shipwrecked with Alonso on Prospero's magic isle.

Gough, Robert.   d. 1624. English actor. He is included in the list of principal actors in the First Folio (1623) of Shakespeare's plays, and was a member of the King's Men, becoming a shareholder in 1611.

Governor of Harfleur.   In *Henry V*, the governor who surrenders his town to Henry (IV.iv).

Gower.   In *2 Henry IV*, an officer in the royal army. In *Henry V*, he tells Fluellen that the King has ordered all the prisoners killed (IV.vii).

Gower.   In *Pericles*, a character who appears as chorus. He is the poet Gower, speaking octosyllabic couplets or sometimes decasyllabics, in couplets or alternating quatrains. In view of this style, Shakespeare is thought not to have written his part.

Grandpré. In *Henry V,* a French lord who vividly describes the worn and desperate appearance of the English army on the morning of Agincourt (IV.ii).

Gratiano. In *The Merchant of Venice,* one of Bassanio's companions. He is a voluble and witty character and one of Shylock's chief persecutors. He marries Nerissa.

Gratiano. In *Othello,* the brother of Brabantio. As the uncle of Desdemona, he succeeds to Othello's fortunes after Othello has killed both Desdemona and himself.

Green. In *Richard II,* a servant of the King.

Greene, Robert. b. at Norwich, England, c1560; d. at London, Sept. 3, 1592. An English dramatist, novelist, and poet. He was educated at St. John's College and at Clare Hall, Cambridge, where he took his master's degree in 1583, and was incorporated at Oxford in 1588. After leaving the university he seems to have led a dissolute life abroad for some time. In 1592, after ten years of reckless living and hasty literary production, he died, according to tradition from an excess of pickled herring and Rhenish wine, deserted by all his friends. Gabriel Harvey attacked him shortly after his death in *Four Letters and Certain Sonnets;* Meres, Chettle, Nash, and others defended him, and Nash, who had also been attacked, published his *Strange News,* directed more against Harvey than in defense of Greene. The quarrel was prolonged. Greene's fame rests mostly on the songs and eclogues that are interspersed through his prose works. Among his works are the tracts and pamphlets *Mamilia* (entered on the Stationer's Register, 1580 and 1583), *Gwydonius, the Carde of Fancie* (1584), *Arbasto, the Anatomie of Fortune* (1584), *Planetomachia* (1585), *Euphues his Censure to Philautus* (1587), *Perimedes the Blacke-Smith* (1588), *Pandosto, the Triumph of Time* (1588; called in later editions *Dorastus and Fawnia*), *Alcida* or *Greene's Metamorphosis* (licensed 1588), *Menaphon: Camilla's Alarum to Slumbering Euphues* (1589; this appeared as *Greene's Arcadia* in 1599), *Greene's Mourning Garment* (1590), *Greene's Never too Late* (1590) and its sequel *Francesco's Fortunes* (1590), *Greene's Farewell to Folly* (1591), *A Notable Discovery of Coosnage* (1591), *The Second and last part of conny-catching* (1592), *The Thirde and last part of conny-catching* (1592), *A Disputation, betweene a Hee conny-catcher and a Shee conny-catcher* (1592), *The Blacke Bookes Messenger* (1592), and *Greene's Groatsworth of Wit Bought with a Million of Repentance* (published at his dying request; licensed 1592). In this last, Greene exhorts other playwrights (Marlowe and probably Peele and Nash) to repent from their evil ways; it is in this pamphlet that Greene made his famous attack on the young Shakespeare, the countryman trying to write plays, the actor attempting to enter the circle of university men, the "upstart Crow ... an absolute *Iohannes fac totum* .. the onely Shake-scene in a countrey" Greene's plays include *The Comicall History of Alphonsus, King of Arragon* (c1588), *A Looking Glass for London and England* (c1590; with Lodge), *The Historie of Orlando Furioso, one of the Twelve Peeres of France* (c1591), *The Honourable History of Friar Bacon and Friar Bungay* (c1591; acted 1594), *The Scottish Historie of James IV* (c1591), and *George-a-Greene, the Pinner of Wakefield* (ascribed to Greene but without much evidence). It is thought by some that he took part in writing the original *Henry VI* plays, later revised or rewritten by Shakespeare. Dyce collected and edited his works (1831–58). See **Groatsworth of Wit.**

Gregory.   In *Romeo and Juliet*, a servant to Capulet. He and Sampson fight with the servants of Montague in the first scene.

Gremio.   In *The Taming of the Shrew*, a rich but old suitor of Bianca. In Act III, Scene 2, he brilliantly describes the marriage of Petruchio and Katherina.

Grey, Lady.   In *3 Henry VI*, the historical Elizabeth Woodville. In the play she is the widow of Sir John Grey, and pleads for her husband's confiscated property, getting instead a gross proposal from Edward IV, which results in marriage. This causes Warwick to desert him. In *Richard III*, as Queen Elizabeth, she attempts to make peace between Richard and her relations. When Edward dies, she takes the Prince off to sanctuary, from which Richard fetches them. With the Duchess of York and Margaret she learns to curse Richard, who despoils her of her brothers and children, much as Margaret has been despoiled of hers. Yet in the midst of her cursing, she listens as he solicits her interest in wooing her daughter. Her answer is ambiguous, and later it is learned that her daughter, Elizabeth, has married Richmond.

Grey, Lord.   In *Richard III*, a son of Queen Elizabeth (Lady Grey) by her former husband. Grey and Rivers are executed by order of Richard at Pomfret.

Grey, Sir Thomas.   In *Henry V*, a conspirator with Scroop and Cambridge against the King. When he is discovered, he claims joy that he is "prevented from a damned enterprise" (II.ii).

Griffith.   In *Henry VIII*, a gentleman usher to Queen Katherine.

Groatsworth of Wit.   [Full title, **Greene's Groatsworth of Wit Bought with a Million of Repentance.**] A posthumous tract by Robert Greene. It was licensed in 1592; the earliest existing edition known is 1596. It was edited by Henry Chettle. Roberto, the young man whose conversion and adventures are related, corresponds in some, though not in all, respects to

Robert Greene himself. Marlowe, Peele, and probably Nash are warned to repent of their wild ways. The exhortation to Peele contains a passage obviously attacking Shakespeare, toward whom the university-bred, established dramatists were very often resentful. See **Greene, Robert.**

Grumio.   In *The Taming of the Shrew*, a servant of Petruchio.

Guildenstern.   In *Hamlet*, a former school friend of the Prince. With Rosencrantz, he spies on Hamlet, under Claudius's orders, and is killed when Hamlet substitutes Rosencrantz's and Guildenstern's names for his own in instructions sent by Claudius.

Guiderius.   In *Cymbeline*, the son of Cymbeline. He is disguised under the name of Polydore and brought up as the son of Morgan.

Guildford, Sir Henry.   In *Henry VIII*, a gentleman of the court.

Gurney, James.   In *King John*, a servant of Lady Faulconbridge.

H

Hal, Prince.   In *1* and *2 Henry IV*, the historical Henry, Prince of Wales, a gay and roistering young man who is one of Falstaff's boon companions. See also under **Henry V.**

Hamlet.   In *Hamlet*, the central character. He is seen at first as a young man deeply disillusioned by his mother's undignified behavior and bitterly grieved by his father's death. The revelation by his father's ghost that the death was not a natural one almost drives Hamlet into madness. He plans to devote his whole being to avenging his father's murder. In order to do this, he pretends to be mad, and it is one of the great questions of the play how far Hamlet's madness is assumed and how far real. Despite his determination to carry out the revenge, he delays in the actual execution of it, and his procrastination leads directly to the death of Polonius and Ophelia. He returns from a journey to England a more stable and resolute man, and finally kills Claudius in a confrontation that brings about his mother's death and also his own. The Romantic critics led by Coleridge tended to see Hamlet in psychological terms, as an individual torn by doubt and seeking to form a course of action. It has been suggested, however, that Coleridge was seeing aspects of himself in Hamlet. T. S. Eliot asserted that the play, in a technical sense, is not succcessful because there is no "objective correlative" to the emotions that Hamlet expresses; that is, the actual circumstances of Claudius's assumption of the throne and Gertrude's marriage would not account in themselves for the terrific disgust that Hamlet feels toward life, and he is therefore insufficiently motivated. Much modern criticism of the play concerns the ethics of Hamlet's revenge and the extent to which he can be considered to have delivered it.

Hamlet. [Full title, **The Tragedy of Hamlet, Prince of Denmark.**] A tragedy by Shakespeare, considered by many to be the greatest in the history of English letters. The story of Hamlet is a very old one, and the name in the form Amlotha appears c1230 in a fragment of verse in the *Prose Edda* of the Icelandic poet Snorri Sturluson. The earliest writer to put the story into an extant literary form was the Dane Saxo Grammaticus who included it in his Latin *Historia Danica* at the end of the twelfth century. François de Belleforest expanded Saxo's version in his *Histoires Tragiques* (1582), a collection that Shakespeare had already used, and it is generally thought that Belleforest's tale was the true source of *Hamlet*, although it has been claimed that Shakespeare also knew Saxo's version. In fact, the two versions are substantially similar and contain all the major elements of the play, including fratricide and incest, committed by the wicked King Feng (Claudius), Amleth's uncle, Amleth's desire to avenge his murdered father, his feigned madness, the use of a woman as a decoy to trap Amleth and betray his disguise, the machinations of a spying friend of King Feng's who hides like Polonius in the Queen's bedchamber when Amleth comes to confront her, the murder of this character, and a scene in which Amleth upbraids his mother for her conduct. As in *Hamlet*, the King dispatches Amleth to England with a letter secretly commanding his death, but Amleth discovers this, changes the letter, returns to his home, in this case Jutland, and finally avenges himself by burning Feng's palace and all his followers, and killing Feng after exchanging swords with him. Belleforest made certain alterations to Saxo's tale that Shakepeare did not use, such as making Feng's murder of his brother take place in public at a banquet, but he did add two important details: he referred to Amleth's "over-great melancholy," and he made it clear that Feng and the Queen had committed adultery before the murder. Neither Saxo nor Belleforest includes a ghost, a play equivalent to *The Mousetrap*, Laertes, Fortinbras, the madness and drowning of the Ophelia character, or a graveyard scene. The relationship between Shakespeare's play and Saxo and Belleforest is complicated by the fact that there clearly existed an earlier play of *Hamlet* that seems to have been known by 1589, since there is a reference to it in Thomas Nash's preface to Robert Greene's romance *Menaphon*, published in that year. The passage in question seems to refer also to Thomas Kyd, author of *The Spanish Tragedy*, who is thought by many to have been the author of this first *Hamlet* (usually known as the *Ur-Hamlet*, "Ur" meaning "source"). It is possible that he wrote the *Ur-Hamlet* just after the highly successful *Spanish Tragedy*, which has many features in common with Shakespeare's *Hamlet*, in an effort to capitalize on *The Spanish Tragedy's* popularity. Philip Henslowe refers to a production of *Hamlet* at the Newington Butts playhouse in 1594, and Thomas Lodge in his pamphlet *Wit's Miserie* (1596) speaks of a ghost crying "like an oister wife, Hamlet, revenge," but the ghost in Shakespeare's play has neither these words nor this manner. Dekker in *Satiromastix* (1601) has a character say "My name's Hamlet revenge," and refer to Paris Garden, where the Lord Chamberlain's Men probably acted the *Ur-Hamlet* in 1596. It is therefore very likely that Shakespeare's *Hamlet* was influenced by the *Ur-Hamlet*, and perhaps that he found in it some of the features of his play that were not in Saxo or Belleforest, such as the ghost, *The Mousetrap* play, and the madness and death of Ophelia, all of which would have been likely ingredients of a Senecan revenge play by Thomas Kyd.

A number of other sources are also thought to have contributed to Shakespeare's *Hamlet*. The presentation of the Ghost, if it did not come from the *Ur-Hamlet*, was likely to have been influenced by Seneca's ghosts, in the *Agamemnon* or the *Troades*, both of which were available in translation, and also by contemporary ghost-lore such as that in Reginald Scot's *The Discoverie of Witchcraft* (1584) or Lavater's *Of Ghosts and Spirites*. The murder of Gonzago perhaps came from contemporary accounts of the death, said to be by poison, of Francesco Maria I, Duke of Urbino, in 1538, although the use of the play "The Murder of Gonzago" (*The Mousetrap*) to discover Claudius's guilt may have been suggested by the anonymous play, *A Warning for Faire Women* (1599), in which there is a discussion of murders miraculously revealed. Aeneas's tale to Dido probably came from Marlowe's *The Tragedie of Dido Queene of Carthage* (1594) and perhaps from Virgil also. The similarities between *Hamlet* and the *Oresteia* of Aeschylus are fascinating, particularly in the matters of the hero's madness, the part played by the faithful friend, and the question of revenge taken against the Queen, but Shakespeare did not know Aeschylus's trilogy in Greek and no translation was available. *Hamlet* was played in 1600 or 1601 and printed first in 1603. It was entered on the Stationers' Register on July 26, 1602, "A booke called the Revenge of Hamlett Prince Denmarke as yt was latelie Acted by the Lord Chamberleyne his Servantes." This was a very imperfect text, known as the first quarto, possibly based on the *Ur-Hamlet*, and less than half the length of the second quarto. The second quarto, published in 1604, was a good text, thought to be as Shakespeare left it. The third quarto was a reprint of the second, and the fourth appeared in 1611. There is a fifth quarto, undated. No others appeared during Shakespeare's lifetime. The four folios are essentially the same text, which differs from the quartos by 200 lines, these being omitted (probably by acting cuts). The German play *Der Bestrafte Brudermord, oder Prinz Hamlet aus Doennemark* (Fratricide Punished, or Prince Hamlet of Denmark) is now thought to be a corrupt version of the *Hamlet* produced at Dresden in 1626, with resemblances to the "bad" first quarto and also to the "good" second quarto and the First Folio. It is suggested that it was constructed from a player's memory of the first quarto, the second quarto, and the *Ur-Hamlet*.

Dramatis Personae

Claudius, King of Denmark	Bernardo, *an Officer*
Hamlet, *Son to the late, and*	Francisco, *a Soldier*
Nephew to the present King	Reynaldo, *Polonius's Servant*
Fortinbras,Prince of Norway	*A Captain*
Horatio, *Friend to Hamlet*	*English Ambassadors*
Polonius, *Lord Chamberlain*	*Players*
Laertes, *his Son*	*Two Clowns, Grave-diggers*
Voltemand, *Courtier*	Gertrude, Queen of Denmark,
Cornelius, *Courtier*	*and Mother to Hamlet*
Rosencrantz, *Courtier*	Ophelia, *Daughter to Polonius*
Guildenstern, *Courtier*	*Lords, Ladies, Officers,*
Osric, *Courtier*	*Soldiers, Sailors, Messengers,*
A Gentleman	*and Attendants*
A Priest	*Ghost of Hamlet's Father*
Marcellus, *an Officer*	

The Story. Hamlet, Prince of Denmark, returns to the royal castle of Elsinore to find that his father has recently died and his mother, Gertrude, has married his father's brother

Claudius, now ruling as King. Hamlet's initial dismay at the unseemly haste of the marriage turns to horror and disgust when he learns from his father's Ghost that his father was murdered by Claudius, and he determines to avenge his father by killing the murderer. At this point in the play Hamlet's fatal tendency toward hesitation and the urge to justify too meticulously every action before he takes it are not yet apparent; his wrath is great, and seemingly vengeance will not be too long delayed. To conceal his designs from Claudius, Hamlet feigns madness and spurns Ophelia, the daughter of the Lord Chamberlain Polonius, whom he had previously courted. To test the truth of the Ghost's information he stages a play before the King that re-enacts the circumstances of the murder. Utterly convinced of the King's guilt by his reaction to this, Hamlet nevertheless hesitates to kill Claudius when he comes upon him at prayer, and instead goes to his mother's room and violently reproaches her for her "incestuous" marriage. Hearing a noise behind the arras and thinking it is Claudius, he kills the eavesdropping Polonius. Claudius, now keenly aware of Hamlet's purpose, sends Hamlet to England with instructions that he be killed, but Hamlet escapes when his vessel is intercepted by pirates and returns to Denmark to discover that in his absence Ophelia has gone mad and drowned herself. Laertes, son of Polonius and a former close friend of Hamlet, has meanwhile returned to avenge his father's death and is persuaded by Claudius that he should participate in a seemingly foolproof scheme to kill Hamlet. A fencing match is arranged between the two young men, for which Laertes's foil is to be poisoned. Laertes wounds Hamlet and thus ensures his death, but Hamlet seizes the poisoned foil and kills Laertes, who, dying, reveals the treachery. Gertrude also dies, having drunk unwittingly from a poisoned chalice prepared by Claudius for Hamlet; and Hamlet then stabs the King with the poisoned sword and compels him to drain the chalice left unfinished by Gertrude.

Harcourt.   In *2 Henry IV*, a member of the King's party who announces to Henry the victory of the sheriff of Yorkshire (IV.iv).

Harpier.   In *Macbeth* (IV.i), a demon or (possibly) harpy.

Harvey.   In *1 Henry IV*, apparently the original name of Bardolph. The change was made, it is assumed, because of protest by someone of that name at the royal court.

Hastings, Lord.   In *2 Henry IV*, a rebel who is arrested after making peace with Prince John.

Hastings, Lord.   In *3 Henry VI*, and *Richard III*, a loyal supporter of Edward IV, whom he helps to escape from prison. Although Edward's Queen is his enemy, he refuses to help

Richard to the throne after Edward's death, is accused by Richard of treachery, and is executed.

Hathaway, Anne. b. c1556; d. 1623. The maiden name of the wife of William Shakespeare. According to the records of the diocese of Worcester, England, a license was issued on Nov. 27, 1582, for the marriage of William Shakespeare and Anne Whateley of Temple Grafton. On November 28, certain friends of the deceased father of Anne Hathway or Hathaway of Stratford posted a bond as security in the matter of the marriage of this Anne to William Shakespeare. It is generally supposed that the name Whateley in the first entry was a clerical error. The license in question was a special one permitting the marriage after only one publication of the banns; the normal triple publication would have made it impossible, for various reasons, to proceed with the ceremony in less than two months; this evidently was judged inadvisable, in view of the fact that Anne was already pregnant. Her first child, Susanna, presumably Shakespeare's child, was christened on May 26, 1583. Subsequently, she bore twins, who were christened Hamnet and Judith on Feb. 2, 1585, and these three, so far as the records show, were her only children. Anne lived to the year 1623, and the inscription on her tombstone says she was sixty-seven years of age at her death, which indicates that she was eight years older than her husband.

Hecate. In *Macbeth*, a superior of the Witches, borrowed from lore already old in Shakespeare's day (actually, she stems from Greek mythology, where she has threefold powers involving the moon and night, the earth, and the lower world, whence her later association with demons and witchcraft). In *Macbeth* (III.v), she scolds the Witches for acting without her advice. Some authorities have attributed her speeches to Thomas Middleton, who later (about 1612) wrote a play called *The Witch*.

Hector. In *Troilus and Cressida*, a son of Priam, King of Troy, and husband of Andromache. He challenges the Greeks to single combat, fights with Ajax, and is later murdered by the jealous Achilles.

Helen. In *Cymbeline*, an attendant of Imogen.

Helen. In *Troilus and Cressida*, the beautiful wife of Menelaus. Her elopement with Paris caused the Trojan War.

Helena. In *All's Well That Ends Well*, the heroine, who pursues the unwilling Bertram until she fulfills the conditions he has set for acknowledging her as his wife. She is a woman of great integrity, ingenuity, and perseverance whose wit and fidelity win her the man she loves.

Helena. In *A Midsummer Night's Dream*, an Athenian maiden in love with Demetrius, who is himself in love with Hermia when the play opens. Puck accidentally contrives that both Demetrius and Lysander should fall in love with her, but at Oberon's instruction restores both lovers to their senses, and in the end Helena obtains Demetrius.

Helenus.   In *Troilus and Cressida*, a Trojan prophet, son of Priam. He favors giving Helen back to the Greeks.

Helicanus.   In *Pericles*, the faithful minister of Pericles.

Heming, John.   [Also, **Hemminge**] b. at Shottery, England, c1556; d. at Aldermanbury, England, Oct. 10, 1630. An English actor. In 1593 he belonged to Strange's Men, a company of Elizabethan actors, and toured with Edward Alleyn. He probably joined the Lord Chamberlain's Men in 1594, about the time the company was formed, and he seems to have been treasurer of the King's Men, later formed from the Lord Chamberlain's company. He played in *1 Henry IV*, and in Jonson's *Volpone*, *The Alchemist*, and several other of his plays. With Henry Condell he edited the First Folio of Shakespeare in 1623. He was a quarter owner, apparently, of the Globe and Blackfriars theatres, and closely associated with Shakespeare, who mentions him in his will. This intimacy has been one of the reasons for accepting the thirty-six plays in the First Folio as actually Shakespeare's.

Henry IV.   See **Bolingbroke, Henry.**

1 Henry IV.   [Full title, **The First Part of King Henry the Fourth.**] A historical play by Shakespeare, first acted c1597 and printed in 1598. With *2 Henry IV* and *Henry V* it comprises a trilogy on the youth and young manhood of the victor at Agincourt, conceived of as the ideal of kingship by the ardently nationalistic English population of the Elizabethan period. However, the plays are usually taught, and always staged, as separate works. (For purposes of quick identification the two parts of *Henry IV* are often referred to by Shakespeare scholars as *1 Henry IV* and *2 Henry IV*, and the reader will find that this system of reference has been used throughout this book.) Shakespeare's main source was Holinshed's *Chronicles* (2nd ed., 1587). The action of the play takes place over a year, from June 1402 to July 1403. Although this was a shorter space of time to be dramatized than in many of Shakespeare's histories, nonetheless a number of events recorded in Holinshed had to be omitted and others compressed or rearranged. Henry IV's references to a crusade are taken from Holinshed's account of the last year of his reign, and he is depicted as an old man, although at the time of the battle of Shrewsbury he was only thirty-seven. The defeat of Mortimer at the hands of Glendower and the victory of Sir Walter Blunt's forces at Holmedon over the Earl of Douglas did not take place on the same day, as recorded in Act I, Scene 1, Prince Henry did not slay Hotspur at Shrewsbury, nor were they in fact the two young rivals that Shakespeare depicts; Prince Henry was fifteen and Hotspur thirty-nine. The character of Hotspur's wife, whom Shakespeare called Kate and Holinshed Elinor, was virtually Shakespeare's invention. Shakespeare probably supplemented Holinshed's account with the *Mirrour for Magistrates* (1559), which contained accounts of Glendower and Northumberland, although he does not take over the *Mirrour's* characterization of Glendower as a man of evil life who deserved his wretched death. Some details in the play come from Samuel Daniel's *"The First Fowre Bookes of the Civile Wars* (1595), in which Hotspur was presented as a rash young man and Hal saves his father on the battlefield from death at the hands of the Earl of Douglas. Daniel's view of Henry IV's reign as overshadowed by an avenging nemesis on account of his usurpation of the throne may also have influenced Shakespeare. An anonymous play called *The Famous Victories of Henry the Fifth*, published in 1598, though possibly written ten years earlier, supplied elements and characters for the comic plot of *1 Henry IV*, including the robbery at Gadshill, Prince Henry's tavern life, the parodying of authority, and the characters of Ned Poins, Gadshill, and "Jockey Old Castle," whom Shakespeare took over, transformed, and renamed Falstaff. The character of Falstaff has no historical justification at all, the original Oldcastle having been a Lollard leader, burned at the stake for his heretical views. Various aspects of his large personality may have had literary sources, such as the braggart *miles gloriosus* in plays like Udall's *Ralph Roister Doister*, the foolish Sir Tophas in Lyly's *Endimion*, and the many tempters and misleaders of youth in medieval Morality plays. The character of Tressilian in the anonymous play *Thomas of Woodstock*, which Shakespeare may have used for *Richard II*, was perhaps another influence, especially in the scene where Tressilian's servants ambush country people on their way to market, as Falstaff and his friends ambush the travelers in *1 Henry IV* (II.ii). In *1 Henry IV* we receive no inkling of the heights that Henry (here called Prince Hal) is eventually to reach; he is here overshadowed as a character by both Sir John Falstaff (one of Shakespeare's most richly human portraits, in the vein of broad comedy) and Hotspur (Harry Percy).

Dramatis Personae

King Henry the Fourth	Sir John Falstaff
Henry, Prince of Wales	Sir Michael
(Prince Hal)	Poins
Prince John of Lancaster	Gadshill
Earl of Westmoreland	Peto

Sir Walter Blunt	Bardolph
Thomas Percy, Earl of Worcester	Lady Percy, *Wife of Hotspur*
Henry Percy, Earl of	Lady Mortimer
Northumberland	Mistress Quickly
Henry Percy (Hotspur)	*Lords, Officers, Sheriff,*
Edmund Mortimer	*Vintner, Chamberlain,*
Richard Scroop	*Drawers, Carriers, Travelers,*
Archibald, Earl of Douglas	*and Attendants*
Owen Glendower	
Sir Richard Vernon	

The Story. When Henry IV refuses to ransom Lady Percy's brother, Edmund Mortimer, rightful claimant to the throne, from his captor Owen Glendower, the Percys refuse to give their Scottish prisoners to Henry. Moreover, Henry Percy (nicknamed Hotspur), with his father, Northumberland, and his uncle, Worcester, determine to raise a rebellion against Henry with York, Glendower, Mortimer, and Douglas. Meanwhile Prince Hal, the young Prince of Wales, is amusing himself with the carefree companionship of Sir John Falstaff and his carousing friends; when the play opens they are laying their plans to rob a group of travelers. But Prince Hal and Poins arrange not to be present at the robbery so that they may be able to attack and put to flight Falstaff and his companions; this they are able to do easily and without being recognized. The prank is revealed at the Boar's Head Tavern after Falstaff has given his exaggerated version of the adventure (from which Sir John emerges, by his own account, as a valiant warrior, afraid of no man), and much merriment ensues. Hal is then strongly rebuked by his father for his irresponsibility and is given part of the royal forces to lead against the rebels, who have, meanwhile, been arguing about how to divide the kingdom when they have captured it. At Shrewsbury, Hotspur and Douglas learn that they have been deserted by Northumberland and Glendower, but prepare nevertheless to meet the advancing royal army. Worcester does not deliver to his rebel allies the King's offer of peace terms, and in the following battle the rebels are severely defeated. Hal's conduct in the battle does not lack for valor (indeed, he is able to slay Hotspur), but one is not yet convinced that he has, or will ever have, the capacity for greatness (although a hint of his largeness of heart is revealed by his willingness to let Falstaff take the credit for killing Hotspur). In this play, taken by itself, Hotspur rather than Hal emerges as the personification of manly honor.

2 Henry IV. [Full title, **The Second Part of King Henry the Fourth.** A historical play by Shakespeare, first acted c1598 and printed in 1600. As in *1 Henry IV* Shakespeare's main source for the historical part of his play was Holinshed's *Chronicles* (2nd ed., 1587), on which he depended more than for the first play, since Samuel Daniel's *The First Fowre Bookes of the Civile Wars* (1595) was of less use to him. He had both a wider span of time to compress, the period from 1403 to Henry V's accession in 1413, and less interesting historical material to deal with. In various ways Shakespeare adjusted and modified Holinshed to make his long account more tractable. The rebellions against Henry IV by Northumberland's faction and the Archbishop of York are condensed from a number of separate uprisings. Northumberland's crafty escape to Scotland so as to avoid confrontation with the royal forces at Gaultree is Shakespeare's invention; in Holinshed, the Archbishop moved too quickly for Northumberland to keep up with him, although Northumberland finally died bravely in battle. Henry IV's illness is predated so as to add force to the presentation of chaos in the realm from the start; this may be due to the influence of Daniel, where the King's bad conscience is related to his sickness, for in Holinshed his illness is not mentioned before 1411. In Shakespeare the King hears the news of Northumberland's death shortly before his own death, although the events actually took place five years apart. Daniel's poem influenced Shakespeare's presentation of Henry IV, especially of the burden of guilt that the King expresses in Act IV, Scene 5, although Shakespeare makes little use of Daniel's facts. John Stowe's *Chronicles of England* (1580) and *Annales of England* (1592) may also have been used for this scene, particularly Stowe's emphasis on the advice given by the dying King to his son; the solemn vows of Henry V in Act V, Scene 2, to rule his realm justly may also have been influenced by Stowe. The anonymous play, *The Famous Victories of Henry the Fifth*, published in 1598 though written earlier, is an important source; Shakespeare takes up its theme of the Prince's ambiguous attitude toward his father but makes it very clear that Hal's apparent indifference and cynicism are only a pose. He makes use of the scene in which the Prince repents at his father's bedside for Act IV, Scene 5, in particular in the details of the music that the King calls for, the King's dozing and then awakening to find the crown gone, and the Prince's weeping. In *The Famous Victories* the Prince is shown boxing the ears of the Lord Chief Justice, whereas in *2 Henry IV* this incident is mentioned but not presented. At Henry V's coronation, Shakespeare uses the scene from the older play where the new King's former companions await his arrival, expecting to be taken to the royal favor but instead finding themselves banished, though it is Ned (Poins) in *The Famous Victories* who steps forward to present himself to the

King, not, as in Shakespeare's infinitely superior conception, Falstaff. But *The Famous Victories* does not account for much of the comic plot. Mistress Quickly, Doll Tearsheet, and the characters of the Gloucestershire countryside are Shakespeare's invention. It has been thought that Shakepeare wrote this play because of the tremendous welcome given by audiences to the character of Sir John Falstaff in *1 Henry IV* (most of the characters, and many of the situations, are carried over from that work), but Prince Hal has drawn away at the end from Falstaff and his cronies to assume the mantle of kingly responsibility, thus providing an explicit bridge in characterization between the carousing youth of *1 Henry IV* and the great king of *Henry V*. It is likely either that Shakespeare intended a two-part play from the start, or that during the writing of *1 Henry IV* he realized that he had too much material for a single play and so made provision for a sequel. The popularity of Falstaff was too great for him to be utterly eliminated from future consideration, and the Epilogue to this play (*2 Henry IV*) promises another one that will include both Falstaff and Henry (thus creating a situation that troubles many people in their reading of the three plays about Henry V: as Henry attains greatness he must sacrifice his close friendship with Falstaff, and because Falstaff is one of the most irresistibly human of all of Shakespeare's characters this process is impossible without causing some people to feel Henry's kingly greatness was obtained at the expense of a true friendship, and that Henry was therefore perhaps more the king, but also less the man).

Dramatis Personae

Rumour, *the Presenter*
King Henry the Fourth
Henry, Prince of Wales,
    afterwards King Henry
    the Fifth
Thomas of Clarence
Prince John of Lancaster
Humphrey of Gloucester
Earl of Warwick
Earl of Westmoreland
Earl of Surrey
Gower
Harcourt
Blunt
Lord Chief Justice
A Servant of the
    Chief Justice

Lord Bardolph
Sir John Coleville
Travers *and* Morton
Falstaff, Bardolph, Pistol,
    and a Page
Poins *and* Peto
Shallow *and* Silence,
    Country Justices
Davy, *Shallow's Servant*
Mouldy, Shadow, Wart, Feeble,
    and Bullcalf, *Recruits*
Fang *and* Snare,
    Sheriff's Officers
Lady Northumberland
Lady Percy
Mistress Quickly
Doll Tearsheet

Earl of Northumberland	*Lords and Attendants; Officers,*
Scroop, Archbishop of York	*Soldiers, Messenger, Porter,*
Lord Mowbray	*Drawers. Beadles, Grooms, etc.*
Lord Hastings	*A Dancer Speaker of the*
	Epilogue

The Story. As the play opens, Westmoreland and Lancaster are preparing to lead an army against the remaining rebels. In London the King has commissioned Falstaff to go on the expedition to enlist soldiers en route. Prince Hal and Falstaff finally leave their friends at the Boar's Head Tavern and set out for the north. In Gloucester, at the home of Justice Shallow, Falstaff allows recruits to buy themselves off and enlists only a few poor and ragged men. Northumberland again deserts the rebels, and York, Mowbray, Hastings, and the others face the royal forces with a low morale. Lancaster tricks them into disbanding by promising to redress their wrongs, and then has them executed. The King is too sick and weary of his duties to rejoice over the defeat of the rebels, but he indicates before he dies that he now has confidence in his son (a confidence that Hal demonstrates not to have been misplaced by the tone of his speeches in the last scene of the play). Hearing that Hal is now Henry V, Falstaff hurries to London, but is there coldly rejected by the new King.

Henry V. In *Henry V*, the king of England. Historically, he came to responsibility early and when not yet sixteen was commander of the royal forces at Shrewsbury against the Percys; an unfounded legend says that he personally killed Harry Percy (Hotspur) at that battle. He succeeded to the throne on March 20, 1413, and immediately set about arranging matters to secure domestic peace, among other things restoring to their former positions those who had lost their titles or lands. In 1415, a plot by Richard, Earl of Cambridge, to make the Earl of March king was discovered. Cambridge was executed. Against the rebellious Lollards Henry V firmly enforced the anti-Lollard statute *De Heretico Comburendo* of 1401, Sir John Oldcastle being one of those burned (1417) for his part in the revolt of 20,000 Lollards in 1414. Henry decided to embark on a career of reconquest in France, principally because of French support of the Welsh during Glendower's rebellion in his father's reign, but also, according to some historians, to divert attention from domestic complaints. He crossed to France in 1415, besieged and took Harfleur, and marched on Calais. At Agincourt, his army of 13,000, thinned by disease, was faced by 50,000 French; on Oct. 25, 1415, St. Crispin's Day, the battle was fought; the French were routed with great loss, and Henry continued on to Calais.

He returned almost at once to England. In 1417, having completed preparations, Henry again crossed the Channel. He took Caen and besieged Rouen; most of Normandy fell into his hands, and after the fall of Rouen in 1419 his army approached Paris. By the Treaty of Troyes (May 21, 1420), he attained his principal aims. He was to marry Catherine of Valois, daughter of Charles VI of France; he would serve as regent for the insane king; and he was to be the king's heir, the Dauphin being specifically excluded. On June 2, he married Catherine; in December he made a triumphal entry into Paris. He returned with his queen to England to have her crowned and to have the treaty ratified, but in his absence a revolt occurred in Normandy. Henry returned to France and, while besieging Meaux (1421–22), weakened his health and died the following summer. He was succeeded by his nine-month-old son Henry VI. Henry is often considered the ideal knightly king, and he modeled himself deliberately in the image of King Arthur and Godfrey of Bouillon. He is said on doubtful authority to have been wild and dissolute in his youth (probably a story spread by prejudiced religious controversialists who disliked his friendship with the Lollard Oldcastle), and is so represented by Shakespeare; but Shakespeare took him as the model king and as the culmination of English greatness before Elizabeth.

Henry V. [Full title, **The Life of King Henry the Fifth.**] A historical play by Shakespeare, first acted before 1600 (it may have been the first play in the new Globe theatre), printed in 1600 in an incomplete pirated edition, and included in the folio of 1623, where there is a fair text (which Dover Wilson believes to be from Shakespeare's manuscript). The main historical source was Book III of Holinshed's *Chronicles* (2nd ed., 1587), but Shakespeare also went independently to Holinshed's source, Hall's *The Union of the Two Noble and Illustre Famelies of Lancastre and Yorke* (1548) for some details. The main outline of the historical events is common to both, but some passages in the play can be separately derived from one or the other. For instance, Fluellen's reference to the effects of countermining (III.ii) comes from Holinshed, as does Westmoreland's wish for more men (IV.iii) and Henry's threat to the French horsemen (IV.vii), The Archbishop of Canterbury's speech on the Salic Law (I.ii) follows Holinshed very closely. From Hall come Henry's conversation with his nobles on England's relations with Scotland (I.ii), the placing of the tennis balls incident after the proroguing of Parliament, and the stress on the theme of the unity of England and France. Shakespeare may also have used other chronicles including the *Vita et Gesta Henrici Quinti* by "Titus Livius," translated into English in 1513. Earlier plays on the life of Henry V were in existence, including the anonymous *The Famous Victories of Henry V*, which Shakespeare had already used for his Henry IV plays, and a lost play, referred to by Nash in 1599, that may have been a source both for Shakespeare's three plays dealing with Henry V and also for *The Famous Victories*. *The Famous Victories* included the tennis ball scene, scenes showing the attitude of the common people to the war, the encounter of an English clown with a French soldier, and a moving scene with Henry as a blunt and matter-of-fact suitor, all of which Shakespeare may have used. He rearranged the material of the sources so as to concentrate on the heroic struggle between England and France, and in particular on the battle of Agincourt, and to show Henry as the ideal king, brave, active, and fully aware of his responsibilities and duties. The play is one of the few that can be dated exactly as to its composition, this being between March and September, 1599, from a reference to the Earl of Essex's expedition to Ireland in the Chorus to Act V. With *1 Henry IV* and *2 Henry IV* it comprises a trilogy on the youth and young manhood of the victor at Agincourt. Here we see Hal grown into the mighty king, having cast off completely the carousing companions and devil-may-care manners of his youth. Falstaff appears not at all; his death is announced briefly at an early point in the development of the plot.

Dramatis Personae

King Henry the Fifth
Humphrey of Gloucester
Duke of Bedford
Duke of Exeter
Duke of York
Earls of Salisbury, Westmoreland, *and* Warwick
Archbishop of Canterbury
Bishop of Ely
Earl of Cambridge
Lord Scroop
Sir Thomas Grey
Sir Thomas Erpingham, Gower, Fluellen, Macmorris, Jamy
Bates, Court, Williams
Pistol, Nym, Bardolph
Boy
A Herald

Charles the Sixth, King of France
Lewis, the Dauphin
Dukes of Burgundy, Orleans, *and* Bourbon
The Constable of France
Rambures *and* Grandpré
Montjoy
Governor of Harfleur
Ambassadors to the King of England
Isabel, Queen of France
Katherine, *Daughter to Charles and Isabel*
Alice
Hostess of a tavern in Eastcheap, formerly Mistress Quickly, *and now married to Pistol*
Lords, Ladies, Officers, French and English Soldiers, Citizens, Messengers, and Attendants
Chorus

The Story. Henry V, supported in his claim to the throne of France by the arguments of the Archbishop of Canterbury, and angered by the insulting gift of tennis balls from the French Dauphin (a gift meant to underline the fact of Henry's youthful follies), sets forth to invade France. Before he leaves he discovers the conspiracy of Grey, Scroop, and Cambridge and orders their execution. At the Boar's Head Tavern, Mistress Quickly describes the death of Falstaff, and his old cronies (Pistol, Nym, and Bardolph) thereupon enlist in the army. In France, before Harfleur, Henry urges on his men, "Once more into the breach, dear friends, once more; / Or close the wall up with our English dead" (III.i). He captures Harfleur and proceeds to face a much larger French army at Agincourt. The evening before the battle, the King, disguised as a common soldier, mingles in the ranks to test their confidence in him. Later in the evening he rejoices with his nobles that the English are outnumbered five to one. He would not wish for one man more who would lessen the honor that "We few, we happy few, we band of brothers" (IV.iii) will have in facing such a superior force. The English are victorious on the following day, and in the Treaty of Troyes, Henry wins the hand of the Princess Katherine and the promise of the French throne upon the death of the French king then reigning.

Henry VI. In *1, 2,* and *3 Henry VI,* the King of England. Historically, he succeeded to the English throne at the age of not quite nine months, under the protectorship of his uncle John, Duke of Bedford, the protectorship being exercised in England by Bedford's brother Humphrey, Duke of Gloucester, during Bedford's absence as regent in France. He married Margaret of Anjou in 1445; their only son Edward was born in 1453. Henry was a weak king, and the rule was always in the hands of others. Then York claimed the throne for himself and the nobles divided into factions and took arms; the Wars of the Roses began. Henry was restored as King in 1470, but in 1471 Queen Margaret's army was defeated at Tewkesbury, where Prince Edward was killed. Henry died in the Tower soon afterwards, probably murdered. In the play Richard of Gloucester is the murderer.

1 Henry VI. [Full title, **The First Part of King Henry the Sixth.**] A historical play attributed to Shakespeare, written between 1589 and 1591 and first acted on March 3, 1592 (if Henslowe's reference in his diary entry of that date to a performance of "Harry the VI" can be taken to apply to this play). It is now thought that the play is largely Shakespeare's own, although many critics have found possible evidence of collaboration, particularly with Greene or Nash. (For purposes of quick identification, this and the other two parts of *Henry VI* are often referred to by Shakespeare scholars as *1 Henry VI, 2 Henry VI,* and *3 Henry VI*, and the reader will find that this system of reference has been used throughout this book.) The three plays can hardly be viewed as a trilogy (and are thus contrasted to *1 Henry IV*, *2 Henry IV*, and *Henry V*), but there is a consistent theme: that punishment is being visited upon Henry VI as the heir in the third generation of the usurper, Henry IV, and this punishment is climaxed when Henry VI is overthrown in favor of Edward IV. Shakespeare's main sources were chronicles of English history, first Edward Hall's *The Union of the Two Noble and Illustre Famelies of Lancastre and Yorke* (1548), perhaps Richard Grafton's *A Chronicle at Large* (1569), which plagiarized from Hall, and also Holinshed's *Chronicles* (2nd ed., 1587) and Robert Fabyan's *The New Chronicles of England and France* (1516). He did not follow the sequence of events given in these chronicles, and he departed much more violently from historical fact than in his later histories. For instance, the first scene of the play shows Henry V's funeral, which took place in 1422, interrupted by news from France combining events from 1436 (the loss of Paris) and 1429 (the crowning of the Dauphin), and concludes with Bedford's departure to fight at Orleans (1428–29) and Winchester's confession that he intends to steal away the baby King Henry VI (1425?). In order to write a patriotic play, probably one intended to be topical at a time when English forces were fighting in France, Shakespeare had to distort history completely by turning the two-year truce that preceded Henry VI's marriage with Margaret of Anjou (V.v) into a triumphant peace with Charles the Dauphin swearing allegiance to Henry VI. Shakespeare used Holinshed most in Act I, but not very much afterwards, except for the Joan of Arc material. The presentation of Joan in the play is much more savage than in Holinshed or any other chronicle; the view of her as a fiery woman of loose morals and an inclination to black magic seems to have been Shakespeare's own invention. Hall's chronicle supplied the main material for Acts II to V, supplemented by Fabyan, Geoffrey of Monmouth's *Historia Regum Britanniae* and Hardyng's *Chronicle* for the account of Bedford carried to battle in a litter (III.ii), and a journal of the *Siege of Rouen* (1591) probably by Sir Thomas Coningsby. Some scenes, for instance the Temple Garden scene (II.iv), those concerning Talbot and his son (IV.vi–vii), and the wooing of Margaret by Suffolk (V.iii) have no basis in the chronicles. Shakespeare's powers of construction are already evident in his arrangement of the material so as to show two aspects of the history of the period: on the one hand the heroic tradition perpetuated by Salisbury, Talbot, and Bedford, and on the other the internal dissension that split the country in the rivalry of Gloucester and the bishop of Winchester, the hatred between the Yorkist and Lancastrian factions, and the machinations of Suffolk.

Dramatis Personae

King Henry the Sixth
Humphrey of Gloucester
Duke of Bedford
Thomas Beaufort, Duke of
    Exeter
Henry Beaufort, Bishop of
    Winchester
John Beaufort, Earl of Somerset
Richard Plantagenet,
    Duke of York
Earl of Warwick
Earl of Salisbury
Earl of Suffolk
Lord Talbot
John Talbot
Edmund Mortimer
Sir John Fastolf, Sir William
    Lucy, Sir William Glansdale,
    Sir Thomas Gargrave
Mayor of London
Woodvile
Vernon
Basset
Mortimer's Keepers
A Lawyer

Charles, Dauphin, *afterwards*
    King of France
Reignier, Duke of Anjou
Duke of Burgundy
Duke of Alençon
Bastard of Orleans
Governor of Paris
Master-Gunner of Orleans
    and his Son
General of the French Forces
    in Bordeaux
A French Sergeant
A Porter
An old Shepherd, Father to
    Joan la Pucelle
Margaret
Countess of Auvergne
Joan la Pucelle (*called* Joan of
    Arc)
Lords, Warders of the Tower
    Heralds, Officers, Soldiers,
    Messengers, and Attendants
    Fiends appearing to Joan la
    Pucelle

The Story. The play begins with the death of Henry V and the accession of the boy king Henry VI to the throne. With the strong hand of Henry V no longer controlling the realm, dissension immediately breaks out between the great nobles, particularly between Gloucester and Winchester, and between the factions of York and Lancaster (thus portending the Wars of the Roses). The English domain in France fares worst of all: Orléans is relieved and the English are driven steadily back toward the coast by the French under Joan of Arc (here portrayed, not unnaturally from the English point of view, as a whore and a witch). Talbot, who meets his death during the course of the play, is the only really powerful figure on the English side, and the play comes to an end as Henry prepares to enter upon marriage with Margaret of Anjou in an effort to bolster the crumbling fortunes of his realm.

2 Henry VI. [Full title, **The Second Part of King Henry**

the Sixth.] A historical play attributed to Shakespeare, written between 1589 and 1591 and published in 1594 in a bad quarto that is thought to be a memorial reconstruction made from the piece as performed. The date of first performance is not known, but the play appears in the folio of 1623. Its original title was *The First Part of the Contention betwixt the two Famous Houses of York and Lancaster* . . . As with *1 Henry VI* and *3 Henry VI*, controversy has existed as to the matter of Shakespeare's authorship, Marlowe, Greene, Kyd, Lodge, and even Nash being mentioned as the authors of greater or lesser portions of the work. The main source was either Hall's chronicle, *The Union of the Two Noble and Illustre Famelies of Lancastre and Yorke* (1548) or Grafton's plagiarized version of it, *A Chronicle at Large* (1569). Shakespeare supplemented this with some elements from Holinshed's *Chronicles* (2nd ed., 1587), and perhaps John Foxe's *Acts and Monuments of Martyrs* (1583 edition), for the false miracle of Simpcox (II.i), and an anonymous play, *The Life and Death of Jack Staw* (published 1593/4) for the Jack Cade scenes. Shakespeare departed from history much less than for *1 Henry VI*, although he did make some modifications to the outline of the events of eleven years from 1444 to 1455, as given in Hall and Grafton. The fall of Gloucester is accentuated when he is accused in the play (III.i) of crimes that were in fact ascribed to others and it was Shakespeare, not the chroniclers, who made Suffolk an accomplice in Gloucester's murder. Some details for Jack Cade's rebellion came from Holinshed's or Grafton's account of the Peasants' Revolt of 1381, and Shakespeare showed Cade's followers as much more unruly than in the chronicles. The character of York is both blackened and made more dynamic than historical fact would suggest, in order to give the play a developing center of interest and to prepare for York's part in *3 Henry VI* as the father of the diabolic Richard of Gloucester. York's sons Edward (the future Edward IV) and Richard (Richard III), already a "heap of wrath, foul indigested lump" (V.i), are introduced at the end of the play to look forward to the sequel, although in 1455 when the battle with which the play ends took place Richard was a child of three. Shakespeare structures his play so as to emphasize the disorder brought about by the selfish ambitions of powerful men like Suffolk, Beaufort the Bishop of Winchester, and York and the triumph of these people over good men like Duke Humphrey and the weak Henry VI.

Dramatis Personae

King Henry the Sixth	John Hume *and*
Humphrey, Duke of Gloucester	John Southwell

Cardinal Beaufort
Richard Plantagenet,
  Duke of York
Edward, Earl of March
Richard, Duke of Gloucester
Duke of Somerset
Duke of Suffolk
Duke of Buckingham
Lord Clifford
Young Clifford
Earl of Salisbury
Earl of Warwick
Lord Scales
Lord Say
Sir Humphrey Stafford
William Stafford
Sir John Stanley
Sir William Vaux
Matthew Goffe
Walter Whitmore
A Sea Captain, Master, and
  Master's-Mate
Two Gentlemen, Prisoners
  with Suffolk

Bolingbroke
Thomas Horner
Peter
Clerk of Chatham
Mayor of Saint Alban's
Simpcox
Jack Cade
George Bevis, John Holland,
  Dick the Butcher, Smith the
  Weaver, Michael, *etc.*
Alexander Iden
Two Murderers
Margaret, *Queen to*
  King Henry
Eleanor, Duchess of
  Gloucester
Margery Jourdain
Wife to Simpcox
Lords, Ladies, and
  Attendants; Herald; Peti-
  tioners, Aldermen, a Beadle,
  Sheriff, and Officers;
  Citizens, Prentices,
  Falconers, Guards, Soldiers,
  Messengers, etc.
A Spirit

The Story. The marriage of Henry to Margaret of Anjou has worsened rather than helped Henry's position in England; it has added to Henry's other troubles Gloucester's resentment at the cession of Maine and Anjou as the price of the marriage and added no equivalent stabilizing factor to his rule. Margaret, supported by York and Suffolk, intrigues against Gloucester, contriving first to have the Duchess of Gloucester arrested as a sorceress and finally securing the murder of Gloucester himself. Various other historical events, including the uprising under Jack Cade and the banishment of Suffolk, Margaret's lover, are also brought into the action of the play. At the end, the York-Lancaster dissension culminates in the initial struggle of the Wars of the Roses; the play ends with the death of Somerset in 1455 at the Battle of St. Albans.

3 Henry VI. [Full title, ***The Third Part of King Henry the Sixth.***] A historical play attributed to Shakespeare, written between 1589 and 1591 and published in 1595. It was first performed sometime before September, 1592, and appears in the folio of 1623. Its original title was *The true Tragedie of Richard*

Duke of York, and the Death of Good King Henry the Sixt . . .
(it was reprinted, under this title, with *2 Henry VI* under its
original title, in 1619 as the second half of a two-part work entitled *The Whole Contention betweene . . . Lancaster and Yorke
. . .*), and the amount of Shakespeare's contribution to it is as
conjectural as it is with *1 Henry VI* and *2 Henry VI*. Indeed, it
was long thought, on a basis of Greene's sharp remark in *A
Groatsworth of Wit* about an "upstart Crow beautified with our
feathers," that Shakespeare had stolen all or most of *2 Henry VI*
and *3 Henry VI*, but most authorities now believe that Greene
was here simply venting his spleen at Shakespeare as an upstart,
without intending a charge of plagiarism in addition. As in *2
Henry VI* the main source was Hall's chronicle, *The Union of
the Two Noble and Illustre Famelies of Lancastre and Yorke*
(1548), or less probably Grafton's plagiarized version of it, *A
Chronicle At Large* (1569). Shakespeare also used Holinshed's
Chronicles (2nd ed., 1587), especially for the savage scene of
York's death at the hands of Clifford and Queen Margaret
(I.ii), and probably Fabyan's *The New Chronicles of England and
France* (1516). He knew the *Mirrour for Magistrates* and may
have taken from it the idea that Richard of Gloucester murdered
Henry VI. As in *2 Henry VI* the events of several years (1460–
71) are compressed and rearranged, though Shakespeare shows
more respect for historical fact than in *1 Henry VI*. Acts I and II
deal with the battles of 1460–61 in which York and his young
son Rutland are slain by Clifford, and Clifford slain and his body
brutalized by York's other sons, Acts III and IV with Edward IV's
marriage to Lady Grey (1464), its political repercussions, and
the rival diplomacy of the different factions, and Act V with the
campaigns of 1471. One of Shakespeare's central aims was to
develop the character of Richard of Gloucester (b. 1452), who
was historically only a youth during the events of this play, and
to contrast him with the weak but saintly Henry VI; it seems
that *Richard III* was already in the playwright's mind. In fact,
Richard and his brother George (Clarence) were in France for a
period in 1461, and could not have been present at the battles
in Act II, Scenes 3–6, where Richard is called a "foul misshapen
stigmatic" by Queen Margaret and drawn into combat with
Clifford. Richard's development from the fiery youth who
avenges his father's death to the Machiavellian schemer who
plots against his brothers is Shakespeare's invention.

Dramatis Personae

King Henry the Sixth	Sir Hugh Mortimer
Edward, Prince of Wales,	Henry, Earl of Richmond
his Son	Earl Rivers

Lewis the Eleventh, King of France

Sir William Stanley
Sir John Montgomery
Sir John Somerville
Duke of Somerset
Duke of Exeter
Earl of Oxford
Earl of Northumberland
Earl of Westmoreland
Lord Clifford
Richard Plantagenet, Duke of York
Edward, Earl of March, afterwards King Edward the Fourth
Edmund, Earl of Rutland
George (Duke of Clarence)
Richard (Duke of Gloucester)
Duke of Norfolk
Marquess of Montague
Earl of Warwick
Earl of Pembroke
Lord Hastings
Lord Stafford
Sir John Mortimer

Tutor to Rutland
Mayor of York
Lieutenant of the Tower
A Nobleman
Two Keepers
A Huntsman
A Son that has killed his Father
A Father that has killed his Son
Queen Margaret
Lady Grey, *afterwards Queen to Edward the Fourth*
Bona
Soldiers, and other Attendants on King Henry and King Edward, Messengers, Watchmen.

The Story. Henry yields to York the succession to the throne, whereupon Queen Margaret, furious that her son should be disinherited, seeks (with the help of Clifford) to resolve the matter on the field of battle. At Wakefield, she is victorious; York himself is captured and subsequently killed. But York's sons Edward (who is to rule England as Edward IV) and Richard (who is also to rule England, as Richard III) vanquish Margaret and the Lancastrians at Towton, capturing Henry himself (now only a figurehead in the affairs of the kingdom) and making possible the crowning of Edward as king. However, the matter is not yet settled; dissension within the Yorkist ranks makes further fighting inevitable, and the throne remains in dispute until the Lancastrian faction is finally defeated at Tewkesbury. Margaret's son is slain, and Richard ruthlessly murders Edward VI.

Henry VII. See under **Richmond, Henry Tudor, Earl of.**
Henry VIII. King of England (1509–47); second and only surviving son of Henry VII and Elizabeth of York. After the death of his older brother Arthur, he became (1503) Prince of Wales. He succeeded his father on April 22, 1509, and on June 3 married his betrothed, Catherine of Aragon, widow of his brother. Henry's marriage had required a papal dispensation, one about

which both the pope and the archbishop of Canterbury had had
doubts at the time. When, in the course of years, Catherine had
a long series of miscarriages, there was talk, in 1514, of a dis-
solution of the marriage; but the accession of Francis I in
France brought closer ties with Spain and the matter was
dropped. Catherine bore a daughter in 1516, the future queen
Mary I, but again the miscarriages began. Henry, knowing he
was not at fault, earnestly desired a son; were he to die leaving
only a daughter, the civil strife that had plagued England in the
Wars of the Roses in his father's time might again break out. He
was a firm adherent of the Church of Rome, but his position
as head of the English nation was paramount in his thoughts
and in 1527 be began proceedings for a divorce from the forty-
two-year-old Catherine, alleging the invalidity, despite the papal
dispensation, of the marriage with a deceased brother's wife.
How large a part Henry's desire for Anne Boleyn played in his
decision to divorce Catherine is conjectural; it is certain that unless they married their children could not inherit the throne and
that she conducted the affair very cleverly. Pope Clement VII
temporized. He appointed (1528) a commission to sit in England,
composed of Wolsey, appointed papal legate for the purpose,
and Lorenzo Campeggio, bishop of Salisbury, the regular papal
legate, to hear and decide on the case; but in 1529, Campeggio
having delayed a decision on papal orders, the case was called to
Rome for hearing. Wolsey was very shortly dismissed and
Cranmer was put in charge of the negotiations. Cranmer held
that the marriage was invalid and that the Pope had been incompetent to grant a dispensation. Anne Boleyn was carrying
Henry's child, and the marriage had to be arranged quickly.
Cranmer secretly performed the ceremony on Jan. 25, 1533, and
on May 23, as archbishop of Canterbury since March, declared
the marriage with Catherine void and that with Anne Boleyn
valid (May 28, 1533). Elizabeth, the future queen, born on Sept.
7, 1533, was thus legitimatized. Henry's marriage to Anne
Boleyn ended on May 19, 1536, when she was executed for
adultery. The next day he was married for the third time, to
Jane Seymour. Elizabeth, daughter of Anne Boleyn, was declared illegitimate. Henry had earlier possessed as one of his
mistresses Mary, Anne's sister, and this was believed to attaint
Elizabeth. Jane Seymour gave birth to the future Edward VI
and then died on Oct. 24, 1537. Henry's fourth wife (Jan. 6,
1540) was Anne of Cleves; their divorce took place on June 24,
1540. On August 8, 1540, the day Cromwell was executed for
being too zealous a Protestant, Henry married Catherine Howard. Catherine Howard was beheaded in less than two years
(Feb. 12, 1452) for adultery, apparently a more justifiable

charge than the one against Anne Boleyn. Henry's sixth wife
was Catherine Parr; they were married on July 12, 1543, and she
survived him. By these six marriages, Henry had three children:
Mary, daughter of Catherine of Aragon, who reigned as Mary I;
Elizabeth, the daughter of Anne Boleyn; Edward VI, the son of
Jane Seymour, who was Henry's immediate successor. Henry's
advisors, besides the great Wolsey, More, Cranmer, and Cromwell, included his early mentors William Warham, archbishop of
Canterbury, who crowned Henry king, Richard Foxe, bishop of
Winchester, and Thomas Howard, Earl of Surrey. Wolsey, deprived of his magnificence, died in disgrace. More was beheaded
for his adherence to the original succession, and Cromwell for
treason. Cranmer alone of the king's principal aides outlived
him, to die at the stake in 1556. Henry's intention throughout
his reign was to strengthen his country and to strengthen the
position of the monarch; it was his boast that he did nothing
unconstitutional, but often the constitutionality of his acts depended on laws enacted after the acts they legitimized.

Henry VIII. [Full title, *The Famous History of the Life of
King Henry the Eighth.*] A historical play, ascribed to Shakespeare, who has been thought to have written only parts of the
play (I.i, ii; II.iii, iv; III.ii. 1–203; V.i) in collaboration with
another writer, possibly John Fletcher Many critics now concede
the play to be wholly by Shakespeare. It was first acted on June
29, 1613 (an exact date is possible, because we know that cannon
fired during the performance started the fire that burned the
Globe theatre to the ground on that day), and published in the
folio of 1623. The main source was Holinshed's *Chronicles*
(2nd ed., 1587), but Shakespeare also relied heavily on an earlier play about Henry VIII, Samuel Rowley's *When You See Me
You Know Me*, published in 1605 and reprinted in 1613. Rowley
also used Holinshed, so that certain similarities between his play
and Shakespeare's were almost inevitable, but there is plenty of
evidence to show that Shakespeare undoubtedly did use his play.
In both plays King Henry is similarly presented, leaning on the
shoulder of one of his intimates as he walks in his gallery,
growing angry when interrupted in his privacy, influenced by
the persuasive rhetoric of Wolsey; Wolsey's downfall is accounted for in similar terms; the announcement of Elizabeth's
birth, the rewarding of the person who brings the news, and
the allusion to the baby's resemblance to her father in Shakespeare's play resemble the same incidents in Rowley's. But
Shakespeare omits Rowley's scenes with the King's fools and
also the account of the King's night visit in disguise to the city
when he becomes involved in a brawl and is put in prison.
Shakespeare presents a king who is by no means without his

weak and sensual side but nonetheless has strength and dignity. Rowley's play is not much concerned with Wolsey's fall, and he does not deal with the divorce from Katherine or the marriage to Anne Boleyn; Shakespeare goes to Holinshed for these. Shakespeare concentrates the events of twenty years into his play, often anticipating time, as when he places Henry's meeting with Anne before Buckingham's condemnation, when in fact Buckingham was executed in 1521 and Henry did not meet Anne until 1526 or 1527, and he makes Katherine die before Elizabeth was born whereas she actually died three years afterward. He made a little use of Hall's *The Union of the Two Noble and Illustre Famelies of Lancastre and Yorke* (1548), for instance, for Suffolk's announcement that Cardinal Campeius has stolen away to Rome (III.ii), and also of John Speed's *History of Great Britain* (1611) for some of the images in Wolsey's speeches (III.ii), and Foxe's *Actes and Monuments of Martyrs* (1583 edition) for the intrigues of Gardiner against Cranmer (V.i). *Henry VIII* forms an appropriate finale to Shakespeare's presentation of English history, "ritualistically expanding through conflict into grace and happy augury" (B. Bullough, *Narrative and Dramatic Sources of Shakespeare*, 1962, IV, 450). An actor, John Lowin, was supposed to have been instructed by Shakespeare himself in the role of King Henry. Betterton acted it in 1664 and it was produced thereafter with much attention to the pageant element. It is unlike any of the other Shakespeare historical plays, being more like the medieval morality tales about the falls of famous men. The alternative name "All Is True" (first mentioned in 1613, from the repeated insistence in the Prologue on the truth of the events to be recounted) was unquestionably applied to the play at an early date, and has been accepted by the late George L. Kittredge and other eminent Shakespearians as historically authentic; however, neither Kittredge nor any other scholar now uses it as a variant name for the play.

Dramatis Personae

King Henry the Eighth	Griffith
Cardinal Wolsey	*Three Gentlemen*
Cardinal Campeius	*Garter King-at-Arms*
Capucius	Doctor Butts
Cranmer	*Surveyor to the Duke of Buckingham*
Duke of Norfolk	Brandon
Duke of Suffolk	*Door-keeper of the Council-chamber*
Duke of Buckingham	*Porter, and his Man*
Earl of Surrey	*Page to Gardiner*
Lord Chamberlain	*A Crier*
Lord Chancellor	Queen Katherine

Gardiner
Bishop of Lincoln
Lord Abergavenny
Lord Sandys
Sir Henry Guildford
Sir Thomas Lovell
Sir Anthony Denny
Sir Nicholas Vaux
Secretaries to Wolsey
Cromwell

Anne Bullen
An old Lady
Patience
Several Lords and Ladies in the
Dumb-shows; Women attending
upon the Queen; Scribes.
Officers, Guards, and other
Attendants
Spirits

The Story. Buckingham, about to expose the ambitious Cardinal Wolsey to the King, is arrested for high treason at the instigation of Wolsey. Queen Katherine (in history, Catherine of Aragon, mother of Queen Mary) pleads with Henry to remove certain oppressive taxes and to pardon Buckingham. The first request the King grants, but the trial and execution of Buckingham are carried out. Meanwhile, the King has met Anne Bullen (in history, Anne Boleyn, mother of Queen Elizabeth) at a party given by Wolsey and has fallen in love with her. He hopes to get a divorce from Katherine on the grounds that his marriage was not permissible for reasons of near relationship, Katherine being his brothers' widow (in the eyes of the Elizabethans, this made the match almost incestuous). Wolsey halts proceedings on the divorce because he realizes that if they are completed Henry will marry Anne, and he opposes her on religious grounds. The King discovers the duplicity of Wolsey, and the Cardinal retires. Cranmer, Archbishop of Canterbury, annuls the marriage to Katherine, who shortly dies of a broken heart. Henry secretly marries Anne, but Cranmer, accused of heresy, is brought to trial; however, the King gives him a ring for protection, and later honors him by asking him to be the godfather of Elizabeth. The christening is the final scene of the play.

Henry, Prince.   In *King John*, the son of John. After John's death the lords swear loyalty to him (as Henry III).

Henry, Prince of Wales.   See **Henry V.**

Henry Bolingbroke.   See **Bolingbroke, Henry.**

Henry Percy.   See **Hotspur.**

Henslowe, Philip.   d. 1616. An English theatre manager. He was a servant of the bailiff of Viscount Montague, whose town house was in Southwark (now part of London). Henslowe took care of the property there, and gradually made money and bought property. He owned the Boar's Head and other inns. In 1585 he bought land on the Bankside, and in 1591 built the Rose theatre there. In 1592 he began to keep the accounts of his theatrical ventures in his Diary. In it he gives the dates of new plays, the amounts he paid for them or advanced to the usually impecunious playwrights, and similar material of great value to students of the drama. In 1600 he built, with Edward Alleyn, his son-in-law, the Fortune theatre. The *Diary* and other papers were lost in a mass of printed material at Dulwich College until 1790, when Edmund Malone recovered them for his variorum edition of Shakespeare. The *Diary*, as edited by W.W. Greg, is a record of the years 1592–1603, in two sections: one, companies performing at the Rose, names of plays, and Henslowe's receipts as theatre owner for performances; and two, after 1597, a listing of his advances to the Lord Admiral's Men for plays, costumes, properties, and licensing fees, and to the actors themselves.

Herbert, Sir Walter. In *Richard III*, a supporter of Richmond.

Herbert, William. [Title, **3rd Earl of Pembroke.**] b. at Wilton, Wiltshire, England, April 8, 1580; d. at London, April 10, 1630. An English statesman and patron of poets. He was educated privately by Samuel Daniel, author of the *Delia* sonnets, and later at New College, Oxford. Soon after he became (1601) Lord Herbert of Pembroke, he was disgraced, imprisoned, and exiled from Court because of his affair with Mary Fitton, maid of honor to Elizabeth. He was the patron of Jonson, Massinger, Inigo Jones the architect, and William Browne, author of *Britannia's Pastorals*. He was chancellor (1617–30) of Oxford University, Pembroke College (formerly Broadgates Hall) being renamed (1624) in his honor. He has been suggested by several scholars as the "Mr. W.H." celebrated by Shakespeare in the earlier sonnets. To him and his brother Philip, Heming and Condell dedicated one of the most famous books in English literature, the First Folio (1623) of Shakespeare; it is this dedication and his patronage of poets and dramatists that are his chief claims to fame. He was the author of *Poems* (1660).

Hereford, Duke of. See under ***Bolingbroke, Henry.***

Hermia. In *A Midsummer Night's Dream*, an Athenian lady, the daughter of Egeus, in love with Lysander. She differs from Helena in being short and quick-tempered.

Hermione. In *The Winter's Tale*, the Queen of Sicilia, wife of the jealous Leontes. She is the Bellaria of Greene's *Pandosto*, the story from which *The Winter's Tale* was taken.

Hero. In *Much Ado About Nothing*, the daughter of Leonato, and friend and cousin of Beatrice. When denounced by Claudio at the church as unchaste, she faints, and on Friar Francis's advice it is announced she is dead. When Claudio repents his false accusation of her, she is brought to him veiled, and the two are reconciled.

Heywood, Thomas. b. in Lincolnshire, England, c1575; d. 1641. An English dramatist and miscellaneous writer. He speaks of his residence at Cambridge in his *Apology for Actors,* but there is no record of him there. He was an actor, a member of the Lord Admiral's, Earl of Southampton's, Earl of Derby's, Earl of Worcester's, and the Queen's companies. After the death of the queen (1603) he went back to the Earl of Worcester's company. He was a prolific writer. Among his plays are *The Four Prentices of London* (produced c1600; printed 1615), *Edward IV* (c1599; in 2 parts), *If You Know not Me, You Know Nobody; or, The Troubles of Queene Elizabeth* (1605–06; in 2 parts), *The Royal King and the Loyall Subject* (printed 1637; acted much earlier), *A Woman Killed with Kindness* (acted 1603; printed 1607), *The Golden Age* (1611), *The Silver Age* (1612–13), *The Brazen Age* (1612–13), *The Iron Age* (1632; in 2 parts), *A Fair Maid of the West, or A Girl Worth Gold* (acted 1617; printed 1631), *The English Traveller* (printed 1633), *Love's Mistress, or The Queen's Masque* (1636), *The Wise Woman of Hogsden* (c1604; printed 1638), *Fortune by Land and Sea* (with William Rowley, c1607; printed 1655), *The Rape of Lucrece* (c1607), *A Challenge for Beauty* (c1635), and *A Maidenhead Well Lost* (c1633). He wrote the lord mayor's pageants for many years. Among his miscellaneous works are selections from Lucian, Ovid, and others; *Troia Britannica,* a long heroic poem (1609); *An Apology for Actors* (1612; reprinted with alterations by William Cartwright in 1658, with the title *The Actors' Vindication*); *England's Elizabeth* (1631); and *The Hierarchy of the Blessed Angels,* a long didactic poem (1635).

Hippolyta. In *A Midsummer Night's Dream,* the Queen of the Amazons, betrothed to Theseus.

Hippolyta. In *The Two Noble Kinsmen,* the wife of Theseus and sister of the heroine, Emilia. She begs Theseus to spare Palamon and Arcite.

Hobbididence. In *King Lear,* a fiend ("prince of dumbness") mentioned by Edgar (IV.i).

Holland, John. In *2 Henry VI,* a follower of Jack Cade.

Holofernes. In *Love's Labour's Lost,* a pedantic schoolmaster who takes the part of Judas Maccabaeus in the masque of the Nine Worthies.

honorificabilitudinitatibus. A word in *Love's Labour's Lost* (V.i) thought by some to be an anagram referring to Francis Bacon.

Hope, the. A playhouse built for Philip Henslowe on the Bankside, Southwark, London, in 1613. Ben Jonson's *Bartholomew Fair* was produced on the occasion of its opening in October, 1614. It also doubled as a pit for the baiting of bears and bulls. It was a cylindrical building near the Globe and was demolished in 1656.

Horatio. In *Hamlet,* a close friend and confidant of Hamlet, charged by Hamlet at the end of the play to "report me and my cause aright / To the unsatisfied" (V.ii).

Horner, Thomas. In *2 Henry VI,* an armorer accused of treasonous sayings by his apprentice. In a combat with the apprentice, Peter Thump, he is mortally wounded and confesses his treason.

Hortensio. In *The Taming of the Shrew,* a suitor of Bianca. He persuades Petruchio to marry Katherina, Bianca's older sister, so that he may marry Bianca, but she marries Lucentio, and he marries a widow instead.

Hortensius. In *Timon of Athens,* a servant.

Host. In *Two Gentlemen of Verona,* the hospitable character who takes Julia in search of Proteus (IV.ii).

Host (of the Garter Inn). In *The Merry Wives of Windsor,* an innkeeper who participates in the schemes of his guests. He urges Dr. Caius to fight with Evans, and when the two realize that they have been fooled they steal his horses. He helps Fenton court Anne Page.

Hotspur. In *Richard II* and *1 Henry IV,* Sir Henry (or Harry) Percy, son of Northumberland. He leads the northern rebellion against Henry IV and is killed at Shrewsbury. His romantic pursuit of honor and his glorification of fighting make him an easy victim of the intrigues of his unscrupulous relatives, the earls of Northumberland and Worcester. Shakespeare makes him the same age as Prince Hal (the historical Hotspur was twenty years Hal's senior) to sharpen the contrast between the man who thinks "it were an easy leap / To pluck bright honor from the pale-faced moon" (*1 Henry IV,* I.iii) and Prince Hal, who has not yet shown his mettle.

Hubert de Burgh. In *King John,* the King's chamberlain. Ordered to kill John's young nephew, Hubert is softened by Arthur's entreaties, lets him live unharmed, and reports to the King that Arthur is dead. When Arthur is discovered dead (he is accidentally killed while trying to escape), Hubert is suspected of responsibility.

Hume, John. In *2 Henry VI,* a priest bribed to undertake witchcraft on behalf of the Duchess of Gloucester.

Humphrey. In *3 Henry VI,* one of the keepers. Sinklo is the other.

Hymen. The classical god of marriage. He appears as a character in *As You Like It* and in *The Two Noble Kinsmen.*

Iachimo.   In *Cymbeline*, a worldly and affected Roman courtier who deceives Posthumus in order to win a wager that the latter's wife, Imogen, is unchaste.

Iago.   In *Othello*, the malignant villain, filled with jealousy of Othello's rank and power. His chief motive is the hatred of goodness and the desire to destroy happiness whenever he sees it. He works on Othello by undermining his self-confidence and persuading him of Desdemona's infidelity with Cassio. A cynical and worldly man, he manages to make the noble and idealistic Othello come to see the world from his point of view. His villainy is finally revealed by his wife, but only after Desdemona's death.

Iden, Alexander.   In *2 Henry VI*, the slayer of Jack Cade.

Ides of March.   In *Julius Caesar*, the fifteenth of March, the day on which Caesar is murdered. According to the Roman calendar the Ides occurred on the fifteenth of March, May, July, and October, and on the thirteenth of the other months.

Illyria, Duke of.   See **Orsino.**

Imogen.   In *Cymbeline*, the daughter of Cymbeline, and wife of Posthumus. She is a chaste and faithful wife who continues to love her husband despite his rejection of her. As a result of Iachimo's deceptions, she undergoes much suffering for Posthumus' sake, but they are finally reunited.

Inns of Court.   Legal societies at London that have the exclusive privilege of calling candidates to the bar, and maintain instruction and examination for that purpose; also, the precincts or premises occupied by these societies respectively. They are the Inner Temple, Middle Temple, Lincoln's Inn, and Gray's Inn. The first two originally belonged to Knights Templars (whence the name Temple). These inns had their origin about the end of the thirteenth century.

Iras.   In *Antony and Cleopatra*, one of the two female attendants (the other being Charmian) who die with Cleopatra.

Iris.   In *The Tempest*, a character in the masque celebrating the betrothal of Ferdinand and Miranda.

Isabel. In *Henry V*, the Queen of Charles VI of France. She is present at the meeting of the two kings (V.ii).

Isabella. In *Measure for Measure*, the sister of Claudio, and object of the passion of Angelo (but married in the end to Vincentio, the Duke). Her status as a novice nun makes it impossible for her to agree to Angelo's proposal that she become his mistress in order to save her brother's life, but it is nonetheless hard not to see something cold and unfeeling in her attitudes. Like Angelo, she is a character quite ignorant of the working of human emotion, and this is something she begins to learn in the play.

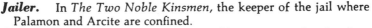

J

Jailer. In *The Two Noble Kinsmen*, the keeper of the jail where Palamon and Arcite are confined.

Jailer's Daughter. In *The Two Noble Kinsmen*, the daughter of the Jailer. She loves Palamon, whom she frees.

James I. [Also, **James VI** (of *Scotland*).] b. in Edinburgh Castle, June 19, 1566; d. March 27, 1625. King of England, Scotland, and Ireland (1603–25); son of Lord Darnley and Mary, Queen of Scots. He became king of Scotland as James VI on July 24, 1567, on the abdication of his mother; and by virtue of his descent, through both his father and his mother, from Margaret Tudor, daughter of Henry VII, succeeded to the English throne when Elizabeth died without issue on March 24, 1603. He was crowned king of England (and Ireland) on July 25, 1603. He was a learned but pedantic, weak, and incapable monarch, whence he was aptly characterized by the Duc de Sully as the "wisest fool in Europe." In domestic politics he sought to assert the theory of the divine right of kingship and of episcopacy; in his foreign relations he strove to maintain peace at all hazards, even to the prejudice of his natural allies, the Protestant powers on the Continent.

Jamy. In *Henry V*, a Scottish captain. He does not appear in the quarto of 1600, possibly through fear of offending the feelings of James VI of Scotland.

Jaquenetta. In *Love's Labour's Lost*, a country maid with whom Costard and Armado are in love.

Jaques. In *As You Like It*, a philosophical companion of the exiled duke. He is usually spoken of as "the melancholy Jaques" and serves as a kind of cynical commentator upon the extravagances of the others. At the end of the play he is the only character who does not desert the forest for the court.

Jaques. [Also, **Jaques de Boys** (or **de Bois**).] In *As You Like It*, an elder brother of Orlando and second son of Sir Rowland de Boys.

Jessica. In *The Merchant of Venice*, the daughter of Shylock. She elopes with Lorenzo, taking her father's jewels and money.

Joan of Arc. [In the Dramatis Personae, **Joan la Pucelle**; also, **La Pucelle**.] In *1 Henry VI*, a leading character. She convinces the Dauphin of her marvelous powers, raises the siege of Orleans, persuades Burgundy to desert the English cause, and finally conjures up fiends to whom she offers herself in exchange for French victory. When captured by the English, she claims to be royal in blood and a virgin, but later states that she is with child, when she is sentenced to burning. Unlike the heroic conception of her that Schiller popularized, Shakespeare, following the Elizabethan viewpoint, portrays her as a coarse instrument of the devil and makes even the French somewhat dubious of her divine attributes.

Jockey of Norfolk. In *Richard III*, the name by which the Duke of Norfolk is addressed in a warning note he receives before Bosworth:

> Jockey of Norfolk, be not so bold,
> For Dickon thy master is bought and sold (V.iii).

John, Don. In *Much Ado About Nothing*, the bastard brother of Don Pedro. It is he who causes Claudio to suspect Hero's chastity. In his malicious determination to do all the evil he can he is like an early study for Iago.

John, Friar. In *Romeo and Juliet*, a Franciscan friar sent by Friar Laurence to tell Romeo about Juliet's feigned death. He is prevented from going by constables who think he may be infected with the plague. Romeo does not find out, therefore, that Juliet is merely sleeping and, upon arriving at the Capulets' tomb, believes her to be dead.

John of Gaunt, Duke of Lancaster. In *Richard II*, the father of Bolingbroke and uncle of the King. On his deathbed he utters the well-known speech beginning "This royal throne of Kings, this sceptr'd isle" and warns Richard of the result of his careless practices (II.i).

John, King. The chief character of *King John.* Historically he was the youngest son of Henry II and seized the throne on the death of Richard I. It is clear that Shakespeare does not regard his title as certain, but he does represent him as a champion of English unity against the Papacy and the French.

Jones, Inigo. b. at London, July 15, 1573; d. there, June 21, 1652. An English architect. He went to Italy to study painting and architecture and resided there many years, especially at Venice, whence he was called (1604) to Denmark by King Christian IV. He returned to England in 1605. As court architect to the Queen, and, after her death, to James I and Charles I, he designed the sets and staging for the court masques by Jonson, Shirley, Carew, and other writers of the time. In 1620 he was appointed commissioner of repairs of Saint Paul's, which, however, were not commenced before 1631. In 1643 he was thrown out of his office, and in 1646 fined 345 pounds for being a royal favorite and a Roman Catholic, having been taken in arms at the capture of Basing House. He is supposed to have died of grief, misfortune, and old age at old Somerset House on the Strand. He sat twice for Vandyck, and a portrait by this master was sent with the Houghton collection to St. Petersburg. Among his works are the banqueting hall in Whitehall (1619–22), the Covent Garden Piazza, the famous gateway of St. Mary's, Oxford (1632), the equally famous portico of old Saint Paul's and the reconstruction of that church (1631–41), and other architectural works. He introduced to England the classical style of Palladio, which, superseding the Jacobean, developed into the Georgian style of the next century.

Jonson, Ben. b. at Westminster (now part of London), c1573; d. Aug. 6, 1637. An English actor, poet, dramatist, and essayist. His father, whom he never knew, was a minister, and his stepfather, whose trade he followed for a short time (thoroughly detesting it), was a bricklayer. He studied at Westminster School and attended Cambridge University, but did not take a degree, although both Cambridge and Oxford were later happy to award him an honorary M.A. He fought in Flanders under Sir Francis Vere and Prince Maurice of Nassau. He seems to have been back at London about 1592 and to have begun his connection with the theatre about 1595. Various entries in Henslowe's *Diary* indicate that Jonson worked for him in 1597. The next year was one of the most important in his career. In 1598 he wrote one of his best comedies, *Every Man in His Humour,* in which Shakespeare acted; he was cited in the famous *Palladis Tamia: Wits Treasury* of Francis Meres as "one of the best for tragedy" (a viewpoint that is no longer held); and he fought a duel with, and killed, a fellow actor, Gabriel Spenser, for which he was

imprisoned and was saved from hanging only by pleading benefit of clergy. Some of his best plays are *Every Man Out of His
Humor* (1599), *Volpone, or the Fox* (1606), *Epicoene, or the
Silent Woman* (1609), *The Alchemist* (1610), considered by many
to be his masterpiece, and *Bartholomew Fair* (1614). Other plays,
all comedies, are *Cynthia's Revels* (1600) and *The Poetaster*
(1601,) in both of which he attacks rival dramatists, *The Devil is
an Ass* (1616), *The Staple of News* (1625), *The New Inn* (1629),
a failure, *The Magnetic Lady* (1632), and *A Tale of a Tub*
(1633), a title later used by Swift. *Sejanus* (1603) and *Catiline*
(1611) are Roman tragedies, superior in scholarship and historical accuracy, but in no other respect, to the Roman plays of
Shakespeare. *The Hue and Cry After Cupid* (1608; unfinished),
The Masque of Queens (1609), and *Oberon* (1611) are court
masques, entertainments combining music, dancing, singing,
with a thin plot. He wrote at least thirty of these masques.
Timber, or Discoveries Made upon Men and Matter (published
1640) is an example of his prose. As a poet he is best remembered for the lovely "Drink to me only with thine eyes" (*To
Celia*), for his tribute to Shakespeare, *To the Memory of My
Beloved Master, Mr. William Shakespeare, and What He Hath
Left Us* (written for and published in the 1623 Folio), for the
lines *To the Reader* (also in the First Folio), *Hymn to Diana*, *The
Triumph of Charis*, the pathetic *Epitaph on Salathiel Pavy*, and
for some short pieces taken from his comedies. His classical
knowledge is evidenced not only through his observance of the
Unities in his plays, but also by his verse translation of Horace's
Art of Poetry. As a literary dictator, in the manner of Dryden,
Pope, and Samuel Johnson, his word was law at the Mermaid, the
Dog, the Sun, the Triple Tun, the Devil, and other inns, where
his disciples, "the sons o' Ben," gathered. With Marlowe and
Shakespeare he ranks as one of the three great Elizabethan
dramatists. His powers as a conversationalist have been recorded in the *Conversations* of William Drummond of Haw-
thornden, whose work (published 1832) does in a small way
for him what Boswell did for Samuel Johnson. Some of his
comedies are still occasionally produced, but he does not hold
the modern stage as well as does Shakespeare. He himself best
summed up the difference between himself and his rival in his
famous line, "He was not of an age, but for all time!" Jonson
is buried in Westminster Abbey, where his grave is marked by
the inscription, "O Rare Ben Jonson."

Jourdain, Margery. In *2 Henry VI*, a witch who summons a
spirit for the Duchess of Gloucester (I.iv).

Julia. In *Two Gentlemen of Verona*, the young woman who
loves Proteus.

Juliet.   In *Measure for Measure,* Claudio's betrothed. Claudio is
sentenced to death when, through her pregnancy, it becomes
known that he has seduced her. Later, she and Claudio are
married.

Juliet.   The heroine of *Romeo and Juliet.* She is the daughter of
Capulet and loves Romeo, the heir of the rival family of Montague. Beginning as a demure young girl who listens to the advice of her mother, she becomes a woman of courage and action,
even willing to die for her husband. In the famous balcony
scene she carefully questions the circumstances of Romeo's love
and wittily refuses his vows. When she next appears, the girlish
reserve has gone and she impetuously asks for news of Romeo.
Very simply she says that her wealth of love is so great, she
cannot sum up half. As her forebodings of Romeo's doom are
borne out by events, her mind dwells on the terrors of the
grave, questioning the action she must take, just as she questioned Romeo's love. Yet when the thought of Romeo enters her
mind, she acts quickly in taking the sleeping potion, and her
actions are even more decisive when she finds Romeo dead beside her. The poison that she had feared becomes the kiss of
Romeo's poisoned lips, and symbolically death is turned into an
act of love.

Julius Caesar.   [Full title, **The Tragedy of Julius Caesar.**]
A historical tragedy by Shakespeare, written and produced
c1599 (a performance date of Sept. 21, 1599, at the Globe
theatre has been tentatively accepted). It was printed in the
folio of 1623. Shakespeare's main source was North's translation
of the lives of Marcus Brutus, Julius Caesar, and Marcus Antonius from Plutarch's *Lives of the Noble Grecians and Romans.*
It is possible that the structure of *Julius Caesar* may have been
influenced by a lost play on the same subject, since it seems
that one may have been in existence in the early 1590's, but the
many verbal echoes of North's *Plutarch* make it clear that Shakespeare went directly to this source. At some points he followed
North very closely, as for instance in the scenes of Artemidorus
preparing his petition (II.iii), the mob falling on Cinna the poet
(III.iii), and especially that of Brutus with Portia (II.i), but elsewhere he modified his source considerably. Caesar's Triumph
for his victory over Pompey in fact took place four months before the feast of the Lupercal, but in Act I, Scenes 1 and 2,
Shakespeare puts them on the same day, together with the dis-
robing of Caesar's images by the tribunes, which took place
still later. For dramatic effect, Shakespeare has the murder of
Caesar followed on the same day by Antony's incitement of the
mob, whereas in fact Antony's reading of the will took place a
few days later, after a meeting of the senate. Antony's actual

speeches at this crucial point in the play are Shakespeare's invention. Shakespeare also telescopes two battles at Philippi into a single encounter. The major figures were characterized in some detail by Plutarch, and Shakespeare makes much use of him; but he did make important changes. Shakespeare's Caesar is more noble than his original, and no references are made to his insults to the senate or his affair with Cleopatra; Shakespeare emphasizes his physical weakness. Plutarch's Brutus had more motivation for the assassination, since Caesar had shown clear signs of imperalist ambition; Shakespeare emphasizes Brutus's lack of judgment and his self-righteousness, as well as the idealism that is in Plutarch. Casca's character is mainly Shakespeare's invention. Several details of the play may have come from other sources. Appian's *Anncient Historie and exquisite Chronicle of The Romane Warres*, of which a translation was published in 1578, emphasized Antony's subtlety and command of rhetoric. Two plays, the anonymous *Caesar's Revenge*, published in 1607 but written earlier, and Kyd's *Cornelia*, a translation of the Senecan play by Garnier, have also been suggested as sources. The treatment of the revenge theme in *Caesar's Revenge* may have influenced Shakespeare, especially in Antony's prophecy of civil war (III.i); Kyd's *Cornelia* also emphasized the horrors of civil war.

Dramatis Personae

Julius Caesar	Flavius *and* Marullus, Tribunes
Octavius Caesar, *Triumvir*	Artemidorus, a Sophist of Cnidos
Mark Antony, *Triumvir*	*A Soothsayer*
M. Aemilius Lepidus, *Triumvir*	Cinna, *a Poet. Another Poet*
Cicero, *Senator*	Lucilius, Titinius, Messala,
Publius, *Senator*	Young Cato, Volumnius
Popilius Lena, *Senator*	Varro, Clitus, Claudius, Strato,
Marcus Brutus, *Conspirator*	Lucius, Dardanius, *Brutus's*
Cassius, *Conspirator*	Servants
Casca, *Conspirator*	Pindarus, *Cassius's Servant*
Trebonius, *Conspirator*	Calphurnia, *Wife to Caesar*
Ligarius, *Conspirator*	Portia, *Wife of Brutus*
Decius Brutus, *Conspirator*	Senators, Citizens, Guards,
Metellus Cimber, *Conspirator*	Attendants.
Cinna, *Conspirator*	

The Story.   Caesar's triumphal return to Rome (of which he has already been made dictator), after a series of military victories in Spain, brings to a climax the fear held by a faction of Roman leaders that the traditional freedoms of the republic may perish through Caesar's overweening ambition, and a plot to assassinate him begins to take shape. Cassius (the chief conspi-

rator, motivated by jealousy fully as much as by a love of freedom), Casca, Cinna, and others persuade Caesar's close friend
Marcus Brutus (a somewhat ambiguous figure; initially a very
strong character, motivated by lofty idealism, he later succumbs
almost to petulance) to join their faction, and that night at
Brutus's house they complete their plans. The night is disturbed,
stormy, and full of portents of disaster. Caesar, despite both the
warning from a soothsayer that he should beware the Ides of
March and the ominous dream of his wife Calphurnia, goes to
the Senate where, as planned by the conspirators, he is stabbed
to death. Mark Antony, in a clever and unscrupulous speech at
Caesar's funeral, arouses the crowd to fury at the assassination.
He then joins Octavius and Lepidus to form a governing triumvirate. The conspirators leave Rome and take refuge at Sardis.
There, as Antony's army approaches, Cassius and Brutus quarrel, but they are reconciled when Brutus tells Cassius of the
suicide of his (Brutus's) wife Portia (in this very moving scene
Cassius reveals a depth of sympathetic understanding hardly
consistent with the stereotype of cold villainy that tradition has
attached to him). In an unwise military move, the conspirators
meet Antony's army on the plains of Philippi and are there
defeated. Cassius and Brutus both die honorably.

Junius Brutus.   See **Brutus, Junius.**

Juno.   In *The Tempest*, a character appearing in the masque
celebrating the betrothal of Ferdinand and Miranda.

Jupiter.   In *Cymbeline*, an apparition that appears to Posthumus
while he is asleep. Jupiter descends amid thunder and lightning,
seated upon an eagle (V.iv).

K

Katherina.   In *The Taming of the Shrew*, the "Shrew." The
daughter of Baptista, she is married to Petruchio and is then
tamed by his rough treatment. She concludes the play with a long
speech advocating the total submission of wives to their husbands.

Katherine.   In *Henry V*, "fair Kate," daughter of Charles VI of
France, whom Henry woos (V.ii). Henry insists on her hand as

part of the peace treaty with France. The historical Catherine of Valois (1401–37) was the mother of Henry VI and after the death of Henry V married Owen Tudor; her grandson became Henry VII.

Katherine.   In *Henry VIII*, the historical Catherine of Aragon, first wife of King Henry, and one of those whose fall from power is depicted. When she receives the news of Henry's divorce she regrets the downfall of Wolsey, whom she has previously taken to be the source of her troubles.

Katherine.   In *Love's Labour's Lost*, a lady in attendance on the Princess of France. She is wooed by Dumain.

Kempe, William.   [Also, **Kemp.**] fl. 1585–1603. A comic actor and dancer, he was one of the original shareholders in the Lord Chamberlain's Men and in the Globe theatre, and was one of the principal actors listed in the First Folio (1623) of Shakespeare's plays. He was known as a comic actor before joining the Chamberlain's company, where he played mostly fools and clowns. He seems to have favored a slapstick style of clowning, much like that of Tarlton, and Shakespeare is thought to have written the parts of Peter in *Romeo and Juliet* and Dogberry in *Much Ado About Nothing* for him. He probably left the company in 1599, and the following year danced a marathon morris-dance from London to Norwich, reported in his *Kemps Nine Daies Wonder* (1600). He may have returned to the Chamberlain's for a time in 1601, but left to act with other companies.

Kent, Earl of.   In *King Lear*, an upright and faithful counselor. He defends Cordelia to her father although this causes his banishment, and his love for Lear is such that he returns in disguise to serve his master, even though he risks death. He stays with Lear throughout his sufferings on the heath, but never wins recognition from him. At the end of the play he refuses part rule of the country, saying that he must follow his master.

Kind-Hart's Dream.   Full title, **Kind-Hart's Dreame. Conteining fiue Apparitions with their Inuectives against abuses raigning.**] A pamphlet written by Henry Chettle in 1592. In the preface is the first allusion to Shakespeare after that in Robert Greene's *Groatsworth of Wit*: "Because myselfe haue seene his demeanor no lesse ciuill, than he excelent in the qualitie he professes: Besides, diuers of worship haue reported his vprightnes of dealing, which argues his honesty, and his facetious grace in writting, that aprooues his Art."

King John.   See **John, King.**

King John.   [Full title, **The Life and Death of King John.**] A historical play by Shakespeare, written probably in 1596 or 1597, but perhaps earlier, and first printed in the 1623 folio. The question of the play's sources is complicated by its relationship to the anonymous play *The Troublesome Raigne of John King of England*, printed in two parts in 1591. Some critics have thought that Shakespeare wrote part or even all of this play, since the edition of 1611 was published as "written by W.Sh." At one time it was generally accepted as earlier than *King John* and Shakespeare's main source, but some recent critics have suggested that the two plays were written within a few months of each other in 1590 or 1591, and that *King John* was the earlier. *The Troublesome Raigne*, which was based on Holinshed's *Chronicles* and Foxe's *Actes and Monuments of Martyrs*, is in many ways very close to *King John*, though for *King John* Shakespeare consulted Holinshed independently and made use of other historical material, including Hall's *The Union of the Two Noble and Illustre Famelies of Lancastre and Yorke* (1548) and possibly Radulph of Coggeshall's *English Chronicle*. Shakespeare's play is shorter and more compact than *The Troublesome Raigne*; it contains less comedy and it curbs the strong anti-Catholic bias in *The Troublesome Raigne*. The two plays differ in their presentation of John's right over that of his nephew Arthur to succeed Richard I as king, and Shakespeare emphasizes the case against John by making the bastard Philip Faulconbridge relate it (II.i) and by taking a sympathetic attitude to the rebel barons. The scene when Hubert prepares to blind Arthur (IV.i) is distinctly more pathetic in *King John*, where Arthur is a frightened child rather than, as in *The Troublesome Raigne*, an eloquent young man. But *King John* omits the scene in which John is poisoned by a monk, thereby losing an opportunity for dramatic action. Both plays cover the whole reign of John (1199–1216) without any presentation of what may now be thought the most outstanding event of that time, the signing of the Magna Carta, but *King John* has a rather different political emphasis. Shakespeare presents the barons' revolt against John as motivated not by John's efforts to curtail their rights but by disgust at his treatment of Arthur. Salisbury, Pembroke, and Bigot, the major rebels, are seen as good men torn between their horror at John's crime and their equal horror at rebelling against their own king and country.

Dramatis Personae

King John	Lymoges, Duke of Austria
Prince Henry, *Son to the King*	Cardinal Pandulph, *Papal Legate*
Arthur, Duke of Britain,	Melun, *a French Lord*
Nephew to the King	Chatillon, *Ambassador from*
The Earl of Pembroke	*France*
The Earl of Essex	Queen Elinor, *Mother to King*
The Earl of Salisbury	*John*

The Lord Bigot
Hubert de Burgh
Robert Faulconbridge
Philip the Bastard,
   his half-brother
James Gurney
Peter of Pomfret, *a prophet*
Philip, King of France
Lewis, the Dauphin

Constance, *Mother to Arthur*
Blanch of Spain, *Niece to King*
   John
Lady Faulconbridge
Lords, Ladies, Citizens of Angiers,
   Sheriff, Heralds, Officers,
   Soldiers, Messengers, and other
   Attendants

The Story. John refuses the demand of King Philip of France that he surrender his throne to his youthful nephew Arthur, and invades France with an army under the leadership of Philip Faulconbridge (Philip the Bastard), the most gallant and wittiest figure in the play. After an indecisive battle at Angiers, a peace is arranged and sealed by the marriage of the Dauphin to John's niece, Blanch. However, the peace proves to be a short one; Pandulph, a papal legate, excommunicates John for not seating his (Pandulph's) choice as Archbishop of Canterbury, and orders Philip and the Dauphin to recommence the war. During the ensuing hostilities, Arthur is captured by the English. John thereupon orders his chamberlain, Hubert, to kill the boy and (although Hubert spares him) the English nobles suspect a murder when Arthur (who actually died escaping) is found dead. The disaffected nobles desert John and join the French army that, at Pandulph's insistence, has invaded England. To regain Pandulph's support, John surrenders his crown to the papal legate and receives it back in fief. During the battle at St. Edmundsbury, Melun, a dying French lord, tells the English deserters that the Dauphin plans to execute them when John is defeated, and the nobles return to John. John, however, dies of poison administered by a monk at Swinstead Abbey. An honorable peace follows and the English are unified under the new king, Henry III.

King Lear.   See *Lear, King.*

King Lear.   [Full title, *The Tragedy of King Lear.*] A tragedy by Shakespeare, written c1605, performed in 1606, and printed in 1608. The quarto of 1608 and First Folio of 1623 differ, the former lacking about 100 lines which the latter has, but the folio having 300 lines of the quarto omitted. The story of the king who imposes a love-test on his daughters and ill-treats the one who loves him most is an old one and appears in many forms in European folk-lore. The story of Lear came into England first in Geoffrey of Monmouth's *Historia Regum Britanniae* (c1135), which Shakespeare probably used, perhaps in the original Latin. It was a popular story, and since many versions of it were available to him, Shakespeare seems to have taken details from a number of them. Holinshed's *Chronicles* (2nd ed., 1587) supplied the names of Cornwall and Albany, but little else specifically; in William Harrison's story in his *Description of England* (printed in Holinshed's *Chronicles*) Shakespeare found a chapter on the religion of the ancient Britons, and in John Higgins's addition to the *Mirrour for Magistrates* (1574 and 1587) a detailed account of the reduction of Lear's retinue. It was Spenser's account in *The Faerie Queene*, Book II Canto X, that provided the form of Cordelia's name and her death by hanging, since in the other sources she committed suicide. An earlier anonymous play on the Lear story, *The True Chronicle Historie of King Leir and his three daughters*, published in 1605 but written much earlier, is a more important source, although Shakespeare modified what he used of its plot very extensively. Shakespeare took material mainly from the earlier part of the play including the seven scenes which he condensed into I.i, the division of the kingdom, and a hint for Kent in the figure of Perillus who remains faithful to Leir throughout, though he is not banished, and Shakespeare also adapted from the old play the scene of Leir and Cordella symbolically kneeling toward the end. He changed the play's ending, in which Leir was restored to his throne and Cordella did not die, made Lear much older and more tragic than Leir, added the storm scene and Lear's madness. The Fool and the Gloucester subplot are both absent from the older play; the former is Shakespeare's invention, while the latter comes from an episode in Sidney's *Arcadia*. In the *Arcadia*, the heroes meet the King of Paphlagonia, accompanied by his good son Leonatus, and hear how he was deceived by his bastard son Plexirtus, blinded, and cast out of his realm. The use Shakespeare makes of this story as a counterpart to that of Lear, comparing and contrasting the two fathers in their folly and progress toward self-knowledge, and the behavior of good and bad children in each family, is a wonderful example of his skill in combining material from different sources. Two contemporary events seem also to have influenced the play. In 1603, an old knight, Sir Brian Annesley, who had three daughters, was reported unfit to look after his estate; his eldest daughter tried to have him declared insane, but his youngest, Cordell, defended her father and prevented his humiliation. He died in 1604, leaving most of his estate to Cordell; the eldest daughter and her husband disputed the will, but the Court of Chancery upheld it. No direct connection between this case and Shakespeare's play can be proved, although the similarity to Lear's situation is evident, but the other event, an apparent case of demoniac possession and the exposure of it as false in a pamphlet by Samuel Harsnett, *A Declaration of Egregians Popishe Impostures* (1603), is a direct source. The pamphlet describes how a group of household servants were encouraged to believe themselves possessed by devils and then "exorcised" by Jesuit priests. Shakespeare took from this the details of the language for Edgar's counterfeit madness, some descriptions from his storm scenes, and many words and phrases. Finally, the play was also influenced by Montaigne, especially by the language of Florio's translation of the *Essais* (1603), and probably also by Montaigne's skeptical thought. Shakespeare's own play suffered somewhat after 1679 by being altered. Nahum Tate, a dramatist of the Restoration period, gave it a happy ending and his version was acted by Betterton, Garrick, Kemble, and Kean.

Dramatis Personae

Lear, King of Britain	*Doctor*
King of France	*Fool*
Duke of Burgundy	*An Officer*
Duke of Cornwall	*Gentleman*
Duke of Albany	*A Herald*
Earl of Kent	*Servants to Cornwall*
Earl of Gloucester	Goneril, *Daughter of Lear*
Edgar, *Son of Gloucester*	Regan, *Daughter of Lear*
Edmund, *Bastard Son of Gloucester*	Cordelia, *Daughter of Lear*
Curan, *a Courtier*	*Knights of Lear's train,*
Oswald, *Steward to Goneril*	*Officers, Messengers,*
Old Man, *Gloucester's Tenant*	*Soldiers, and Attendants*

The Story.   Lear, intending to divide his kingdom between his three daughters, demands, with some arrogance, protestations of love from them. When Cordelia, whose love for him is genuine, declines to affirm it, he disinherits her, banishes her supporter Kent, and divides the kingdom between his other daughters, Goneril and Regan, and their husbands, Albany and Cornwall. Goneril, with whom Lear first stays, treats him disrespectfully, and he goes to Regan, who refuses to admit him (and puts Kent, who in disguise has become a servant to Lear, in stocks). Lear, driven to the point of madness by rage and sorrow at the ingratitude of his daughters, rushes into a violent storm with Kent and the Fool. On the heath they meet Edgar, the legitimate son of the Duke of Gloucester (who has banished him because Edmund, the Duke's illegitimate son, has falsely persuaded the Duke that Edgar plans to murder him). Edgar is disguised as the mad Tom o'Bedlam. Lear has by this time utterly lost his mind; Gloucester has been blinded by Cornwall for aiding Lear. Lear, with Kent, and Gloucester, with Edgar, separately make their way to the coast to meet Cordelia, who is landing with her husband, the King of France, to rescue Lear. There Edgar saves the life of his father and Cordelia tenderly cares for Lear, although they are taken prisoners by the English forces. Meanwhile, Regan and Goneril have fallen in love with Edmund, and the jealous Goneril poisons Regan and takes her own life when Edmund is killed by Edgar. It is revealed—but too late to avert further tragedy—that Edmund has ordered Cordelia's execution, and Lear then enters carrying his dead daughter. Lear dies of a broken heart, believing at the last moment before his death that Cordelia still lives. Gloucester too has died from "joy and grief" upon learning the identity of Edgar. The kingdom is left to Albany.

King of Antioch. See **Antiochus.**

King of Bohemia. See **Polixenes.**

King of France. In *All's Well That Ends Well,* the ailing King whom Helena cures and who later suspects Bertram of having murdered Helena. He speaks the Epilogue to the play.

King of France. In *King Lear,* the husband of Cordelia. He arrives with an army to rescue Lear, but he does not appear on stage after the first scene.

King of Naples. See **Alonso.**

King of Navarre. See **Ferdinand.**

King of Pentapolis. See **Simonides.**

King of Sicilia. See **Leontes.**

King of the Fairies. See **Oberon.**

King's Men. See **Lord Chamberlain's Men.**

L

Laertes. In *Hamlet,* the son of Polonius and brother of Ophelia. It is he who cautions Ophelia against Hamlet's love and receives from her the reply that he should not be one who "the primrose path of dalliance treads / And recks not his own rede" (I.iii). Later he seeks a duel with Hamlet (who has killed his father,

Polonius, and whom he holds responsible for Ophelia's death) and he falls in readily with Claudius's plot to ensure Hamlet's death by using a poisoned foil.

Lafew.   [Also, **Lafeu.**] In *All's Well That Ends Well*, a sagacious old lord.

Lancaster, Prince John of.   In *1* and *2 Henry IV*, the younger brother of Prince Hal, and son of Henry IV. In *1 Henry IV*, he is at the battle of Shrewsbury, where he is commended for his conduct in battle by Hal (V.iv). In *2 Henry IV*, he leads an army against the rebels and in a most dishonorable manner executes them after he has promised them pardon if they disband. He is cold and rather dull, with none of the virtues of his brother Hal; according to Falstaff, "a man cannot make him laugh; but that's no marvel, he drinks no wine" (IV.iii). In *Henry V*, he appears as Duke of Bedford, and in *1 Henry VI*, as Regent of France, he captures Orleans and Rouen, where he dies (III.ii).

La Pucelle.   See **Joan of Arc.**

Lartius.   See **Titus Lartius.**

Launce.   In *Two Gentlemen of Verona*, a servant of Proteus, noted for his remarks to his dog Crab.

Laurence, Friar.   In *Romeo and Juliet,* a Franciscan friar, the confidant and adviser of Romeo and Juliet. He marries them in a secret ceremony in his cell.

Lavatch.   [Also, **Lavache.**] A clown in *All's Well That Ends Well.*

Lavinia.   In *Titus Andronicus*, the daughter of Titus. She is ravished and mutilated by Tamora's sons, Demetrius and Chiron, and is finally killed by Titus.

Lear, King.   In *King Lear*, the King of Britain, the chief figure of the drama. He tests the devotion of his daughters by requiring a public profession of their love for him, in return for which each will receive a third of his kingdom. This brings a gradual alienation from his family, as he first denies parental affinity with Cordelia, then after he is rejected by both Regan and Goneril, who are by that time in possession of his kingdom, he invokes the curse of sterility upon Goneril, desiring that the storm "crack nature's molds, all germens spill at once / That make ungrateful man" (III.i). In his attempt to extort the tributes of love from his children we see a tyrant indulging in an unrestrained display of egotism, but his pride soon suffers as he recognizes the true feelings of his cold and selfish elder daughters. As his madness begins, he insists vehemently on his proper entourage, but the sisters insist that he needs no one. Unable to weep at the tragic truth that they now deny him even the smallest portion of his need, Lear rushes into the storm. The violence of the storm and the physical privations he endures combine with his tremendous mental anguish to drive him mad. This madness, paradoxically, helps him finally to obtain sanity, as he comes to a better understanding both of himself and of the miseries and injustices of human society. He reaches a new humility and is reunited with his loving daughter Cordelia, of whom he begs forgiveness. He dies, not of madness, but of old age and a broken heart, after the death of Cordelia.

Le Beau. In *As You Like It*, a courtier in attendance on Frederick, the usurping duke.

Lena, Popilius. In *Julius Caesar*, a senator. His conversation with Caesar just before the assassination alarms the conspirators, who fear that their plan has been discovered.

Lennox. In *Macbeth*, a Scottish thane. Convinced of Macbeth's guilt (after the murder of Banquo and as a result of MacBeth's behavior at the banquet), he joins the anti-Macbeth faction headed by Malcolm.

Leonardo. In *The Merchant of Venice*, the servant of Bassanio.

Leonato. In *Much Ado About Nothing*, the governor of Messina; the uncle of Beatrice and father of Hero.

Leonine. In *Pericles*, the attendant of Dionyza, employed to murder Marina. As he prepares to do so, he is attacked by pirates and runs off. However, he tells Dionyza that Marina is dead, and Dionyza poisons him.

Leontes. In *The Winter's Tale*, the King of Sicilia and husband of Hermione. His jealousy, unlike that of Othello, is willful and tyrannical. He is the Pandosto of Robert Greene's *Pandosto*, from which the play was taken.

Lepidus, M. Aemilius. In *Julius Caesar*, the historical Marcus Aemilius Lepidus, a Roman leader who becomes one of the triumvirate after Caesar's death. He witnesses the assassination and joins Octavius in the civil strife following, but is referred to in slighting fashion by Antony. In *Antony and Cleopatra*, he attempts to serve as a moderator between his fellow triumvirs, Antony and Octavius.

Lewis, the Dauphin. [Also, **Louis**.] In *Henry V*, the son of Charles VI of France. He sends Henry a present of tennis balls to mock his claim upon the French throne. He later boasts of French prowess when preparations are being made for the battle of Agincourt.

Lewis, the Dauphin. In *King John*, the historical Louis (VIII), son of Philip II of France. To bring about peace with France a marriage is arranged between him and John's niece Blanch of Spain.

Lewis XI. In *3 Henry VI*, the historical Louis XI, King of France. He promises aid to Margaret in her fight against Edward IV, then turns against her when Warwick offers to arrange Edward's marriage to Lewis's sister-in-law, Lady Bona. When Edward marries Lady Grey, Lewis is reconciled to Margaret and pledges arms to help restore Henry to the throne.

Lieutenant.   In *Coriolanus*, an officer in Aufidius's army, whose account of Coriolanus's popularity and superiority on the battlefield arouses Aufidius's jealousy (IV.vii).

Lieutenant.   In *3 Henry VI*, the Lieutenant of the Tower who apologizes to King Henry for having kept him prisoner (IV.vi).

Ligarius.   In *Julius Caesar*, one of the conspirators against Caesar. He does not, however, take part in the assassination.

Lincoln, Bishop of.   In *Henry VIII*, the historical John Longland. The King asks him to admit that he formerly advocated the divorce (II.iv).

Lion.   In *A Midsummer Night's Dream*, the part played by the joiner, Snug, in the interpolated play.

Lodovico.   In *Othello*, a kinsman of Brabantio. He produces the letters (found in Roderigo's pockets) that incriminate Iago and, after Othello's death, vehemently denounces Iago.

Lodowick, Friar.   In *Measure for Measure*, the name assumed by the disguised Duke Vincentio.

London Prodigal, The.   A comedy published in 1605, attributed to Shakespeare at that time, and included by Chetwood in the second issue of the third folio (1664). It is not now considered to have been by Shakespeare.

London Stone.   A stone preserved at London from some old monument. In *2 Henry VI*, Jack Cade uses it as a symbol of the city when he announces that London is taken (IV.vi).

Longaville.   In *Love's Labour's Lost*, one of the three lords attending the King of Navarre at his rural academy. He falls in love with Maria.

Lord Admirals' Men.   [also: *Admiral's Men*; until 1585, *Lord Howard's Company*; after 1596, *Earl of Nottingham's Company*; after 1603, *Prince Henry's Company*; finally, *the Elector Palatine's Company*, or *Palsgrave's Company*.]   An Elizabethan and Jacobean theatrical company, led for a time by Edward Alleyn. This company and the Lord Chamberlain's Men were the two most important companies of the many that were performing on the Elizabethan stage. Henslowe's *Diary* gives more information about this company than is available about any other. When their first patron, Charles Howard, became, in 1585, Lord High Admiral, they changed their name from Lord Howard's Company to Lord Admiral's Men. For a time they joined Strange's Men and toured (1593–94) the provinces under the leadership of Edward Alleyn. In London after 1594, Henslowe (whose stepdaughter had married Alleyn) was the backer and manager of the company and received one half of the entrance money. They played at his Rose theatre every weekday from October to Lent and from Easter to midsummer, when they left to tour the provinces for three months. After 1600 Alleyn, who had temporarily retired, resumed his acting career, and the company moved to the Fortune theatre on the north side of the Thames. In 1596 they took the newest title of their patron as their name and were called the Earl of Nottingham's Company. In the reign of James I they became known as Prince Henry's Company; later they were under the patronage of the Elector Palatine and were consequently called the Elector Palatine's Company, or, sometimes, the Palsgrave's Company.

Lord Chamberlain. In *Henry VIII*, an official at Wolsey's feast and at the arraignment of Cranmer. He is in charge of the christening of the infant Elizabeth.

Lord Chamberlain's Men. [Also: *Chamberlain's Men;* until 1594, *Strange's Men* or *Derby's Men;* after 1603, *King's Men.*] An Elizabethan theatrical company. They had formerly been Strange's Men, or Derby's Men (after Lord Strange became the Earl of Derby in 1572). This earlier company, in existence from the 1560's, was a group of traveling actors until they began to perform in the 1580's at Court. In 1591 they played at the Curtain, in 1592 at the Rose. Their members are thought to have included James and Richard Burbage, William Kempe, Thomas Pope, John Heming, and Augustine Phillips. In the reorganization of companies during 1594, most of the members of Derby's Company formed a new company under the patronage of Henry Carey, who became Lord Chamberlain in 1585, and his son, George Carey, who became Lord Chamberlain in 1597. About 1594 Shakespeare and Richard Burbage joined the newly formed Lord Chamberlain's Men as shareholders as well as actors. From that time on, Shakespeare wrote plays for no other company, and the company also performed many of Jonson's plays. They are thought to have performed at the Theatre, the Swan, and the Curtain until the Globe was built in 1599. Between 1594 and 1603 they gave thirty-two performances at Court. By the time they became the King's Men, in 1603, they had presumably acted Shakespeare's *Two Gentlemen of Verona, A Comedy of Errors, Love's Labour's Lost, Midsummer Night's Dream, The Merchant of Venice, Richard II, Richard III, Henry IV, King John, Titus Andronicus,* and *Romeo and Juliet.* As the King's Men they continued acting at the Globe, and in 1609 they took Blackfriars Theatre as their winter quarters. Between 1603 and 1616, they gave approximately twelve performances at Court each year. Shakespeare is last mentioned as an actor in their performance of Jonson's

Sejanus, first acted in 1603. In 1611 they performed *Macbeth, Cymbeline, The Winter's Tale,* and Jonson's *Catiline.* In 1619, when they were issued a new patent, some new shareholders, including Nathan Field, joined them. The company dissolved in 1642 when the theatres were closed, but the actors of the Chamberlain's collaborated in publishing (1647) the first folio edition of Beaumont and Fletcher.

Lord Chancellor.   In *Henry VIII,* the historical Sir Thomas Wriothesley. He is president of the Council arraigning Cranmer.

Lord Chief Justice.   In *2 Henry IV,* the historical Sir William Gascoigne, the judge who warns Falstaff and orders him to repay Mistress Quickly. He later fears that Prince Hal as King may hold a grudge against him, because once Hal was imprisoned by his order. The new King, however, confirms his impartial justice and orders him to enforce the penalties against Falstaff and his followers.

Lord Howard's Company.   See **Lord Admiral's Men.**

Lorenzo.   In *The Merchant of Venice,* a Venetian gentleman in love with Jessica. He elopes with her, taking part of Shylock's treasure.

Lovel, Lord.   In *Richard III,* a follower of Richard. He executes Hastings and brings in his head (III.v).

Lovell, Sir Thomas.   In *Henry VIII,* a courtier in King Henry's confidence.

Love's Labour's Lost.   A comedy by Shakespeare, first acted c1595, printed in quarto in 1598. The full original title (*A Pleasant Conceited Comedie called Love's Labour's Lost as it was presented before her Highness this last Christmas, Newly corrected and augmented by W. Shakespere. Imprinted 1598*) marks the first appearance of Shakespeare's name on a play's title page. The earlier version, which some have thought to be implied by this title, probably does not exist. From 1605 to 1839, when it was staged at Covent Garden, the play had no performances in London, a neglect that can perhaps be attributed to its bewildering array of topical references, plays on contemporary literary and philosophic terms, and satires of personalities unknown to later audiences. No one source has been found for the slender plot, which is perhaps Shakespeare's invention, and the origins of the individual characters and themes are not easily traced. John Lyly was clearly an influence on the play's style, especially in the comic use of pedantry and the mockery of the language of logic and rhetoric, for instance in the dialogues of Armado and Moth in I.ii and III.i and Armado's letter in IV.i. The treatment of characters such as the braggart Armado and the pedant Holofernes recalls the Italian *commedia dell'arte.* The theme of the withdrawal of a group of young men from involvement with women and with the world in order to study was not a new one; perhaps Shakespeare took it from Pierre de la Primaudaye's *Académie Française* (1577), in which such retreat is advocated. The *Académie Française* was dedicated to Henry III of France, brother-in-law to Henry of Navarre whose amorous adventures may be alluded to in *Love's Labour's Lost*. Many of the names in the play, including Berowne (or Biron), Longaville, Dumain, Boyet, and Mercade, were those of contemporary French noblemen, supporters of Henry of Navarre, whom Elizabeth at this time supported. *Love's Labour's Lost* was one of Shakespeare's most topical plays. The Muscovite masque in V.ii may well have been influenced by his recollection of the Christmas revelry at Gray's Inn in 1594–95, when Twelfth Night entertainment was provided by revellers dressed as ambassadors from Russia.

Dramatis Personae

Ferdinand, King of Navarre	Moth, *Page to Armado*
Berowne	*A Forester*
Longaville	The Princess of France, *wooed*
Dumain	*by Ferdinand*
Boyet	Rosaline, *wooed by Berowne*
Marcade	Maria, *wooed by Longaville*
Don Adriano de Armado	Katherine, *wooed by Dumain*
Sir Nathaniel, *a Curate*	Jaquenetta, *a country Wench*
Holofernes, *a Schoolmaster*	Officers and Others, Attendants
Dull, *a Constable*	*on the King and Princess*
Costard, *a Clown*	

The Story.   It is a highly stylized play with a very simple plot, hinging upon the revenge of Cupid on four men (Ferdinand, King of Navarre, and his attendant lords Berowne, Longaville, and Dumain) who have vowed to deny love for three years and devote themselves to study. The ladies (the Princess of France and her attendant ladies Rosaline, Maria, and Katherine), having come upon the academic retreat, are forbidden to enter, and thereupon determine to punish the foolish ascetics by causing them to break their vows. This is accomplished (although not without some remorse on the part of each lord, but as Berowne argues, women in themselves provide a worthy subject of study and, in addition, forswearing their vows may be less dangerous than denying love's power), but when the smitten lovers woo their ladies in Russian costume, the ladies confuse them by wearing masks and then exchanging them. In their own persons, the lovers then engage their ladies in a game of wit and sit with them to watch a pageant, but their revels are cut short by the news of the death of the father of the Princess. The ladies depart, and a year's penance is laid on each lover before he may have his lady. Contrast to the main plot concerning the courtly lovers is provided by the subplot of the rivalry of Armado and Costard for the affections of a country girl, Jaquenetta. It seems clear that this play was written for a courtly audience that would appreciate the many literary and topical allusions.

Lowin, John.   b. 1576; d. 1659. An English actor of the Jacobean period. He is mentioned as one of the principal actors of Shakepeare's plays, in the First Folio (1623). It is recorded that he acted "with mighty applause" the parts of Falstaff, Volpone (in Jonson's comedy of that name), and Epicure Mammon (in Jonson's *The Alchemist*). It is supposed that Shakespeare himself instructed him in the acting of the part of Henry VIII for the première of the play of that name. Lowin ended his days keeping the *Three Pigeons*, a tavern at Brentford.

Luce.   In *The Comedy of Errors*, a female servant to Adriana.

Lucentio.   In *The Taming of the Shrew*, an accomplished young student from Pisa, whose skillful wooing of Bianca forms the subplot of the play.

Lucetta.   In *Two Gentlemen of Verona*, a waiting-woman to Julia.

Luciana.   In *Comedy of Errors*, the sister of Adriana.

Luciano.   In *Hamlet*, a character in the play presented before the King. He is the murderer of the sleeping Gonzago.

Lucilius.   In *Julius Caesar*, a friend of Brutus and Cassius. He describes (IV.ii) the coldness with which Cassius received Lucilius as Brutus's emissary.

Lucilius.   In *Timon of Athens*, a servant of Timon. One of Timon's generous acts is to give Lucilius enough money to win the girl he wants to marry.

Lucio.   In *Measure for Measure*, a "fantastic" (i.e., profligate), but nevertheless sincere, friend of Claudio who urges Isabella to intercede for Claudio. Not recognizing the Duke in a friar's disguise, he slanders the Duke and then reports that a friar has been maligning the Duke. The Duke finally orders him to marry a woman he has wronged.

Lucius.   In *Julius Caesar*, a boy, servant to Brutus.

Lucius.   In *Timon of Athens*, a flattering lord; also, in the same play, a servant of this lord who is sent to recover a debt from Timon.

Lucius.   In *Titus Andronicus*, a son of Titus. After his brothers are executed, his sister Lavinia raped, and his father mutilated, he joins the invading Goths. The emperor Saturninus is overthrown, Tamora and Aaron are killed, and Lucius becomes the ruler of Rome. He has a son who is also named Lucius.

Lucius, Caius.   In *Cymbeline*, a Roman general who invades Britain. He discovers Imogen, disguised as a boy, and she follows his army. When Lucius and Imogen are captured by the Britons, Cymbeline recognizes his daughter and frees Lucius.

Lucullus.   In *Timon of Athens*, a flattering lord.

Lucy, Sir William.   In *1 Henry VI*, a leader who implores York and Somerset to go to Talbot's body after his defeat.

Lychorida.   In *Pericles*, the nurse of Marina.

Lymoges.   See *Austria, Duke of.*

Lysander.   In *A Midsummer Night's Dream*, a young Athenian in love with Hermia. He runs off with her and while sleeping in the woods is mistaken by Puck for Demetrius. Puck squeezes in his eyes the juice of a magic herb, making him fall in love with Helena, and recriminations follow between him and Hermia. Oberon orders Puck to restore the lovers to their natural state, and Theseus then sanctions Lysander's marriage with Hermia.

Lysimachus.   In *Pericles*, the governor of Mytilene.

M

Macbeth.   The chief figure of *Macbeth.* He is a brave and skillful soldier, driven by his misguided ambition and the persuasion of his evil wife to commit the murder of Duncan, the initial and unforgivable crime from which all else in the tragedy stems. When the first murder does not provide him with the security he craves he finds himself impelled to commit further crimes. The tragedy lies in the way his intense and sensitive nature is brutalized and coarsened by his life of crime until he is no better than a "dead butcher" (V.vii).

Macbeth, Lady.   In *Macbeth*, the wife of Macbeth. Unlike her husband, she is in all matters utterly realistic and intensely practical. She cannot sympathize with Macbeth's fears of damnation. After he returns from Duncan's chamber with blood on his hands, she says calmly that it can be washed off. But she is eventually punished for her efforts to stifle all her humanity and her imagination; in the sleepwalking scene (V.i) she shows herself to be obsessed by the impossibility of freeing herself from the guilt of Duncan's murder, and she finally commits suicide.

Macbeth.   [Full title, **The Tragedy of Macbeth.**] A tragedy
by Shakespeare, probably written in 1605 or 1606. Its first recorded production is April 20, 1610 but it is thought to have
been played before. It was printed in the 1623 folio, but there
is some probability that cuts were made from the stage manuscript. The Hecate scenes are probably Middleton's. In the Restoration period D'Avenant made it into an opera. Shakespeare's
main source was Holinshed's *Chronicles*, probably in the 1587
edition that he used elsewhere, although he may also have seen
illustrations from the 1577 edition. He used Holinshed not only
for the account of Macbeth's life but also for the story of the
murder of King Duff by Donwald, and for the description of
ancient Scottish life and customs. Shakespeare altered Holinshed's account of Macbeth's life in a number of ways; the involvement of Banquo, supposedly King James' ancestor, was
omitted and Banquo's character generally whitewashed, while
Macbeth was made more villainous. Holinshed's Duncan was a
weak and unsatisfactory monarch whom Macbeth assassinated
with the help of friends, and after the murder Macbeth ruled
in a just and beneficent way for ten years before he was overcome by guilt and proceeded to further crimes. Holinshed's account of the murder of King Duff in fact bears more resemblance
to the murder of Duncan in Shakespeare's play, although the
subsequent career of Duff's murderer, Donwald, does not parallel Macbeth's. Holinshed describes Duff as a good king and
Donwald as a kinsman whom he especially trusted; Donwald,
urged on by his wife, secretly murdered Duff by cutting his
throat while Duff was a guest in his home. After Duff's murder
monstrous events took place in the kingdom. There were a
number of other chronicles of Scottish history available to
Shakespeare. He probably did not use William Stewart's *The
Buik of the Chronicles of Scotland*, which was available in manuscript in King James' private library, although this has been
disputed, but he may well have seen the *Rerum Scoticarum Historia* (1582) by George Buchanan, which contains a Macbeth
very similar in character to Shakespeare's and also describes the
remorse felt by a royal murderer, King Kenneth, in much fuller
terms than Holinshed. John Leslie's *De Origine Scotorum* (1578)
supplied a Macbeth who killed Duncan without any assistance
from Banquo, and Shakespeare may have seen this, although it
was only available in Latin. James's interests were a significant
consideration in the composition of *Macbeth*, and Shakespeare
may well have read some of James's own work for it, especially
the *Daemonologie* (1597), which could have provided hints for
the treatment of the witches. The chronicle sources for *Macbeth*
provided Shakespeare with very little dialogue and few detailed
encounters; these he may have derived from some of Seneca's

tragedies. *Medea* or *Agammemnon* may have suggested ideas for the characterization of Lady Macbeth, and both of these had been translated by John Studley. The atmosphere of concentrated evil is particularly Senecan, although Shakespeare seems to have drawn also on his own early works, the poem *The Rape of Lucrece*, and *Richard III*, to evoke it. Finally, as might seem appropriate in a tragedy of damnation, Shakespeare drew heavily on the Bible.

Dramatis Personae

Duncan, King of Scotland	Boy, *Son to Macduff*
Malcolm, *Son of Duncan*	*An English Doctor*
Donalbain, *Son of Duncan*	*A Scottish Doctor*
Macbeth, *General of the Army*	*A Sergeant*
Banquo, *General of the Army*	*A Porter*
Macduff, *Scottish Nobleman*	*An old Man*
Lennox, *Scottish Nobleman*	Lady Macbeth
Ross, *Scottish Nobleman*	Lady Macduff
Menteith, *Scottish Nobleman*	Gentlewoman *to Lady Macbeth*
Angus, *Scottish Nobleman*	Hecate, *and Three Witches*
Caithness, *Scottish Nobleman*	Lords, Gentlemen, Officers,
Fleance, *Son of Banquo*	*Soldiers, Murderers,*
Siward, Earl of Northumber-	*Attendants, and Messengers*
land, *General of the English*	The Ghost of Banquo, and
Forces	*other Apparitions*
Young Siward, *his Son*	
Seyton, *Officer to Macbeth*	

The Story. Macbeth and Banquo, Scottish generals, are returning from a victorious campaign when they meet upon the heath three Witches who hail them, prophesying that Macbeth will be Thane of Cawdor and King hereafter, and that Banquo will beget kings. Part of the prophecy is immediately fulfilled when a messenger announces that Duncan, King of Scotland, has promoted Macbeth to Thane of Cawdor. Lady Macbeth, having learned of the Witches, plays upon her husband, already tempted by dreams of royal power, to kill the King, who falls into their hands when he arrives for a visit at the castle of Macbeth. But when the murder is done, Macbeth is completely unnerved; in his own words:

> Will all great Neptune's ocean wash this blood
> Clean from my hand? No. This my hand will rather
> The multitudinous seas incarnadine, . . . (II.ii)

Lady Macbeth, also nervous, must return to Duncan's room with the daggers that Macbeth has neglected to leave behind. Into this scene of horror comes the sound of knocking at the gate. The murder is discovered, and Macbeth puts the grooms to death to conceal his action. Duncan's sons, Malcolm and Donalbain, flee from Scotland, and Macbeth is crowned. He then hires murderers to kill Banquo and his son, Fleance, but the latter escapes. At a banquet given by Macbeth, the ghost of Banquo appears to him, and Lady Macbeth, vainly trying to make light of her husband's agitation, dismisses the guests. Macbeth returns to consult with the Witches, who show him apparitions that tell him to beware Macduff, that "none of woman born / Shall harm Macbeth," and that he shall be safe until "Birnam Wood to high Dunsinane Hill / Shall come" (IV.i). However, he is then also shown a procession of future kings, all descendants of Banquo. Macduff, meanwhile, has gone to England to raise an army with Malcolm to defeat Macbeth and there learns that his wife and children have been killed at the order of Macbeth. Macbeth, preparing to meet the invading army, learns of Lady Macbeth's death, and he conceives that her dying is merely part of the timeless flux that is his life: "Life's but a walking shadow, . . . a tale / Told by an idiot, full of sound and fury, / Signifying nothing" (V.v). The army advances, bearing branches cut from Birnam Wood for concealment, and Macduff who was "from his mother's womb / Untimely ripped" (V.vii) kills Macbeth. Malcolm is crowned King of Scotland.

Macduff.   In *Macbeth*, the Thane of Fife. He discovers the murdered Duncan and is probably the first to suspect Macbeth. He goes to England to beg Malcolm to return with him to fight Macbeth, and there hears of the slaughter of his wife and children. He was "from his mother's womb untimely ripped," (V.vii) and thus not naturally "of woman born" (V.vii). Therefore, according to the Witches' prophecy, he is the only agent capable of destroying Macbeth, whom he kills in battle.

Macduff, Lady.   In *Macbeth*, Macduff's wife. She and her son are murdered on Macbeth's orders.

Macmorris.   In *Henry V*, an Irish captain.

Maecenas.   In *Antony and Cleopatra*, a friend of Octavius who tries to reconcile the triumvirs. He later supports Octavius against Antony.

Mahu.   In *King Lear*, a fiend ("of stealing") alluded to by Edgar (IV.i).

Malcolm.   In *Macbeth*, a son of Duncan. He flees to England when Duncan is murdered and is there approached by Macduff, who hopes he will return and claim the throne. To test Macduff's loyalty he represents himself as a man of disgraceful and vile character (IV.iii). At Macbeth's defeat he is crowned King of Scotland.

Malcolm III.   [Also: **Malcom III MacDuncan;** called **Can-**

more.] d. near Alnwick, Northumberland, Nov. 13, 1093. King of Scotland (1054–93); son of Duncan I. He ascended the throne on the defeat of the usurper Macbeth by Earl Siward of Northumbria July 27, 1054, which was followed by his own victory at Lumphanan in Aberdeenshire, where Macbeth was slain. Shakespeare introduces him in *Macbeth*.

Malvolio. In *Twelfth Night*, Olivia's steward, a conceited, grave, self-important personage forced into comic situations (in the most ludicrous of which he imagines Olivia to be in love with him). He was probably intended as a satire on the Puritans.

Mamillius. In *The Winter's Tale*, the young Prince, son of Leontes and Hermione. He gives the play its title, when he says, "A sad tale's best for winter" (II.i). His death is later reported.

Marcade. In *Love's Labour's Lost*, the messenger who brings the news of the death of the King of France.

Marcellus. In *Hamlet*, an officer on watch upon the battlements who has twice seen the Ghost (of Hamlet's father) when the play opens.

March, (5th) **Earl of.** See **Mortimer, Edmund.**

Marcius. [Also, **Young Marcius.**] In *Coriolanus*, the young son of Coriolanus.

Marcus Andronicus. In *Titus Andronicus*, a tribune of the people and the brother of Titus. Unlike most of the other characters in the play, he is not bloodthirsty and vengeful, but gently tries to comfort Titus and to assist Lavinia after her mutilation, showing her how, in order to reveal the wrongdoers, to hold a stick in her mouth and write in the sand.

Mardian. In *Antony and Cleopatra*, a eunuch in attendance on Cleopatra. He is sent by Cleopatra to tell Antony that she is dead (IV.xiv).

Margarelon. In *Troilus and Cressida*, a bastard son of Priam, King of Troy.

Margaret. In *1, 2,* and *3 Henry VI* and *Richard III*, the historical Margaret of Anjou, a protagonist against the Yorkist party. She is first depicted as a timid young girl, the daughter of Reignier, then after her marriage with Henry VI a determined enemy of York and Gloucester and in love with Suffolk. In *3 Henry VI*, she is characterized as a cruel but politically righteous woman fighting to keep the throne for her son. Her last appearance, in *Richard III*, is as an old woman who leads Queen Elizabeth and the Duchess of York in a chorus of cursing against Richard. This last is unhistorical, but Shakespeare makes her an almost ghostly figure whose suffering is transmuted into a kind of externalized conscience for the villainous Richard.

Margaret. In *Much Ado About Nothing*, a gentlewoman attending Hero, whom she impersonates in a pretended assignation with Borachio.

Maria. In *Love's Labour's Lost*, a lady attending the Princess of France. She is wooed by Longaville.

Maria. In *Twelfth Night*, Olivia's witty waiting-woman. She sets up the plot to prove Malvolio mad by writing a love letter in a hand like Olivia's.

Mariana. In *All's Well That Ends Well*, a Florentine girl.

Mariana. In *Measure for Measure*, a lady betrothed to Angelo, but after the loss of her dowry, rejected by him. She takes Isabella's place in an assignation with Angelo, and later the Duke orders him to marry her. It was in allusion to her that Tennyson wrote his *Mariana in the Moated Grange* and *Mariana in the South*.

Marina. In *Pericles*, the extraordinarily virtuous and beautiful daughter of Pericles and Thaisa. Rescued by pirates from the murderous jealousy of Dionyza, she is sold to the keeper of a brothel, where nevertheless she keeps her virtue. She is finally reunited with Pericles and marries Lysimachus, Governor of Mytilene. In Gower's *Confessio Amantis*, from which Shakespeare got his plot, she is called Thaise.

Mark Antony. [Also: **Antony**; Latin, **Marcus Antonius**.] In *Julius Caesar*, one of the triumvirs with Octavius and Lepidus after Caesar's death. Brutus mistakenly believes him to be merely a dissolute minion of Caesar, and therefore allows him to deliver a funeral oration over Caesar's dead body as it lies in front of the Capitol. The famous speech beginning "Friends, Romans, countrymen, lend me your ears" (III.ii), although at first seeming to praise the conspirators, as Antony has promised, in fact cleverly turns the populace against them, and Antony is gradually revealed as an unscrupulous opportunist. With Octavius, he later defeats Brutus and Cassius at the Battle of Philippi (after somewhat callously dividing the rule of the Roman empire with Octavius). He appears as the hero of *Antony and Cleopatra*, which has its setting in the later years of his life. A much weaker, but also more attractive, person than the Mark Antony of *Julius Caesar*, he succumbs to Cleopatra's charms and in his passion degenerates into a fool, whom Octavius sees at his worst and for whom Lepidus tactfully apologizes when, upon the threat of further civil war, he returns to Rome. After marrying Octavia as a political expedient to bind Octavius closer to him, Antony returns to Cleopatra in Egypt. As a result, war with Octavius breaks out. His fleet is defeated at Actium, and he stabs himself upon hearing a false report of Cleopatra's death.

Marlowe, Christopher. b. at Canterbury, England, Feb. 6, 1564; d. at Deptford, England, May 30, 1593. An English poet and dramatist, son of a shoemaker, he secured a good education at Cambridge University, taking his B.A. in 1584 and M.A. in 1587. He was forced to appear at the Middlesex Sessions in London in 1588, but the charge is unknown. It appears that by 1587 he was attached to the Lord Admiral's Men as a playwright, enjoying the familiar acquaintance of Sir Walter Raleigh and other writers, adventurers, and men about town, and probably living a gay and roistering life. He was the "gracer of tragedians" reproved for atheism by Greene in his *Groatsworth of Wit* (1592). Chettle is probably referring to him when he speaks of "one he cares not to be acquainted with." Marlowe freely avowed the heretical and even atheistic views for which eventually, in 1593, he was called to account. An information against him was lodged with the authorities, but before he could be brought to trial, he was slain by an Ingram Frisar in a tavern brawl at Deptford. This is the generally accepted circumstance of his death, although many other accounts have been circulated. Some have advanced the theory that Marlowe, secretly involved in politics (perhaps as a French agent), was the victim of a conspiracy. It has been said that if Shakespeare, born in the same year with Marlowe, had like the latter died at the age of twenty-nine, Marlowe's name would have come down in literary history as the greatest of the Elizabethan dramatic poets. *Tamburlaine,* in two parts, probably first acted about 1587 and licensed for printing in 1590, is universally ascribed to him on internal evidence alone. *Doctor Faustus* appears to have been first acted in 1588, but it was not entered on the Stationers' Register for publication until 1601. It is known to have been produced by Henslowe twenty-four times between 1594 and 1597, and subsequently it was performed frequently by English companies in several of the chief German cities. *The Jew of Malta,* another tragedy, was written and first produced probably in 1589, was frequently acted in England between 1591 and 1596, and was also given by English companies on the Continent. In 1818 Edmund Kean revived it at the Drury Lane Theatre in a modernized version. Marlowe's historical play *Edward II* was entered on the Stationers' Register in 1593. About the same time, he collaborated with Thomas Nash in writing *The Tragedy of Dido, Queen of Carthage,* and wrote *The Massacre at Paris* alone. *Lust's Dominion, or the Lascivious Queen,* published in 1657, has been attributed to him, but without much substantiation. It is generally thought that he had a hand in fashioning some of the earlier plays of the Shakespeare canon. The greatest of his nondramatic works was an unfinished paraphrase of the *Hero and Leander* of Musaeus, which was completed by George Chapman; but he is now most often remembered for one of the most famous of English lyrics,

The Passionate Shepherd to His Love, which begins with the much-quoted line, "Come live with me and be my love." His advent in the London theatre marked the beginning of great drama in England, and there are few who will deny that he was surely a dramatist of authentic genius (there are many readers who will insist, indeed, that no list of the greatest Elizabethan plays is complete which fails to include at least *Doctor Faustus* and *The Jew of Malta* from among Marlowe's works).

Marston, John. [Pseudonym, **W. Kinsayder.**] b. c1575; d. at London, June 25, 1634. An English dramatist, satirist, and divine. He studied at Brasenose College, Oxford, taking his B.A. in 1594. Under his pseudonym, he published *The Metamorphosis of Pigmalions Image, and certaine Satyres* (1598) and *The Scourge of Villanie* (1598), poems so coarsely erotic that they were burned (1599) by order of John Whitgift, Archbishop of Canterbury. Marston's reputation among writers was not harmed by this episode and he soon began writing for the stage. *The History of Antonio and Mellida* (1599) and its sequel, *Antonio's Revenge* (1600), were both published in 1602. Their overdone melodrama, in addition to an attack on the comedy of humors contained in the induction to the first play, caused Ben Jonson to attack Marston in *The Poetaster* (1601), with the result that Marston, collaborating with Thomas Dekker, caricatured Jonson in *Satiromastix* (1602). Jonson and Marston soon became friends, however, and Marston dedicated *The Malcontent* (1604) to Jonson. They collaborated (1605) with George Chapman in *Eastward Ho*, and all three were imprisoned for a time for certain scenes in the play ridiculing the Scots, who had become numerous in London after the accession (1603) of James I. Among Marston's other plays are *What You Will* (1601), *The Dutch Courtezan* (1604), *Parasitaster, or the Fawn* (c1605), *The Wonder of Women, or the Tragedy of Sophonisba* (c1605), and parts of *Histriomastix* (c1599) and *Jack Drum's Entertainment* (c1600). He gave up writing for the stage in 1616 to become rector of Christchurch, Hampshire.

Martext, Sir Oliver. In *As You Like It*, a country curate.

Martius. In *Titus Andronicus*, one of the four sons of Titus.

Marullus. In *Julius Caesar*, a tribune. He and Flavius fear the growing power of Caesar and attempt to stop a triumphal celebration from being held for him.

masque. [Also, **mask.**] A type of dramatic entertainment originating from the silent entrance by masked figures into a banquet or gathering of distinguished guests, and completed by a dance between the masquers and those already present. Lyly and Jonson established the term in the French form "masque" in preference to "mask." The players in a masque (the masquers) wear facial masks, this being especially appropriate for Court performances in Jacobean and Caroline times, when although there was no real secrecy, a disguise would be appropriate for a noble amateur who would ordinarily disdain theatrical performances. The form started in Italy, where it received much of its original form and style at the court of Lorenzo de' Medici. Later it appeared in France, and appeared in England in the late fifteenth century, where there occurred a separation of the masquers and spectators (the early masque in France had its spectacular climax in the masquerade, in which everyone had a part). In the reign of Henry VIII the first masque was performed at Court, no disguises being worn, but the masquers already having rich costumes. By the time of Elizabeth an allegorical element was present (used as a means of flattering her, especially in the course of her various progresses through the country). The greatest development of the masque was under James I, partly because Queen Anne loved to participate in entertainments. Whereas the Elizabethan masque was mimetic, having only a few speeches by a presenter, when Ben Jonson began to write masques (*The Masque of Blackness, The Masque of Queens, The Hue and Cry After Cupid*) dialogue was used. Earlier masques had comic characters but Jonson was the first to make them a formal part of the masque. Unfortunately, Jonson and Inigo Jones, who did the elaborate scenery and stage devices for Court masques under James I and Charles I, could not agree over the primacy of their contributions: should the scenery be more important or the dialogue itself? Jones won, and the later masques (particularly those of James Shirley) had complicated stage machinery but very little else. The influence of the masque may be noted in Shakespeare's *Love's Labour's Lost, Romeo and Juliet, The Tempest, Timon of Athens,* and his and Fletcher's *Henry VIII.* The masque was important later as the source of scenery and staging for Restoration plays.

Master Gunner of Orleans.   A minor character in *1 Henry VI.*

Mayor of London.   A character in two of Shakespeare's plays: In *1 Henry VI,* he stops the fighting between followers of the Bishop of Winchester and those of the Duke of Gloucester. In *Richard III,* he supports Richard's claim to the throne.

Mayor of York.   In *3 Henry VI,* Thomas Beverly, who reluctantly admits Edward IV into the town.

Measure for Measure.   A comedy by Shakespeare, first acted in 1604 or 1605, printed in the folio of 1623. *Measure for Measure* was based on a pre-existing play, *Promos and Cassandra* (1578) by George Whetstone, which was itself based on an Italian source, a tale from Geraldi Cinthio's *Hecatommithi*

(1565). Cinthio also wrote a play on the same subject, *Epitia* (1583). Shakespeare knew both Whetstone's play and Cinthio's collection of fables, which he also used for the plot of Othello, and he may well have known *Epitia* too, since, like *Measure for Measure* but less like *Promos and Cassandra*, it is very much concerned with the nature of justice and authority, and contains characters who contrast in their attitudes to justice much as Angelo and Escalus do. Other contemporary versions of the story were contained in the second part of Thomas Lupton's *Siuquila* (1581), an allegory about a kind of Puritan Utopia, and the narrative that Whetstone created out of his play and published in his *Heptameron of Civil Discourses* (1582). From *Promos and Cassandra* Shakespeare took the story of a virtuous girl whose brother is condemned to death for rape under severe new laws; the King's deputy, Promos (Angelo), who has made the judgment, agrees to pardon the brother if his sister Cassandra (Isabella) will sleep with him. She does so, but afterwards Promos breaks his promise and orders the young man to be executed. He is, however, secretly preserved by his jailor. Cassandra, believing him dead, reveals the story to the King and asks him for justice; the King then orders Promos to marry Cassandra and afterwards be executed. But she has fallen in love with Promos, and begs for his life; at first, the King refuses, but when the brother is revealed alive he agrees, and all ends happily. Shakespeare changed this plot in three important ways. Perhaps influenced by the characterization of King Leonarchus in Barnaby Rich's pamphlet *The Adventures of Brusanus, Prince of Hungaria* (1592), he turned the minor figure of the King into the ambiguous Duke Vincentio, who stage-manages the action of the play and becomes its hero. He made Isabella a novice, unlike any of the sources or analogues, thus giving her a compelling reason for not agreeing to Angelo's demand and also a Christian motivation for forgiving him. And, perhaps following an incident in his own *All's Well That Ends Well*, he provided Mariana to substitute for Isabella in Angelo's bed, and thus give a different emphasis on Angelo's character. The title of the play and its theme of justice transcended by mercy perhaps came from Luke, 6:36–42. Often referred to as a "problem play," *Measure for Measure* gives certain indications of having been started as a tragedy and converted, somewhat abruptly, into a comedy during the course of its writing. Certainly, without the Duke as a *deus ex machina*, the play would have proceeded to an unhappy ending; moreover, the characters of Mariana (loyal to the man who has abandoned her), Angelo (rather too quick in his repentance at the end), and Isabella (convent-bound at the beginning, but conveniently willing to marry the Duke at the end) give the impression of having been forced into molds quite different from those that the beginning of the play would suggest.

Dramatis Personae

Vincentio, Duke of Vienna	Froth, *a foolish Gentleman*
Angelo, *the Deputy*	Pompey, *Mistress Overdone's*
Escalus, *an ancient Lord*	*Servant*
Claudio, *a young Gentleman*	Abhorson, *an Executioner*
Lucio, *a Fantastic*	Barnadine, *a dissolute Prisoner*
Two other Gentlemen	Isabella, *Sister to Claudio*
Provost	Mariana, *betrothed to Angelo*
Thomas, *a Friar*	Juliet, *beloved of Claudio*
Peter, *a Friar*	Francisca, *a Nun*
A Justice	Mistress Overdone, *a Bawd*
Varrius	*Lords, Officers, Citizens, Boy, and*
Elbow, *a simple Constable*	*Attendants*

The Story. Unwilling to be directly connected with the enforcement of certain long-neglected laws against unchaste behavior, Vincentio, Duke of Vienna, has entrusted to his deputy Angelo all governmental powers during his supposed absence (actually, however, he remains in the city, disguised as a friar). Angelo immediately arrests Claudio, who has got with child Juliet, his (Claudio's) betrothed, and sentences him to death. Claudio sends for his sister Isabella, who is about to enter a nunnery, to try to prevail upon Angelo for mercy. Angelo is at first adamant, but the beauty of Isabella arouses his lust and he offers to pardon Claudio if she will yield herself to him. She refuses indignantly and returns to the prison to tell Claudio, who begs her to sacrifice her chastity for his life. The Duke, still disguised as a friar, overhears the conversation and suggests that Isabella agree to Angelo's request, but that they get Mariana, formerly the fiancée of Angelo, to substitute for Isabella at the assignation. After his meeting with this spurious "Isabella" (by whom he is nevertheless utterly deceived), Angelo breaks his word and orders the execution of Claudio. However, the Provost of the prison prevents this by the dexterous substitution of a prisoner already awaiting execution for another offense and then sending Angelo the head of a prisoner who died of fever. The Duke then lays aside his disguise, hears the complaints, and straightens everything out; judgment is given upon Angelo (who still assumes that Claudio is dead) with the words: "An Angelo for Claudio, death for death! . . . and Measure still for Measure" (V.i) Angelo, pardoned upon Mariana's plea, marries her, while the Duke marries Isabella, and Claudio, Juliet.

Melun. In *King John*, a French lord who warns the English nobles who have deserted to the French side that the Dauphin intends to kill them when he has defeated John.

Menas.   In *Antony and Cleopatra,* a pirate who proposes to Pompey that they fall upon the triumvirs as they are feasting.

Menecrates.   In *Antony and Cleopatra,* a pirate (associated with Pompey).

Menelaus.   In *Troilus and Cressida,* the husband of Helen.

Menenius Agrippa.   In *Coriolanus,* the talkative, sometimes witty friend of Coriolanus. To calm the plebeians and tribunes, he tells them the fable of the belly and members; later he urges Coriolanus to control his wrath and to speak less arrogantly to the populace.

Menteith.   In *Macbeth,* a Scottish thane.

Merchant of Venice, The.   A comedy by Shakespeare, entered on the Stationers' Register in 1598, published in quarto in 1600, 1619, 1637, and 1652, and in folio in 1623. It was probably written in 1596 or 1597. To construct his play Shakespeare combined two stories, the Bond of Flesh and the Casket Choice, both of them with long traditions in folklore. The Bond of Flesh story involving Antonio, Bassanio, Portia, and Shylock seems to have originated in India, for a version is found in the *Mahabharata* (compiled between 500 and 200 B.C.), but Shakespeare's sources were probably tales from the *Gesta Romanorum,* a medieval compilation, and the collection of prose romances, *Il Pecorone* (1558), by Ser Giovanni Fiorentino. The Bond story in the *Gesta Romanorum* existed only in manuscript, and *Il Pecorone* must have been known to Shakespeare either in a manuscript translation or in Italian, since there was no published English translation known in his day. In the *Gesta Romanorum* the Bond story was linked with a tale of wooing, and here Shakespeare could have found several elements of the plot such as the triple love test, the disguising of the lady, and the lady's judgment that the flesh must be taken without loss of blood. The Shylock figure in this was not, however, a Jew. In the story from *Il Pecorone,* which is closer to the *Merchant of Venice,* a young man tries to woo the lady of Belmonte, a rich widow who has agreed to marry the first man that sleeps with her on condition that if he fail he must forfeit all his wealth. On two occasions he is given drugged wine and so prevented, and in consequence deprived of all his money; on the third occasion his godfather borrows a large sum from a Jew to equip him, and he is successful. He marries the lady, but he forgets to inform his godfather until the day for redeeming the Jew's bond is past; the lady sends him to Venice with the money, and herself follows disguised as a lawyer, but the Jew refuses it and demands instead his pound of flesh. The disguised lady steps forward, and all is resolved as in *The Merchant of Venice,* even down to the affair of the rings. Another version of the Bond of Flesh story that Shakespeare might have used is contained in *Zelauto* (1580) by Anthony Munday, although here the moneylender is no Jew but a usurer, and the forfeit demanded is the young man's eyes. There was also a contemporary ballad "shewing the cruel-tie of Germutus a Jew," but this may be of later date than Shakespeare's play. The Caskets plot apparently derived from the *Gesta Romanorum,* and there was a translated version of this story made by Richard Robinson in 1595. Shakespeare interchanged the mottos on the gold and silver caskets in the original, and completely changed that on the lead casket. The story of Jessica, Shylock, and Lorenzo was probably suggested by the elopement of the usurer's daughter in *Zelauto* and perhaps also by the treatment of Abigail, the Jew's daughter, in Marlowe's *The Jew of Malta.* Shylock's cry at hearing of Jessica's elopement, "My daughter, O my ducats, O my daughter," (II. viii) is very like Barabas's speech as Abigail throws down his money bags to him from a window. Another probable source for Jessica's elopement was a tale in the fifteenth century collection *Il Novellino,* by Masuccio, in which a young man falls in love with the daughter of a miser, ingratiates himself with the old man, and borrows money from him, giving as security a slave; the slave then helps the daughter steal her father's wealth and elope with the young man. Shakespeare's decision to write a play centered on a Jew may have been influenced by the revivals of Marlowe's play in 1594 and 1596, and probably also by the trial and execution of Roderigo Lopez, a Portuguese Jew, for allegedly attempting to poison the Queen. Poor versions and adaptations of *The Merchant of Venice* were made by Dryden, Otway, Shadwell, Lansdowne, and others, which held the stage until 1741, when Macklin restored Shakespeare's version. Two of Shakespeare's most famous characters are in this play: Portia, the woman turned lawyer, and Shylock, for the Elizabethan age an unusually sympathetic characterization of a Jew.

Dramatis Personae

Duke of Venice	Old Gobbo, *Father of Launcelot*
Prince of Morocco	Leonardo, *Bassanio's Servant*
Prince of Arragon	Balthasar, *Portia's Servant*
Antonio, *a Merchant of*	Stephano, *Portia's Servant*
Venice	Portia, *a rich Heiress*
Bassanio, *his Friend*	Nerissa, *her Waiting-maid*
Gratiano	Jessica, *Daughter of Shylock*
Solanio	*Magnificoes of Venice, Officers*
Salerio	*of the Court of Justice, Jailer,*

Lorenzo, *in love with*
    Jessica
Shylock, *a rich Jew*
Tubal, *a Jew, his Friend*
Launcelot Gobbo, *a Clown,*
    Shylock's Servant

Servants to Portia, and other
Attendants

The Story.   Antonio, the merchant of Venice, is asked for
a loan by his well-born but impecunious friend Bassanio in
order that the latter may be enabled to pursue his courtship of
the heiress Portia. Antonio, whose money is tied up in ships that
have not yet returned to port, borrows 3,000 ducats from the
Jewish usurer Shylock, who makes Antonio promise to forfeit a
pound of flesh if he is unable to pay on the agreed date. Meanwhile, at Belmont, Portia has turned away two suitors, the
Prince of Morocco and the Prince of Arragon, both of whom
fail to pass the test (set by the terms of Portia's father's will)
of selecting from three caskets (one each of gold, silver, and lead)
the one containing Portia's portrait. Bassanio chooses the correct casket, the lead one, but as they are rejoicing in the thought
of an early marriage, word comes that Antonio has been unable to pay his debt and that Shylock is demanding the pound
of flesh. After a hasty wedding, Bassanio returns to Venice and,
as soon as he has left, Portia and her maid, Nerissa (who has
married Bassanio's friend Gratiano), leave also for Venice, disguised respectively as a lawyer and a clerk. In court, the disguised Portia first pleads with Shylock for mercy; rebuffed in
this approach, she concedes the legality of Shylock's claim, but
points out that if he exacts more than a pound of flesh, or if one
drop of blood is shed, his life and lands are forfeit. Moreover,
she points out, death is the penalty for conspiring against the
life of a Venetian citizen. The Duke of Venice pardons Shylock
from the death sentence, but orders that his fortune be divided
between Antonio and the state. Antonio returns his share to
Shylock, with the stipulation that he must leave it in his will
to his daughter Jessica, disinherited when she eloped with
Lorenzo, a Christian, and finally that Shylock himself must
become a Christian. Portia and Nerissa (whose real identity remains unknown to the others) will accept as payment only the
rings Bassanio and Gratiano have received from their wives.
Back at Belmont, the wives reproach their husbands for no
longer having the rings, but, after much teasing, reveal the fact
of their disguise, and with the news that Antonio's ships have
also returned, all ends happily.

Mercutio.   In *Romeo and Juliet*, a friend of Romeo, slain in an
encounter with Tybalt. He is endowed with courage, an easy

mind, wit, fancy, and a light heart. He is remembered particularly for his Queen Mab speech (I.iv).

Mermaid Tavern. An Elizabethan literary gathering place, at London. Sir Walter Raleigh, Ben Jonson, Francis Beaumont, John Fletcher, John Selden, and probably William Shakespeare were among the notable figures who frequented it.

Merry Wives of Windsor, The. A comedy by Shakespeare, produced c1600. It was first printed as we know it in the folio of 1623 from an authoritative manuscript. In 1602 an imperfect and unauthorized version in quarto was printed (reprinted in 1619). This version seems to have been based on an actor's report (probably by one who played the Host) and has passages from other works by Shakespeare (*Henry IV* and *Hamlet*). No major source has been found for the whole plot of this play, but various influences have been suggested for the four main components of it. The way in which Shakespeare interweaves elements of multifarious origin is very typical of the synthesizing process by which many of his plays were composed. The devices by which the amorous Falstaff is exposed to ridicule when he concurrently woos the two merry wives, Mistress Page and Mistress Ford, may well have come from the Italian novelle, in particular from Ser Giovanni Fiorentino's *Il Pecorone* (1558), Day 1 Novella 2, and G.F. Straparola's *Le Piacevoli Notti*, Night 4, Fable 4. In both stories the lover undergoes three ordeals and triumphs over the cuckolded husband; in *Il Pecorone* the lover is hidden by the wife under a pile of newly washed linen, which perhaps suggested the episode where Falstaff has to make his escape from Ford's house in a basket of dirty linen (III.iii). Straparola's story appeared in an English version in Tarlton's *Newes out of Purgatorie* (1590), which Shakespeare undoubtedly knew. He also knew Barnaby Rich's *A Farewell to the Militarie Profession* (1581) which contained the story of Mistress Doritie, who makes her two suitors, a doctor and a lawyer, look ridiculous. The situation of Anne Page in *The Merry Wives of Windsor*, who is wooed by two suitors chosen by her parents while herself preferring a third, owes something to *Casina*, a comedy by Plautus. In this play, a man and his wife propose different husbands for their slave-girl; a wedding is arranged, but a man takes the bride's place and she is enabled to escape and marry the man of her choice. The obscure references to visiting Germans who borrow horses but do not return them (IV.iii,v), to "cosen-garmombles" (IV.v. Q.text), and to the Ceremony of the Garter (V.iv), may relate to a matter of topical interest, the visit of Frederick Count Mompelgard of Würtemberg to England in 1592, his indefatigable travels about the kingdom, and his persistent application to be admitted to the

Order of the Garter, as he finally was in 1597. It has been thought that the play was written for the Garter Installation feast of 1597. The fairy scene in Windsor Park where Falstaff disguises himself with a buck's head is related to the story of Actaeon from Ovid's *Metamorphoses* II, 138–252; Actaeon, a famous hunter, came upon the goddess Diana naked as she was bathing with her nymphs in a stream, and was punished by being changed into a stag and hunted to death. In Shakespeare's time "Actaeon" became a cant-name for a cuckold. An opera, *Die lustigen Weiber von Windsor*, by Otto Nicolai, words from Shakespeare by Mosenthal, was produced at Berlin in 1849. John Dennis, an English critic of the early eighteenth century, maintained that this comedy was written at the request of Queen Elizabeth, who wanted to see Falstaff in love.

Dramatis Personae

Sir John Falstaff	Pistol, *Follower of Falstaff*
Fenton, *a Gentleman*	Nym, *Follower of Falstaff*
Shallow, *a Country Justice*	Robin, *Page to Falstaff*
Slender, *Cousin to Shallow*	Simple, *Servant to Slender*
Ford	Rugby, *Servant to Dr. Caius*
Page	Mistress Ford
William Page, *Son to Page*	Mistress Page
Sir Hugh Evans, *a Welsh Parson*	Anne Page, *her Daughter*
Doctor Caius, *a French Physician*	Mistress Quickly, *Servant to*
Host of the Garter Inn	*Dr. Caius*
Bardolph, *Follower of Falstaff*	*Servants to Page, Ford*

The Story. Sir John Falstaff decides to pay court to Mistress Page and Mistress Ford, the merry wives of Windsor, hoping thereby to obtain some money (the two women are known to have charge of their husbands' purse strings). He sends identical notes to them and they, comparing them, decide to make a fool of the corpulent knight by appearing to encourage him. Meanwhile, Nym and Pistol, the cast-off cronies of Falstaff, inform the husbands of Falstaff's intentions (at this stage Ford himself is not confident of his wife's fidelity, and, in disguise, retains Falstaff to plead with her for him, as still another suitor). Mistress Ford, knowing all this, arranges an assignation with Falstaff, during which Ford returns, and Falstaff is hidden in a basket of dirty laundry and dumped in a muddy stream. At the second assignation, Ford again appears, and Falstaff tries to flee disguised as a woman ("the fat woman of Brentford"), but is beaten by Ford as a witch. Meanwhile, Anne Page, daughter of Mistress Page, has been courted by Slender, who is favored by Page, by Dr. Caius, who is favored by Mistress Page, and by Fenton, whom Anne loves. Mistress Quickly, Dr. Caius's serv-

ant, bears messages from all of them to Anne and encourages
them all impartially. In the last act, everyone gathers in Windsor Forest: Falstaff to meet the wives, who leave him to be
tormented by mock fairies; Slender to elope with Anne who, as
Page tells him, is to be dressed in white; Caius also to elope
with her, but thinking her to be dressed in green; and Fenton,
who succeeds in carrying her off. Slender and Caius discover
that they have eloped with boys disguised as fairies.

Messala.   In *Julius Caesar*, a friend of Brutus and Cassius.

Metamorphoses.   Poetical work by Ovid, in fifteen books. The
work is a collection of some 250 stories taken from Greek mythology, Roman and Latin folk tales, legends, and myths, including also some tales from the East. The unifying element in
the collection is that all of the stories have to do with transformations: for an infinite variety of causes, gods, men, and
animals are transformed in an infinite variety of ways. Ovid
dexterously maneuvered through intricate plots and relationships
so that one story led almost imperceptibly to another, making
the work a whole rather than a collection of separate, uncon-
nected tales. His treatment of the stories is notable in the
compassion that is shown for the human protagonists and in
the lightly irreverent treatment of the immortal gods. Besides
being a literary production of interest, charm, and artistry, the
Metamorphoses is a treasury of myth and legend, gleaned by
Ovid from the works of ancient poets and other writers and
transformed by him into a literary masterpiece of immortal
interest. His work has been an undiminished source of inspiration and influence for western European literature, as indeed
Ovid thought it would be, for in the closing lines of the *Metamorphoses* he wrote: "My work is complete: a work which
neither Jove's anger, nor fire nor sword shall destroy, nor yet
the gnawing tooth of time. . . . If there be any truth in poets'
prophecies, I shall live to all eternity, immortalized by fame."
Shakespeare, who found Ovid an invaluable source of plots,
subplots, characterization, and other ideas, could have made
the same kind of statement about the immortality of his work.

Michael.   In *2 Henry VI*, a follower of Jack Cade.

Michael, Sir.   In *1 Henry IV*, a priest or knight who is in the
service of the Archbishop of York and is sent by him with letters to the rebels (IV.iv).

miching malicho.   A phrase in *Hamlet* (III.ii) and glossed as
"skulking mischief" by Tucker Brooke. The quarto has "munch-
ing Mallicho." *Miching* is a participle form of the Middle English verb *miche*, meaning "to skulk." The last word may be
from the Spanish *malhecho*, i.e., "misdeed." Eric Partridge has
suggested that it was a Gypsy word.

A Midsummer Night's Dream. A comedy by Shakespeare, written in 1595 or 1596, and certainly staged several times within the next four years, although the date of first performance is not known. It is mentioned by Francis Meres in his *Palladis Tamia*, which was issued in 1598, was entered on the Stationers' Register Oct. 8, 1600, and was first published in 1600. It is included in the folio of 1623 with a few added stage directions but no scene markings. This is one of those plays for the plot of which Shakespeare depended on no one main source. There are five interwoven strands to the plot: (1) the marriage of Theseus and Hippolyta; (2) the quarrel between Titania and Oberon; (3) the assorted relationships of the four human lovers; (4) the adventures of Bottom; (5) the Pyramus and Thisbe play. No known source combines all these stories, and although Shakespeare took names and details for each of them from various subsidiary sources he did not rely heavily on the work of any other writer for any element of his play. Theseus and Hippolyta may have come from North's translation of Plutarch's *Life of Theseus* in which Theseus is depicted as a lawgiver and statesman, or perhaps from Chaucer's *Knight's Tale*, where the marriage of the mature couple, Theseus and Hippolyta, is contrasted with the unhappy situation of the two young men who both love the same girl. It may also be that this love-triangle provided a starting point for the relationships between the human lovers of *A Midsummer Night's Dream*. Oberon and Titania are · literary fairies and may be traced accordingly; Oberon comes from the romance *Huon of Bordeaux*, translated by Lord Berners (c1534), and perhaps also from Robert Greene's *James IV*, while Titania comes from Ovid's *Metamorphoses*, iii. 173. But the main fairy background and the figure of Puck come from English folk lore. Bottom's transformation and his brief love affair with Titania have various literary analogues but no specific sources: Midas and his ass's ears, the transformation of the amorous Apuleius in *The Golden Asse*, and various tales from Reginald Scot's *Discoverie of Witchcraft* (1584) may have contributed. Numerous sources have been discovered for the Pyramus and Thisbe play, which was very popular in Elizabethan times as a story of the misfortunes of thwarted love. Shakespeare undoubtedly read and was influenced by Golding's translation of Ovid's *Metamorphoses* (1567), iv. 67–201, which was written in the heavily-stressed fourteeners that readily lend themselves to parody. Other versions of the story that he may also have used include "A New Sonet of Pyramus and Thisbe" from the anthology *A Handfull of Plesant Delites* (1584), *A Gorgeous Gallery of Gallant Inventions* (1578), and perhaps Thomas Mouffet's didactic poem *The Silkewormes and Their Flies* (1599), which Shakespeare may have seen in manuscript. Though the work is now ranked as one of the best of the comedies, it was not always so highly esteemed (a performance in 1662 merited Pepys's comment: "The most insipid, ridiculous play that ever I saw in my life").

Dramatis Personae

Theseus, Duke of Athens
Egeus, *Father of Hermia*
Lysander, *in love with Hermia*
Demetrius, *in love with Hermia*
Philostrate, *Master of the Revels*
Quince, *a Carpenter*
Snug, *a Joiner*
Bottom, *a Weaver*
Flute, *a Bellows-mender*
Snout, *a Tinker*
Starveling, *a Tailor*
Hippolyta, Queen of the
    Amazons, *betrothed to*
    Theseus

Hermia, *in love with*
    Lysander
Helena, *in love with*
    Demetrius
Oberon, King of the Fairies
Titania, Queen of the
    Fairies
Puck, *or* Robin Goodfellow
Peaseblossom, *a Fairy*
Cobway, *a Fairy*
Moth, *a Fairy*
Mustardseed, *a Fairy*
Other Fairies attending their
    King and Queen
Attendants on Theseus and
    Hippolyta

The Story. To the court of Theseus, Duke of Athens, who is about to marry Hippolyta, come Hermia and her father, Egeus, who insists that she marry Demetrius (who now loves Hermia, but who has earlier avowed love for Hermia's friend Helena, by whom he is still loved). Lysander also loves Hermia, and it is his suit that she favors. Theseus invokes the Athenian law, which gives her four days in which to agree to her father's request; if she persists after that time in her disobedience she must become a nun or be condemned to death. However, she and Lysander arrange to meet that night in a neighboring wood, whence they plan to flee beyond the reach of Athenian law. She tells her plan to Helena, but Helena tells Demetrius, hoping thus to regain his love. Demetrius follows Hermia and Lysander into the wood, and Helena follows Demetrius. In the wood also, but unbeknownst to them, are fairies who have arrived from India for the wedding of Theseus and Hippolyta. Titania and Oberon, the Queen and King of the fairies, are quarreling about the possession of a changeling boy who has caught Titania's fancy. Oberon, to spite Titania, drops on her eyelids as she sleeps a magic liquid squeezed from a certain flower so that when she awakens she will fall in love with the first creature she sees. This happens to be Bottom, a weaver, one of a group of Athenian artisans who have gone into the wood to rehearse a play in honor of the forthcoming marriage of Theseus and Hippolyta; Puck, Oberon's mischievous servant, has playfully given Bottom the head of an ass. Oberon, having overheard Demetrius berating Helena for following him, seeks to help them out of their difficulty by ordering Puck to anoint Demetrius so that he may fall in love with Helena. But Puck confuses Lysander with Demetrius, and drops the liquid on the eyes of the wrong man; Lysander, upon awakening, sees Helena, and loves her. Seeking to correct the mistake, Oberon himself now anoints Demetrius, who also first sees Helena upon awakening, so that both young men are now in love with Helena, exactly the reverse of the situation at the beginning. Neither Helena nor Hermia has any inkling of what has caused the situation; Hermia upbraids Helena (who, far from wanting the attentions of Lysander, has thought he was making sport of her in offering them). Titania, meanwhile, has been entrapped by the unique (to her) beauty of Bottom's donkey's ears and velvet muzzle; never, in her bewitched eyes, has there been an object of such surpassing beauty. Oberon pities her humiliation and removes the spell; they are reconciled and she agrees to give up the changeling boy. Puck, by enclosing the human lovers in a dense fog, arranges that Lysander will awaken to love Hermia once more, and Demetrius to love Helena. Theseus and Hippolyta arrive in the wood, discover the couples, and arrange a triple wedding which takes place in the palace. At the ceremony, the artisans' play, the "most lamentable comedy" of Pyramus and Thisbe, is presented. After the lovers retire, the fairies dance through the palace, leaving Puck to deliver the Epilogue.

Milan, Duke of.   In *Two Gentlemen of Verona*, the father of Silvia.

Milan, Duke of.   See also **Antonio** and **Prospero.**

miracle plays.   See **mystery plays.**

Miranda.   In *The Tempest*, the daughter of Prospero. She is loved by Ferdinand. She represents the innocence and charm of the girl of good birth who is raised away from the corrupting influence of society.

Modo.   In *King Lear*, a fiend ("of murder") mentioned by Edgar (IV.i). The name is taken from Samuel Harsnett's *Popish Impostures*.

Montague.   In *Romeo and Juliet*, the family name of Romeo. Montague is Romeo's father and a bitter enemy of Capulet. This feud between the houses of Montague and Capulet plays an important part in the separation of the lovers that leads to the eventual tragedy. However, Montague is reconciled after Romeo and Juliet's deaths, promising to erect a statue of Juliet.

Montague, Lady.   In *Romeo and Juliet*, the mother of Romeo.

Montague, Marquess of. In *3 Henry VI*, the historical John Neville, Marquis of Montague, a supporter of York who later joins the Lancastrians under Henry VI and is killed at the battle of Barnet.

Montano. The name of Reynoldo in the first quarto of *Hamlet*.

Montano. In *Othello*, the Governor of Cyprus.

Montgomery, Sir John. In *3 Henry VI*, a supporter of Edward, Earl of March. He urges Edward to fight for the throne (IV.vii).

Montjoy. In *Henry V*, a French herald who asks whether Henry will offer ransom before he is forced to engage in battle with the French army at Agincourt. Later he acknowledges French defeat.

Moonshine. In *A Midsummer Night's Dream*, the part played by Starveling, the tailor, in the interpolated play.

Mopsa. A shepherdess in *The Winter's Tale*.

morality plays. [Also, **moralities.**] Plays developed in the early fifteenth century, having the didactic purpose of inculcating good behavior in their hearers. Generally speaking, the morality play presents abstract virtues and vices struggling for possession of a man's soul. There is usually a debate between Body and Soul in which the Soul moralizes against the Body, which has led it unwillingly down the road to damnation. Finally, after death, abstractions representing heavenly judgment decide whether Man shall be given mercy or harsh punishment. These heavenly abstractions are often the Four Daughters of God: Mercy and Peace (for salvation), Righteousness and Truth (for damnation). The earliest morality play is *The Pride of Life* (c 1400), and others include *The Castle of Perseverance* (c1405), *Mind, Will, and Understanding* (c1460), *Mankynd* (c1475), and the well-known *Everyman* (late fifteenth century).

Morgan. In *Cymbeline*, the assumed name of Belarius.

Morocco, Prince of. In *The Merchant of Venice*, an unsuccessful suitor of Portia. He chooses the golden casket as the one containing her portrait; it doesn't, and he thus fails to win her.

Mortimer, Edmund. In *1 Henry IV*, a prisoner of Owen Glendower, whose daughter he marries. His sister is Hotspur's wife and he and Glendower join Hotspur against Henry IV. Shakespeare confused the historical Sir Edmund (1376–1409) with his nephew, Edmund, 5th Earl of March.

Mortimer, Edmund. (5th) Earl of March. In *1 Henry VI*, an old nobleman. He tells Richard that he is imprisoned by the Lancastrians because he is the real heir to the throne and Richard is his heir. Shakespeare apparently confused the historical Earl with his uncle, Sir Edmund Mortimer, or with another member of the family.

Mortimer, Lady.   In *1 Henry IV*, the daughter of Owen Glendower and wife of Edmund Mortimer. She can speak only Welsh. Hotspur tries to imitate Mortimer's amorous wooing of his Welsh bride.

Mortimer, Sir John and **Sir Hugh.**   In *3 Henry VI*, illegitimate sons of Roger Mortimer and uncles of Richard, Duke of York.

Morton.   In *2 Henry IV*, the retainer who brings Northumberland news of Hotspur's death.

Morton, John.   In *Richard III*, the Bishop of Ely, an adherent of Richmond after having escaped from Richard. The historical Morton became Archibishop of Canterbury in Henry VII's reign and Sir Thomas More lived in his house. More got material from him for his *History of King Richard III*, which Shakespeare used as a source for *Richard III*.

Moth.   In *Love's Labour's Lost*, a witty, knavish page of Armado.

Moth.   A fairy in *A Midsummer Night's Dream*.

Mouldy, Ralph.   In *2 Henry IV*, a recruit whom Falstaff allows to purchase his freedom.

Mousetrap play, The.   See *Hamlet* (the play).

Mowbray.   In *2 Henry IV*, one of the lords opposing Henry.

Mowbray, Thomas.   In *Richard II*, the Duke of Norfolk. Bolingbroke accuses him of treason before Richard, and Mowbray, to defend his honor, challenges Bolingbroke to single combat. At the last moment, Richard calls off the tournament and banishes Bolingbroke for ten years and Mowbray for life.

Mowbray, Thomas.   [Titles: Earl of **Nottingham,** 12th Baron **Mowbray,** 1st Duke of **Norfolk.**] d. at Venice, 1399. An English nobleman. He was created Earl of Nottingham in 1383, earl marshal in 1384, and was one of the lord appellants of 1387, but afterward joined the king. He was created Duke of Norfolk in 1397. Having been accused of treason by Henry Bolingbroke, Earl of Hereford (afterward Henry IV), in 1398, he challenged the latter to single combat, and the lists were set at Coventry in the presence of Richard II, who banished both disputants on the eve of the contest, Norfolk for life and Hereford for ten years. Shakespeare introduces him in *Richard II*.

Mucedorus.   A play, perhaps by George Peel, Robert Greene, or Thomas Lodge, printed anonymously in 1598 and reprinted with additions in 1610. It was erroneously assigned to Shakespeare by Edward Archer in 1656.

Much Ado About Nothing.   A comedy by Shakespeare, produced c1598. It may have been written in 1598 or 1599, although some authorities have thought that its verse is earlier in style. It was first printed in 1600, and its registration that year marked the first appearance of Shakespeare's name in the Stationers' Register. The story of Hero and Claudio belongs to a long tradition dating back to a Greek romance and was available to Shakespeare in both dramatic and non-dramatic versions. He probably knew Sir John Harrington's translation of the fifth canto of Ariosto's epic poem *Orlando Furioso*, which appeared in 1591, and the variant of this by Matteo Bandello in the twenty-second of his *Novelle*. Bandello's version was translated into French by François de Belleforest in his *Histoires Tragiques* (1574), but not into English in Shakespeare's lifetime. Edmund Spenser had included a version of this story in *The Faerie Queene* (1590), Book II Canto IV, in the account of Phedon (Claudio) deceived as to the chastity of Claribella (Hero) by a plot between her maid and his best friend, which Shakespeare probably also knew, and there was a play, perhaps by Anthony Munday, called *Fedele and Fortunio* (1585) that contains a similar situation. Shakespeare took some of the names, notably Don Pedro and Leonato, and the setting in Messina, from Bandello, but he altered the situation so that Hero and Claudio were of the same rank, whereas in Bandello and several of the sources the Claudio figure was of higher rank and greater wealth. He also changed the circumstances of the deception so that evidence of Hero's guilt seem greater and the censure of Claudio correspondingly less. But the parts of the play that are probably most attractive to modern audiences, the "merry war" between Beatrice and Benedick, and the comic misunderstandings of Dogberry and the Watch, are Shakespeare's own invention, as is the villainous Don John. The subplot, apparently invented by Shakespeare, concerns the love of Benedick and Beatrice. The constable, Dogberry, and his assistants are also Shakespeare's.

Dramatis Personae

Don Pedro, Prince of Arragon
Don John, *his bastard Brother*
Claudio, *a young Lord of Florence*
Benedick, *a young Lord of Padua*
Leonato, *Governor of Messina*
Antonio, *his Brother*
Balthasar, *Servant to Don Pedro*
Borachio, *Follower of Don John*
Conrade, *Follower of Don John*
Dogberry, *a Constable*

Verges, *a Headborough*
Friar Francis
A Sexton
A Boy
Hero, *Daughter of Leonato*
Beatrice, *Niece of Leonato*
Margaret, *Gentlewoman to Hero*
Ursula, *Gentlewoman to Hero*
Messengers, Watch, Attendants

The Story. Claudio and Benedick, officers in the army of Don Pedro, Prince of Arragon, are with him when he visits Leonato, the Governor of Messina. Claudio falls in love with Hero, Leonato's daughter and despite the scheming of Don John, the vindictive bastard brother of the Prince, the wedding is arranged. Meanwhile, Beatrice, the niece of Leonato, and Benedick bait each other in verbal skirmishes, each professing to oppose the very idea of love or marriage, but are tricked into love for each other when Claudio and Don Pedro contrive that each shall overhear a conversation touching on the love that the other is supposed to feel, but is unwilling to express, for the listener. In the affair of Claudio and Hero, however, things are somewhat less happy. Don John persuades Borachio to converse at midnight through a window with Hero's maid Margaret, who is dressed as Hero, and arranges that Claudio and Don Pedro shall witness the conversation and thereby be brought to suspect the virtue of Hero. The wicked scheme succeeds, and at the wedding ceremony on the following day Claudio and Don Pedro denounce Hero, who swoons (whereupon Friar Francis, convinced of her innocence, persuades her father to announce her death). In the following scene the love of Beatrice and Benedick is declared, and Beatrice lays as a task on Benedick that he should kill Claudio for impugning her cousin Hero's virtue. However, Claudio is not to suffer for his mistrust; Borachio boasts of his exploit and is arrested by Dogberry and Verges. A repentant Claudio, believing Hero to be dead, agrees to marry Leonato's niece, who when she is unveiled turns out to be Hero. Benedick and Beatrice (with some manifestly feigned reluctance on the part of the latter) also marry, and word comes that Don John has been apprehended and is being returned for punishment.

mummer. One who mums, or masks himself and makes diversion in disguise; a masker; a masked buffoon; specifically, in England, one of a company of persons who go from house to house performing a mumming play.

Mustardseed. A fairy in *A Midsummer Night's Dream.*

Mutius. In *Titus Andronicus,* the youngest son of Titus. He is killed by his father as he attempts to protect Lavinia.

Myrmidons. In *Troilus and Cressida,* the soldiers of Achilles.

mystery plays. [Also, **miracle plays.**] Plays developed in the fourteenth and fifteenth centuries for secular performance but with religious themes. They are the successors of earlier, simpler dramatizations of episodes in the Christian story that were presented in church. As such dramatic presentations grew more elaborate, they passed out of the church into the market place and the streets of the town and out of the hands of the clergy into those of the guilds. (The word *mystery* in this connection was apparently influenced by the now archaic *mystery,* "a craft or trade"). In a number of larger towns cycles of such plays developed. They were often performed on "pageants," movable platforms that were wheeled through the streets. As each platform reached a designated point (at York at one time there were fourteen) it stopped and the play was presented. Then it moved on and another took its place. In some places the platforms were stationary and the audience moved from one to the next in succession. The great occasion for these performances was Corpus Christi Day, and most cycles were given then. The particular subjects were often assigned according to the association of a given guild with the event depicted. Thus the York cycle has the shipwrights' guild performing the story of Noah and his ark, the fishermen and mariners doing the ark's voyage, the bakers doing the Last Supper, the vintners performing the miracle of the wedding feast at Cana, and the cooks doing the harrowing of hell. At its peak, this cycle had fifty-seven pageants, more than that of any other town. There are four cycles preserved more or less fully, those of York (1415) with forty-eight plays, Wakefield (best known as the Towneley Plays, fifteenth century) with thirty-two plays, Chester (1328) with twenty-five plays, and the Hegge cycle (in a manuscript of 1468) with forty-two plays, as well as two Coventry plays and one each from Norwich and Newcastle. There are three plays in the Digby series (the Digby Plays) of the fifteenth century. The Beverley cycle of thirty-eight plays (1423) has vanished. The term "miracle play" has also been used to refer to this type of drama, and a technical distinction has sometimes been made between a play concerning an event in the life of Christ as given by the gospels (mystery) and a play concerning the activities of a saint, or a subject taken from the Bible or apocryphal sources (miracle). See also **morality plays.**

N

Nash or **Nashe, Thomas.**   [Pseudonym, **Pasquil.**] b. at Lowestoft, England, 1567; d. c1601. An English satirical pamphleteer, poet, and dramatist. He took the degree of B.A. at Cambridge (Saint John's College) in 1585. His earliest work is a preface to Robert Greene's *Menaphon* (1589); the *Anatomy of Absurdity* appeared in 1589. Using his pseudonym, he entered (1589) the Martin Marprelate controversy on the side of the bishops and is generally credited with writing *A Countercuffe to Martin Junior, Martins Months Minde,* and *Pasquils Apologie,* though no definite ascription is possible. In 1591 he edited, without authorization, Philip Sidney's poems, and the next year began his long and scurrilous "paper war" with Gabriel Harvey in *Pierce Pennilesse, his supplication to the Devil.* In it he attacked Richard Harvey for criticizing *Menaphon.* Greene's death in degraded circumstances gave fuel to the Harveys' side of the conflict and the ensuing years saw publication by Nash, in answer to attacks by Harvey, of *Strange Newes of the intercepting certaine Letters* (1592), *Christs Teares over Jerusalem* (1593, a conciliatory effort followed by a renewal of the attack in a new edition in 1594), and *Have with You to Saffronwalden, or Gabriell Harveys Hunt is Up* (1596). The whole affair was ended by the intervention (1599) of John Whitgift, archbishop of Canterbury, who officially suppressed it. Nash wrote a pioneering realistic novel of adventure, *The Unfortunate Traveller or the Life of Jack Wilton* (1594), a satirical masque, *Summers Last Will and Testament* (1592), and *Lenten Stuffe* (1599, a tongue-in-cheek praise of Yarmouth and the red herring). He is thought to have completed (1596) Christopher Marlowe's play *Dido Queen of Carthage.* The lost play *The Isle of Dogs* (1597), written in collaboration with others, contained material considered seditious and slanderous, for which he was sentenced to the Fleet prison, but he does not appear to have served his sentence.

Nathaniel.   In *The Taming of the Shrew,* one of Petruchio's servants.

Nathaniel, Sir.   A curate in *Love's Labour's Lost.*

Nerissa.   In *The Merchant of Venice,* the clever waiting-maid of

Portia. When Portia disguises herself as a lawyer, Nerissa acts as a clerk.

Nestor. In *Troilus and Cressida*, a Greek commander. Old and greatly venerated by the other warriors, he remarks that adversity is the test of valor (I.iii).

Neville. The name of a family prominent in English history, several of whose members appear as characters in Shakespeare's historical plays, as follows: Anne Neville is Lady Anne in *Richard III*; John Neville is the Marquess of Montague in *3 Henry VI*; a Ralph Neville is the Earl of Westmoreland in *1* and *2 Henry IV* and in *Henry V*; another of the same name and title appears in *3 Henry VI*; a Richard Neville is the Earl of Salisbury in *2 Henry VI*; and another Richard Neville, the famous "Kingmaker," is the Earl of Warwick in *2* and *3 Henry VI*.

Newgate. The western gate of London wall by which the Watling Street left the city. It was at first called Westgate, but later Chancellor's Gate. In the reign of Henry I Chancellor's Gate was rebuilt and called Newgate, and at the same time began serving as a prison. Newgate had an unsavory reputation and resisted efforts at reform.

Newington Butts Theatre. A theatre in Newington, Surrey, in which plays were performed from about 1580 onwards.

New Place. The house of Shakespeare's (later) residence and death at Stratford-upon-Avon. The foundations still remain. It is now believed to have been built c1490. Shakespeare bought it for £60 in 1597. At that time there were two barns, two gardens, and two orchards belonging to it, and Shakespeare afterward enlarged the gardens. He retired there permanently in 1610. The house was torn down in 1759, but the site was bought by subscription in 1861.

Nicanor. In *Coriolanus*, the Roman who chats wth the Volscian and tells him of the banishment of Coriolanus (IV.iii).

Nine Worthies. In *Love's Labour's Lost*, the masque presented before Ferdinand, King of Navarre, the Princess of France, and the rest of the court. In the masque, Costard is Pompey, Sir Nathaniel is Alexander, Moth is Hercules, and Armado is Hector. It is intended as a parody on a pageant familiar to Elizabethans and often given on state occasions.

Norfolk, Duke of. In *3 Henry VI*, a supporter of the Yorkist (White Rose) faction.

Norfolk, (1st) **Duke of.** In *Richard III*, the historical John Howard, a supporter of the King. He is killed at Bosworth.

Norfolk, (1st) **Duke of.** In *Richard II*, see **Mowbray, Thomas.**

Norfolk, (2nd) **Duke of.** In *Henry VIII*, the historical Thomas Howard, a strong opponent of Wolsey. He appears as the Earl of Surrey, son of the 1st Duke of Norfolk, in *Richard III*.

Northumberland, Earl of.   In *Macbeth*, see **Siward.**

Northumberland, (1st) ***Earl of.***   In *Richard II*, the elder Henry Percy, who joins Bolingbroke on his return to England and later orders Richard to Pomfret and his queen to France. In *1 Henry IV*, he pretends illness to avoid committing himself against Henry IV (Bolingbroke) in battle and is not present at Shrewsbury when his son Hotspur is killed. In *2 Henry IV*, he encourages Archbishop Scroop to rebel but then flees to Scotland. Later it is announced that he has been defeated.

Northumberland, (3rd) ***Earl of.***   In *3 Henry VI*, the historical Henry Percy, grandson of Hotspur, a supporter of the King and of the Lancastrian (Red Rose) faction. He is killed at Towton.

Northumberland, Lady.   In *2 Henry IV*, the wife of the (1st) Earl of Northumberland. She advises her husband to flee to Scotland.

Nurse.   In *Romeo and Juliet*, a go-between during the early romance who later (after Romeo is banished) urges Juliet to forget Romeo. A very practical woman, and a major source of comic relief in the play, she has come to be one of the best-known minor characters in Shakespeare.

Nurse.   In *Titus Andronicus*, a witness of the birth to Tamora of Aaron's bastard son, and therefore killed by Aaron.

Nym.   In *The Merry Wives of Windsor*, a thief and sharper, the companion of Falstaff, "an amusing creature of whimsey." He also appears with Pistol and Bardolph in *Henry V*. It has been thought that he may be a parody of characters in the Jonsonian humour comedies, since he is constantly referring to his "humour."

O

Oberon.   In *A Midsummer Night's Dream*, the King of the Fairies, who quarrels with his wife Titania. It is the magic liquid that he drops into her eyes (and thus causes her to fall in love with the first creature she sees on awakening), and that

Puck drips into the eyes of various human participants in the play, that makes possible the various misunderstandings and misdirected affections upon which the plot depends.

Obidicut.   In *King Lear*, a fiend ("of lust") mentioned by Edgar (IV.i).

Octavia.   In *Antony and Cleopatra*, the rather conventional wife of Antony. She accepts marriage with Antony in an effort to reconcile him and her brother Octavius, but Antony deserts her for Cleopatra.

Octavius Caesar.   In *Julius Caesar*, one of the triumvirs after Caesar's death and a victorious general in the civil war against Cassius and Brutus. Shakespeare's *Antony and Cleopatra* has him marrying off his sister Octavia to Antony, ridding himself of Lepidus, the other triumvir, and making war on Cleopatra and Antony after the latter has deserted Octavia and fled to Egypt. Defeating Antony at Actium, he then invades Egypt and after the suicides of Antony and Cleopatra is left in control of the Roman Empire. The historical Octavius (63 B.C.–A.D. 14) was Caesar's nephew and became emperor of Rome in 27 B.C.

Old Lady.   In *Henry VIII*, a companion to Anne Bullen (II.iii). She somewhat resembles the Nurse in *Romeo and Juliet*.

Old Man.   In *King Lear*, one of Gloucester's tenants. He leads the blinded Earl and is sent by him for clothes for Tom o'Bedlam (IV.i).

Old Man.   In *Macbeth*, a minor character (III.iv).

Oliver.   In *As You Like It*, the elder brother of Orlando. He plots to kill Orlando, who thereupon flees to the forest. Later Oliver is saved from a lion, repents, and marries Celia. In Lodge's *Rosalynde*, from which the plot is taken, he is called Saladyne.

Olivia.   A principal character in *Twelfth Night*. Like Orsino, she is absorbed in herself and her own situation, but her infatuation with the disguised Viola gives her a new awareness of life.

Ophelia.   In *Hamlet*, the daughter of Polonius. A timorous and dutiful girl, she obeys her father and repulses Hamlet's overtures, thus adding to the Prince's sense of betrayal and solitude. Hamlet's subsequent cruelty to her and the shock of her father's death combine to drive her mad, and she drowns herself.

Orlando.   In *As You Like It*, the younger brother of Oliver and lover of Rosalind.

Orleans, Duke of.   In *Henry V*, the historical Charles d'Orléans, the cousin and close companion of the Dauphin. He brags of the French superiority, but is captured at Agincourt.

Orsino.   In *Twelfth Night*, the Duke of Illyria. He is a self-indulgent character, obsessed with his own emotions and his unrequited love for Olivia. Finally he comes to realize that it is actually Viola whom he loves.

Osric.   In *Hamlet*, an affected courtier.

Ostler, Williams.   fl. 1601–23. An English actor, one of the per-formers listed in the First Folio (1623) of Shakespeare's plays.

Oswald.   In *King Lear*, Goneril's steward. He is a haughty, in-sulting person, who, having angered Lear, is struck by him. He is called a "serviceable villain" (IV.vi) by Edgar, who kills him.

Othello.   The hero of the tragedy *Othello*. By nature he is a noble and idealistic man who has won a high reputation as a soldier. All of his experience has been in the military world, so that he comes to his marriage in middle age with complete inno-cence of women and of civilian life. He readily falls victim to the wiles of the experienced Iago, and gradually his trust in his wife and his confidence in himself are totally eroded. When he real-izes that he has been tricked into murdering his pure and loving wife, he immediately executes justice on himself by committing suicide.

Othello.   [Full title, ***The Tragedy of Othello, the Moor of Venice.***] A tragedy by Shakespeare, probably written in 1602, first acted in 1604, and printed in 1622 in a quarto and in 1623 in the First Folio. The folio is better than the quarto, but both were apparently prepared from the Shakespeare manuscript, the folio containing revisions made during the playing. The play's main source was Giraldi Cinthio's *Gli Hecatommithi* (Decade 3, Story 7), first published in 1565, which Shakespeare perhaps read in the French translation made by Gabriel Chappnys in 1584, no English version being known until 1753. Shakespeare alters both the circumstances of the story and the characteriza-tion. In Cinthio, the Moor and his wife Disdemona have been married for several years before the story starts, and all the events take place over a much longer period of time than in Shakespeare's play. The Ensign (Iago) is motivated by thwarted love for Disdemona; he steals her handkerchief while she is caressing his child. The murder of Disdemona is contrived to look like an accident; the Moor and the Ensign beat her to death with a stocking filled with sand and then cause the ceiling of the room to collapse, thus burying the body. After her death the Moor becomes half mad with grief and misery; he dismisses the Ensign, who thereupon plots with the Corporal (Cassio) to bring him to trial for murder. Finally, all is revealed and God avenges Disdemona's death. In this account the Moor is a totally passive and ignoble victim of the malicious Ensign. No character corresponding to Shakespeare's Roderigo appears. Shakespeare may also have used Geoffrey Fenton's translation of a story from Belleforest's *Histories Tragiques*, adapted from the Italian *Cer-taine Tragicall Discourses* by Matteo Bandello, published in 1567. This story tells of a soldier husband who becomes needlessly jealous of his young wife a month after their marriage and stabs her in bed in a paroxysm of fury. The wife does not die immediately but in fact survives her husband, who immediately commits suicide. After his death she pardons him. The ending of this perhaps suggested Desdemona's last words to Emilia. Some details of the background of the Venetian-Turkish war in *Othello* may have been drawn from Richard Knolles's *History of the Turks* (1603) and perhaps also from William Thomas's *History of Italy* (1549) and Sir Lewis Lewkenor's *The Commonwealth and Government of Venice*, translated in 1599 from the Italian version of G. Contarini's *De Magistratibus et Republica Venetorum* of 1543. In his play, Shakespeare concentrates on the betrayal of a good man by a completely wicked man whose evil flows out of the boundless and irrational nature of all evil. With diabolical adroitness Iago links Cassio's utterly innocent activities with the supposed faithlessness of Desdemona and thus contrives to build in Othello's mind a hideous structure of suspicion. But Iago does not work toward this by plain words; his strategy is marked by disingenuous indirection, leaving Othello always with the suspicion that he (Iago) knows more than he has hinted at. The play, which contains some of the most beautiful poetry in all of Shakespeare, is well plotted and moves at a rapid pace. The double time scheme, by which the actual stage events are spaced within the compass of two days whereas the actual sequence of time for the plot development is several months, contributes to this unity.

Dramatis Personae

Duke of Venice	Montano, *Governor of Cyprus*
Brabantio, *a Senator*	Clown, *Othello's Servant*
Other Senators	Desdemona, *Othello's Wife*
Gratiano, *Brabantio's Brother*	Emilia, *Iago's Wife*
Lodovico, *Brabantio's Kinsman*	Bianca, *Cassio's Mistress*
Othello, *a noble Moor*	Sailor, *Messengers, Herald,*
Cassio, *Othello's Lieutenant*	*Officers, Gentlemen,*
Iago, *Othello's Ancient*	*Musicians, and Attendants*
Roderigo	

The Story. Othello, a Moorish general in the service of Venice, has secretly married Desdemona, a Venetian beauty. While he is explaining their love to her father, Brabantio, and the Senate, news comes that war has broken out in Cyprus, and he must leave immediately. Desdemona follows him, accompanied by Othello's ensign, Iago, who is angry that a promotion has been given to Cassio rather than himself. This is the ostensible motive for the course of treachery he immediately starts to follow. Iago manages to get Cassio drunk and consequently demoted for disorderly behavior; then suggests to him that he approach Othello through Desdemona for reinstatement. At the same time, Iago manages to suggest to Othello that Desdemona and Cassio are having an affair. Then, getting Emilia (his wife) to pick up a handkerchief that Desdemona inadvertently drops, he contrives that Cassio should give the handkerchief to his mistress Bianca and that Othello should see her sewing upon it. The handkerchief itself has magic in it, as Othello tells Desdemona, and thus it is more than a mere incriminating clue. It becomes for Othello the symbol of Desdemona's supposed wantonness, for in giving it to Cassio, as he believes, she has betrayed the scant regard that she attaches to his love. In the last act, Othello is a ruthless avenger, bent (as he now thinks) on preventing Desdemona from betraying other men. Just as he has always done his duty on the field of battle, Othello must do his duty now, even though it breaks his heart. He asks Iago to kill Cassio; the deed is attempted by Iago's dupe Roderigo but fails, and Iago kills Roderigo to avoid betrayal. Othello thereupon goes to Desdemona and smothers her in her bed. But his love for her is not dead, and at this climactic moment he is overwhelmed by a poignant realization of his loss. At the same time, he does not yet suspect the perfidy of Iago and he keeps repeating the ironic refrain, "Honest, honest Iago" (V.ii). Emilia, however, questions Iago and almost instantly perceives the truth, crying "Villainy, villainy!" (V.ii). Meanwhile, letters have been found on Roderigo's body that incriminate Iago. With this, Othello's world collapses, and he bitterly renounces his honor, "But why should honor outlive honesty? / Let it go all" (V.ii). After trying, and failing, to kill Iago, he recalls the service he has done on the battlefield and asks that Cassio and the others remaining do him the justice of reporting things honestly as they have happened. With a return to the quiet dignity that is perhaps his most essential characteristic, he says simply that they should, in referring to him, speak of "one that loved not wisely but too well" and one "perplex'd in the extreme" (V.ii). He stabs himself and, falling on Desdemona's bed, dies.

Overdone, Mistress.   In *Measure for Measure*, a bawd who is sent to prison.

Ovid.   [Full Latin name, **Publius Ovidius Naso.**] b. at Sulmo, Italy, 43 B.C.; d. at Tomi (now Constanta), near the Black Sea, A.D. 18. A Roman poet, one of the leading writers of the Augustan age. He lived at Rome, and was exiled for an unknown reason to Tomi on the Euxine (Black Sea) in Moesia, about A.D. 9. His chief works are elegies and poems on mythological subjects, *Metamorphoses, Fasti, Ars Amatoria, Heroïdes,* and *Amores.*

Oxford, Earl of. In *3 Henry VI*, the historical John de Vere, a supporter of Margaret and the Lancastrians. He is captured at the battle of Tewkesbury. In *Richard III*, he joins Richmond and fights at Bosworth.

P

Page. In *The Merry Wives of Windsor*, the easy husband of Mistress Page.

Page to Falstaff. In *2 Henry IV*, a small boy who serves Falstaff and who talks rather precociously. In *Henry V*, he is the "Boy" who serves Bardolph, Nym, and Pistol, upon whose antics he comments caustically. He is killed by the French while guarding the army supplies of the English.

Page, Anne. In *The Merry Wives of Windsor*, the daughter of the Pages, wooed and finally won by Fenton. She rejects both Slender and Dr. Caius, her parents' choices.

Page, Mistress. In *The Merry Wives of Windsor*, one of the married women to whom Falstaff professes love. She fools him into believing that she responds but in fact devises the Windsor Forest incident, the climax of all the pranks played on Falstaff.

Page, William. In *The Merry Wives of Windsor*, the young brother of Anne Page. The scene where he appears was first printed in the folio of 1623.

Palace of Pleasure, The. A collection of tales published in two volumes (a third was projected, but never written) by William Painter in 1566–67. Translations of the stories of Livy, Boccaccio, Bandello, and Margaret of Navarre appear here (Painter originally intended to translate only from Livy, but changed his plan and added the later French and Italian stories). The two volumes contain a hundred tales, making this the largest prose work between *Morte d'Arthur* and North's *Plutarch*, and it is a source for the plots of many Elizabethan dramas.

Palamon. In *The Two Noble Kinsmen*, one of the principal characters, the cousin and friend of Arcite.

Palamon and Arcite.   Two noble youths, the story of whose love for Emelye (or Emilia) has been told by Chaucer in *The Knight's Tale* (derived from Boccaccio's *Il Teseida*), and by numerous others, including a play by Fletcher and another author (perhaps Shakespeare) called *The Two Noble Kinsmen* (written about 1612–13, registered 1634).

Palsgrave's Company.   See **Lord Admiral's Men.**

Pandarus.   In *Troilus and Cressida*, the uncle of Cressida. An older and more corrupt character than Chaucer's Pandarus, he takes a salacious pleasure in fostering Cressida's affair. At the end of the play he predicts his own death and bequeaths his diseases to his fellow bawds.

Pander.   In *Pericles*, the owner of the brothel in Mytilene to which Boult brings Marina. His trade is nearly lost by her persuading his clients to desist from their vice.

Pandulph, Cardinal.   In *King John*, the papal legate who forces the French king to break his peace with John. He persuades the Dauphin to invade England, but then vainly tries to make him withdraw when John accepts the Pope's (and Pandulph's) candidate for Archbishop of Canterbury.

Panthino.   In *Two Gentlemen of Verona*, the servant of Antonio.

Paris.   In *Romeo and Juliet*, a young nobleman to whom Capulet has betrothed his daughter Juliet, against her will.

Paris.   In *Troilus and Cressida*, a son of Priam and lover of Helen. He, of course, opposes Hector's suggestion that Helen be returned to the Greeks so that the war may end, and fights with Menelaus, Helen's former husband (V.vii).

Parolles.   In *All's Well That Ends Well*, a braggart whose poltroonery is humorous and droll. One of Shakespeare's best comic parts, he has been compared with Falstaff, but his boasting dominates him, whereas Falstaff's does not. Like Pistol, he is pompous and lacks a sense of humor. When exposed, he takes his dishonor calmly and decides to make use of his talents: "There's place and means for every man alive" (IV.iii).

Pasquil.   Pseudonym of **Nash** (or **Nashe**), **Thomas.**

Patroclus.   In *Troilus and Cressida*, a Greek commander. He urges his friend Achilles to stop sulking and rejoin the war, but it requires his death at Trojan hands finally to rouse Achilles to action.

Patience.   In *Henry VIII*, a gentlewoman to Queen Katherine.

Paulina.   In *The Winter's Tale*, the wife of Antigonus and defender of Hermione. She brings Leontes the young Perdita and announces Hermione's death. Years later she produces Hermione before Leontes and there is a reconciliation. Antigonus having died, Leontes persuades Paulina to marry Camillo.

Peaseblossom. A fairy in *A Midummer Night's Dream.*

Pedant. In *The Taming of the Shrew,* a teacher who pretends to be Vincentio, the father of Lucentio, and is useful in arranging Lucentio's marriage to Bianca. When the real father of Lucentio appears, Pedant runs away, but he reappears in the happy scene at the end of the play.

Pedro, Don. In *Much Ado About Nothing,* the Prince of Arragon. He arranges for the marriage of Claudio and Hero, but by the scheme of his bastard brother, Don John, is convinced of Hero's unfaithfulness. Later he makes amends when the truth is discovered. He arranges also for Benedick to overhear that Beatrice is in love with him, and for Beatrice to be similarly entrapped.

Pembroke, Earl of. In *3 Henry VI,* the historical William Herbert, a Yorkist whom Edward IV orders to secure men for his cause against King Henry.

Pembroke, (1st) Earl of. In *King John,* the historical William Marshal, 1st Earl of Pembroke and Striguil. He disapproves of submission to the Pope and later joins the other English lords in their defection to the French after Arthur's supposed murder. When these lords find that the French have sworn to kill them after defeating John, they return to his side.

Percy, Henry. In historical plays, three characters, based on historical figures, appear under the name of Henry Percy: the (1st) Earl of Northumberland, father of Hotspur, in *Richard II* and *1* and *2 Henry IV;* Hotspur, in *1 Henry IV;* and the (3rd) Earl of Northumberland, grandson of Hotspur, in *3 Henry VI.* See also **Northumberland, Earl of.**

Percy, Sir Henry. [Called **Hotspur.**] b. 1364; killed in the battle of Shrewsbury, England, 1403. An English soldier; son of Henry Percy (1342–1408), 1st Earl of Northumberland. In 1402 he fought alongside his father at Homildon Hill and captured the Earl of Douglas. He attempted to arrange an exchange of prisoners with Henry IV, seeking to use Douglas as ransom for his (Percy's) brother-in-law Edmund Mortimer. Henry IV refused, and Percy, angered by this refusal, associated himself with Owen Glendower in his war against the King. It was during this war that Percy was killed at Shrewsbury, in 1403. Shakespeare introduces him (on the basis of the accounts in Holinshed) as a gay, jesting, fiery-tempered soldier, in *1 Henry IV.*

Percy, Lady. In *1 Henry IV,* the wife of Hotspur and sister of Mortimer. In a domestic scene she pleads with Hotspur to tell what plans he has in hand. He refuses to talk to her about the rebellion, but she follows him when he goes to Wales to join Mortimer and Glendower. In *2 Henry IV,* she speaks proudly of her husband, noting that every courtier is affecting his lisp. She urges Northumberland to be avenged for his son's death at Shrewsbury.

Percy, Thomas, Earl of Worcester. See **Worcester, Thomas Percy, Earl of.**

Perdita.   In *The Winter's Tale*, the daughter of Leontes and Hermione. Leontes orders that she be abandoned in some desert place, but she is rescued and raised as a shepherdess. Florizel falls in love with her, and she is finally restored to her mother and penitent father.

Pericles.   The Prince of Tyre, the hero of *Pericles*. He is an upright and noble character who undergoes much suffering, losing both wife and daughter, but is eventually rewarded when they are restored to him.

Pericles.   [Full title, **Pericles, Prince of Tyre.**] A play by Shakespeare, written possibly in 1607 or 1608. It must have been first performed in the interval January, 1606–November, 1608 (probably nearer to the latter date), as we have a report from the Venetian ambassador that he saw it in London in that span of time. It was published in 1609, in quarto, in a corrupt and probably unauthorized text, and again in quarto in 1611, 1619, 1630, and 1635. Not in the folio of 1623, it appeared first in folio in 1664. It is now generally agreed that Shakespeare did not write the entire play, and it was probably not included in the folio of 1623 for that reason. It has been suggested that Shakespeare took two acts by an inferior playwright and added three more (except possibly for the Gower choruses). The main sources for the play are the story of Apollonius of Tyre from Book VIII of John Gower's *Confessio Amantis* (1343) and Laurence Turine's romance, *The Patterne of Painefull Adventures* (c.1594), a version of story 153 from the Medieval Latin collection *Gesta Romanorum*. Material from Gower and Turine is interwoven throughout the play. In Gower, the hero's name is Apollinus, and in Turine, the more usual Apollonius; Shakespeare's name Pericles has been thought to come from Pyrodes in Sidney's *Arcadia* (1590), whose adventures are to some extent similar, and other suggestions for its source have included North's translation of Plutarch's *Lives*, which also contains the names Cleon and Lysimachus. Marina's name is perhaps Shakespeare's invention, for she is called Thaise in Gower and Tharsia in Turine, a name that Shakespeare or his coauthor adapted for her mother. The relationship of *Pericles* with its main sources is somewhat complicated by the existence of George Wilkins's novel, *The Painfull Adventures of Pericles, Prince of Tyre*, published in 1608, a year before the play; this is mainly founded on Turine's book, which was reissued in 1607, and on a *Pericles*, performed by the King's Men. This *Pericles* may have been the one Shakespeare partly wrote, an earlier version of it, or a completely different play that Shakespeare too used as a source. The Shakespearean *Pericles* differs from Gower and Turine in the addition of the character Gower, who acts as a chorus or presenter. The play omits details of Antiochus' incest with his daughter, adds a test enforced by Simonides to prove Pericles's love for Thaisa, and generally strengthens the contrast between the different father-daughter relationships. The brothel scenes are elaborated and made more realistic anu sordid in the play, although Lysimachus's character is made purer so that he may be a fitting husband for Marina. It is difficult to generalize on the use of the sources in this play, since Shakespeare's part in it is still not certain and the text is corrupt. In 1660 Betterton acted the play on the Restoration stage (some have thought that it was the first of Shakespeare's work to take the stage again after the Restoration).

Dramatis Personae

Antiochus, King of Antioch	Boult, *the Pander's Servant*
Pericles, Prince of Tyre	*Marshal*
Helicanus, *a Lord of Tyre*	*The Daughter of Antiochus*
Escanes, *a Lord of Tyre*	Dionyza, *Wife of Cleon*
Simonides, King of Pentapolis	Thaisa, *Daughter of Simonides*
Cleon, *Governor of Tarsus*	Marina, *Daughter of Pericles*
Lysimachus, *Governor of*	Lychorida, *Marina's Nurse*
Mytilene	*A Bawd*
Cerimon, *a Lord of Ephesus*	*Lords, Ladies, Knights, Gentle-*
Thaliard, *a Lord of Antioch*	*men, Sailors, Pirates, Fisher-*
Philemon, *Cerimon's Servant*	*men, and Messengers.*
Leonine, *Dionyza's Servant*	Diana
A Pander	Gower, *as Chorus*

The Story.   Pericles discovers early in his courtship of the daughter of Antiochus of Antioch that the father and daughter are entangled in an incestuous romance, and is therefore placed in peril of his life by Antiochus. Deputizing his loyal minister, Helicanus, to rule Tyre in his stead, he boards ship for Tarsus, but is cast up on the shores of Pentapolis, the sole survivor of a shipwreck. He participates in a tourney for the hand of Thaisa, daughter of King Simonides of Pentapolis, and their marriage follows shortly on the heels of his victory. Thus far, in the first two acts (which Shakespeare is believed not to have written), the play has followed a very straightforward plot, but at this point manifold complications are introduced. Pericles is informed by Helicanus of the death of Antiochus, and the hero therefore sets out at once for Tyre with his wife, who is now with child. A violent storm arises, and the terrified Thaisa gives birth to a daughter and, a few moments later, falls into a state of unconsciousness so deep as to simulate death. Pericles, believing her dead, places her in a chest and casts the chest into the sea. Thaisa is washed ashore at Ephesus and restored to consciousness by Cerimon. Convinced that her husband has perished, she enters the temple of Diana as a votaress. Pericles, meanwhile, leaves the daughter, Marina, in Tarsus with Cleon and his wife Dionyza. Sixteen years later Dionyza, violently jealous of this child, now become a woman more beautiful than her own daughter Philoten, seeks to rid herself of Marina by ordering a servant to kill her. The servant is frightened off by pirates, however, and Marina is carried off to a brothel in Mytilene. Humbled by her chastity and beauty, the patrons of this establishment leave her untouched, and one of them, Lysimachus, governor of the city, buys her freedom. Meanwhile, Pericles sees Marina's tomb in a dream and sets out to visit it; cast ashore at Mytilene, he recognizes and is joyfully reunited with Marina. Another dream then sends him to Ephesus with Marina, and there he encounters Thaisa. Marina is forthwith married to Lysimachus, and it is related that Dionyza and Cleon have been murdered by the Athenians.

Peter. In *Measure for Measure*, a confidant of Vincentio, the Duke of Vienna.

Peter. In *Romeo and Juliet*, the servant of Juliet's nurse.

Peter of Pomfret. In *King John,* a prophet who predicts that John will yield up his crown before Ascension Day. He is hanged for this.

Peto. In *1 and 2 Henry IV*, an associate of Sir John Falstaff.

Petrarch. [Italian, **Francesco Petrarca**; original name, **Petracco**.] b. at Arezzo, Italy, July 20, 1304; d. at Arqua, near Padua, July 19, 1374. An Italian poet, second in importance among Italian poets of the Middle Ages only to Dante. In 1327 he first saw the Laura idealized and celebrated in his sonnets. Her real identity is unimportant: what is important is the effect she had on Petrarch's lyric poems of unrequited love and consequent melancholy, together with his inner conflict between desire and religious duty. These reactions were distilled into verse of remarkable elegance, clarity of expression, and formal perfection. From the outset of his career he was an avid student of antiquity, his passion for which was evidenced in his Latin works of erudition, such as his collection of biographies *De viris illustribus* (On Famous Men, 1338 *et seq.*), and in his first major work, the Latin epic poem *Africa* (1338–42), celebrating the exploits of Scipio Africanus. Primarily in recognition of the promise shown in the *Africa*, he was crowned poet laureate by the senate in Rome April 8, 1341 (he had received on the same day as the invitation to Rome a similar invitation from the University of Paris). In 1347 he built a house at Parma, but resided partly at Vaucluse until 1353, when he settled at Milan. He was patronized by nobles and ecclesiastics and employed on various diplomatic missions, principally by the Visconti, whom he represented at the court of King John II of France, conducting the marriage of a young Visconti with the daughter of the king. In 1362 he removed to Padua, where he had held a canonry since 1347, and to Venice, in the same year, where he saw Boccaccio for the last time, having first met him in 1350 at Florence. In 1370 he went to Arqua, where he died. Posterity remembers him chiefly for his personal utterances, in his *Canzoniere* (collected lyric poems, in Italian) and such Latin works as his *Epistles* (1326–74), and for his philosophic-religious treatises *Secretum* (Innermost Thoughts, 1343), *De vita solitaria* (On Solitary Life, 1346–56), *De otio religiosorum* (On Monastic Freedom from Care, 1347–56), and *De remediis utriusque fortunae* (On the Remedies for Good and Bad Fortune, 1350's–1366). An effort to rival Dante in an Italian allegorical and didactic poem, *I Trionfi* (The Triumphs, c1352–74), was unsuccessful. The English sonnet, perhaps the principal verse form in the language, stems directly from Petrarch through Henry Howard, Earl of Surrey, and Sir Thomas Wyatt, whose translations of his sonnets appeared early in Elizabeth's reign and inspired in the next fifty years a great flow of English lyric poetry.

Petruchio. In *The Taming of the Shrew,* a Veronese gentleman who determines to wed and tame the shrew, Katherina. Despite her display of temper on their first meeting, he calls her "passing courteous" and "modest as the dove" (II.i). By asserting his dominance (in such ways as arriving late and in old clothes for the wedding, refusing to let her stay for the dinner, taking her food and new clothes from her, and making her call the sun the moon) he makes her a gentle and submissive wife.

Phebe. In *As You Like It,* a shepherdess loved by Silvius. She falls in love with the disguised Rosalind but finally marries Silvius.

Philario. In *Cymbeline,* an Italian gentleman, the friend who tries to prevent Posthumus and Iachimo from making their wager.

Philemon. In *Pericles,* a servant of Cerimon.

Philip, King of France. In *King John,* the historical Philip II, who supports Arthur's claim to the English throne.

Philip Faulconbridge. See **Faulconbridge, Philip.**

Philip the Bastard. See **Faulconbridge, Philip.**

Phillips, Augustine. d. May 1605. English actor and musician. He was one of the original shareholders in the Lord Chamberlain's Men (formed 1594) and of the Globe (1599) and is listed as a principal actor in the First Folio (1623) of Shakespeare's plays.

Philo. In *Antony and Cleopatra,* a friend of Antony.

Philostrate. In *A Midsummer Night's Dream,* Theseus's master of the revels.

Philoten. In *Pericles,* the daughter of Cleon and Dionyza. She is so far surpassed in beauty by Marina that the latter's murder is plotted by the jealous parents of the plainer girl. She does not appear on stage. In Lillo's adaptation of the play, she instigates the attempt to murder Marina.

Philotus. In *Timon of Athens,* a servant to one of Timon's creditors.

Phoenix, the. A London theatre near Drury Lane. It was altered (1616) from a pit for fighting cocks and its earlier name was the Cockpit. It was pulled down in 1649 by the Puritans here but not completely destroyed.

Phoenix and the Turtle, The. A poem generally accepted as being by Shakespeare, first published in an appendix to a book called *Love's Martyr,* by Robert Chester, in 1601.

Phrynia. In *Timon of Athens,* a mistress of Alcibiades.

Pinch. In *The Comedy of Errors,* a schoolmaster who believes Antipholus and Dromio of Ephesus to be mad and orders them confined.

Pindarus. In *Julius Caesar,* a servant to Cassius. When Cassius thinks the battle is lost at Philippi, he makes Pindarus stab him.

Pirithous. In *The Two Noble Kinsmen,* an Athenian general.

Pisanio. In *Cymbeline,* the servant of Posthumus. When he receives his master's letter ordering him to kill Imogen, he disguises her as a boy and bids her join the Roman army.

Pistol. In *The Merry Wives of Windsor,* in *2 Henry IV,* and also in *Henry V,* a bully and swaggerer, a companion of Falstaff. He is a modification of the stock type of Italian comedy, the "Thrasio" or cowardly boaster. In *Henry V* he is married to Mistress Quickly, and after her death he decides to become a pimp. Shakespeare may have intended him as a satire upon the acting of Edward Alleyn, the well-known Elizabethan tragedian and leader of the rival Lord Admiral's Men.

Plantagenet, Lady Margaret. In *Richard III,* a young daughter of Clarence who mourns his death.

Plantagenet, Richard. See **York,** (3rd) **Duke of.**

Players. In *Hamlet,* the company that comes to play at the Court. They travel because they could not find city employment. The "late innovation" (II.ii) is a Shakespearean reference to contemporary conditions in the London theatrical world, either to the child companies whose popularity had temporarily surpassed that of the adult companies or to the banning of plays in London because of Essex's recent rebellion (1601). They perform the "Murder of Gonzago" (*The Mousetrap* play), in which Hamlet has inserted a few pertinent speeches. Hamlet's advice to the actors (III.iii) is of documentary interest in illustrating the stylized acting of the Elizabethan stage.

Players. In the Introduction to *The Taming of the Shrew*, the company represented as about to enact the play itself, for the entertainment of Christopher Sly.

Plays. In all, there are now some thirty-eight plays that are generally attributed to Shakespeare, with John Fletcher as coauthor of *Henry VIII* and *The Two Noble Kinsmen*, and the first two acts of *Pericles* most probably written by another author. There is still some question as to whether *The Two Noble Kinsmen* can actually be attributed to Shakespeare, even as coauthor, and this play is often omitted from listings of Shakespeare's plays. The dates of composition of the plays can be given only tentatively, since many were written some time before they were registered or printed, and the probable revision of some of the plays makes the problem even more difficult. In some cases letters, journals, and other sources have aided in a closer determination of when the plays were first acted, and parodies of various lines or references to some of the plays in other plays of the period have also aided in dating the plays. In many cases, internal evidence, such as references to contemporary events, has also proved helpful. The following is an alphabetical listing of the plays, with tentatives dates of composition:

All's Well That Ends Well (c1593; rewritten 1602–04)
Antony and Cleopatra (1606–07)
As You Like It (1599–1600)
The Comedy of Errors (1592–93)
Coriolanus (1607–08)
Cymbeline (1609–10)
Hamlet (1600–1601)
1 Henry IV (c1597)
2 Henry IV (c1598)
Henry V (1598–99)
1 Henry VI (1589–91)
2 Henry VI (1589–91)

3 Henry VI (1589–91)
Henry VIII (1612–13)
Julius Caesar (c1599)
King John (1596–97)
King Lear (c1605)
Love's Labour's Lost (1594–95; possible rev. 1597)
Macbeth (1605–06)
Measure for Measure (1604–05)
The Merchant of Venice (1596–97)
The Merry Wives of Windsor (1597–1601)
A Midsummer Night's Dream (1595–96)

Much Ado About Nothing	The Tempest (1611–12)
(c1598)	Timon of Athens (1605–08)
Othello (c1602)	Titus Andronicus (1593–94)
Pericles (1607–08)	Troilus and Cressida (1598–1601)
Richard II (1595–96)	Twelfth Night (1599–1600)
Richard III (1592–93)	Two Gentlemen of Verona
Romeo and Juliet (1594–96)	(1594–95)
The Taming of the Shrew	The Two Noble Kinsmen (1612–13)
(1593–94)	The Winter's Tale (1610–11)

Poins.   In *1* and *2 Henry IV*, a dissolute, witty companion of Prince Henry and Falstaff.

Polack.   A Pole; the term is used in *Hamlet (I.i,* and elsewhere).

Polixenes.   In *The Winter's Tale,* the King of Bohemia, father of Florizel.

Polonius.   In *Hamlet,* the father of Ophelia, and the King's chamberlain. He is an unscrupulous and interfering old man who spies on the activities of his children and does not hesitate to use Ophelia as a bait to trap Hamlet. Appropriately, he is killed by Hamlet when hiding in Gertrude's chamber to spy on her encounter with her son.

Polydore.   In *Cymbeline,* the name under which Guiderius is raised by Morgan (actually Belarius).

Pompey.   [Also, **Sextus Pompeius.**] In *Antony and Cleopatra,* a leader of the rebellion against the triumvirate. When Antony returns from Egypt, Pompey makes peace with him and Octavius and entertains them on his galley. In the war between Antony and Octavius, he sides with Antony. In history he was the younger son of Pompey the Great.

Pompey.   In *Measure for Measure,* the clownish servant of Mistress Overdone.

Pope, Thomas.   fl. 1586–1603. English actor, comedian, and acrobat. He is listed in the First Folio (1623) of Shakespeare's plays as a principal actor and was an original shareholder in the Lord Chamberlain's Men (formed 1594).

Porter.   In *Macbeth,* the drunken doorman who admits Macduff and Lennox to Macbeth's castle just as Macbeth has murdered Duncan. He is the only comic character in the tragedy.

Portia.   In *Julius Caesar,* the wife of Marcus Brutus. She goes insane from anxiety over her husband, and her death (from swallowing fire) is reported (IV.iii).

Portia.   In *The Merchant of Venice,* an heiress in love with Bassanio. Portia is noted for her law-court defense of Bassanio's friend Antonio against the demand of Shylock for a pound of flesh from Antonio's body. It is she who (disguised as Balthasar, a learned doctor of law) delivers the famous speech beginning

"The quality of mercy is not strain'd" (IV.i), a plea for Shylock's mercy. In her adherence to the exact letter of the law she beats Shylock at his own game and brings about his ruin.

Posthumus Leonatus. In *Cymbeline*, the husband of Imogen. His wager as to her fidelity is a turning point of the play.

Priam. In *Troilus and Cressida*, the King of Troy. He debates with his sons about returning Helen to the Greeks and later pleads with Hector not to fight Achilles.

primrose path. A gay and easy way to evil and hell; used by Ophelia (to Laertes) in *Hamlet*, in contrast to the difficult way to heaven:

> Do not as some ungracious pastors do
> Show me the steep and thorny way to heaven,
> Whiles, like a puff'd and reckless libertine,
> Himself the primrose path of dalliance treads
> And recks not his own rede. (I.iii)

Prince Henry's Company. See **Lord Admiral's Men.**

Prince of Bohemia. See **Florizel.**

Prince of Verona. See **Escalus.**

Princess of France. In *Love's Labour's Lost*, a visitor to the "little Academe" (I.i) of the King of Navarre. The King falls in love with her and thus breaks his vow to deny love for three years.

Proculeius. In *Antony and Cleopatra*, a friend of Octavius. He is sent to capture Cleopatra at the end of the play but is frustrated in his purpose when she kills herself.

Prospero. In *The Tempest*, the rightful Duke of Milan. He is represented as a wise and good magician (not a necromancer or wizard) living in exile on an island with his daughter Miranda. Through his use of magic he makes Ferdinand fall in love with Miranda, after having caused the shipwreck that brought Ferdinand to the island. Later in the play, Prospero again uses magic, to thwart the plan of Caliban, Stephano, and Trinculo for murdering him. Alonso, the King of Naples, Antonio, Prospero's brother and the usurping Duke of Milan, and the evil Sebastian, who were also brought to the island in the shipwreck, are humbled by Prospero and forgiven when they repent their crimes. He thereupon renounces his magic: "But this rough magic / I here abjure" (V.i). This is said after the beautiful speech in which he dissolves the masque presented before the lovers, Ferdinand and Miranda:

> These our actors
> As I foretold you, were all spirits, and
> Are melted into air, into thin air:
> . . . . the great globe itself,

Yea, all which it inherit, shall dissolve
And like the insubstantial pageant faded,
Leave not a rack behind. We are such stuff
As dreams are made on, and our little life
Is rounded with a sleep. (IV.i)

Proteus. In *Two Gentlemen of Verona*, one of the "two gentle-men." He is faithless to Julia, his betrothed, and betrays his friend Valentine, but eventually repents and is happily wedded to Julia at the end of the play.

Provost. In *Measure for Measure*, the prison custodian. He sympathizes with Claudio and agrees to execute Barnardine in his stead, but finally sends Angelo the head of another prisoner who has already died.

Publius. In *Julius Caesar*, a senator who is astonished by the conspiracy against Caesar.

Publius. In *Titus Andronicus*, the son of Marcus Andronicus.

Puck. [Also, **Robin Goodfellow.**] In *A Midsummer Night's Dream*, the servant of Oberon. He plays many pranks in the woods near Athens, including changing the head of Bottom to that of an ass. Puck was a mischievous household spirit of English folklore, and Shakespeare transmuted him from a rather malicious sprite, often called Robin Goodfellow, to the gay and joking fairy of the play.

Pyramus and Thisbe. In classical legend, two Babylonian lovers. They were forbidden to see each other by their parents, but continued secretly to talk together through a crack in the wall that separated their gardens. They finally planned to meet at a certain tomb. Thisbe, who arrived first, was terrified by a lion and fled, dropping her cloak. Pyramus arrived a few min-utes later, found the cloak bloodstained from the lion's mouth (the lion, according to the traditional account, had eaten some-one else just before it saw Thisbe), believed Thisbe dead, and killed himself. When Thisbe returned and found her lover dead, she too killed herself. Their story is celebrated by Ovid in his *Metamorphoses*, and Shakespeare introduces it (as "Pyramus and Thisby") in the interlude of *A Midsummer Night's Dream*, presented by Bottom, Flute, and the other artisans in honor of the marriage of Theseus and Hippolyta. Various elements of their story are reminiscent of that of Romeo and Juliet, espe-cially the feuding families and the double deaths at the tomb.

Q

Queen.   In *Cymbeline*, the wife of Cymbeline and the mother of Cloten by a former husband. In her efforts to secure the throne for her son, she tries to marry him to Imogen, then attempts to poison Imogen, Cymbeline, and Pisanio. She goes mad and confesses her crimes before she dies.

Queen.   In *Richard II*, the historical Isabel of France, Richard's queen. She overhears a gardener talking about an orchard and contrasting his husbandry with that of Richard. She bids farewell to Richard as he goes to the Tower.

Queen Elizabeth's Men.   An Elizabethan theatrical company formed by Edmund Tilney, Master of the Revels under Queen Elizabeth. They were the most important company in London from 1583 to 1590.

Queen of the Amazons.   See **Hippolyta.**

Queen of the Fairies.   See **Titania.**

Queen of the Goths.   See **Tamora.**

Quickly, Mistress.   In *The Merry Wives of Windsor*, the housekeeper of Dr. Caius. She assists Anne Page's suitors and later plays the Queen of the Fairies. Some critics argue that she is not identical with the Mistress Quickly in the historical plays. In *1* and *2 Henry IV* and *Henry V*, the simple-minded and garrulous Hostess of the Boar's Head, the tavern that Falstaff and his friends frequent. In *2 Henry IV*, she claims that Falstaff has promised to marry her, and that he owes her £100. He talks her out of it, even though she will have to pawn the tavern furnishings. Later she goes to prison with Doll Tearsheet for beating up a man. In *Henry V*, it appears that she has married Pistol. She movingly describes the death of Falstaff (II.i).

Quinapalus.   In *Twelfth Night*, an imaginary authority cited by the clown: "For what says Quinapalus? 'Better a witty fool than a foolish wit' " (I.v).

Quince, Peter.   In *A Midsummer Night's Dream*, a carpenter. He is stage manager and speaks the Prologue in the interpolated play.

Quintus.   In *Titus Andronicus*, one of the four sons of Titus.

R

Raleigh, Sir Walter. [Surname as he preferred to spell it, *Ralegh.*] b. at Hayes, Devonshire, England, c1552; executed at London, Oct. 29, 1618. An English courtier, colonizer, and poet. He came into great favor at court; according to legend this was due to his gallant action of spreading his cloak over a puddle so that the queen might not wet her shoes. Actually, his personal charm, good looks, and powerful sponsors at court all probably facilitated his rapid rise. He introduced cultivation of the potato, in Munster, on lands he was granted by the queen; he is also credited with introducing the "drinking" of tobacco (as smoking was then called). In 1588 he took an active part against the Armada. During this period he became a friend of Edmund Spenser, whom he had met in Ireland some years earlier. He introduced Spenser to Elizabeth and persuaded him to publish the *Faerie Queene.* He had, however, gradually fallen out of the queen's favor as she became more and more infatuated with Robert Devereux, 2nd Earl of Essex. Raleigh became the center of a group of poets and scientists, known as the "school of night," that included Christopher Marlowe, Thomas Harriot, George Chapman, Walter Warner, and Matthew Royden, among others. This brilliant group, containing some of the best minds in England, gained notoriety for their free attitude toward such matters as religion, in those days so closely tied to government in the person of the monarch that atheism was tantamount to treason; Marlowe was killed before the Privy Council could examine him on his opinions, but an official investigation was made into Raleigh's beliefs in 1594, the charges eventually dying for lack of decisive evidence. On the accession of James in 1603, Raleigh was stripped of his honors and estates and charged with a plot to place Arabella Stuart on the throne. He was imprisoned in the Tower, tried very unfairly in November, 1603, and sentenced to death. The sentence was not carried out, but Raleigh remained a prisoner in the Tower until 1616. While in the Tower he devoted himself to chemical experiments and began writing his *History of the World,* which was left unfinished when he was released from the Tower in 1616. He commanded another expedition to Guiana and the Orinoco, but the expedition was a failure from the start. Ships were lost in storms; his men melted away as the result of disease and desertion; a group got into a fight with the Spaniards and Raleigh's son was killed. On his return, when the Spanish ambassador made an official complaint about the destruction of a Spanish town by Raleigh, an old sentence was invoked, and Raleigh was executed. In addition to the incomplete *History of the World*, which contains a famous apostrophe to Death, he wrote a number of other prose works, including accounts of the Azores fight and the discovery of Guiana, and he was the author of several poems: *Cynthia* (which is his longest extant poem and may be a fragment of a much longer work), *The Lie*, *The Pilgrimage*, *The Nymph's Reply* (to Marlowe's *The Passionate Shepherd*), the sonnet appended to the *Faerie Queene* "Methought I saw the grave where Laura lay," and others.

Rambures.   In *Henry V*, the Master of the Cross-bows and one of the French lords who boast about the power of the French army before the battle of Agincourt.

Rape of Lucrece, The.   [Also, *Lucrece.*] A narrative poem by Shakespeare, published in 1594, taken from the Roman story of Lucretia. (See article, "Shakespeare's Major Poetry.")

Rape of Lucrece, The.   A tragedy by Thomas Heywood, published in 1608 and revised in 1636. It was produced in 1612. Possibly it was written in 1607, since the Roman theme may have been suggested by an edition of Shakespeare's *Rape of Lucrece* that appeared in that year; however, Heywood used Livy for the historical material in the play.

Ratcliff, Sir Richard.   In *Richard III*, a follower of the King who leads Richard's various victims to execution. He is killed at Bosworth with Richard.

Ratsey's Ghost.   [Also, *Ratsei's Ghost.*] A very rare tract, printed without date but supposed to have been published in 1605. It mentions the play *Hamlet* by name during a discussion of Ratsey's criminal career.

recorder.   A small flutelike wind instrument of wood with a whistle-shaped mouthpiece and eight holes, much used in Shakespeare's day. In *Hamlet* the courtiers Rosencrantz and Guildenstern are carrying recorders. Guildenstern claims he cannot play, and Hamlet counters, " 'Tis as easy as lying" (III.ii).

Red Bull, the.   A public playhouse built in Clerkenwell, now part of London, about 1604.

Regan.   In *King Lear*, the second daughter of Lear; like her sister Goneril, she hypocritically flatters Lear in order to win his land, but her feeling for him is soon revealed as scorn and derision. She is cruel and pitiless toward Gloucester, and encourages her husband Cornwall to blind him. Finally she finds herself in competition with Goneril for the favors of Edmund and dies of poison at her sister's hand.

Reignier, Duke of Anjou. In *1 Henry VI*, the supporter of the Dauphin and Joan of Arc, and the assumed King of Naples, Sicily, and Jerusalem. He agrees to the marriage of Margaret, his daughter, with Henry if he can have the territories of Maine and Anjou.

Retort Courteous. In *As You Like It* (V.iv), the first (and now probably the best known) of the seven possible retorts to an insult, or "degrees of the lie," cited by Touchstone as causes of a quarrel. The others, in order, are the Quip Modest, the Reply Churlish, the Reproof Valiant, the Countercheck Quarrelsome, the Lie Circumstantial, and the Lie Direct.

Revels Office. An official body existing in England from about the middle of the sixteenth century to the late seventeenth century, headed by the Master of the Revels and charged with supervising Court performances of plays and other entertainments. Sir Thomas Cawarden was the first permanent Master. Court Revels were held from Nov. 1 to the beginning of Lent in the time of Henry VIII; under Elizabeth they were concentrated around Christmas; and James I (who greatly enjoyed the theatre) lengthened the season again. It is presumed that in most cases plays licensed by the Master of the Revels for playing were automatically licensed for printing.

Reynaldo. In *Hamlet*, a servant to Polonius. In the first quarto he is called Montano.

Rice, John. fl. 1607–20. An English actor. He acted in Shakespeare's plays and is mentioned as a principal actor in the First Folio (1623) of Shakespeare's works.

Richard, Duke of Gloucester. See **Gloucester, Richard, Duke of.**

Richard, Duke of York. See **York, Richard,** (5th) **Duke of.**

Richard II. In *Richard II*, the king of England, a poetic and charming man but a fatally weak monarch. Unable to follow any decisive course of action, he fails in his royal duties (but with his keen sense of the dramatic, he takes a kind of satisfaction in posing as the wronged and wretched king). Before his death he comes to some recognition of the duties involved in kingship and of his own failure to perform them.

Richard II. [Full title, **The Tragedy of King Richard the Second.**] A historical play by Shakespeare, produced probably in 1595, and published in 1597. The deposition scene unquestionably carried particular significance for Queen Elizabeth (whose right to the throne was questioned by a fair number of her subjects for most of her reign). Understandably, therefore, it was omitted in the first quarto (1597); however, by the time of the fourth quarto (1608) it was restored. The play was also given a special performance at the Globe theatre on Feb. 7, 1601, the day before Essex started his rebellion. It was paid for by Essex's supporters, but none of the actors was punished for putting it on. Shakespeare took material for the play from a number of sources but his main source was Holinshed's *Chronicles* (2nd ed., 1587), from which he took most of the names and events in his play, following, with certain alterations, Holinshed's account of the end of Richard's reign from April 1398 to March 1400. In several instances he telescoped and rearranged the sequence of events for greater dramatic effect; the death of Gaunt, Richard's departure for Ireland, and the return of Bolingbroke from banishment all take place in a single scene (II.i), whereas in Holinshed they happen over a matter of months, and the events of Act IV are also compressed. The accusations of Bagot and Fitzwater were made on separate occasions in October 1598 after the actual abdication of the king, which was in September, and the Abbot of Westminster's plan for conspiracy was not formed until December. Other changes from Holinshed reflect on Shakespeare's planning of the characterization in his play. He omits an episode in which Northumberland tricked Richard into an ambush on the way to Flint Castle that might have reflected badly on Bolingbroke, and he totally changes the ages of Northumberland's son, Henry Percy (Hotspur), and Bolingbroke's son, the future Henry V. Hotspur was in fact two years older than both Richard II and Bolingbroke, whereas in *Richard II* he is a youth; and Bolingbroke's son was only twelve in 1399, when Shakespeare has Bolingbroke speak of him as a dissolute young gallant. He used another chronicle, *The Union of the Two Noble and Illustre Famelies of Lancastre and Yorke* (1548) by Edward Hall, for the point of departure of his play, since Hall's account of Richard II's reign also begins with the quarrel between Mowbray and Hereford, but for little otherwise. He undoubtedly knew the anonymous contemporary play, *Woodstock*, which deals with events from 1382 to 1399 and especially with the life of Richard II's uncle, Thomas of Woodstock, Earl of Gloucester, who is referred to several times in *Richard II*, although critics have differed as to how far this play influenced him. There are a number of verbal echoes of *Woodstock* in *Richard II*, and it is possible that Shakespeare presumed on his audience's knowledge of the older play in his passing allusions to Richard's extravagance and extortion. Shakespeare also knew the *Mirrour for Magistrates*

(1599) in which Richard II is presented as a proud and tyrannous king, a classic example of the idea that "lawles life, to lawles death ey drawes," but he plainly departed very far from this moralistic view of Richard II's life and death. Froissart's *Chronicles,* translated by Lord Berners in 1525, was also available to him, and from this he may have taken hints for the conception of Gaunt as a wise but rejected counsellor, for the important part Northumberland played in calling back Bolingbroke, and for Bolingbroke's popularity with the people, although he could have found these elsewhere. Two other French chronicles, the *Chronicque de la Traison et Mort de Richard Deux Roy Dengleterre* and the *Histoire du Roy d'Angleterre Richard II* by Jean Créton, both known to Holinshed and Hall, may have been used independently by Shakespeare. The *Traison* is evidence of a tradition more favorable to Richard II than that of the Tudor chronicles, and it may have helped Shakespeare to form his relatively sympathetic portrait of Richard II, especially in the account of Richard's leave-taking from his Queen, although in the *Traison* the event takes place before Richard's departure for Ireland. From Créton may have come the comparison between Richard's betrayal and that of Christ. The *Traison* and Créton's account also influenced Samuel Daniel in his poem *The First Fowre Bookes of the Civile Wars* (1595), which it is likely that Shakespeare knew and used. Many parallels between *Richard II* and Daniel's poem may be incidental, but Shakespeare seems to owe to Daniel the conception of the Queen—she was in fact a child of nine at the time—and he may also have used Daniel for the account of the contrasted entries of Richard and Bolingbroke into London (V.ii). Finally, Marlowe's *Edward II,* although in no way a source for Shakespeare's play, may well have provided some ideas and inspiration in its treatment of the fall of a weak monarch.

Dramatis Personae

King Richard the Second
John of Gaunt
Edmund of Langley, Duke of York
Henry Bolingbroke, Duke of Hereford, *later* Henry IV
Duke of Aumerle
Thomas Mowbray, Duke of Norfolk
Duke of Surrey
Earl of Salisbury
Lord Berkeley
Lord Ross
Lord Willoughby
Lord Fitzwater
Bishop of Carlisle
Abbot of Westminster
Lord Marshal
Sir Stephen Scroop
Sir Pierce of Exton
Captain of a Band of Welshmen
Queen to King Richard
Duchess of Gloucester
Duchess of York

Bushy	*Lady attending on the Queen*
Bagot	*Lords, Heralds, Officers, Soldiers,*
Green	*Gardeners, Keepers, Messen-*
Earl of Northumberland	*ger, Groom, and other Attend-*
Henry Percy (Hotspur)	*ants*

The Story. In the presence of the King, Bolingbroke ac-cuses Mowbray of causing the death of the Duke of Gloucester. It is agreed that each man may defend his honor in a tourna-ment, but just as each is about to attack the other, the King dramatically halts the proceedings and banishes them both. Shortly thereafter, upon the death of John of Gaunt (Boling-broke's father), Richard seizes his estates in order to finance an Irish campaign. This additional evidence of Richard's disregard for the rights of his nobles arouses the ire of both York and Northumberland, and the latter, with other nobles, goes to join Bolingbroke (who has returned, despite his exile, to claim his dukedom). When Richard returns from Ireland, he learns that his army has dispersed and his favorites, Bushy and Green, have been executed by Bolingbroke. Richard takes refuge in Flint Castle, and when Bolingbroke meets him there (ostensibly to claim his estates) submits to being taken as a prisoner to Lon-don. Before Parliament, he is forced to confess his crimes against the state, and despite the protests of the Bishop of Carlisle, he hands over his crown to Bolingbroke, who is already acting as king. Aumerle, the son of York, has meanwhile plotted against the new ruler. When York discovers this he hastens to inform Bolingbroke, but Aumerle and his mother, York's wife, plead for and are granted clemency. Richard is imprisoned in Pomfret Castle, where he is murdered by Sir Pierce of Exton (who mis-takenly believes that Bolingbroke wishes Richard's death). Bo-lingbroke, however, regrets the murder and vows to lead a Crusade to ease his conscience. In its theme, the play touches a principle which was to tear England apart half a century later: the right, conferred by God, of a king to hold his throne. This right is here examined in a situation in which the king is a poor ruler but an attractive person, and the usurper, whose abilities may merit the throne, must nevertheless bring "disorder, horror, fear, and mutiny" to England by taking it. As Richard points out, he himself is a traitor to the crown by giving it up, and Bolingbroke is aspiring beyond his reach in accepting the crown.

Richard III. See **Gloucester, Richard, Duke of.**

Richard III. [Full title, **The Tragedy of King Richard the Third.**] A historical play, written by Shakespeare in 1592–93. It was printed anonymously in quarto in 1597; in a 1598 quarto Shakespeare's name appears; other quartos were published in

1602, 1605, 1612, and 1622; it appears also in the folio of 1623. In 1700, Cibber produced an alteration, using parts of other Shakespeare plays, that was long considered the only acting version of the text. Cibber himself acted in the role of Richard until 1739. Shakespeare's main sources were the two prose chronicles, Holinshed's *Chronicles* (2nd ed., 1587) and *The Union of the Two Noble and Illustre Famelies of Lancastre and Yorke* (1548) by Edward Hall, which Holinshed had used as a source, although Shakespeare consulted it independently. Both Hall and Holinshed had the story of the fiend-like Richard, which in many respects owes more to Tudor propaganda than to historical fact, from chronicles composed in the reign of Richard's successors Henry VII and Henry VIII, Sir Thomas More's *History of King Richard III*, printed in English in 1557 and in Latin in 1566, and Polydore Vergil's *Historia Angliae* (1534). Shakespeare might have consulted More or Vergil himself, but he is more likely to have come to their work through the medium of Hall and Holinshed. As was usual in his history plays, Shakespeare had to select from, rearrange, and compress events taking place over a considerable period of time, in this instance fourteen years, from Henry VI's death in May 1471 to the Battle of Bosworth in August 1485. For instance, in the play the arrest of the Duke of Clarence takes place before the burial of Henry VI and his execution before the death of his brother Edward IV, whereas in fact Henry was buried in 1471, Clarence was executed in 1477, and Edward died in 1483. As well as using Hall and Holinshed for the major events of the play and the characterization of the hero, Shakespeare took various minor details from their accounts; the bleeding of Henry VI's corpse during the funeral procession comes from Holinshed, the two murderers of Clarence from Hall's account of the murder of the Princes in the Tower, the demise of the credulous Hastings (III.iv) from Hall, and the contrasting orations of Richmond and Richard before the battle from both. Other details were taken from sixteenth-century plays and poems. From the *Mirrour for Magistrates* (1559) Shakespeare took the idea of the ghosts of Richard's victims appearing at his bedside the night before the battle and also the account of Clarence's wretched death; the *Mirrour* was the first work to suggest that Richard was in part responsible for Clarence's death. He may have found a precedent for his use of the women characters from the Latin tragedy *Richardus Tertius* (1579) by Thomas Legge; in *Richard III* the women are distinctly more significant than in Shakespeare's earlier histories and Queen Margaret, who in fact never came back to England after she was ransomed but died in 1383 in France, is unhistorically introduced into several scenes to prophesy and curse. Legge used various Senecan plays such as *Hercules Furens,* translated by Jasper Heywood in 1561, for some of Queen Elizabeth's part, and Shakespeare may also have drawn on Seneca, either in the original or in one of the contemporary translations. The relationship of Shakespeare's *Richard III* to the anonymous play, *The True Tragedy of Richard III,* published in 1594 but written earlier, is not clear; the plays have many features in common, especially in their fusion of elements from the Senecan revenge play with the English chronicle play, but owing to uncertainty over the dating of *Richard III* it is impossible to say which play borrowed from the other. The problem is complicated by the fact that the extant version of *The True Tragedy* is textually very corrupt, and must have come from an earlier, accurate version, now unfortunately lost.

Dramatis Personae

King Edward the Fourth
Edward, Prince of Wales,
    afterwards King Edward V
Richard, Duke of York
George, Duke of Clarence
Richard, Duke of Gloucester,
    afterwards King Richard III
A young Son of Clarence
Henry, Earl of Richmond;
    afterwards King Henry VII
Cardinal Bourchier
Thomas Rotherham,
    Archbishop of York
John Morton
Duke of Buckingham
Duke of Norfolk
Earl of Surrey
Earl Rivers
Marquess of Dorset
Lord Grey
Earl of Oxford
Lord Hastings
Lord Stanley (Earl of Derby)
Lord Lovel

Sir Thomas Vaughan
Sir Richard Ratcliff
Sir William Catesby
Sir James Tyrrel
Sir James Blunt
Sir Walther Herbert
Sir Robert Brakenbury
Christopher Urswick, *a Priest*
Another priest
Tressel *and* Berkeley
Lord Mayor of London
Sheriff of Wiltshire
Elizabeth, *Queen to*
    King Edward IV
Margaret, *Widow of King*
    Henry VI
Duchess of York
Lady Anne
Margaret Plantagenet
Lords and other Attendants; a
    Pursuivant, Scrivener,
    Citizens, Murderers,
    Messengers, Soldiers
Ghosts of those murdered by
    Richard III

The Story. Richard, Duke of Gloucester, having determined to obtain the crown, sets out to dispose of every obstacle, whether a person or a right, that may stand in his way. He manages to get his elder brother, the Duke of Clarence, imprisoned by the dying Edward IV, and orders his murder in the

Tower. As the funeral procession of Henry VI passes by, he greets Lady Anne, the widow of Henry's son, and is soundly cursed by her; nevertheless, he proposes to her and is accepted. Margaret the widow of Henry VI, Elizabeth the widow of the now dead Edward IV, and the Duchess of York, the mother of Edward, Clarence, and Richard, all curse the scheming Richard and mourn the loss of their loved ones. While appearing to arrange the coronation of young Edward (whom he has imprisoned with his younger brother in the Tower), Richard executes Hastings, Rivers, Grey, and Vaughan, supporters of Elizabeth and her son. Buckingham, Richard's supporter, goes to the Guildhall and persuades the citizens to offer Richard the crown. When he is crowned he disposes of all who might oppose him, including the young princes in the Tower. His henchman, Buckingham, having refused to kill the princes, flees to join Richmond but is murdered on the way. Meanwhile Richmond, the champion of justice, has landed and marches toward London, and at Bosworth Field the two forces meet. On the eve of the battle, Richard sees the ghosts of all his victims, and the following day he is slain by Richmond, who is then crowned Henry VII, the first Tudor king.

Richmond, Henry Tudor, Earl of. In *3 Henry VI*, a young boy who Henry prophesies shall be king one day. In *Richard III*, he lands with an army, bent on dethroning the tyrannical Richard. He defeats Richard at Bosworth and is proclaimed Henry VII. His reign is foreseen as bringing peace to England. The historical Henry VII, first of the Tudor dynasty, unified the Lancastrians and Yorkists by his marriage with Edward IV's daughter, Elizabeth.

Rinaldo. In *All's Well That Ends Well*, the steward of the Countess of Rossillion.

Rivers, Earl. In *3 Henry VI*, the brother of Elizabeth, Lady Grey, who is later the Queen of Edward IV. In *Richard III*, he is executed on Richard's order because he has urged the coronation of young Prince Edward.

Roan Barbary. In *Richard II*, the favorite horse of King Richard.

Robin. In *The Merry Wives of Windsor*, Falstaff's page. He may be the same person as the Page who appears in *2 Henry IV* with Falstaff and in *Henry V* with Bardolph, Nym, and Pistol.

Robin Good Fellow. See **Puck.**

Robinson, Richard. d. 1648. An English actor, celebrated as an impersonator of female characters. He appears in the lists of actors of the Shakespeare (1623) and Beaumont and Fletcher (1647) folios. He is known to have acted in Jonson's *Catiline* (1611) and Fletcher's *Bonduca* (1611).

Roderigo.   In *Othello*, a foolish gentleman in love with Desdemona. Iago uses him to involve Cassio in a quarrel, hoping the
latter will be killed, but then stabs Roderigo while he is
scuffling with Cassio. The letters incriminating Iago in the plot
to play upon Othello's jealousy are found on Roderigo's body.

Rogero.   In *The Winter's Tale*, a gentleman of Sicilia.

Romeo.   The hero of *Romeo and Juliet*. He is moody at first,
then reveals to Benvolio his longing for the haughty Rosaline.
When he sees Juliet he is gay and lyrical (even Tybalt gets no
harsh words), but his happiness is ruined when he is forced into
a duel with Tybalt by the latter's killing of Mercutio. In Friar
Laurence's cell he is distracted, threatens suicide, and has to be
warned that this would betray his love for Juliet. He must face
banishment in accordance with the Prince's edict. He revives
at the hope of meeting Juliet but, when he hears she is dead,
his own death is his inevitable next thought.

Romeo and Juliet.   [Full title, **The Tragedy of Romeo and
Juliet.**] A romantic tragedy by Shakespeare, printed in an unauthorized edition in 1597, which is 800 lines shorter than the
quarto of 1599, and known to have been produced before 1597.
It was written between 1594 and 1596 and the textual critics
Dover Wilson and Alfred Pollard have suggested that it is
basically a revision of an older play. Shakespeare's main source
for this play was a long narrative poem in fourteeners called *The
Tragical Historye of Romeus and Juliet* by Arthur Brooke, published in 1562, from which he had already taken a few phrases
for his poem *Venus and Adonis*. Brooke's poem was in turn based
on a French translation by Pierre Boiastuau of an Italian novella
by Matteo Bandello. The story of two young lovers who persist
in their romance despite the enmity of their families only to
come to a tragic conclusion had long been popular in Renaissance Italy in several forms, the earliest known version being
the story of Mariotto and Gianozza of Siena told by Masuccio in
Il Novellino (1476). In Luigi da Porto's *Istoria novellamente
ritrovata di due Nobili Amanti* (pub. c1530), for the first time the
story is set in Verona, the lovers are aristocrats, and the feuding
families are the Montecchi and the Cappelleti. Shakespeare did
not know the Italian versions of the story and probably not
Boiastuau's French one, but apart from Brooke's poem he may
also have known William Painter's translation of Boiastuau in
his *Palace of Pleasure* (1567). Brooke, in his preface to the
reader, says that he has seen the story "lately set foorth on
stage," but no stage version before Shakespeare's is known. It
is clear that the story of Romeo and Juliet was popular in
Elizabethan England. Brooke's poem was reprinted in 1582, and
reissued in 1587. Shakespeare followed it quite closely. Romeo's

former love, the meeting of Romeo and Juliet at the ball, the helpful intervention of Friar Laurence, the clandestine marriage, Romeo's fight with Tybalt and subsequent banishment, Juliet's sleeping potion, the ill-luck with the messenger sent to Romeo, the suicide of Romeo followed by the immediate revival of Juliet and her death, are all essential features of Shakespeare's play to be found in Brooke. Shakespeare alters his source principally by speeding up the action and filling out the characters. In Brooke, the story takes place at a leisurely pace over several months; in Shakespeare the lovers meet, mature, and die in a few hectic days. The characters of Mercutio and Tybalt are developed from the briefest descriptions; their enmity and their opposition to the world Romeo discovers through his love for Juliet are entirely Shakespeare's invention. The lovers are younger than in the source; in Brooke, Juliet is sixteen, in Shakespeare only fourteen. Apart, of course, from filling out the bare language of his source with amazing poetry, Shakespeare's main alteration was to the tone of the story. Brooke says his aim is to describe "a couple of unfortunate lovers, thralling themselves to unhonest desire, neglecting the authorities and advise of parents and frendes . . . and by all meanes of unhonest lyfe, hastyng to most unhappye deathe." His is a moral tale, emphasizing the rashness of youth and the inconstancy of fortune. Shakespeare takes from him the theme of ill-luck and "inauspicious stars," but his emphasis is rather on the beauty and pathos of Romeo and Juliet's sacrificial passion than on their "unhonest lyfe." *Romeo and Juliet* was adapted by Otway in 1680 as *Caius Marius*; in altered form it was the object of a competition in 1750 between Garrick and Anne Bellamy at Drury Lane and Barry and Mrs. Theophilus Cibber at Covent Garden. Indeed, it was not until 1850 (and then as a vehicle for the American actress Charlotte Cushman) that the play was again performed as Shakespeare wrote it.

Dramatis Personae

Escalus, Prince of Verona	Peter, *Servant to Juliet's*
Paris, *Kinsman to the Prince*	*Nurse*
Montague	Abram, *Servant to Montague*
Capulet	*An Apothecary*
Uncle to Capulet	*Three Musicians*
Romeo, *Son to Montague*	*Page to Paris; another Page*
Mercutio, *Friend to Romeo*	*An Officer*
Benvolio, *Friend to Romeo*	Lady Montague
Tybalt, *Nephew to Lady Capulet*	Lady Capulet
Friar Laurence	Juliet, *Daughter to Capulet*
Friar John	*Nurse to Juliet*

Balthasar, *Servant to Romeo*

Sampson, *Servant to Capulet*

Gregory, *Servant to Capulet*

Citizens of Verona; Kinsfolk of both Houses; Masquers, Guards, Watchmen, and Attendants

Chorus

The Story.   In Verona live the feuding families of Montague and Capulet. Romeo, the son of Montague, is infatuated with "the fair Rosaline" (I.ii), Capulet's niece. Learning that she is invited to a ball at Capulet's, he joins with some masquers and attends, in disguise, but there falls in love with Juliet, the daughter of Capulet. That night he steals into Capulet's orchard and, standing under Juliet's balcony, hears her declare her love for him, "O Romeo, Romeo! wherefore art thou Romeo? . . . be but sworn my love, / And I'll no longer be a Capulet" (II.iii). At this, he steps forward and declares his love for her, and they plan to be secretly married the following day. Romeo arranges with Friar Laurence for the marriage, and with the aid of Juliet's voluble nurse, the two are wed at the Friar's cell. That same afternoon, in a chance meeting with Tybalt, a Capulet, Romeo is challenged to a duel, but he refuses, knowing Tybalt is Juliet's cousin. Romeo's friend Mercutio accepts the challenge and is killed, at which Romeo avenges his death by killing Tybalt. Since such fighting had been declared unlawful, Romeo is banished by the Prince, and after one night with Juliet he leaves for Mantua, reassured by Friar Laurence that in time all will be reconciled. Meanwhile, Juliet's parents announce that she is to be married immediately to Paris, a kinsman of the Prince. Her parents refuse to postpone the marriage, and her nurse advises that a handsome and noble second husband in Verona is of more use than a first husband in banishment. Now alone with her problem, Juliet obtains from Friar Laurence a sleeping potion that will make her seem as if dead, for forty-two hours, during which time he will send a message to Romeo, who will come and free her from the tomb. However, Friar John, with the message for Romeo, is delayed by constables who think he may be infected with the plague, so Romeo hears only of Juliet's death. He returns to Verona, fights with and kills the mourning Paris at Juliet's tomb, then enters the tomb, drinks poison, and dies at Juliet's side. Juliet awakens as Friar Laurence, who has just heard of his plans going awry, enters the tomb to rescue her. On seeing the dead Romeo, she refuses to leave the tomb, and when the Friar is frightened away, she first tries to poison herself with the remains of Romeo's poison, then stabs herself. Alerted by Paris's page, the watch arrives, discovers the bodies, and captures Friar Laurence, who tells of the secret marriage, the sleeping potion, and the double death. At this tragedy, Montague and Capulet repent of their enmity.

Rosader.   In Thomas Lodge's *Rosalynde* the younger brother of Torrismond the Usurper, and lover of Rosalynde. He became Orlando in Shakespeare's adaptation of the story, *As You Like It.*

Rosalind.   In *As You Like It,* the daughter of the exiled duke, in love with Orlando and the heroine of the play. She is a vigorous and witty character who controls the romantic action of the play and contrives the reunions and marriages in the final scene. At the same time she is a woman deeply in love, and Shakespeare manages to make her satirize the extravagance and artifice of romantic love while herself falling a victim to it.

Rosaline.   In *Love's Labour's Lost,* an attendant to the Princess of France. Berowne falls in love with her.

Rosaline.   In *Romeo and Juliet,* a Capulet with whom Romeo is in love at the beginning of the play. She does not appear.

Rose, the.   An Elizabethen playhouse on the Bankside, built in 1587 by Philip Henslowe and his partner John Cholmley. Shakespeare may have acted there in his early days with the Admiral's Men. The excavation of part of its foundations in 1989 reveals it to have been a polygonal structure, originally with a raked floor in the yard sloping toward the stage, which was tapered at the front, and erected to the north-north-west of the theatre. It probably had a thatched roof and walls of timber and plaster with a lower section of brick. It was rebuilt by Henslowe in 1592 to enlarge and level the yard, and to relocate the stage, possibly providing a roof over it.

Rosencrantz.   In *Hamlet,* an old schoolfellow of Hamlet, sent for, along with Guildenstern, by the King to spy upon Hamlet.

Ross.   In *Macbeth,* a Scottish thane who must tell Macduff that his wife and children have been killed on Macbeth's orders.

Ross, Lord.   In *Richard II,* one of the noblemen who join Bolingbroke when he comes to claim his estates.

Rossillion.   [Also, **Ronsillion**] **Countess of.** In *All's Well That Ends Well,* the mother of Bertram and the guardian of Helena, who tries to bring Bertram back when he abandons Helena.

Rotherham, Thomas.   In *Richard III,* the Archbishop of York. He resigns when he hears that Rivers and Grey have been imprisoned.

Rowe, Nicholas.   b. at Little Barford, Bedfordshire, England, 1674; d. Dec. 6, 1718. An English dramatist and poet, appointed (1715) poet laureate. He was educated for the bar. His chief tragedies are *The Ambitious Stepmother, Tamerlane* (1702), *The Fair Penitent* (1703), *Ulysses* (1706), *The Royal Convert* (1707), *Jane Shore* (1714), and *Lady Jane Grey* (1715). He also wrote

The Biter (1704), a comedy. He translated Lucan's *Pharsalia*. His edition (1709) of Shakespeare included a collection of traditions gathered at Stratford by Thomas Betterton; Rowe used his knowledge of the stage to divide the plays into acts and scenes, to indicate exits and entrances, to add a *dramatis personae* to each play, and to amend the many errors of spelling and punctuation in the text.

Rowley, William.   b. c1585; d. 1626 (or, according to some authorities, c1642). An English dramatist. He is mentioned as an actor in the Duke of York's Company in 1610, and also acted with Princess Elizabeth's Company at the Cockpit theatre in 1623. In 1621 he was writing for this latter company, both alone and with Thomas Middleton. He joined the King's Men in 1625 and did his last work for them. Five of his plays are extant: *A New Wonder: A Woman never Vext* (printed 1632), *A Match at Midnight* (printed 1633), *A Shoemaker a Gentleman* (printed 1638), and *The Birth of Merlin* (printed 1662), which bore Shakespeare's name as coauthor when it was printed, although it is now thought that not Shakespeare but possibly Middleton collaborated on it. *The Thracian Wonder* is no longer considered Rowley's, although his name appears on its title page. He was a collaborator on a play for Queen Anne's Men in 1607. He worked with Middleton on *A Fair Quarrel* (printed 1617), *The Spanish Gypsy* (acted c1623, printed 1653), *The Changeling* (acted 1624, published 1653), and *A Game of Chess* (licensed and acted 1624, printed 1625). A play (c1615) that is thought to be a first revision of Middleton's lost play, *The Old Law*, is credited to Rowley. With John Ford and Thomas Dekker he wrote *The Witch of Edmonton* (acted 1623, printed 1658); with Dekker, *Keep the Widow Waking* (now lost); with John Webster, *A Cure for a Cuckold* (printed 1661); and with Thomas Heywood, *Fortune by Land and Sea* (printed 1655). It is thought that Rowley also worked on some of the plays attributed to Beaumont and Fletcher.

Rugby, John.   In *The Merry Wives of Windsor*, a servant to Dr. Caius.

Rumour.   In the Induction to *2 Henry IV*, a stage direction reads "Enter Rumour painted full of tongues." He brings false news to Northumberland of Hotspur's victory at Shrewsbury. Rumour was a common figure in the masques.

Rutland, Edmund, Earl of.   In *3 Henry VI*, a son of the Duke of York, killed by Clifford to avenge the death of his father.

S

Sackerson. [Also, **Sackarson.**] A famous performing bear seen at Paris Garden in Shakespeare's time. Slender mentions him to Anne Page in *The Merry Wives of Windsor* (I.i).

Saint Nicholas' clerks. Highwaymen, a reference to Saint Nicholas as the patron of thieves; used by Gadshill in *1 Henry IV* (II.i).

Salisbury, Earl of. In *2 Henry VI*, the historical Richard Neville. He is the enemy of Suffolk, whom he has banished, and also of Cardinal Beaufort, whose death he witnesses. He joins the Duke of York and fights at St. Albans. In *3 Henry VI*, Warwick says that the Yorkist side caused Salisbury's death at Wakefield.

Salisbury, (3rd) **Earl of.** In *King John*, the historical William de Longespée (or Longsword), illegitimate son of Henry II. Disapproving of John's second coronation and suspecting him of responsibility for Arthur's death, he resolves to join the Dauphin, but on learning of the French treachery returns to John.

Salisbury, (3rd) **Earl of.** In *Richard II*, the historical John de Montacute (or Montagu), a loyal supporter of Richard. He tries to keep Richard's Welsh troops in order, and later he rebels against Henry IV but is captured and executed.

Salisbury, (4th) **Earl of.** In *Henry V*, the historical Thomas de Montacute (or Montagu). He is present at Agincourt. In *1 Henry VI*, he is killed by a cannon blast.

Salisbury Court Theatre. An old London theatre. It was built in 1629 and became one of the principal playhouses. It was destroyed in 1649.

Sampson. In *Romeo and Juliet*, a servant of Capulet.

Sandys, Lord. [Also, **Sir William Sandys** (or **Sands**).] In *Henry VIII*, a courtier.

Saturninus. In *Titus Andronicus*, the son of the late emperor of Rome. When Titus withdraws from the election, Saturninus is chosen emperor. He marries Tamora, Queen of the Goths. Discovering the body of his brother Bassianus, he orders Titus's sons executed for his murder. He kills Titus and is himself killed by Lucius.

Say, Lord. In *2 Henry VI*, the Lord Treasurer. Cade captures him and accuses him of various crimes against the populace. He is executed and his head put on a pole.

Scales, Lord. In *2 Henry VI*, the commander of the Tower who is solicited for aid during the rebellion of Cade. In *1 Henry VI*, a messenger reports that he has been captured at Patay.

Scarus. In *Antony and Cleopatra*, a friend of Antony. He describes the flight of Cleopatra's fleet at Actium and remains loyal to Antony.

Scogan, Henry. [Also, *Scoggin*.] b. c1361; d. 1407. English poet and scholar. He was a friend of Chaucer (some of his poems were long thought to be actually by Chaucer) and tutor to the sons of Henry IV (whence the suggestion made by some authorities that Shakespeare was referring to him in *2 Henry VI*; however, from the context of the play, it is clear that Shakespeare was thinking of the famous jester John Scogan, even though he put him a century before his time).

Scogan, John. [Also, *Scoggin*.] fl. c1480. A person said to have been the favorite jester of Edward IV, now chiefly remembered from a work known as *Scogan's Jests*, compiled and published by a certain Andrew Boorde (or Borde) in 1526. Some sources, including the *Dictionary of National Biography*, are inclined to suspect that he may have been a fictional character, invented as someone upon whom to hang a collection of witticisms now attributed to him. There is an allusion to him (but within the wrong century) in *2 Henry IV*.

Scroop, Lord. In *Henry V*, a traitor who, with Cambridge and Grey, plots to murder the King. He is discovered (it is not explained how) and given a warrant for his death that be believes at first to be a commission for the French campaign. He had been one of Henry's most trusted counsellors.

Scroop, Richard. In *1 and 2 Henry IV*, the historical Richard le Scrope, Archbishop of York. He joins Hotspur's rebellion in *1 Henry IV* but is not present at the crucial battle. In *2 Henry IV*, he is tricked into making an armistice and dismissing his forces, after which he is arrested. He supports the justice of the rebellion even though Prince John censures him for using his authority to subvert the English people.

Scroop, Sir Stephen. In *Richard II*, a supporter of Richard who reports the death of Bushy and Green.

Sea Captain. In *Twelfth Night*, the captain of the ship wrecked on the Illyrian coast. He promises to present Viola, disguised as a page, to Orsino, the Duke.

Seacole. In *Much Ado About Nothing*, the Second Watchman, who arrests Borachio and Conrade.

Sebastian. In *The Tempest*, the brother of the King of Naples.

He is ready to murder Alonso for his power, but is easily prevented by Ariel. At the end of the play he shows no sign of repentance.

Sebastian.   In *Twelfth Night*, the twin brother of Viola.

Second Maiden's Tragedy, The.   A play of unknown authorship, at one time attributed to George Chapman and also to Shakespeare. On the basis of internal evidence, it has also been suggested that it may have been a collaborative work by Philip Massinger and Cyril Tourneur.

Second Part of King Henry the Fourth.   See **2 *Henry IV*.**

Second Part of King Henry the Sixth.   See **2 *Henry VI*.**

Sejanus His Fall.   A tragedy by Ben Jonson, acted in 1603 and published in 1605. It is said that Shakespeare played in it.

Seleucus.   In *Antony and Cleopatra*, the treasurer of Cleopatra.

Sempronius.   In *Timon of Athens*, one of the lords who refuse to help Timon.

Sempronius.   In *Titus Andronicus*, a kinsman of Titus.

Servilius.   In *Timon of Athens*, one of Timon's servants.

Setebos.   A supposed Patagonian god, mentioned by Caliban in *The Tempest*, and by Browning in *Caliban upon Setebos*.

Sextus Pompeius.   See ***Pompey*.**

Seyton.   In *Macbeth*, an officer attending Macbeth. He reports the death of Lady Macbeth.

Shadow, Simon.   In *2 Henry IV*, a man pressed into military service by Falstaff.

Shakespeare's Cliff.   [Also, ***Hay Cliff*.**] A cliff in SE England, in Kent, about 2 miles W of Dover. It is traditionally considered to be the locale of one of the climactic scenes of *King Lear*.

Shallow.   A solemn, insignificant country justice in *The Merry Wives of Windsor* and *2 Henry IV*. He has fictitious memories of having been a roaring blade in his youth. In *2 Henry IV*, when Hal denounces Falstaff, Shallow loses both his hope of advancement and his loan of £1,000 to Falstaff, who had promised him the favor of the new king. In *The Merry Wives*, he threatens a suit against Falstaff for his tricks and tries to secure the hand of Anne Page for Slender, his cousin.

Shank, John.   d. January 1636. An English actor. A member of Pembroke's, Queen Elizabeth's, and the King's Men (c1615), he is also mentioned as a principal actor in the First Folio (1623) of Shakespeare's plays.

Shepherd.   In *1 Henry VI*, the father of Joan of Arc.

Shepherd, Old.   In *The Winter's Tale*, the reputed father of Perdita, but who actually has found her on the shore and has brought her up as his daughter. He is condemned to death by Polixenes for permitting Florizel's infatuation with her and flees with the lovers to Sicilia.

Shipmaster. [Also, **Sea Captain.**] In *2 Henry VI*, the captor of the Duke of Suffolk.

Shylock. In *The Merchant of Venice*, a Jew, one of the principal characters. He lends Bassanio 3,000 ducats on condition that if they are not repaid at the promised time he shall be allowed to cut a pound of flesh from the body of Antonio, Bassanio's friend and surety. He claims the forfeiture but is defeated by Portia, who reminds him that he loses his life if he sheds one drop of blood or takes more or less than his lawful pound of flesh. Down to the time of Charles Macklin the part was played by the low comedian and was grotesque to the extent of buffoonery. Macklin transformed it from "the grimacings of low comedy to the solemn sweep of tragedy," and made Shylock a vengeful, inexorable moneymaker. Shakespeare was ahead of his time in seeing that the bitterness and spite of Shylock resulted in part from his cruel and inhuman treatment at the hands of a Christian society.

Sicinius Velutus. In *Coriolanus*, a tribune of the people. Junius Brutus is the other.

Sidney, Sir Philip. b. at Penshurst, Kent, England, Nov. 30, 1554; d. at Arnhem, Holland, Oct. 17, 1586. An English soldier, statesman, poet, and critic, brother of Mary Herbert, Countess of Pembroke. Educated (1568–71) at Christ Church, Oxford, he made the grand tour (1572–75), traveling in France, Flanders, Germany, Hungary, and Italy. He served in Parliament (1581) for Kent. Knighted in 1583, he was a favorite, at various times, of Queen Elizabeth. He was appointed (1585) governor of Flushing, and was shot (Sept. 22, 1586) at the Battle of Zutphen, where, suffering pangs of thirst, according to a story that well illustrates (whatever its truth) the esteem in which he was held as a gracious knight and a chivalrous gentleman, he gave the water he had called for and was about to drink to a wounded soldier, saying "Thy necessity is greater than mine." Author of *Arcadia* (written 1580–83; published 1590), a combination of prose romance and poetry, *Apologie for Poetrie* (published 1595, in two editions, one entitled *Defense of Poesie*), historically important as the first good example of English literary criticism, and *Astrophel and Stella* (1591), a series of 11 songs and 108 sonnets addressed to Penelope Devereux (wife of Robert Rich). Despite this feverish literary attachment to Stella, to whom he continued to address sonnets even after his marriage, he married (1583) Frances Walsingham, daughter of Elizabeth's secretary of state. The *Arcadia*, written for his sister's amusement, was used by William Shakespeare, James Shirley, Edmund Spenser, Francis Beaumont and John Fletcher, and many others, in the Elizabethan and later periods, as source material for plays, poems, and stories; the *Apologie* was an answer to the *Schoole of Abuse* (1579), an attack on plays and poetry by Stephen Gosson, a clergyman; Sidney's sonnets anticipated and influenced those by Shakespeare.

Silence.   In *2 Henry IV*, a dull country justice.

Silius.   In *Antony and Cleopatra*, an officer under Ventidius.

Silvia.   In *Two Gentlemen of Verona*, the daughter of the Duke of Milan, loved by Valentine.

Silvius.   In *As You Like It*, a shepherd in love with Phebe.

Simonides.   In *Pericles*, the King of Pentapolis and father of Thaisa. He calls Pericles a traitor to test him before he consents to his marriage to Thaisa.

Simpcox, Saunder.   In *2 Henry VI*, an impostor who pretends to be lame until he is whipped and runs away. His wife is also present and is whipped with him.

Simple.   In *The Merry Wives of Windsor*, a servant of Slender.

Sinklo.   In *3 Henry VI*, one of the keepers; Humphrey is the other. The name derives from that of John Sincler, an actor of Shakespeare's day, who is indicated by the stage directions in the folio of 1623 to have played the part.

Sir Thomas More.   A chronicle play, based on the life of More as told in Hall's *Chronicles*. Parts of it have been attributed to Shakespeare on the basis of handwriting, as well as to Munday and Dekker, by W.W. Greg and others, who have examined the manuscript, the form in which it remained until the nineteenth century. If the handwriting could be proven to be Shakespeare's, the knowledge would be a valuable aid in determining the authorship of other manuscripts. The insurrection scenes in this play bear a similarity to Jack Cade's rebellion in *2 Henry VI*, and the tone of the scene in which More entertains the Lord Mayor, and of his speech on degree after his fall from favor is much like Shakespeare. Chambers dates the play about 1596; but Shucking, on the basis of its similarity to the work of Shakespeare, dates it 1604–05.

Siward.   [Title: **Earl of Northumberland;** called "Siward the Strong."] d. 1055. A Danish soldier in England. He is introduced as a character in *Macbeth*, where he leads an army of 10,000 English soldiers sent by Edward the Confessor. His son, Young Siward, is killed in a fight with Macbeth.

Slender.   In *The Merry Wives of Windsor*, a foolish gentleman, cousin to Shallow, and suitor to Anne Page, favored by her father.

Sly, Christopher.   A tinker in the Induction to *The Taming of the Shrew*. He is found in a drunken sleep by a nobleman, who has him taken to his own home, as a jest; and when he wakes he is made to believe that he is the lord of the manor, just recovered from fifteen years of insanity. The "Taming of the Shrew" is played for his entertainment before his illusion is broken.

Sly, William. d. 1608. An English actor. He is listed as a principal actor in the First Folio (1623) of Shakespeare's plays and may have joined the Lord Chamberlain's Men at their formation in 1594. He was an original shareholder in Blackfriar's (1608).

Smith the Weaver. In *2 Henry VI*, a follower of Jack Cade.

Smolkin. A fiend mentioned in *King Lear*.

Snare. In *2 Henry IV*, one of the two sheriff's officers (Fang is the other) sent to arrest Falstaff in Mistress Quickly's suit.

Snout, Tom. In *A Midsummer Night's Dream*, a tinker who is cast in the part of the father of Pyramus in the interpolated play. However, he finally plays the part of the wall.

Snug. In *A Midsummer Night's Dream*, a joiner who plays the part of the Lion in the interpolated play.

Solanio and Salerio. (Also, **Salanio and Salarino.**) Two minor characters in *The Merchant of Venice*. They play roles in incidents involving Lorenzo and Antonio.

Solinus. In *The Comedy of Errors*, the Duke of Ephesus.

Somerset, (2nd) Duke of. In *2 Henry VI*, the historical Edmund Beaufort, brother of John Beaufort. He carries on a fight with the Duke of York, begun by his brother. Made Regent of France, he later reports that he has lost the English territories. He is killed at St. Albans.

Somerset, (4th) Duke of. In *3 Henry VI*, the historical Edmund Beaufort, son of the 2nd Duke. He joins Warwick against Edward IV, sends Richmond to Brittany for security, and is captured and executed at the battle of Tewkesbury.

Somerset, Earl of. In *1 Henry VI*, John Beaufort, who later becomes Duke. He tries to maintain peace between Gloucester and the Bishop of Winchester but quarrels with the Duke of York.

Somervile, Sir John. In *3 Henry VI*, a supporter of the Yorkist faction.

sonnets. Sonnets (154 in number) written by Shakespeare, probably between 1593 and 1603, published in 1609. It would seem from the contents that the bulk of the sonnets were written to a man (1–126) and most of the remaining (127–152) to a woman (the Dark Lady), but, although there have been various theories, no one has been able to identify these people. (See the article, "Shakespeare's Major Poetry.") The poems are referred to by their first lines, among the best-known of which are:

"Shall I compare thee to a summer's day?"
"A woman's face with Nature's own hand painted"
"When, in disgrace with fortune and men's eyes"
"When to the sessions of sweet silent thought"
"Take all my loves, my love, yea, take them all;"
"When I have seen by Time's fell hand defaced"
"No longer mourn for me when I am dead"
"So oft have I invoked thee for my Muse"
"Some say, thy fault is youth, some wantonness;"
"Let me not to the marriage of true minds"
"The expense of spirit in a waste of shame"
"My Mistress' eyes are nothing like the sun;"
"Thou blind fool, Love, what dost thou to mine eyes,"
"Love is my sin, and thy dear virtue hate,"

Soothsayer.   In *Antony and Cleopatra*, a seer who tells Charmian and Iras that they will outlive Cleopatra.

Soothsayer.   A character in *Cymbeline*. He foretells success to the Romans and interprets Posthumus's vision.

Soothsayer.   In *Julius Caesar*, an old man who warns Caesar to "beware the Ides of March" (I.ii).

Southampton, 3rd Earl of.   [Title of **Henry Wriothesley.**] b. Oct. 6, 1573; d. in the Netherlands, Nov. 10, 1624. An English politician and soldier, a friend and patron of William Shakespeare, who dedicated to him *Venus and Adonis*, and *The Rape of Lucrece.* He was a patron also of several others writers, including Thomas Nash and John Florio. He accompanied Robert Devereux, 2nd Earl of Essex, on the expeditions of 1596 and 1597, and in 1598 married Essex's cousin, Elizabeth Vernon, a marriage that brought down on his head the ire of Queen Elizabeth. He sponsored the performance of Shakespeare's *Richard II*, a play revolving about the deposition of an incompetent king, just before the ill-fated rebellion of Essex (1601) and, being otherwise implicated in the plot, was sentenced to death. The sentence was commuted to life imprisonment, and he was released (1603) on the accession of James I. He was deeply interested in colonization and was a member of the council of the Virginia Company, whose expedition (1605) he helped to finance. He was treasurer of the company from 1620 to 1624.

Southwell, John.   In *2 Henry VI*, a priest who conjures up a spirit for the Duchess of Gloucester.

Speed.   In *Two Gentlemen of Verona*, a servant of Valentine.

Spenser, Edmund.   b. at London, c1552; d. at Westminster (now part of London), Jan. 13, 1599. An English poet. He was educated at the Merchant Taylors' School, London, and at Pembroke College, Cambridge (1569–76), where he associated with Gabriel, Harvey, Edward Kirke, and other men of note. Afterward, he became intimate with Sir Philip Sidney and Robert Dudley, 1st Earl of Leicester, who did much for him. In 1580 he went to Ireland as secretary to Lord Grey of Wilton. Until about 1588 he was resident usually at or near Dublin. Prominent among the men of letters there who were his close friends were Geoffrey Fenton and Lodowick Bryskett. From 1588 to 1598 he resided chiefly on his estate at Kilcolman in Munster in the southwestern part of Ireland. He returned to London with Sir Walter Raleigh in 1589 with the first three books of the *Faerie Queene*, which he published there in 1590, dedicating the work to Queen Elizabeth. In 1591 he returned to Kilcolman Castle, and on June 11, 1594, he married Elizabeth Boyle. In his *View of Ireland* (written c1596; published 1633) Spenser advocates the necessity of severe measures to reform Ireland. Kilcolman Castle was burned by the Irish rebels in 1598, and Spenser fled with his family to Cork, whence he went to London, where he died about four weeks later. He was buried near Geoffrey Chaucer in Westminster Abbey. His first poems, translations from Petrarch and Joachim du Bellay, were published in John van der Noodt's *Theatre* (1569). His chief poems are *The Shepherd's Calendar* (1579), *The Faerie Queene* (1590–96), *Daphnaida* (1591), *Complaints*, including "Tears of the Muses," "Mother Hubbard's Tale," and others (1591), *Colin Clout's Come Home Again, Astrophel, Amoretti,* and *Epithalamion* (1595), and *Four Hymns* and *Prothalamion* (1596).

Stafford, Lord. In *3 Henry VI*, a supporter of the Yorkist faction.

Stafford, Sir Humphrey and **William.** In *2 Henry VI*, brothers, members of an armed force that tries to stop the rebel, Jack Cade, and his men. The two Staffords are killed.

Stanley, Lord. In *Richard III*, a lord attending Richard. He is mistrusted by Richard because his wife is the mother (by Henry Tudor) of Richmond. Richard keeps Stanley's son, George, as hostage when Richmond lands in England, and on the eve of Bosworth, Stanley tells Richmond he cannot openly help him. However, he also refuses to help Richard. In one quarto and the folio he is called the Earl of Derby.

Stanley, Sir John. In *2 Henry VI*, the escort of the Duchess of Gloucester when she goes into exile.

Stanley, Sir William. In *3 Henry VI*, a member of the Yorkist faction.

Starveling, Robin. In *A Midsummer Night's Dream*, a tailor who is cast in the part of the mother in the interpolated play.

He actually has no lines to speak and plays Moonshine instead.

Stephano.   A messenger in *The Merchant of Venice.*

Stephano.   In *The Tempest*, a drunken butler who plots with Caliban to murder Prospero.

Strange's Men.   See **Lord Chamberlain's Men.**

Stratford-on-Avon.   [Also: **Stratford-upon-Avon,   Stratford.**] A municipal borough and market town in C England, in Warwickshire, situated on the river Avon, at the N end of the Cotswolds, ab. 8 mi. SW of Warwick, ab. 101 mi. NW of London by rail. It is famous as the birthplace of William Shakespeare. It contains the Church of the Holy Trinity, with the tomb of Shakespeare; the house where it is thought that Shakespeare was born; and New Place, the site of the house built by Sir Hugh Clopton in the time of Henry VII, and bought by Shakespeare in 1597. Shakespeare's supposed birthplace is now national property and has been restored. The low gabled exterior and the interior rooms preserve their 16th-century character. A Shakespeare Museum has been formed in the house. The Shakespeare Memorial Building (built by popular subscription from the U.S. and Britain) includes a theatre in which the annual Shakespeare Festival takes place, a gallery, and a library. The Shakespeare fountain was erected in 1887 by George W. Childs. Nearby is Shottery, with Anne Hathaway's cottage. (See the article, "A Short Biography of Shakespeare.")

Strato.   In *Julius Caesar*, a servant of Brutus. He is the only one who will consent to hold the sword on which Brutus kills himself (V.v).

Suffolk, (1st) **Duke of.**   In *Henry VIII*, the historical Charles Brandon. He is present in a number of scenes including the coronation of Anne, the arraignment of Cranmer, and the christening of Princess Elizabeth.

Suffolk, (4th) **Earl of.**   In *1 Henry VI*, the historical William de la Pole, a Lancastrian supporter who captures Margaret at Angiers. He arranges her marriage with Henry and becomes her lover. In *2 Henry VI*, he is created (1st) Duke and attains greater power, managing the imprisonment of Gloucester and the banishment of the Duchess of Gloucester. He himself is banished, and later killed by Walter Whitmore.

Surrey, (1st) **Duke of.**   In *Richard II*, the historical Thomas Holland, also 3rd Earl of Kent. He defends Aumerle against a charge of treason, joins the rebellion against Henry IV, and is captured and killed. He is also referred to in the play as Kent (V.vi).

Surrey, Earl of.   In *2 Henry IV*, the historical Thomas Fitzalan, a supporter of the King.

Surrey, Earl of.   In *Henry VIII*, the historical Thomas Howard, a gentleman of the court. He opposes Wolsey and avenges the death of Buckingham.

Surrey, Earl of.   In *Richard III*, the historical Thomas Howard, later the 2nd Duke of Norfolk, a supporter of Richard.

Surveyor.   In *Henry VIII*, the surveyor to the Duke of Buckingham. He swears that his master threatened Henry's life.

Swan, the.   A London playhouse built in 1594 on the Bankside, on the south bank of the Thames. A well-known drawing of the Swan, one of the very few in existence of Elizabethan theatres, shows a circular building with three galleries of three tiers each. A forestage or apron stage comes forward into the pit yard, and halfway back columns support the "shadow" or roof of the stage. It had no inner stage, but merely two doors leading into the dressing rooms. Above the stage were six boxes, including an upper stage, a room for distinguished spectators, and one for musicians. After 1620, it was used for prize fights, and by 1632 a contemporary source referred to it as "fallen to decay." (See cut following page 148.)

"Swan of Avon," the.   In Jonson's *To the Memory of Shakespeare*, a reference to Shakespeare, who was born at Stratford-on-Avon. The phrase has since passed into the language, and is now widely used and generally accepted as denoting Shakespeare.

Sycorax.   A witch, the mother of Caliban in *The Tempest*; she does not appear in the play. In Dryden and D'Avenant's version, she is Caliban's sister.

T

Tailor.   In *The Taming of the Shrew*, a character who brings a dress for Katherina that is refused by Petruchio.

Talbot, John.   In *1 Henry VI*, the son of Lord Talbot.

Talbot, Lord.   In *1 Henry VI*, the commander of the English army. He is captured at Patay through Fastolfe's cowardice, escapes from the Countess of Auvergne, and with his son is surrounded and killed near Bordeaux.

Taming of the Shrew, The. A comedy by Shakespeare, printed in 1623. It is difficult to discuss the source of *The Taming of the Shrew* since its exact relationship to a very similar play, *The Taming of a Shrew*, is not known. The date of Shakespeare's play is uncertain since it was neither published nor mentioned before the First Folio in 1623. *A Shrew* was printed in 1594, at about the same time or just after *The Shrew* is thought to have been written. Three possible relationships between the two plays have been conjectured: that *A Shrew* was a separate earlier play and *The Shrew* was derived from it; that *A Shrew* is an earlier version, or "bad quarto," of *The Shrew*; that both plays derive from a common, but lost, original. This last is now the most generally accepted theory. Both plays are constructed from the same three main elements, the induction and scenes with Sly the Tinker, the wooing and taming of Katherina, and the contrasted wooing of her sister. In *A Shrew* the Sly episode is filled out, with the Tinker making several interruptions to the play and finally going home to tame his own wife, whereas in Shakespeare's play, although the character of Sly is more developed and the preparation for the play more subtly done, the story is never completed, for Sly disappears from the action at the end of the first act. The taming of the shrew, a story long known in fabliaux, is similarly dealt with in both plays, except that Katherina and her husband Petruchio are more fully characterized and brought to life in Shakespeare's play. The two versions of the Bianca plot differ considerably. In *A Shrew* Kate has two sisters who are wooed by two friends; like Bianca they cannot marry until their sister is provided for, so they produce a husband for her, but the disguises and intrigues of their suitors are not very similar to those in the subplot of Shakespeare's play. Shakespeare took his subplot partially from the classical comedy *Supposes* (1566) by George Gascoigne, a prose version of Ariosto's *I Suppositi* (1509), which has a willing girl wooed by rivals, her real suitor having disguised himself as his servant to get access to her, as Lucentio does in *The Taming of the Shrew*. The substance of *A Shrew* is combined with a number of elements from *Supposes* in Shakespeare's play to produce a sharp and witty comedy of love and marriage.

Dramatis Personae

A Lord	Hortensio, *Suitor to Bianca*
Christopher Sly, *a Tinker*	Tranio, *Servant to Lucentio*
Hostess, Page, Players,	Biondello, *Servant to Lucentio*
Huntsmen, and Servants	Grumio, *Servant to Petruchio*
Baptista Minola, *of Padua*	Curtis, *Servant to Petruchio*
Vincentio, *old Gentleman of Pisa*	A Pedant

Lucentio, *Son to Vincentio, in*   Katherina, *the shrew,*
    love with Bianca   *Daughter to Baptista*
Petruchio, *Gentleman of Verona,*   Bianca, *Daughter to Baptista*
    suitor to Katherina   Widow
Gremio, *Suitor to Bianca*   Tailor, Haberdasher, and
                                              Servants

The Story.   In the Induction, Christopher Sly is found in a drunken sleep by a nobleman who decides to have some fun with him. Sly is taken to the nobleman's house, treated lavishly, and persuaded (with some difficulty) that he is himself a nobleman just recovered from fifteen years of insanity. For his entertainment a group of strolling players present "The Taming of the Shrew": Baptista Minola has two daughters, the hot-tempered, cantankerous Katherina, and the sweet and gentle Bianca. Baptista will not allow the younger to wed until Katherina has found a husband. Petruchio resolves to woo her, partly to help his friend Hortensio gain Bianca, and partly for Katherina's large dowry. At their first meeting she rails at him, but he pretends that he finds her soft-spoken and gentle, and commences his taming of her. He arrives late at the wedding, riding on a tired nag and dressed in disreputable clothes. He embarrasses her at the ceremony, refuses to let her stay for the wedding dinner, takes her to his country house, where his cruelty to his servants forces her to defend them, gives her nothing to eat, tosses in bed all night so that she can get no sleep, and sends her new clothes away. After these and other pranks she is so exhausted and bewildered that she is quite submissive. Meanwhile young Lucentio, in the guise of a tutor, has won Bianca; Hortensio, the disappointed rival, consoles himself with a rich widow. At Lucentio's wedding feast, Petruchio easily wins a wager that he has the most docile and obedient wife of any husband in the room.

Tamora.   In *Titus Andronicus*, the Queen of the Goths. Taken a prisoner by Titus, with her three sons, she plots with her lover, Aaron, to avenge the sacrifice of her eldest son. Titus, in turn, avenges the death of his sons, the rape and mutilation of his daughter, and the loss of his own hand, first by serving Tamora a pie in which her sons' bodies have been baked, and then by killing her.

Tarlton, Richard.   d. at London, 1588. An English clown and comic actor. He is said to have been brought to London from Shropshire, and to have been a "prentice in his youth" in the city of London, later a "water-bearer." He was enrolled (1583) as one of the twelve of Queen Elizabeth's Men, and became a kind of court jester as well. He was celebrated for his extemporaneous rhymes and for his "jigs" (comic songs with a dance), which he invented. His popularity and audacity were both unbounded. He fell into disgrace and was dismissed from court for scurrilous reflections upon Robert Dudley, 1st Earl of Leicester, and Sir Walter Raleigh. He then kept a tavern in Paternoster Row. He wrote *The Seven Deadly Sins*, a play that appears to have been the result of his real or pretended repentance of his irregularities. The second part, extant in manuscript form, was once thought to be a sketch for a performance similar to the Italian *commedia dell' arte*, but it is now known to be a summary of the episodes and a cue sheet. A collection of jokes and humorous anecdotes compiled in the 1590's was attributed to him as *Tarlton's Jests*, though the material is much older. He is said to have been the person Shakespeare had in mind in writing about "poor Yorick," in *Hamlet*.

Taurus. In *Antony and Cleopatra*, Octavius's commander at Actium.

Taylor, Joseph. d. at Richmond, England, in November, 1652. An English actor. He was the successor of Richard Burbage in *Hamlet* and *Othello* and is supposed to have been the original Iago. It is said that Shakespeare personally instructed him in the playing of Hamlet, and the remembrance of this performance enabled Sir William D'Avenant to give the traditions of Shakespeare's directions; however, he seems not to have joined the King's Men until 1619, three years after Shakespeare's death.

Tearsheet, Doll. In *2 Henry IV*, a whore, Falstaff's mistress. She quarrels with Pistol (II.iv). Later she is taken to prison.

The Tempest. A play by Shakespeare, written and first performed in 1611 or 1612 and first printed in the folio of 1623. It was his last finished play. No source has been discovered for the plot or characters, although there are several analogues. It is clear that Shakespeare was interested in the colonization of America, and in particular in the shipwreck of a colonizing vessel, the *Sea-Adventure*, that took place off the coast of Bermuda in 1609, and this incident may have provided some ideas for the play. He read three accounts of it, Sylvester Jourdain's *Discovery of the Bermudas* (1610), the Council of Virginia's *True Declaration of the State of the Colony in Virginia* (1610), and William Strachey's letter, known as the *True Repertory of the Wracke*, dated 1610 and published in 1625. Strachey's letter, which Shakespeare must have read in manuscript, and Jourdain's pamphlet supplied details for the storm at sea as described by Ariel (I.ii), the conversations of Alonso and his fellows in II.i, and Stephano's and Trinculo's scattered remarks about their preservation. The *True Declaration* emphasizes the idea that providence was responsible for the safety of the shipwrecked colonists, a notion that Shakespeare makes into an important theme in his play. Shakespeare had also read Montaigne's essay "On Cannibals" in Florio's translation, which influenced Gonzalo's description of the ideal commonwealth, and perhaps also the general contrast between civilized and natural manners and societies in the play. Prospero's speech renouncing his magic powers (V.i) was partly based on Ovid's *Metamorphoses* (VII, 197–209), for which Shakespeare probably used the original Latin as well as the translation made by William Golding in 1587. Contemporary folklore contributed something to Ariel as did the tradition of the wild man and the ideas of the native inhabitants of America to Caliban, but little otherwise can be said with any certainty of Shakespeare's sources for this play; it seems that both the plot, which in its major lines and ideas resembles the plots of his other late plays, and the strange and original characters of Ariel and Caliban came largely from Shakespeare's own imagination.

Dramatis Personae

Alonso, King of Naples	*Master of a Ship*
Sebastian, *his Brother*	*Boatswain*
Prospero, *the right* Duke of Milan	*Mariners*
Antonio, *his Brother, the usurping* Duke of Milan	Miranda, *daughter to Prospero*
Ferdinand, *Son to the King*	Ariel, *an airy Spirit*
Gonzalo, *an honest old Counsellor*	Iris, *a Spirit*
Adrian, *a Lord*	Ceres, *a Spirit*
Francisco, *a Lord*	Juno, *a Spirit*
Caliban, *Prospero's Slave*	Nymphs, *Spirits*
Trinculo, *a Jester*	Reapers, *Spirits*
Stephano, *a drunken Butler*	*Other Spirits attending on Prospero*

The Story. Prospero, whose brother, Antonio, with the aid of Alonso, King of Naples, has usurped his rightful claim to the duchy of Milan and set him adrift in a boat with his lovely daughter, Miranda, now, twelve years later, is living not unhappily with Miranda on an enchanted tropical isle. Prospero has used his knowledge of the art of magic to release the airy spirit Ariel, who had been imprisoned in a tree, and to force the brutish Caliban, son of the witch Sycorax, to serve him. Learning, with the help of Ariel, that his former enemies are sailing near the island, Prospero summons a tempest to force them into his power, and they presently reach the shore from their wrecked ship in separate groups. Ferdinand, the son of the King of Naples, wanders to the cave of Prospero and, there meeting

Miranda, falls in love with her, and she with him. Meanwhile, most of the other survivors (who believe Ferdinand to be dead) are lulled to sleep by Ariel's music, but Antonio and Sebastian, Alonso's brother, remain awake and plot the murder of Alonso. Ariel, however, prevents this by awakening the others just in time. Another group from the ship, Stephano, a drunken butler, and Trinculo, a jester, have met Caliban and have given him some of their liquor, which delights and bemuses him. Caliban offers to serve them, suggesting that they should murder Prospero and seize the island, and that Stephano should then marry Miranda. But Ariel has overheard these plotters too, and warns Prospero, who, with Ariel's aid, sets out to punish and reward all according to their just deserts. To punish Alonso and Antonio, Prospero and Ariel set before the hungry men a magnificent banquet that vanishes each time they try to eat. Ariel, disguised as a harpy, then rebukes Alonso for his crimes against Prospero. Prospero next presents a graceful masque before the now betrothed Ferdinand and Miranda, but suddenly interrupts it when he remembers Caliban's plot. These conspirators, however, are easily distracted by the gaudy clothes Ariel has hung upon a line, and run away howling as spirits in the shape of dogs chase them around the island. The other group of conspirators are now led by Ariel's music to the cave of Prospero, where Prospero reveals his identity and demands the return of his dukedom. He shows the repentant Alonso Ferdinand and Miranda playing chess; the other conspirators return, sore from the pinching they have received; Prospero renounces his magic, setting free Ariel and Caliban, who says he will try to be wiser and to seek for grace. The entire group plans to sail for Naples with "calm seas, auspicious gales" (V.i) on the following day. Because *The Tempest* is Shakespeare's final comedy, some critics have interpreted the role of Prospero as Shakespeare bidding farewell to his own art. In some respects, this is a tenable interpretation, although other critics deny its plausibility. But whether or not *The Tempest* is a conscious conclusion to Shakespeare's career, the play is, in a way, a summation of his work. The themes of reconciliation and concord, which appear throughout Shakespeare's dramas, are nowhere more ideally worked out than here. The conspiracies are never actually dangerous, because Prospero and Ariel never allow them to reach fruition; yet Prospero happily renounces his supernatural power to return to normal society. The play abounds in contrasts: Ariel and Caliban, delicate music and crude jesting (by Trinculo and Stephano), love and discord, storm and calm. The poetry in the play ranks with Shakespeare's best, and even the ugly Caliban is given some beautiful lines:

> the isle is full of noises,
> Sounds and sweet airs that give delight and hurt not.
> Sometimes a thousand twangling instruments
> Will hum about mine ears. (III.ii).

Thaisa. In *Pericles*, the daughter of Simonides and wife of Pericles.

Thaliard. In *Pericles*, a lord of Antioch.

Thane of Cawdor. See **Cawdor, Thane of.**

Thane of Fife. See under **Macduff.**

Thane of Glamis. See **Glamis, Thane of.**

Theatre, the. The first London theatre. It was a wooden building erected by James Burbage, the father of Richard Burbage, in 1576–77, on the site of the priory of Saint John the Baptist, Shoreditch, which had been destroyed during the Reformation. It was taken down in 1598, and the Globe, Bankside, was built from the materials.

Thersites. In Greek legend, the most impudent of the Greeks assembled before Troy. He assailed the name of Agamemnon and was beaten by Odysseus (Ulysses). When he taunted Achilles, Achilles killed him. In *Troilus and Cressida*, his bawdiness is contrasted with Troilus's romantic nature, and he acts as a Chorus. Possibly he was meant to be the playwright, John Marston, alluding to a current controversy in London.

Theseus. In *A Midsummer Night's Dream*, the Duke of Athens, engaged to marry Hippolyta. He also appears in *The Two Noble Kinsmen*.

Thisbe. In classical legend, a maiden of Babylon, loved by Pyramus. The two made love secretly through a hole in the wall between their houses, their parents being opposed. Pyramus killed himself when he saw blood that he mistakenly believed to be Thisbe's. In *A Midsummer Night's Dream*, the part of "Thisby" in the interpolated play is taken by Flute. See also **Pyramus and Thisbe.**

Thomas. In *Measure for Measure*, the head of an order of friars. He permits the Duke of Vienna to disguise himself as a friar of the order so that he may spy on Angelo.

Thomas, Lord Cromwell. [Also, **The Life and Death of Thomas, Lord Cromwell.**] A play published in 1602 and included in the second issue of the Third Shakespeare Folio (1664), but now considered not to be Shakespeare's.

Thomas Percy, Earl of Worcester. See **Worcester, Thomas Percy, Earl of.**

Thump, Peter. In *2 Henry VI*, an apprentice to Horner. He accuses his master of treasonous speech and in a fight with sandbags kills him. The King believes the outcome to be an indication of God's power and justice (II.iii).

Thurio.   In *Two Gentlemen of Verona*, a rival to Valentine for
Silvia. He is foolish and cowardly. Proteus pretends to be wooing Silvia for him after Valentine has been banished, and in the
final act Thurio claims Silvia, but gives her up as soon as Valentine challenges him.

Thyreus.   In *Antony and Cleopatra*, a follower whom Octavius
sends to Cleopatra to persuade her to desert Antony.

Timandra.   In *Timon of Athens*, a mistress of Alcibiades.

Time.   In *The Winter's Tale*, Time acts as Chorus, bridging the
gap (sixteen years) between Acts III and IV.

Timon.   In *Timon of Athens*, the noble Athenian who is the
hero of the play. Although he is at first a trusting and warm-
hearted person, the ingratitude of his friends (when he loses
his fortune) causes a violent reaction in him and he becomes a
bitter misanthrope, only occasionally revealing glimpses of his
former goodness, as in his touching words to Flavius. He dies in
solitude, a bitter and cynical man. The historical Timon lived in
the last part of the fifth century B.C.

Timon of Athens.   [Full title, ***The Life of Timon of Athens.***]
A tragedy by Shakespeare, probably all by his hand, although
some scholars have doubted it. It is now thought that the play
is incomplete; perhaps Shakespeare realized that Timon's story
did not provide him with enough material, and set it aside to
write a fuller study of wrath and ingratitude in *Coriolanus*. It
was written between 1605 and 1608, was printed in the folio of
1623, and was adapted by Shadwell. There is no record of performance before 1678 and this was Shadwell's adaptation (not
until 1851 was there a performance of Shakespeare's play). The
main source was North's translation of Plutarch's *Lives of the
Noble Grecians and Romans*, from which Shakespeare used the
Life of Marcus Antonius and the *Life of Alcibiades*. He found
in the former Timon's misanthropy, the idea that he had been
abandoned by his friends, the relationships with Alcibiades and
Apemantus, the anecdote of the fig-tree (V.i)., and the two epi-
taphs for the tomb. He may also have been influenced by the
description of Antony's life, which mentioned his trusting nature
and the sycophants who took advantage of it. *The Life of Alcibiades* supplied very much that Shakespeare did not use for his
rather incomplete portrait of the soldier, but he did take the fact
of Alcibiades's turning against Athens and his resolution to
harm the city, and also the courtesan Timandra, although he
changes the reason for Antony's leaving Athens and omits
Plutarch's account of Timandra's genuine affection for Alcibiades. Another important source was Lucian of Samosata's dialogue *Timon*, which was not translated into English in Shakespeare's time, although he could have read it in Erasmus's
Latin version, in Italian, or in French. From this he may have

taken elements not in Plutarch, such as Timon's kindness to his friends, the hypocritical offers of money made to him only when he was not in need, and the incident of his driving away the parasites who approach him after he has dug up the unwanted gold. The character and manner of speech may have been modeled on Diogenes in John Lyly's play *Campaspe* (1584), in which the philosopher talks with Alexander the Great much as Apemantus does with Timon. Shakespeare probably also knew the story of Timon in William Painter's *The Palace of Pleasure* (1560), one of his favorite source-books, although he does not seem to have used it. An anonymous academic play called *Timon*, also based on Lucian, did exist, but it was possibly written after Shakespeare's play, and in any case Shakespeare probably never knew it.

Dramatis Personae

Timon, *a noble Athenian*

Lucius, *a flattering Lord*

Lucullus, *a flattering Lord*

Sempronius, *a flattering Lord*

Ventidius, *a false Friend of Timon*

Alcibiades, *an Athenian Captain*

Apemantus, *a churlish Philosopher*

Flavius, *Steward to Timon*

Flaminius, *a Servant to Timon*

Lucilius, *a Servant to Timon*

Servilius, *a Servant to Timon*

Caphis, Philotus, Titus, Lucius, and Hortensius, *Servants to Timon's Creditors*

Poet, Painter, Jeweller, and Merchant

An old Athenian

Servants to Varro and Isidore, *two of Timon's Creditors*

Three Strangers

A Page

A Fool

Phrynia, *a Mistress of Alcibiades*

Timandra, *a Mistress of Alcibiades*

Lords, Senators, Officers, Soldiers, Thieves, and Attendants

Cupid and Amazons in the Masque

The Story. Timon is a kindly and good Athenian, but perhaps a trifle too lavish as a host. When he suddenly discovers that he is deeply in debt, he asks his friends, whom he has so frequently entertained, for help. They, however, are only "feast-won" and refuse him. As a final gesture, Timon invites them all to a banquet at which he serves only warm water, and this he throws in their faces. Bitterly denouncing all mankind, Timon then retreats to a cave, where he lives on roots grubbed from the earth nearby. One day in his digging he discovers buried treasure, and when he learns that the great captain Alcibiades is preparing to attack Athens he shares his gold with him. Apemantus, the professional misanthrope, visits him, as well as a number of thieves, artists, and others, all anxious now to flatter him, and thus perhaps to secure some of his gold. Flavius, his faithful steward, is the only one to whom Timon speaks kindly, but he too is finally sent away and, as Alcibiades enters Athens, news comes that Timon has died alone by the sea.

Titania.   In *A Midsummer Night's Dream*, the Queen of the Fairies. Shakespeare is said to have been the first to give this name to the queen of the fairies, although Ovid used it as an epithet of Diana.

Titinius.   In *Julius Caesar*, a friend of Brutus and Cassius. He meets Brutus's forces at Philippi, but Cassius thinks he is taken prisoner by the enemy and kills himself. Titinius stabs himself on finding Cassius's body.

Titus.   In *Timon of Athens*, a servant of one of Timon's creditors.

Titus Andronicus.   The hero of *Titus Andronicus*. At the beginning of the play he is a hot-tempered and tyrannical old father who kills one of his sons in a rage. He becomes the victim of the wicked Tamora, her lover Aaron, and her sons, who rape his daughter and kill two of his sons. He is driven mad and revenges himself horribly on Tamora, finally killing his daughter and then committing suicide.

Titus Andronicus.   [Full title, **The Tragedy of Titus Andronicus.**] A tragedy, produced probably in 1593 or 1594, variously attributed to Christopher Marlowe, Thomas Kyd, and William Shakespeare. However, it was published with Shakespeare's plays in the First Folio (1623) and on that ground is generally accepted as one of Shakespeare's plays, though Edward Ravenscroft, who published a revision in 1687, reported that he had heard that Shakespeare merely touched up the play "by a private Author." If it was new in 1594, it was crude for such a date, but possibly Ravenscroft was right (one other reference makes it earlier, 1584–89). The probable source of the play is an anonymous prose tale, *The History of Titus Andronicus*, which exists only in an eighteenth-century version; this tale is closely related to a ballad, "The Lamentable and Tragical History of Titus Andronicus," printed in 1620, although it is not known for certain if the ballad was influenced by Shakespeare's play or vice versa. The prose tale describes Titus's war against the Goths and the marriage between the Goths' queen, Attava, and the Emperor of Rome. Attava has a black child by her lover, a Moor, and together they plot against Titus and his family. They have Titus's surviving sons murdered, and Attava's own sons rape and mutilate Titus's daughter, Lavinia. Titus feigns madness to secure revenge, which takes the form of cutting the throats of Attava's sons and baking them in a pie. Finally Titus kills Attava and her husband;

the Moor confesses his crimes and is horribly put to death; Titus kills his daughter at her own request and then commits suicide. This hideous tale has a few links with historical facts, but is in the main fictitious. Shakespeare's play shares the same basic features but with several changes. In particular, Shakespeare inserts the contrast between the Roman ideals of Titus and the decadence of the Emperor Saturninus, and he enlarges the Machiavellian character of the Empress's Moorish lover. The character of Titus was perhaps influenced by two portraits of the great Roman generals Scipio Africanus and Coriolanus in Plutarch's *Lives* (translated by North, 1579). Some of the names in the play also come from Plutarch. Seneca's tragedy, *Thyestes*, available in a translation of 1560 by Jasper Heywood, was also an important source and provided among other elements the manner of Titus's revenge on the Empress and her sons. The episode of Lavinia's rape comes from the tale of the ravished Philomela, to which Shakespeare refers, from Ovid, *Metamorphoses*, V.i. The references to the rape of Lucrece come from Ovid's *Fasti*, which Shakespeare also used as a source for his poem, *The Rape of Lucrece*.

Dramatis Personae

Saturninus, Emperor of Rome	Aemilius, *a noble Roman*
Bassianus, *Brother of Emperor*	Alarbus, *Son of Tamora*
Titus Andronicus, *Roman*	Demetrius, *Son of Tamora*
General	Chiron, *Son of Tamora*
Marcus Andronicus, *Tribune*	Aaron, *a Moor, Tamora's Lover*
Lucius, *Son of Titus*	*A Captain, Tribune, Messenger,*
Quintus, *Son of Titus*	*and Clown*
Martius, *Son of Titus*	*Goths and Romans*
Mutius, *Son of Titus*	Tamora, Queen of the Goths
Young Lucius, *Son of Lucius*	Lavinia, *Daughter of Titus*
Publius, *Son of Marcus*	*A Nurse and a black Child*
Sempronius, *Kinsman of Titus*	Senators, Tribunes, Officers,
Caius, *Kinsman of Titus*	*Soldiers, and Attendants*
Valentine, *Kinsman of Titus*	

The Story. Titus, a victorious Roman general, brings home as his captives Tamora, Queen of the Goths, and her three sons, the eldest of whom (Alarbus) is sacrificed by Titus's sons. Saturninus, the new emperor, and Bassianus, his brother, both claim the hand of Titus's daughter, Lavinia, but Saturninus renounces Lavinia and marries Tamora, who with her lover, Aaron the Moor, is determined to be revenged on Titus for the death of her son. Her two remaining sons, Demetrius and Chiron, meet Bassianus and Lavinia in the woods. They kill Bassianus, throw his body into a pit, ravish Lavinia, and cut off her hands and tongue. Titus's sons Quintus and Martius fall into the pit and are accused of murdering Bassianus. Aaron informs Titus that they will be pardoned if Titus cuts off one of his hands and sends it as ransom. Aaron, however, returns the hand along with the heads of the two sons. Titus, driven mad, takes revenge by killing Demetrius and Chiron, and serving them baked in a pie to Tamora. He kills Lavinia, Mutius (his youngest son, who is trying to protect his sister), then Tamora, and is himself killed by Saturninus, whom Lucius, the last remaining son, then kills. Aaron, meanwhile, has been captured and is condemned by Lucius, now the new emperor, to be set breast-deep in earth until he starves to death.

Titus Lartius.   In *Coriolanus*, a Roman general who opposes the Volscians.

Tom o'Bedlam.   Formerly, in England, a popular name for a lunatic. "Bedlam" was the colloquial name for the hospital of Saint Mary of Bethlehem, at London, an insane asylum that for a period was so overcrowded that many inmates, uncured but considered harmless, were dismissed and turned beggars. In *King Lear*, Edgar pretends to be one of these mendicants. calling himself "Poor Tom."

Tooley, Nicholas.   d. 1623. He is mentioned as a principal actor in the First Folio (1623) of Shakespeare's plays and was a member of the King's Men, becoming a shareholder in 1605.

To the Memory of My Beloved Master, William Shakespear.   An elegiac poem by Ben Jonson, written upon the death of Shakespeare, whom Jonson calls "soul of the age, the applause, delight, the wonder of our stage." Later in the poem, Jonson refers to Shakespeare as "sweet swan of Avon," which came into popular use as an epithet for Shakespeare. It is Jonson's reference in this poem to Shakespeare's "small Latin and less Greek" that has given rise to the conjectures as to the extent of Shakespeare's schooling. However, some scholars take the phrase to mean simply that Shakespeare didn't rely as heavily as some of his contemporaries on classical sources for his themes.

Touchstone.   In *As You Like It*, an "allowed fool." He is in his facetiousness a fool by profession, not an unconscious clown. His worldly-wise attitudes are used to contrast with and temper the romantic feelings and extravagance of the other characters.

Tragedy.   The twelve works entitled tragedies by Shakespeare are entered under their short titles. They are: *Antony and Cleopatra, Coriolanus, Hamlet, Julius Caesar, King Lear, Macbeth, Othello, Richard II, Richard III, Romeo and Juliet, Titus Andronicus*, and *Troilus and Cressida*.

Tranio.   In *The Taming of the Shrew*, a servant of Lucentio.

Travers.   In *2 Henry IV*, a retainer of Northumberland who brings the news of Hotspur's defeat.

Trebonius.   In *Julius Caesar*, a conspirator who (with Brutus)

opposes the killing of Antony. At the time of the assassination
of Caesar, he leads Antony away from the scene.

Tressel.   In *Richard III*, an attendant to Lady Anne.

Trinculo.   In *The Tempest*, a jester who, with Stephano and
Caliban, plans to murder Prospero.

Troilus.   In *Troilus and Cressida*, the youngest son of Priam and
lover of Cressida. He is faithful, open, and chivalrous, and when
he witnesses Cressida's unfaithfulness, is broken-hearted and
vows to kill Diomedes (who, however, escapes).

Troilus and Cressida.   [Full title, **The Tragedy of Troilus
and Cressida.**] A tragedy written sometime in the period
1598–1601 by Shakespeare, date of first performance unknown.
It was published in 1609 in quarto, and appears in the First Folio
(1623). It was not paged in that edition, apparently having been
withdrawn for a time because of some difficulty over its owner-
ship. Dryden's version of it (with Cressida much altered) was
staged in 1679 with Betterton as Troilus and Mrs. Betterton as
Andromache. A few revivals were staged of this version, but
the original Shakespeare play did not receive another performance until 1907. The love-plot of *Troilus and Cressida* is based
on Chaucer's narrative poem *Troilus and Criseyde*, although the
characterization of the three main figures is very different,
partly because of the influence of Robert Henryson's sequel, *The
Testament of Cresseid*, thought at that time to be by Chaucer,
which Shakespeare also used. The main sequence of events in
Chaucer is followed, with Shakespeare making use of such details as the scene in which Criseyde watches Troilus return from
the war amid popular acclamation (Book II, ll.610–51), the emotional confusion of the lovers at their first meeting, Cressida's
protestation of fidelity in IV.ii (from Book IV, ll.1534–54), and
the letter she finally sends to Troilus after she has gone over to
the Greek camp. Shakespeare's Troilus is close to Chaucer's, a
young and impetuous warrior, but Pandarus is older and coarser
than his medieval counterpart. The character of Cressida is
strongly influenced by Henryson's poem, in which she finally
becomes a leprous beggar after being mistress to a succession
of Greek warriors. The war-plot of the play is influenced by
other sources, John Lydgate's *The Hystorye Sege and Dystruc-
cyon of Troye* (1513), a very long and rather tedious poem,
Caxton's *Recuyell of the Historyes of Troye* (c1474), and George
Chapman's translation of Homer, *The Seaven Bookes of the
Iliades* (1598). Shakespeare's debt to Homer for *Troilus and
Cressida* implies that he used more of the *Iliad* than was contained in Chapman's version, as for instance in the incidents of
Achilles being moved to return to battle by the death of Patroclus and his humiliation of the dead body of Hector. The charac-
ter of the railing Thersites and the emphasis on dissension in
the Greek camp also came from Homer. Lydgate and Caxton may

have supplied inspiration for the encounter between Hector and Ajax in IV.v., for Andromache's dream, and for Hector's fight with the Greek in sumptuous armor that immediately precedes his death. The idea for Ulysses's famous speech on degree (I.iii) comes from Homer, *Iliad* Book II, but many sources have been suggested for the details of it, including Virgil, *Aeneid* I, 430, which supplies the image of bees swarming to the hive, Thomas Elyot's *The Boke named the Governour* (1531), which also uses this image and relates it to the idea of order, the Homily on obedience appointed to be read in churches, Hooker's *Ecclesiastical Polity* (1597), and Florio's translation of Montaigne's *Essais*. It is not necessary to suppose that Shakespeare consciously combined material from all these sources, for the ideas in Ulysses's speech were very conventional ones in Shakespeare's day and the notion of disorder leading to the breakdown of human society, symbolized by cannibalism, can be found also in *Coriolanus*, *King Lear*, and the Shakespearean scenes of *Sir Thomas More*. Of all of the versions of the story of Troilus and Cressida that have been written, Shakespeare's is for many modern readers one of the least satisfactory. His Cressida is at best a thoughtless flirt, at worst a selfish wanton, and Troilus's sorrow at her betrayal of their love thereby loses dignity (to lose one's true love is one thing, but to lose a passing bed-mate, however pleasing she may have been, is quite another, and Cressida's behavior certainly suggests that she was never more than the latter). For this reason, among others, this work is usually grouped with Shakespeare's "problem plays." We see here a world without love, honor, or nobility of character; the atmosphere is one of degeneracy and corruption, from the commanders on either side down to the vulgar and cynical Thersites.

Dramatis Personae

Priam, King of Troy

Hector, *Son of Priam*

Troilus, *Son of Priam*

Paris, *Son of Priam*

Deiphobus, *Son of Priam*

Helenus, *Son of Priam*

Margarelon, *Bastard Son of Priam*

Aeneas, *Trojan Commander*

Antenor, *Trojan Commander*

Calchas, *Trojan Priest*

Pandarus, *Uncle of Cressida*

Agamemnon, *Greek General*

Menelaus, *Brother of Agamemnon*

Achilles, *Greek Commander*

Ajax, *Greek Commander*

Ulysses, *Greek Commander*

Nestor, *Greek Commander*

Diomedes, *Greek Commander*

Patroclus, *Greek Commander*

Thersites

Alexander, *Cressida's Servant*

Servants to Troilus, to Paris, to Diomedes

Helen, *Wife of Menelaus*

Andromache, *Wife of Hector*

Cassandra, *Daughter of Priam*

Cressida, *Daughter of Calchas*

Trojan and Greek Soldiers

The Story. In Troy, during the Trojan War, Troilus, the youngest son of King Priam, has fallen deeply in love with Cressida. Pandarus, her uncle, helps them arrange meetings and otherwise encourages the romance, and they pledge eternal faithfulness. Meanwhile, Calchas, Cressida's father, who has deserted Troy for the Greeks, persuades the Greek commanders to exchange one of their prisoners for Cressida. Cressida parts reluctantly from her lover, but she does not remain long forlorn; very soon we see her in dalliance with various of the Greek commanders, and she even gives to Diomedes, as she embraces him, the token of love that Troilus had given her at the time of their parting. Troilus, in the Greek camp under a safe conduct from Ulysses, witnesses this betrayal of their love by Cressida, and is broken-hearted. He vows to kill Diomedes, but the fight between them at the end of the play ends indecisively. The other part of the plot concerns the Greek decision to redouble their efforts to end the war. In a council meeting, Ulysses arouses the spiritless and weary commanders and, when a challenge to personal combat comes from the Trojan warrior Hector, he suggests giving it to Ajax instead of Achilles, who is moodily sulking in his tent. The fight between Hector and Ajax ends in a truce, and the two armies feast together. On the following day, however, the fighting continues and, when Hector kills Patroclus, Achilles is aroused to avenge his friend. Coming upon Hector resting without his armor, Achilles treacherously kills him. The day ends with defeat for the Trojans.

Tubal. In *The Merchant of Venice*, a Jewish friend of Shylock.

Tullius Aufidius. See **Aufidius, Tullius.**

Tutor to Rutland. In *3 Henry VI*, the companion of Rutland. He begs Clifford not to slay his charge.

Twelfth Night. [Full title, **Twelfth Night; or What You Will.** A comedy by Shakespeare, first acted in 1602 and printed in the folio of 1623. The central situation of the play, that of a girl disguised as a page acting as emissary from the man she loves to the woman he loves, was one that Shakespeare had already used before in *Two Gentlemen of Verona*. For *Twelfth Night*, which has been called "a masterpiece of recapitulation," he took characters and devices from several of his earlier plays including the use of identical twins mistaken for one another from *The Comedy of Errors*, the loyal friend Antonio from *The Merchant of Venice*, the comic possibilities of eavesdropping from *Much Ado About Nothing*, and the girl disguised as a boy unbeknown to the man she loves from *As You Like It*. But there are also important outside sources. There were numerous plays and prose romances available to Shakespeare that combined the device of identical twins, originally from the *Menaechmi* of Plautus, with that of the disguised girl serving her lover as a page.

The plot of the Italian play, *Gl'Ingannati* (The Deceived) (1537) is very close to Shakespeare's, although its tone and mood, those of a bustling and realistic contemporary comedy, are very different; Shakespeare could have known something of it in a Latin version that was performed at Queen's College, Cambridge in 1595 under the title *Laelia*. In *Gl'Ingannati* the heroine disguises herself in order to follow a man who once loved but has now forgotten her; she is employed by him to woo the lady he loves, and this lady falls in love with her. The heroine's troubles are finally solved when her long-lost twin brother appears to woo the lady in her stead, while her old nurse meantime convinces her lover of her devotion. Other possible sources include *Gl' Inganni* (*The Deceiver*, 1597) by Curio Gonzaga, in which the disguised girl takes the name of Cesare, and two plays by Nicolo Secchi, *Gl' Inganni* (1562) and *L' Interesse* (1581), in the latter of which a duel is proposed in which the disguised heroine is to take part, as Viola duels with Sir Andrew. Of the available prose romances, Shakespeare may well have known versions of the story in Bandello's *Novelle* (1554) and Belleforest's *Histoires Tragiques* (1579), but the most important of these is the story of Apolonius and Silla in Barnaby Rich's *A Farewell to the Military Profession* (1581). In this tale Silla, the heroine, is shipwrecked, disguises herself as her brother, Silvio, and woos a wealthy widow on behalf of Apolonius, whom she loves; Silvio appears, and takes over his sister's part with the wealthy widow, getting her pregnant; the disguised Silla is accused of this deed and obliged to reveal her sex to prove her innocence. Apolonius, touched by her devotion, agrees to marry her, and Silvio marries the widow. None of these sources contained the Malvolio subplot, which is Shakespeare's invention, and the character is possibly based on a real figure, Sir William Knollys, controller of the Queen's household, although Shakespeare may have found a hint for the episode of his being imprisoned in the dark and tormented by the fool from one of Rich's stories about a man who locked up his shrewish wife in a dark house to cure her temper. The subplot with Sir Toby Belch, Sir Andrew Aguecheek, and Maria is Shakespeare's invention.

Dramatis Personae

Orsino, Duke of Illyria
Sebastian, *Brother of Viola*
Antonio, *a Sea Captain*
Valentine
Curio
Sir Toby Belch, *Uncle of Olivia*
Sir Andrew Aguecheek
Malvolio, *Olivia's Servant*

Feste, *a Clown, Olivia's Servant*
A Sea Captain
Olivia, *a rich Countess*
Viola, *in love with the Duke*
Maria, *Olivia's Woman*
Lords, Priests, Sailors, Officers, Musicians, and other Attendants

The Story. The Duke of Illyria, Orsino, is courting the wealthy countess Olivia with the aid of his page Cesario, who is really the beautiful Viola disguised as a man. (Viola has been shipwrecked on the coast of Illyria and thus separated from her twin brother, Sebastian.) Olivia refuses the advances of Orsino and falls in love with Cesario (Viola), who has herself fallen in love with Orsino. In the household of Olivia, drunken Sir Toby Belch, Sir Andrew Aguecheek, the clown Feste, Fabian, and Maria plot to trick the stern and melancholy Malvolio by leading him to believe that Olivia is in love with him. They contrive that he shall discover a letter apparently written by Olivia (but actually penned by Maria) that will sustain his amorous hopes, and, as the letter suggests, he appears before the astonished Olivia in yellow stockings, crossed garters, and a constant smile. Because of his strange antics, he is believed insane and, in confinement as a madman, is subjected to further teasing by Feste until finally Olivia releases him. Meanwhile, Sebastian has arrived in Illyria, and Olivia, believing him to be the page, persuades him to marry her. After much confusion resulting from mistaking the twins, Orsino discovers his love for the lovely Viola (whom he too has hitherto thought to be a man) and decides to marry her.

Two Gentlemen of Verona, The. A comedy by Shakespeare, written in 1594 or 1595 and first printed in the folio of 1623. There is no record, however, of any performance until 1672, in the reign of Charles II. The primary source for the story of Julia was the romance *Diana Enamorada* by Jorge de Montemayor (Valencia, 1559), which Shakespeare might perhaps have known in the original Spanish, or more likely in the French translation by Nicolas Collin (1578, 1587); an English translation by Bartholomew Young (or Yonge) was published in 1598, though it had been made sixteen years earlier. In this story Felix (the Proteus character) is sent to a foreign court so that he may not marry Felismena (Julia); Felismena follows him in male disguise and finds him wooing Celia (Silvia). She becomes his page and goes to Celia with Felix's letter, with the result that Celia falls in love with her; Shakespeare made use of this part of this story not in *Two Gentlemen of Verona* but later, with the disguised Viola and Olivia in *Twelfth Night*. Finally Celia dies when the "page" cannot return her love, and Felix goes into exile, but he is pursued, saved from death, and finally re-won by Felismena. Shakespeare changed this story in several ways. He altered the character of Felismena, who is a bold Amazonian shepherdess, for his more gentle Julia, and he added another young man, Valentine, and so provided a rival for Proteus and a happy ending for the second heroine. Some of his changes may be due to

the influence of a lost play, *Felix and Fello(s?)mena*, performed in
1585, which may well have been a pastoral based on Montemayor, but he could also have found the theme of the disloyal
friend in Lyly's *Euphues: The Anatomy of Wit* (1579). Lyly's
plays supplied several ideas for *Two Gentlemen of Verona*;
Endimion included two comic servants who foreshadow Launce
and Speed, a foolish suitor, Sir Tophas, who resembles Sir
Thurio, and a treatment of the conflict between love and friendship in *Euphues*. Lyly's characteristic verbal wit and logic-
chopping perhaps influenced the style of *Two Gentlemen of
Verona*. The basis of Shakespeare's play is the conflict between
love and friendship, a popular Renaissance theme, and Shakespeare could have found other presentations of this in Boccaccio's
La Teseide and the *Decameron* (X.8), in Chaucer's *The Knight's
Tale*, and in Sir Thomas Elyot's *The Governour* (1531). *Two
Gentlemen of Verona*, one of Shakespeare's earliest comedies,
contains many ideas and devices that he was constantly to vary
and re-use in years to come, including the disguised heroine, the
movement of the main characters from court to country, the
rivalry and betrayal in love, and the comic servant.

Dramatis Personae

Duke of Milan	Panthino, *Antonio's Servant*
Valentine, *Gentleman of Verona*	Host, *where Julia lodges*
Proteus, *Gentleman of Verona*	Outlaws, *with Valentine*
Antonio, *Father of Proteus*	Julia, *beloved of Proteus*
Thurio, *Valentine's Rival*	Silvia, *beloved of Valentine*
Eglamour, *a Knight*	Lucetta, *Julia's Woman*
Speed, *Valentine's Servant*	Servants, Musicians
Launce, *Proteus's Servant*	

The Story.   Valentine, one of the two Veronese gentlemen
of the title, travels to the court of Milan, where he falls in love
with the Duke's daughter, Silvia. His friend Proteus, the other
gentleman of Verona, pledges constant faithfulness to his beloved Julia before departing for Milan, but there he, too, falls
in love with Silvia. Determined to have her for himself, he betrays the confidence of his friend by informing the Duke that
Valentine is about to elope with his daughter. Valentine is
thereupon banished and joins a band of robbers. Proteus continues his courting of Silvia, who rejects both him and her
father's choice, the foolish Thurio. Meanwhile, Julia has arrived,
disguised as a page, and offers her services to Proteus. When
Silvia, in search of Valentine, flees her father's court, Proteus
and his "page" follow her and rescue her from robbers. As Proteus is in the act of pressing (perhaps too ardently) his suit with
Silvia, Valentine appears and because Proteus is so overcome

with remorse, even offers to yield Silvia to Proteus. However, at this point the "page" faints, Proteus recognizes her as Julia, and realizes that she, rather than Silvia, is his true love. The Duke and Thurio arrive, but because Thurio is too cowardly to fight Valentine for Silvia, the Duke gives her to the "gentleman of Verona."

Two Noble Kinsmen, The. A play attributed by some to Shakespeare on the basis of the Stationer's Register for 1634 (but this lists John Fletcher as coauthor with Shakespeare), probably written in the period 1612–13 (which would place it after *The Tempest,* usually considered Shakespeare's "last play," if, in fact, this work can be grouped with the body of Shakespeare's plays) and first staged c1619. It was published in 1634 in a good text and included in 1679 in the second folio of Beaumont and Fletcher's plays. D'Avenant produced a version of it as *The Rivals* in 1664.

Dramatis Personae

Theseus, Duke of Athens	*A Gentleman*
Palamon, *Nephew of*	Gerrold, *a Schoolmaster*
Theban King	Hippolyta, *Wife of Theseus*
Arcite, *Nephew of Theban King*	Emilia, *her Sister*
Pirithous, *an Athenian general*	*Three Queens*
Artesius, *an Athenian captain*	*The Jailer's Daughter*
Valerius, *a Theban nobleman*	*Servant to Emilia*
Six Knights	*Country Wenches and Women*
A Herald	*Personating Hymen, Boy,*
A Jailer	*A Laborer, Countrymen,*
Wooer of the Jailer's Daughter	*Messengers, a Man*
A Doctor	*Personating Hymen, Boy,*
Brother of the Jailer	*Executioners, Guards,*
Friends of the Jailer	*Soldiers, Attendants*

The Story. The principal source for the play was Chaucer's *Knights Tale,* which tells the story of Palamon and Arcite ("the two noble kinsmen"), who fight for Thebes against Theseus, are captured and imprisoned, fall in love with Emilia (sister of Hippolyta, the wife of Theseus), and (now out of prison) are discovered by Theseus as they fight each other for the right to woo her. Theseus is at first disposed to condemn them both to death, but substitutes (at the behest of Hippolyta and Emilia) another sentence: Palamon and Arcite must within a month's time each secure three knights and then engage in a tourney for the hand of Emilia. The victor will marry her; the loser will be beheaded. In the tourney, Arcite (who has prayed to Mars) is victorious over Palamon (who has prayed to Venus), but just as Palamon is about to be executed word arrives that Arcite has been mortally hurt by a fall from his horse, and as he dies he surrenders Emilia to Palamon (whom Theseus now spares from death). The story differs from Chaucer's only in its subplot, wherein Palamon is enabled to escape from prison by the Jailer's Daughter, who has fallen in love with him, but who shortly removes herself from further important involvement in the play by going mad for fear her father may be punished for her action and Palamon may be devoured by wolves.

Tybalt.   In *Romeo and Juliet*, the nephew of Lady Capulet. He is a quarrelsome young man who, having discovered Romeo's presence at the Capulet ball, wishes to fight with Romeo when he later meets him on the street. Knowing that Juliet is Tybalt's cousin, Romeo refuses to fight, upon which Mercutio accepts the challenge. Romeo interferes during the fight, and Mercutio is mortally wounded when Tybalt thrusts at him under Romeo's arm. In remorse, Romeo attacks Tybalt and kills him, as a result of which he is banished from Verona. Tybalt is referred to as Prince or King of Cats, an allusion to the tale of *Reynard the Fox*, where Tibert (or Tybalt) is Prince of Cats.

Tyrrel, Sir James.   In *Richard III*, a supporter of Richard. He is ordered to kill the Princes in the Tower, but hires two murderers to do the deed for him.

U

Ulysses.   In *Troilus and Cressida*, one of the Greek commanders. He makes the speech on degree (I.iii) in an attempt to bring order to the Greeks. He also suggests that Achilles be made jealous of Ajax so as to get him into battle again. He goes with Troilus to see Cressida and tries to comfort him when Troilus sees her with Diomedes.

Underwood, John.   d. 1624. An English actor. He is listed as a principal actor in the First Folio (1623) of Shakespeare's plays, and he probably joined the King's Men in 1608.

Ur-Hamlet. The name given by scholars to a lost pre-Shake-spearian play. (Ur means "source.") The existence of such a play is shown by such evidence as a reference in Greene's *Mena-phon* (1589), a performance in June, 1594, which was not a new play, Thomas Lodge's allusion to the Ghost in 1596, and in Dekker's *Satiromastix* (1601), where a character says "My name's Hamlet's revenge" and mentions Paris Garden, where the old *Hamlet* probably was acted in 1596. Possibly this play was by Kyd; some scholars maintain that it is merely a bad version of the final play.

Ursula. In *Much Ado About Nothing,* one of Hero's gentle-women.

Urswick, Christopher. In *Richard III,* a priest who is sent with a message to Richmond (IV.v).

V

Valentine. In *Titus Andronicus,* a kinsman of Titus.

Valentine. In *Twelfth Night,* a gentleman attending on Orsino, Duke of Illyria.

Valentine. In *Two Gentlemen of Verona,* one of the "two gen-tlemen." He is the lover of Silvia.

Valeria. In *Coriolanus,* a friend of Virgilia.

Valerius. In *The Two Noble Kinsmen,* a Theban nobleman.

Varrius. In *Antony and Cleopatra,* a friend of Pompey.

Varrius. In *Measure for Measure,* a friend of the Duke. The Duke merely speaks to him, and he was not listed in the folio of 1623.

Varro. In *Julius Caesar,* a servant of Brutus.

Varro. In *Timon of Athens,* two servants of a usurer, who sends them to collect a debt from Timon. They are both called by the name of their master (who does not appear).

Vaughan, Sir Thomas. In *Richard III,* an enemy of Richard who is executed with Rivers and Grey.

Vaux, Sir Nicholas. In *Henry VIII*, a gentleman of the court who is put in charge of Buckingham when he is arrested.

Vaux, Sir William. In *2 Henry VI*, a messenger who announces that Cardinal Beaufort is dying.

Venice, Duke of. In *The Merchant of Venice*, the judge presiding at the trial of Antonio. He pardons Shylock on the terms suggested by Antonio.

Venice, Duke of. In *Othello*, the ruler of Venice. He tries to persuade Brabantio to accept Othello as his son-in-law, and orders Othello to take charge of the expedition to Cyprus.

Ventidius. In *Antony and Cleopatra*, one of Antony's generals.

Ventidius. In *Timon of Athens*, a false friend of Timon.

Venus and Adonis. A narrative poem by Shakespeare, published in 1593. (See the article, "Shakespeare's Major Poetry.")

Verges. In *Much Ado About Nothing*, a "headborough" (a minor constable), assistant to Dogberry.

Vernon. In *1 Henry VI*, an adherent of the Duke of York. He quarrels with Basset, a supporter of the Lancastrian faction, and both ask for single combat but are refused.

Vernon, Sir Richard. In *1 Henry IV*, one of the rebels. He tells Hotspur of the royal army approaching "all plumed like estridges . . . As full of spirit as the month of May," and describes Hal vaulting on his horse "As if an angel dropped down from the clouds / To turn and wind a fiery Pegasus" (IV.i).

Vincentio. In *The Taming of the Shrew*, an old gentleman of Pisa, Lucentio's father.

Vincentio, Duke of Vienna. In *Measure for Measure*, the reigning duke.

Viola. In *Twelfth Night*, a principal female character, twin sister of Sebastian. She assumes a page's disguise and the name of Cesario when she arrives in Illyria. Unlike Orsino and Olivia, she is a resourceful and practical person who makes the best of her unfortunate situation. She woos Olivia on Orsino's behalf, disguised as his page, but finds herself falling in love with him. Eventually he recognizes the quality of her devotion and marries her.

Violenta. In *All's Well That Ends Well*, a Florentine woman, friend of the Widow.

Virgilia. In *Coriolanus*, the wife of Coriolanus. She, with her son and Volumnia, persuade Coriolanus to spare Rome.

Voltemand. In *Hamlet*, a courtier.

Volumnia. In *Coriolanus*, the mother of Coriolanus. She is a powerful woman who exerts great influence over her son. Her arguments persuade Coriolanus to give up his plan to attack Rome, and as a result she wins a "happy victory to Rome"

(V.iii), but loses her son, who is killed by his Volscian allies under Aufidius (V.vi).

Volumnius. In *Julius Caesar*, a boyhood friend who refuses to hold the sword for Brutus's suicide.

W

Wall. In *A Midsummer Night's Dream*, the wall that separates Pyramus and Thisby (Thisbe) in the interpolated play. It is represented (with spoken lines) by Snout, the tinker.

Wart, Thomas. In *2 Henry IV*, a recruit in Falstaff's army.

Warwick, Earl of. In *2 Henry IV*, *Henry V*, and *1 Henry VI*, the historical Richard de Beauchamp. In *2 Henry IV*, he is a counsellor to the King and reassures him about the rebellion and the behavior of the Prince. In *Henry V*, he is a leader of the English forces in France. In *1 Henry VI*, he plucks a white rose, indicating that he favors Richard Plantagenet.

Warwick, Earl of. In *2* and *3 Henry VI*, the historical Richard Neville, called "the Kingmaker," a member of the Yorkist faction. In *2 Henry VI*, he is convinced that Gloucester was murdered, accuses Suffolk, and later fights on the winning side at the first battle of St. Albans. In *3 Henry VI*, he at first supports Edward but, when he learns that Edward has married Lady Grey instead of Lady Bona, he joins the Lancastrians, captures Edward, and returns Henry VI to the throne. He is killed at Barnet.

Warwick, Edward, Earl of. In *Richard III*, a young son of the Duke of Clarence, eventually imprisoned by Richard.

Westminster, Abbot of. In *Richard II*, a conspirator with Aumerle against Bolingbroke.

Westmoreland (1st) *Earl of.* In *1* and *2 Henry IV* and *Henry V*, the historical Ralph Neville (1365–1425), 1st Earl of Westmoreland, a loyal adherent of the King. He is a leader of the royal forces, in *Henry IV* against the rebels and in *Henry V* against the French.

Westmoreland, Earl of.   In *3 Henry VI*, the historical Ralph Neville (c1404–84), a member of the Lancastrian faction.

W. H., Mr.   See **Herbert, William.**

Whitefriars.   A district in E central London, in the City of London and the County of London. It is named from the convent of an order of Carmelites, established in Fleet Street in 1241. The first monastery of the order in England was founded by Ralph Freshburne near Aterwich, Northumberland, in 1224. In 1580 the Whitefriars' Monastery was given up to a company of players, and known as Whitefriars' Theatre.

White Hart Inn.   A tavern in Southwark, mentioned in *2 Henry VI* (IV.viii) by Jack Cade, perhaps as his headquarters.

White Surrey.   In *Richard III*, a favorite horse of Richard.

Whitmore, Walter.   A character in *2 Henry VI* who, in revenge for losing an eye in a sea battle, beheads his prisoner, Suffolk (IV.i).

Widow.   In *All's Well That Ends Well*, a Florentine woman with whom Helena lodges, the mother of Diana.

Widow.   In *The Taming of the Shrew*, the woman who marries Hortensio.

William.   In *As You Like It*, a country bumpkin in love with Audrey.

Williams, Michael.   In *Henry V*, a soldier who encounters King Henry disguised as an English gentleman before the battle of Agincourt. He challenges the King upon the latter's defending his faithfulness to his troops. Fluellen comes to blows with him.

Willoughby, Lord.   In *Richard II*, a deserter of the King and later a member of Bolingbroke's party.

Winchester, Bishop of.   In *1 Henry VI*, the historical Henry Beaufort, a son of John of Gaunt and great-uncle of Henry VI. He quarrels with Gloucester, the Protector, who accuses him of having Henry V murdered. He crowns Henry VI in Paris and later appears as a Cardinal (V.i). In *2 Henry VI*, he joins York, Suffolk, and others in accusing Gloucester of misdeeds and having him imprisoned. Gloucester is murdered, apparently on his orders, and he repents for this on his deathbed (III.iii).

The Winter's Tale.   A play by Shakespeare, produced c1611, printed in the folio of 1623. The main source was Robert Greene's popular romance *Pandosto* (1588) from which Shakespeare borrowed more words and phrases than from any other romance he used. He altered the story in several ways. He changed the names so as to make them more Greek, even giving a Greek name to his invented comic character, Autolycus. He omitted Greene's account of the growth of friendship between the Queen (Hermione) and Egistus (Polixenes) that partly motivates the jealousy of Pandosto (Leontes), thus emphasizing Hermione's total innocence and Leontes's delusion. He had Leontes's baby daughter, Perdita, left in a remote spot by an invented character, Antigonus (who is then eaten by a bear), rather than having the baby placed in a boat and cast off to sea as in Greene. He altered the ending of the story by having Hermione reappear, posing as her own statue, after sixteen years' absence; in Greene, the Queen died, and the story ended with Pandosto's sudden suicide after a reconciliation with his daughter. This change makes *The Winter's Tale* more like Shakespeare's other late plays, and emphasizes the ideas of forgiveness and reconciliation that seem to have interested Shakespeare at that stage of his writing. Shakespeare added four characters, Antigonus, Paulina, Autolycus, and the Clown; Antigonus and Paulina have important functions in the plot, but Autolycus, whose origins may be found in the Elizabethan cony-catching pamphlets of writers like Greene and Dekker, is needed mainly to evoke the atmosphere of the Bohemian countryside. The clown, son to the old shepherd who saves the baby Perdita, forms with his father a significant part of the pattern of contrasting relationships between older and younger generations, as in Leontes and Mamillius, Polixenes and Florizel. Shakespeare also changed the nature of the relationship between the two young lovers; in Greene, Dorastus (Florizel) regards his instinctive feeling for the shepherdess Fawnia (Perdita) as unworthy, since he is a prince and she of lowly rank, and Fawnia is attracted by the prospect of becoming a queen when she marries Dorastus. Shakespeare's lovers are less class-conscious and thus far more attractive. A minor source for the play is Francis Sabie's blank verse poem based on Pandosto, *The Fisherman's Tale* (1595). Except for *The Tempest*, it is the last of Shakespeare's works to be written by himself alone (*Henry VIII* and *The Two Noble Kinsmen* are both later than either this or *The Tempest*, but for these Shakespeare had a collaborator). The play was revised in the Restoration, and Garrick produced it as *Florizel and Perdita*.

Dramatis Personae

Leontes, King of Sicilia	A Mariner
Mamillius, Prince of Sicilia	A Jailer
Camillo, *a Lord of Sicilia*	Hermione, *Queen to Leontes*
Antigonus, *a Lord of Sicilia*	Perdita, *Daughter to Leontes*
Cleomenes, *a Lord of Sicilia*	*and Hermione*
Dion, *a Lord of Sicilia*	Paulina, *wife to Antigonus*
Polixenes, King of Bohemia	Emilia, *a Lady to Hermione*
Florizel, Prince of Bohemia	Mopsa, *a Shepherdess*
Archidamus, *a Lord of Bohemia*	Dorcas, *a Shepherdess*

An old Shepherd, reputed   Lords, Ladies, and Gentlemen,
   Father of Perdita   Officers, and Servants, Shep-
Clown, his Son   herds and Shepherdesses,
Autolycus, a Rogue   Guards
                                    Time, as Chorus

The Story.   Leontes, King of Sicilia, unjustifiably accuses
his wife, Hermione, of having a love affair with his friend,
Polixenes, King of Bohemia, who is visiting the court at Sicilia.
Leontes tries unsuccessfully to poison Polixenes, who flees to
safety; Hermione is imprisoned, and shortly thereafter gives
birth to a daughter. At the trial of Hermione, the king refuses
to believe the Delphic oracle, which has stated that Hermione is
innocent. The king orders the baby to be abandoned; word
comes of the death of the king's son, Mamillius; and Paulina, a
lady at court, reports the death of Hermione. Meanwhile, the
baby, Perdita, is discovered on the Bohemian "coast" by an old
shepherd, who raises her to young womanhood. Sixteen years
later, Florizel, the son of Polixenes, meets her and falls in love
with her but, because of the opposition of his father to a marriage, flees with her to Sicilia. There the identity of Perdita is
discovered, to the joy of Leontes (who has long since regretted
his distrust of his wife), and Polixenes, who has followed his
son, is reconciled to his old friend. Leontes, however, grieves for
his wife (whom he thinks dead), but Paulina offers to show him
a lifelike statue of her, which turns out to be the actual Hermione. The play ends happily with the betrothal of Florizel and
Perdita.

Witches.   [Also, **Weird Sisters.**] In *Macbeth*, three supernatural women. They appear in the first scene, setting the atmosphere of the play. They hail Macbeth as Thane of Glamis, Thane
of Cawdor, and "King hereafter" (I.iii). When Macbeth learns
immediately afterward that he is indeed to become Thane of
Cawdor, their words seem prophetic, and his ambitions are soon
raised to a feverish pitch as his mind dwells upon the possibility
of the throne being his. Their prophecies upon the second occasion of his consulting them are ambiguous and suggest a security
that is not real. The characters are derived from the Scandinavian
Norns, or Goddesses of Fate, probably by way of the Anglo-
Saxon Wyrdes.

Wolsey, Thomas, Cardinal.   One of the major characters in
Henry VIII.

Woodvile.   In *1 Henry VI*, a Lieutenant of the Tower (of London).

Worcester, Thomas Percy, Earl of.   In *1 Henry IV*, the hot-
headed younger brother of Northumberland. Suspicious of the

King, he fails to tell Hotspur of the King's offer to pardon the rebels.

Wriothesley, Henry. See *Southampton,* (3rd) *Earl of.*

Y

Yorick. In *Hamlet,* the king's jester whose skull is found by the Gravediggers and is apostrophized by Hamlet (V.i).

York, Archbishop of. See *Rotherham, Thomas* (*Richard III*) and *Scroop, Richard* (*1* and *2 Henry IV*).

York, Duchess of. In *Richard II,* the wife of York and mother of Aumerle. She begs Henry to pardon her son's treason.

York, Duchess of. In *Richard III,* the mother of Edward IV and Clarence, whose deaths she laments with Margaret and Queen Elizabeth. She joins the chorus of cursing women who hate Richard.

York, (1st) *Duke of.* In *Richard II,* Edmund of Langley (the historical Edmund de Langley). At first a supporter of Richard, he is left as Lord Protector during Richard's absence in Ireland. As soon as Bolingbroke demonstrates his power, however, he adheres to him, and later he reveals the part of his son Aumerle in the plot against Bolingbroke. Some critics consider York weak, indecisive, or even a sycophant; others consider him correct in his extreme loyalty to the crown, whether held by Richard or Henry.

York, (2nd) *Duke of.* In *Henry V,* a cousin to the King. He is killed at Agincourt. In *Richard II,* he is the Duke of Aumerle, son of the Duke of York.

York, (3rd) *Duke of.* In *1 Henry VI,* the historical Richard Plantagenet, head of the house of York. He picks a white rose in the Temple Garden, indicating his opposition to the house of Lancaster. As regent in France, he fails to aid Talbot and condemns Joan of Arc to death. In *2 Henry VI,* he claims his right to the throne and, with the support of Warwick and Salisbury, wins the battle at St. Albans and there kills Clifford. In

3 Henry VI, he makes peace, being promised the succession to the throne at the King's death. Gloucester urges him to break his oath, and he is captured and killed by the Lancastrians at Wakefield.

York, Richard, (5th) ***Duke of.***   In *Richard III*, a young boy, son of Edward IV, who is murdered in the Tower by Richard.

Yorkshire Tragedy, A.   A play produced and printed n 1608, founded on an event that occurred in 1604. It was formerly attributed to Shakespeare, as his name appeared in full on the title page in the 1608 edition, and it was included in the second issue of the third Shakespeare folio (1664), but is not now considered his.

NTC SPEECH AND THEATRE BOOKS

Speech Communication
ACTIVITIES FOR EFFECTIVE COMMUNICATION, LiSacchi
THE BASICS OF SPEECH, Galvin, Cooper, & Gordon
CONTEMPORARY SPEECH, HopKins & Whitaker
CREATIVE SPEAKING, Frank
DYNAMICS OF SPEECH, Myers & Herndon
GETTING STARTED IN ORAL INTERPRETATION, Naegelin & Krikac
GETTING STARTED IN PUBLIC SPEAKING, Carlin & Payne
LISTENING BY DOING, Galvin
LITERATURE ALIVE, Gamble & Gamble
MEETINGS: RULES & PROCEDURES, Pohl
PERSON TO PERSON, Galvin & Book
PUBLIC SPEAKING TODAY, Carlin & Payne
SELF-AWARENESS, Ratliffe & Herman
SPEAKING BY DOING, Buys, Sill, & Beck

Theatre
ACTING AND DIRECTING, Grandstaff
THE BOOK OF CUTTINGS FOR ACTING & DIRECTING, Cassady
THE BOOK OF MONOLOGUES FOR ASPIRING ACTORS, Cassady
THE BOOK OF SCENES FOR ACTING PRACTICE, Cassady
THE BOOK OF SCENES FOR ASPIRING ACTORS, Cassady
THE DYNAMICS OF ACTING, Snyder & Drumsta
GETTING STARTED IN THEATRE, Pinnell
AN INTRODUCTION TO MODERN ONE-ACT PLAYS, Cassady
AN INTRODUCTION TO THEATRE AND DRAMA, Cassady & Cassady
NTC'S DICTIONARY OF THEATRE AND DRAMA TERMS, Mobley
PLAY PRODUCTION TODAY, Beck et al.
STAGECRAFT, Beck

For a current catalog and information about our complete
line of language arts books write:
National Textbook Company,
a division of *NTC Publishing Group*
4255 West Touhy Avenue
Lincolnwood (Chicago), Illinois 60646-1975 U.S.A.